Collins **Total Revision**

GCSE Geography

Michael Raw
Nicholas Rowles

Series Editor: Jayne de Courcy

Contents

How this book will help you...

It doesn't matter whether you're heading for mocks in Year 11, or in the final run-up to your GCSE exam – **this book will help you to produce your very best.**

Whichever approach you decide to take to revision, this book will provide everything you need:

1 Total revision support
2 Quick revision check-ups
3 Exam practice

1 Total Revision Support

Everything you need to know

This book contains all the topics you'll have studied at school. **It covers all the important topics set by all the Exam Boards.**

Short, easy-to-use sections

If, when you are revising, you need to go over something you haven't understood, you'll have no trouble finding it in this book. We've divided each chapter into a number of **short sections with clear headings.** Just look up the topic you want in the contents list or index. **We've put important geographical terms into bold black type** (e.g. **longshore drift**) so that you can't miss them.

Clear maps and diagrams

There are lots of maps and diagrams. It's often easiest to remember facts if they're presented visually. **All the maps and diagrams are in full colour and clearly labelled.** You'll find them really easy to understand.

...Turn over for QUICK REVISION CHECK-UPS and EXAM PRACTICE...→

2 Quick Revision Check-ups

Check yourself questions

It can be really hard knowing where to start when you're revising. Sitting down and wading through pages of facts isn't easy. You're probably asleep before the third page! This book makes it easy to stay awake – **because it makes revising ACTIVE**.

We came up with the idea of putting **'Check yourself' questions** into each chapter. **The questions test your understanding of all the important geographical concepts and ideas** in each section of the chapter. In this way, you can find out quickly and easily just how much you know. You don't need to read through all the text first – just try the questions. If you get all the questions right, you can move straight on to the next section. If you get several of the questions wrong, you know you need to read through the whole section carefully. **This really cuts down on revision time – and helps you focus on where you need to put most effort**.

Answers and Tutorials

If you want the 'Check yourself' questions to be a genuine test of how much you know, then you need to cover up the answers. But, if you'd rather, you can read through a question, then the answer and then the **'tutorial'**. This will still do you a lot of good – and doesn't require quite as much effort!

We've included 'tutorials', as well as answers, to give you even more help with your revision. The tutorials contain extra information, they point out common mistakes that the authors know candidates make, and give you hints on answering similar questions in exams.

Exam checklists

These are another important revision aid. **The checklists summarise all of the key ideas in each topic**. Use them to tick off the areas that you know about – and to spot the ones where you need to do more work.

3 Exam Practice

Exam technique

Knowing the facts is important. But **it's even more important to know how to use them to answer exam questions correctly.** The authors see hundreds of exam scripts a year and students very often lose marks not because they don't know their facts, but because **they haven't understood how to tackle exam questions**.

Questions and sample students' answers

It's often easiest to explain what to do and what not to do by looking at **actual examples of students' answers to exam questions**. This is why we've included sample answers in this book.

These are typical answers, not perfect ones. They highlight the kind of mistakes students often make. **In the examiner's comments, the authors run through these mistakes and show you clearly what you need to do to score full marks on the questions**.

Questions to Answer

We've also included **lots of past exam questions from different Exam Boards for you to have a go at.** The answers are at the back of the book so it's easy not to cheat. Have a go at the questions yourself and then compare them with the answers. **We've provided comments on the answers to give you extra help** – and if you're still unsure you can go back to the relevant section in the book.

Three final tips:

1 Work as consistently as you can during your whole GCSE Geography course. If you don't understand something, ask your teacher straight away, or look it up in this book. You'll then find revision much easier.

2 Plan your revision carefully and focus on the areas you know you find hard. The 'Check yourself' questions in this book will help you do this.

3 Try to do some exam questions as though you were in the actual exam. Time yourself and don't cheat by looking at the answers until you've really had a good go at working out the answers.

About your GCSE Geography course

Knowledge

All GCSE syllabuses place great emphasis on factual recall.

This book will help you build up your knowledge of:

- the definitions of key terms
- places on the earth's surface which can be used as case studies
- descriptions of geographical features
- themes at a range of scales from local to global
- spatial patterns and distributions across the earth's surface.

Understanding

Understanding relates to your ability to explain the processes that influence the human and physical features on the earth's surface.

Skills

Skills relate to your ability to use a wide range of stimulus material such as maps, photographs, diagrams, graphs and figures

You may be asked to do a practical task such as drawing a graph or extracting the information from a map or diagram.

The questions in the *Check yourself* sections and the *Exam practice* questions test your ability in knowledge, understanding and skills.

If you work through the *Tutorials* and *Examiner's comments*, you will get expert guidance on how to improve your performance in all three areas.

Topics covered

This book covers all the main topics in the new syllabuses of the GCSE Exam Boards. However, it is vital that you are familiar with the details of the syllabus for which you have been entered. Ask your teacher for a copy of your syllabus.

Foundation and Higher tier

There are two levels or tiers in the GCSE exam. The Higher tier is restricted to grades A* to E. If you do not achieve a grade E, you will be unclassified. The Foundation tier is targeted at grades C to G. The coursework element which contributes up to 25% of the total marks will be common regardless of the tier for which you are entered. The difference between the two tiers is in the language and style of question used, rather than the geographical content.

Grading

Most exams have two question papers and a coursework component. You will be graded on each of these components which will be put together to give you the overall grade. If you underperform on one component, it is possible for a good mark on another to compensate.

This book is concerned with improving your performance on the question paper component of the exam. The ways this book helps you to improve your grade are:

- by providing a range of case studies that will allow you to show detailed understanding and so achieve a higher level of response in your answer
- by emphasising the key command words (e.g. describe, explain, etc.) to show you what the examiner is looking for in a particular question
- by explaining the difference between point marking and levels of response marking
- by explaining how to avoid the most common errors that GCSE candidates tend to make.

CHAPTER 1

EARTHQUAKES AND VOLCANOES

1.1 THE INTERIOR OF THE EARTH

The Earth is one of nine planets in the solar system. Earth is a relatively small planet, measuring just 12,740 km from pole to pole. If the Earth were sliced in two, we would see four concentric shells in its cross-section (Fig. 1.1). These shells in order of increasing depth are: the **crust**; the **lithosphere**; the **mantle**; and the **core**:

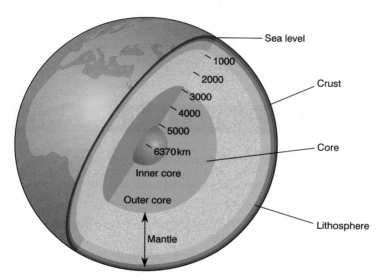

Figure 1.1
The structure of the Earth

- The crust is the outermost, rocky layer. Its main features are the **continents** and **ocean basins** (Fig. 1.2).

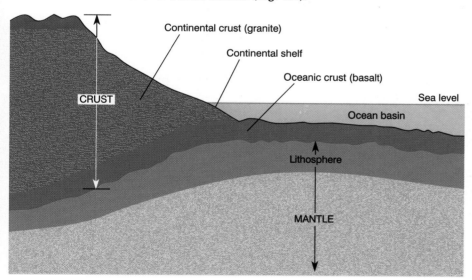

Figure 1.2
The continental and oceanic crust

- Beneath the crust and welded to it is the lithosphere.
- Deeper still, is the mantle which accounts for over 80 per cent of the Earth's volume.
- Finally, deep in the Earth's interior are the outer and inner cores.

Each shell has a different density, rock type, temperature and physical state (i.e. solid, liquid or plastic) (Table 1.1).

Table 1.1		Composition of the Earth			
LAYER		THICKNESS (km)	AVERAGE DENSITY (g/cm^3)	ROCK TYPE	TEMPERATURE (°C)
Crust and Lithosphere	Continental Oceanic	0–70 0–5	2.7 3.0	Granite (solid) Basalt (solid)	10
Mantle		2900	5.5	Peridotite (plastic)	375
Core	Outer Inner	2000 1450	10.0 13.3	Iron/nickel ore (liquid) Iron/nickel ore (solid)	3000

1.2 PLATE TECTONICS

The theory of **plate tectonics** provides us with an explanation for the formation of earthquakes and volcanoes, and for **landforms** such as **fold mountains, ocean trenches, island arcs** and **rift valleys**.

Plate tectonics tells us that:

- The Earth's crust and lithosphere are broken into many large fragments or **plates**.
- There are seven major plates (e.g. the African plate) and dozens of smaller ones (e.g. the Philippine plate) (Fig. 1.3).

Figure 1.3
Major lithospheric plates and distribution of earthquakes and volcanoes around the world

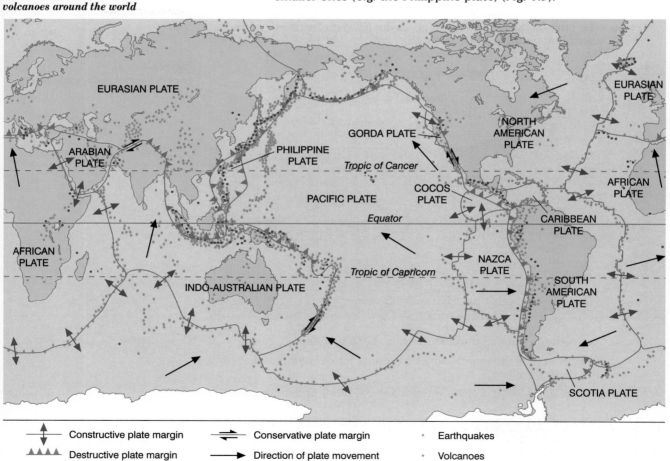

Constructive plate margin	Conservative plate margin	· Earthquakes
Destructive plate margin	Direction of plate movement	· Volcanoes

- Some plates mainly consist of continental crust (e.g. the Eurasian plate); others are largely made up of oceanic crust (e.g. the Pacific plate).
- Plates are constantly moving: they can move away from each other; towards each other; or slide past each other.
- Plate movement has important effects, especially along the plate margins, where plates meet.

There are three types of plate margin: **constructive**, **destructive**, and **conservative**. Now let's examine these three types of plate margin in more detail.

CONSTRUCTIVE PLATE MARGINS

Constructive plate margins are submarine valleys found in mid-ocean. In the Atlantic and Pacific Oceans steep, undersea mountain ranges run for thousands of kilometres along the entire length of these valleys. They are known as **mid-ocean ridges** (Fig. 1.4). Here molten rock (**magma**) rises from the mantle and forms new crust. Slowly the new crust pushes the older crust sideways, away from the ridges. We call this sideways movement **sea floor spreading**. It is like a slow conveyor belt, creeping along at 2 cm a year. This may not seem much, but over millions of years even tiny movements add up to great distances.

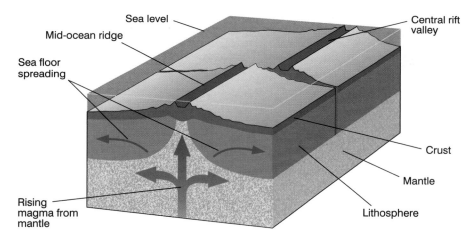

Figure 1.4
Constructive plate margin (mid-ocean ridge)

CONTINENTAL DRIFT

For several centuries scientists speculated that all of the continents had once been joined together. However, scientists were unable to explain how land masses the size of continents could have drifted across the globe. In the 1960s came the discovery of sea floor spreading. Scientists explained that the continents, being lighter than the oceanic crust, simply ride on the conveyor of sea floor spreading. Finally, **continental drift** could be explained.

DESTRUCTIVE PLATE MARGINS

We know that new crust forms at mid-ocean ridges, and yet the Earth is not expanding. How is this possible? There is only one explanation: somewhere old crust is being destroyed at exactly the same rate as new crust forms. The places where this happens are called **subduction zones** (Fig. 1.5).

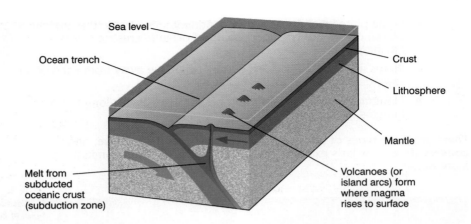

Figure 1.5
*Destructive plate margin
(subduction zone)*

Here oceanic crust, shifted over hundreds of millions of years by sea floor spreading, finally plunges into the mantle. As it does so the oceanic crust buckles the surrounding crust and lithosphere to form a deep ocean trench. Subduction produces other effects, most notably earthquakes and outbursts of volcanic activity.

CONSERVATIVE PLATE MARGINS

At conservative boundaries crust is neither formed nor destroyed. Instead the plates simply grind past each other with a shearing motion. These movements are rarely smooth. Where the plates jar together, enormous pressure can build up. It is the release of this pressure that causes earthquakes.

Check yourself

QUESTIONS

Q1 With the help of Figure 1.3 state what kind of plate margin separates each of the following pairs of plates:

i)   North American plate/Eurasian plate.
ii) Eurasian plate/African plate.
iii) Pacific plate/North American plate.

Q2 Study the diagram on the right.

i)   Is the plate boundary constructive, destructive or conservative?
ii) Name the features at A, B and C.

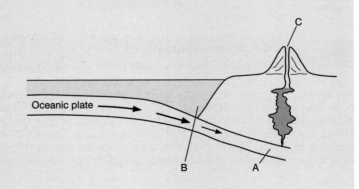

Q3 Figure 1.3 shows that the plate boundary which separates the North American plate from the Eurasian plate runs through Iceland. Use this fact to explain why Iceland is getting larger.

REMEMBER! Cover the answers if you want to.

ANSWERS

A1
i) Constructive plate margin.
ii) Destructive plate margin.
iii) Conservative plate margin.

A2
i) Destructive plate boundary.
ii) A is a subduction zone; B is an ocean trench; and C is a volcano.

A3 The plate boundary is constructive. As the plates move apart at a constructive boundary magma moves up from the mantle. This solidifies to form new crust and eventually new land areas.

TUTORIALS

T1 You do not need to know all the names of the plate margins shown in Figure 1.3. Make sure that you know one example of each type of plate margin for your examination.

T2
i) If a plate is being destroyed as it is forced underneath another one, the plate boundary is destructive. These simple diagrams may help you to remember the difference between the three types of boundaries:

Destructive boundary   → ←

Constructive boundary   ← — →

Conservative boundary   ⤢

ii) The features listed are the ones you are most likely to be asked about in a GCSE examination.

T3 This is an example of sea floor spreading. Iceland is on the Mid Atlantic Ridge. Iceland is a volcanic island formed where a submarine range of mountains appears above the sea surface. You are likely to gain extra credit for using as many other examples as possible to support your answer. This helps to show that you really understand the question. Other examples of sea floor spreading are St Helena and Tristan da Cunha.

1.3 EARTHQUAKES

- Earthquakes occur when rocks which have been compressed or stretched, slip or snap along a **fault** line in the crust.
- Earthquakes release massive amounts of stored energy as shocks or **seismic waves**.
- These waves spread out from the earthquake's origin or **focus** (Fig. 1.6).
- The **epicentre** of an earthquake is the point on the Earth's surface directly above the focus (Fig. 1.6). It is here that the destructive effects of an earthquake are greatest.

If you look at Figure 1.3 you will see that most earthquake epicentres are close to plate boundaries. Although earthquakes are common at mid-ocean ridges, most are fairly shallow and are less powerful than those found along subduction zones. In a subduction zone two plates converge (Fig. 1.5). If the plate descending into the mantle jams, enormous strains build up. Sooner or later the subducting plate slips, creating the powerful shock waves we call an earthquake. Several recent earthquakes such as those in Armenia (1988), Japan (1995) and Iran (1997) occurred along subduction zones.

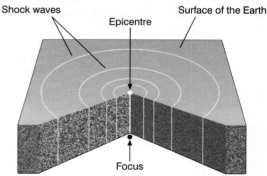

Figure 1.6 *Earthquake focus and epicentre*

Table 1.2	Measuring earthquakes: the Richter and Mercalli scales
Richter scale	The Richter scale measures the strength of earthquakes on a logarithmic scale. This means that an earthquake of magnitude 7 is ten times more powerful than one of magnitude 6, and 100 times more powerful than one of magnitude 5. The most powerful earthquake this century – the San Francisco earthquake in 1906 – measured 8.6 on the Richter scale. The Richter scale goes from 0 to 10.
Mercalli scale	The Mercalli scale measures the physical effects of earthquakes. The scale goes from 1 (rarely felt) to 12 (total damage, waves seen on the surface of the ground, large objects thrown into the air).

1.4 CASE STUDY: EARTHQUAKE IN MAHARASHTRA

On 1 October 1993 the most severe earthquake to hit India for over 100 years struck Maharashtra state, in central India (Fig. 1.7). The earthquake measured 6.4 on the Richter scale and flattened two small towns and thirty villages, killing 22,000 people (Fig. 1.8).

Figure 1.8 *Devastating effects of Indian Earthquake*

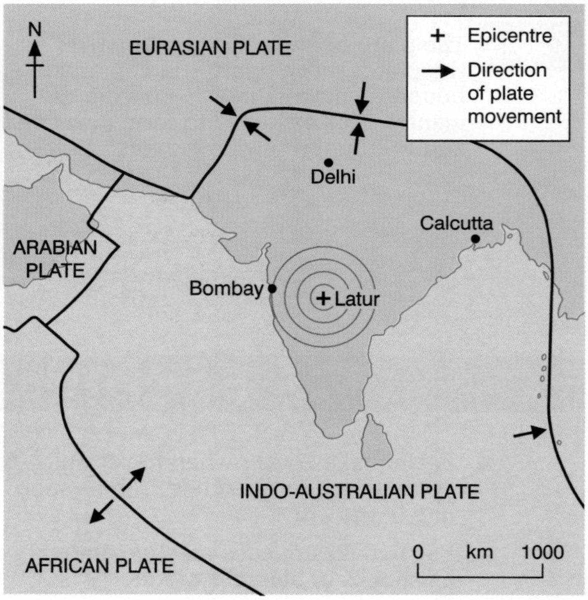

Figure 1.7
The Maharashtra earthquake

The Maharashtra earthquake resulted from a sudden movement of the Earth's crust along a fault line. Like ripples in a pond, the earthquake spread out from its epicentre in Latur (Fig. 1.7). The shock waves were recorded thousands of kilometres away in Calcutta, Delhi and Bombay.

Although the earthquake hit a mainly rural area with few high rise buildings, its effects were none the less devastating. There were two main reasons for this:

● The earthquake struck at 4 a.m. when most people were indoors.

● Few homes were earthquake proof.

The people living in Maharashtra state are poor. Their houses, made of loosely bonded stone and with heavy slab roofs, give little protection against earthquakes. Most of those killed or badly injured were buried under collapsed buildings. In some settlements less than 20 per cent of the houses were left standing. Significantly those houses that survived belonged to the better-off and were built from concrete.

Emergency relief

Getting help to the survivors proved difficult. The region is remote and has poor communications. Emergency aid came from the Indian government, foreign governments and overseas agencies such as the Red Cross and the UN. The priorities were to provide temporary shelter for the homeless, blankets, and safe drinking water. Water contaminated by sewage threatened to spread diseases such as typhoid. The lack of hospitals in the region was a further obstacle to the relief effort.

Reducing the earthquake hazard

In the twentieth century around 1.4 million people have been killed by earthquakes, most of them by collapsing buildings. The majority of deaths have occurred in poor countries. Rich countries such as Japan and the USA can afford to construct buildings which are earthquake proof. Special techniques used in the design of these buildings include:

- Counterweights on the roofs of high-rise blocks which move in the opposite direction to the force of the earthquake.
- Rubber shock absorbers in the foundations which allow buildings to rock.
- Cross-bracing which allows tall buildings to twist.

Yet poor countries can build safer houses at relatively low cost. For instance, houses are more likely to withstand an earthquake if:

- They are roughly cuboid in shape.
- Doors and windows are kept away from corners.
- Foundations are deep.
- 'Through' stones at regular intervals tie together rubble walls.
- Large stones secure the corners.
- Timber wall plates prevent walls from twisting in a earthquake.
- Roofs are made of lightweight materials.
- Lintels above windows and doors run well into the walls on either side.

Check yourself

QUESTIONS

Q1 What is meant by each of the following:
  i) earthquake focus?
  ii) epicentre?

Q2 Why is India prone to earthquakes?

Q3 Why were the effects of the Maharashtra earthquake severe in both the short term and the long term?

ANSWERS

A1
i) The earthquake focus is the place where the earthquake begins.
ii) The epicentre is the point on the Earth's surface which is directly above the earthquake focus.

A2 India is part of the Indo-Australian plate which collides with the Eurasian plate.

A3 In the short term many people lost their homes. Because of the remoteness of this part of India it took a long time for emergency aid to reach victims. Many of those trapped beneath collapsed buildings died because they did not receive medical assistance until it was too late. As India is a Less Economically Developed Country (LEDC) it did not have the resources to repair the damage quickly. As a result thousands of people continued to suffer the effects of the earthquake for a long time after the event.

TUTORIAL

T1 *Geographers sometimes use the term seismic focus instead of earthquake focus. Seismology is the study of earthquakes.*

T2 *Earthquakes most often occur at plate boundaries, particularly along subduction zones. However, the Maharashtra earthquake shows that earthquakes can occur well away from plate boundaries. In this case the cause of the earthquake was a sudden movement of the crust along a fault line. In any answer a good candidate will mention any exceptions to the general rule.*

T3 *It is very likely that in a GCSE question on earthquakes (or volcanic eruptions) you will be asked something about the human responses to these natural disasters. Questions are likely to test: a) the long-term and short-term effects of such disasters; b) why natural disasters tend to cause greater loss of life in Less Economically Developed Countries. The financial loss to a More Economically Developed Country (MEDC) is likely to be greater because it affects a larger economy.*

1.5 VOLCANOES AND VOLCANIC ERUPTIONS

Volcanic eruptions are among the most awesome events in nature. They can change landscapes and alter the global weather and climate. Like earthquakes they also affect the lives of millions of people (Table 1.3).

Table 1.3	Catastrophic volcanic eruptions	
1500 BC	Santorini, Greece	Island destroyed
AD 79	Vesuvius, Italy	Pompeii destroyed
1586	Kelud, Indonesia	10,000 dead
1669	Etna, Italy	20,000 dead
1815	Tambora, Indonesia	90,000 dead
1883	Krakatoa, Indonesia	36,000 dead
1902	Mont Pelee, Martinique	30,000 dead
1985	Nevado del Ruiz, Colombia	25,000 dead

Mount Vesuvius in southern Italy is an **active volcano**. It has erupted more than 50 times in the last 2,000 years. Active volcanoes spew out solid rocks, molten rock (**lava**), ash, steam and hot gases. Layers of ash and lava from old eruptions can accumulate to form a classic cone shaped, composite volcano (Fig. 1.9).

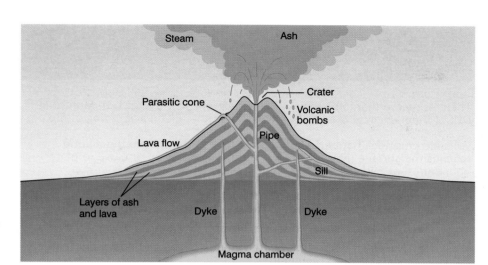

Figure 1.9
A composite volcano

However, not all volcanoes are cone-shaped. Their shape depends on the thickness or **viscosity** of the lava erupted (Fig. 1.10):

- Thick lava (e.g. rhyolite) which doesn't flow very far produces steep-sided **volcanic domes**.

- Thin runny lava (e.g. basalt) may flow for many kilometres. It forms low-angled **shield volcanoes** (Fig. 1.11).

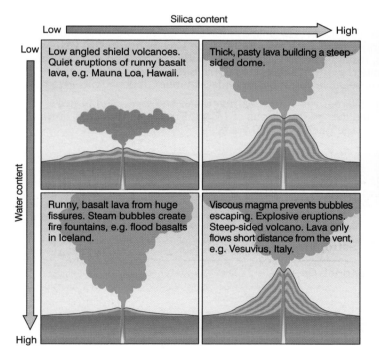

Figure 1.11 *Shield volcano, Mauna Loa, Hawaii*

Figure 1.10
Different types of volcanoes and eruptions

Volcanoes which have been inactive or **dormant** for hundreds of years can suddenly burst into life (e.g. Mount Pinatubo, Philippines in 1991). In fact, some of the worst disasters have been caused by volcanoes thought to be **extinct**, such as Vesuvius in AD 79, which overwhelmed Pompeii.

It may surprise you to know that not all eruptions of molten rock come from volcanoes. In Iceland, for example, **fissure eruptions** are common. Here molten rock reaches the surface through great cracks in the Earth's crust. Such eruptions can produce huge amounts of lava. Over thousands of years they build **lava plateaus** (Fig. 1.12) such as the Antrim plateau in Northern Ireland.

Figure 1.12 *Lava plateau at Thorsmörk, Iceland*

1.6 CAUSES AND EFFECTS OF VOLCANIC ERUPTIONS

There are more than 600 active volcanoes in the world (Fig. 1.3). More than half of them encircle the Pacific Ocean – the so-called Pacific 'ring of fire'.

Volcanic eruptions happen when molten rock and ash from the mantle reaches the surface (Fig. 1.13). Most eruptions occur on or close to plate boundaries, at mid-ocean ridges and subduction zones.

On average around 50 volcanoes erupt each year. A total of 360 million people are at risk from volcanic eruptions. These people face a variety of hazards:

- Lava flows which endanger life and property.
- Nuées ardents: superheated clouds of gas and dust which can engulf whole communities.
- **Lahars**: mudflows caused either by heavy rain or meltwater mixing with volcanic ash.
- Ash falls which smother farmland, block roads and cause buildings to collapse.
- Ash, pumice and rock fragments which avalanche down the slopes of volcanoes.
- Toxic gas clouds which poison/suffocate all they drift over.

Eruptions don't just affect people who live close to active volcanoes. Volcanoes can alter the world's climate. Volcanic ash forced high into the atmosphere can block the sun's rays. After a major eruption there may be one or two years of cooler summers, resulting in smaller harvests, and possibly food shortages in LEDCs. Yet despite the obvious dangers people often choose to live near volcanoes. This is because volcanoes provide a number of economic advantages:

- Rich soils derived from weathered ash and lava. One in five Sicilians live on the slopes of Mount Etna even though it erupts on average once every 10 years.

Figure 1.13
Causes of volcanic eruptions

Island arcs
Where two oceanic plates converge (e.g. western Pacific). One plate is pushed downwards (subducted) into the mantle. As the subducted plate melts, magma rises to the surface forming numerous volcanoes or island arcs, e.g. the Aleutian Islands.

Mid-oceanic ridges
Tension in the crust leads to deep rifts. Magma rises up to the ocean floor along these rifts, forming new crust. The ridges form a continuous line of submarine volcanoes. In places the volcanoes rise above sea level, e.g. Iceland.

Hot spot volcanoes
Rising plumes of magma reach the surface in the centres of plates, e.g. Hawaii.

Continental-oceanic plate margins.
Here the oceanic plate is subducted beneath the thicker continental plate. As it melts some of the lighter oceanic plate magma forces its way to the surface, forming volcanoes, e.g. Andean volcanoes.

Flood basalts
Great cracks or fissures in the crust (caused by tension) allow vast amounts of magma to reach the surface. These eruptions build-up great thicknesses of lava, known as flood basalts.

Island arc
Oceanic crust
Trench
Sea level
Mid-oceanic ridge
Hot spot
Trench
Continental crust
Flood basalt
Lithosphere
Subduction zone
Subduction zone
Lithosphere
Mantle
Mantle

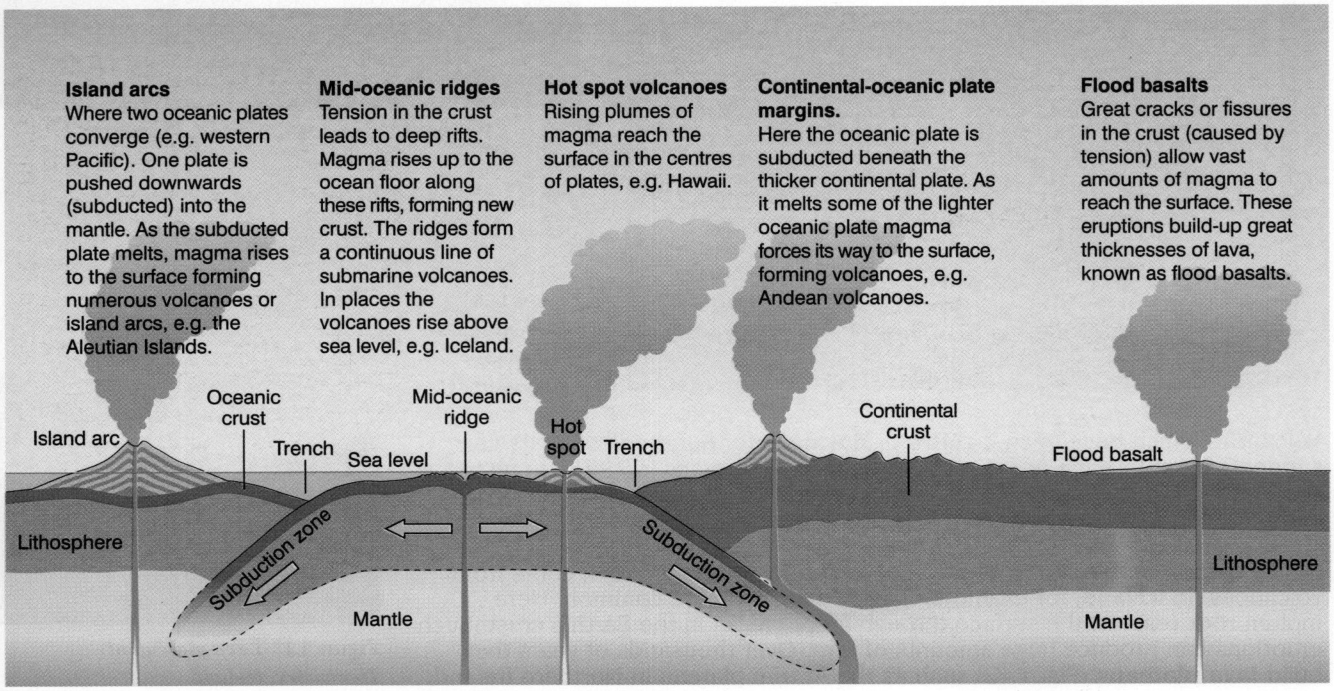

- Hot springs, around which spa resorts such as Bath developed.

- Geysers, boiling mud pots, etc., such as those in Iceland, Rotorua (New Zealand) and Yellowstone (USA) which attract millions of tourists.

- Geothermal energy. In Iceland electricity is generated from steam produced by red hot magma. Hot water for central heating in the capital, Reykjavik, also comes from geothermal sources.

- Mineral veins (e.g. copper, gold, etc.) and diamonds associated with extinct volcanoes.

1.7 CASE STUDY: THE MOUNT PINATUBO ERUPTIONS

The Philippines are a group of volcanic islands in South-east Asia. In this region three great tectonic plates – the Philippine, Eurasian and Pacific plates – meet (Fig. 1.14). Off the east coast of the Philippines, the Philippine plate is subducted beneath the Eurasian plate.

As a result there are 20 active volcanoes on the Philippines. One of them is Mount Pinatubo. On 13 June 1991, Pinatubo erupted for the first time in 600 years. Over the following week there were several further eruptions. These eruptions produced lava flows at temperatures up to 1000 °C and huge columns of ash which rose high into the atmosphere (Fig. 1.15).

The ash settled over a wide area. It blotted out the sun and smothered farmland in up to 35 cm of ash. On the slopes of Pinatubo, the ash mixed with heavy rain causing destructive mudflows or lahars. These overwhelmed villages up to 15 km away. The eruptions killed 97 people and injured thousands of others. They made 100,000 hill farmers homeless and caused the evacuation of 20,000 servicemen and their families from a nearby American airbase.

However, the effects of the Pinatubo eruptions were not confined to the Philippines. The volcano continued to erupt until 1993, pumping huge amounts of ash and sulphuric acid into the atmosphere. The effect of this was that for the next two years the world's climate cooled by 1 °C.

Figure 1.15 *Ash plume from Mount Pinatubo. The green area is the island of Luzon, and the yellow areas are normal clouds.*

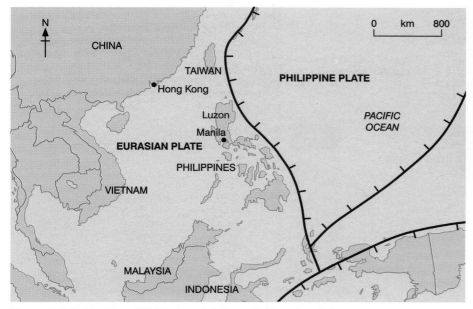

Figure 1.14 *Subduction of Philippine plate beneath Eurasian plate*

Check yourself

QUESTIONS

Q1 What are the differences between active, dormant and extinct volcanoes?

Q2 Why do lavas which are low in silica and water form low angled volcanic cones?

Q3 The following are important volcanic areas:

Iceland, Hawaii, Mount Cotopaxi in the Andes, The Aleutian Islands.

Match each of these locations to one of the following causes of volcanic eruptions:

continental/oceanic plate boundary; constructive plate boundary; convergence of two oceanic plates; a weakness in the centre of a plate (a hot spot).

Q4 Why do people choose to live near to volcanoes despite the possible danger?

REMEMBER! Cover the answers if you want to.

ANSWERS

A1 An active volcano is one that has erupted in living memory. If there is documentary evidence of a volcano erupting in historical times, then the volcano is said to be dormant. With an extinct volcano there is only geological evidence of an eruption ever having taken place.

A2 A lava low in silica and water will be non viscous, so it flows a long way before it solidifies. This results in a low angled volcanic cone such as Mauna Loa in Hawaii.

A3 Constructive plate boundary – Iceland.

Continental/oceanic plate boundary – Mount Cotapaxi in the Andes.

Convergence of two oceanic plates – The Aleutian Islands.

A hot spot – Hawaii.

A4 The attractions are: rich volcanic soils; hot springs (for medicinal properties); geothermal energy; income from tourism; and rich mineral deposits.

TUTORIALS

T1 A volcano classified as extinct is just as likely to erupt as an active or dormant volcano. Questions testing your knowledge of definitions are very common in GCSE examinations.

T2 Some texts give details of the chemistry of different types of lava. This detail is more useful in a geology examination,. Although you would gain credit for it in a geography examination, it is sufficient for you to know simply whether a lava is low or high in silica.

T3 These examples show that the majority of volcanoes are found around the edge of plates. If you are answering a question on the location of volcanic eruptions then you should emphasise the global distribution. A good candidate would give more specific information about how the volcanoes are found at different types of plate margins. It is always important to mention any exceptions to the general rule. In this case the hot spot is the exception because Hawaii is in the middle of the Pacific plate.

T4 It is worth learning a case study. If you can give detailed information, you will reach higher levels in a level marked question.

EXAMINATION CHECKLIST

The facts and ideas that you should know and understand after studying earthquakes and volcanoes are:

- The Earth is made up of different concentric shells.
- The crust is broken up into a series of plates.
- There are three kinds of plate margins: constructive, destructive and conservative.
- What is happening at each of these plate margins.
- The reasons for the pattern of earthquakes over the Earth's surface.
- The difference between the Richter and the Mercalli scales.
- One detailed case study of an earthquake, e.g. the 1993 Maharashtra earthquake in India.
- The difference between short-term and long-term effects of an earthquake.
- The contrasting economic and social impacts of earthquake disasters in LEDCs and MEDCs.
- What can be done to reduce an earthquake hazard.
- The variety of causes of volcanic eruptions.
- The causes of the different shapes of volcanic cones.
- Why people continue to live near volcanoes despite the obvious dangers.
- One case study of a volcanic eruption in detail, e.g. Mount Pinatubo in the Philippines.

KEY WORDS

These are the keywords. Tick them if you think you know what they mean. Otherwise check on them.

crust	rift valleys	focus
lithosphere	plates	epicentre
mantle	constructive	active
core	destructive	lava
continents	conservative	viscosity
ocean basins	mid-ocean ridges	volcanic domes
cores	magma	shield volcanoes
plate tectonics	sea floor spreading	dormant
landforms	continental drift	extinct
fold mountains	subduction zones	fissure eruptions
ocean trenches	fault	lava plateaus
island arcs	seismic waves	lahars

EXAM PRACTICE

Sample Student's Answer and Examiner's Comments

EXAMINER'S COMMENTS

1 i)
This is correct. The candidate would have gained the mark even if the sentence had stopped after the word "plate". The second part of the sentence is elaboration and is necessary only if the question had asked for explanation.

ii)
He gets full marks even though there is a factual error: the Richter scale goes from 0–10. (In an examination you do not lose marks for writing something which is wrong or irrelevant.) The second mark comes from the statement "and increases 10-fold every 1 number up".

iii)
The three credit worthy points are all contained in one sentence, "death", "water and power being down" and "buildings being destroyed".

iv)
This question is marked in levels:

Level 1 Basic understanding: 1–2 marks
Level 2 Clear understanding: 3–4 marks
Level 3 Detailed understanding 5–6 marks

*The answer is marked **as a whole** and it is not necessary to go through all levels.*

The first sentence shows clear understanding, so 3 marks are achieved. The second sentence is another Level 2 statement. If the rest of the answer were made up of further Level 2 statements, he could not go beyond the 4 marks achieved at the top of Level 2. However, both the final two sentences reach level 3. He has referred to a particular example (the San Andreas Fault) and has elaborated on earlier points made by explaining that the earthquake occurs when the build up of pressure is released.

He therefore has reached the top of Level 3 and gains the full 6 marks.

Quake city is holding its breath
DEATH TOLL RISES AS LOS ANGELES BLAZES

The earthquake that struck the sleeping city of Los Angeles early yesterday morning has left at least twenty-four people dead, hundreds more injured and millions without power and water. Those who had their homes destroyed became refugees in their own city.

The tremor, which registered 6.6 on the Richter scale, destroyed houses, shops, offices and roads. It was felt hundreds of miles away, from San Diego in the south, to Las Vegas 275 miles to the east. The main jolt, which occurred at 4.31 a.m. and lasted for 45 seconds, was followed throughout the day by twenty more after shocks. These toppled many buildings weakened by the first quake. Some buildings not flattened by the tremors were engulfed in flames as gas mains cracked open. The resulting explosions sent concrete and glass hundreds of feet into the sky. Power lines were also brought down, disabling phone networks and computer systems. Prevented from mounting a fully co-ordinated rescue operation, the emergency services were further hampered by roads that were warped out of shape and cracked. Despite the chaos, rescue workers tirelessly continued in their attempts to save victims trapped under rubble.

The shell-shocked people of Los Angeles have been warned to brace themselves for more tremors which are a distinct possibility, according to experts.

Source: Associated Press Ltd

1 (i) What is a tremor?
This is a sudden movement of a plate caused by friction suddenly being released.
(1 mark)

(ii) What is the Richter scale?
The Richter Scale is a scale used to measure the violence of plate movements. It goes from 0-12, and increases 10-fold every 1 number up.
(2 marks)

(iii) What were the effects of the earthquake on the people who live in Los Angeles?
The immediate effects are death, water and power being down, and buildings being destroyed.
(3 marks)

(iv) Explain fully the causes of earthquakes.
Earthquakes are caused by two plates pushing together in a destructive way so that the pressure that builds up is suddenly released. The plates that do this are an Oceanic pushing against a Continental. The Oceanic goes underneath because it is heavier. Earthquakes occur only at or near the plate boundary.
In the mantle, convection currents move the plates around. This causes the plates to meet; conservative (San Andreas Fault) and collision (between two continental plates). New crust is formed at the constructive plate margins. This increases the pressure on the other margins, so that the pressure builds and then when it is too much, the plates jerk violently, until they are more stable.
(6 marks)

SEG, 1996

Questions to Answer

The answer to Question 2 can be found in Chapter 18.

2 a) Study Figure 1.3.

   i) Name a major volcano and state which two plates form the plate boundary on which it is located. (1)

   ii) Describe the relationship between plate margins and volcanoes shown in Figure 1.3. (2)

   b) Study the diagram below.

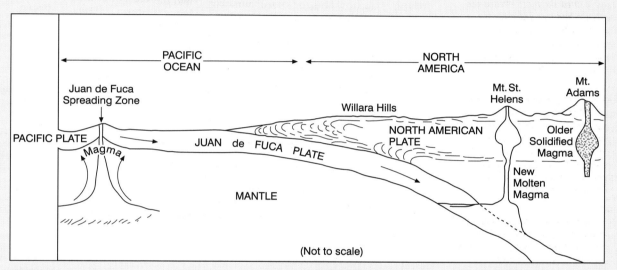

(Not to scale)

   Use the information in the diagram to explain why Mount St Helens is an active volcano. (5)

   c) Describe the hazards to people and the environment during a volcanic eruption. You should refer to either Mount St Helens or another active volcano. (6)

   d) Explain why people still live in areas of active volcanoes. (6)

MEG (specimen paper)

CHAPTER 2

ROCKS AND LANDFORMS

2.1 WHAT ARE ROCKS?

Rocks form the Earth's hard outer layer or crust. They are a mixture of different **minerals** such as quartz, calcite, feldspar and olivine. Granite consists of just three minerals: quartz, feldspar and mica. Limestone is even simpler, often containing only a single mineral – calcium carbonate.

2.2 ROCK TYPES

Although there are hundreds of different kinds of rock, they fall into just three main groups: **igneous**, **sedimentary** and **metamorphic**. We base this simple grouping on how the rocks formed (Fig. 2.1).

Figure. 2.1
How rocks are formed

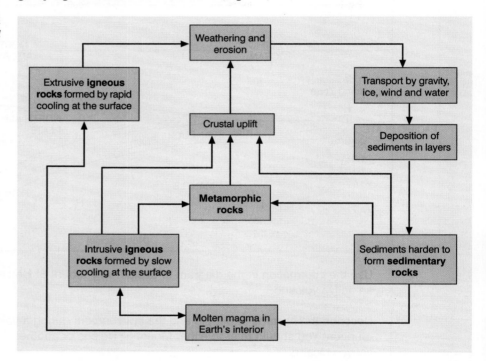

IGNEOUS ROCKS

All igneous rocks start out as molten **magma** deep below the Earth's crust. Igneous rocks form by magma cooling and solidifying either at the Earth's surface or within its crust. You should know that:

- Rocks which cool and solidify at the Earth's surface are known as **lavas**.
- Exposed to the air, lavas cool rapidly.
- Rapid cooling creates fine-grained rocks with tiny mineral crystals.
- **Basalt** is the most common type of lava.
- **Granite** cools slowly, deep inside the crust.
- Slow cooling produces coarse-grained rocks with large mineral crystals.
- Granite is the most common igneous rock and forms most of the continental crust.

SEDIMENTARY ROCKS

Most sedimentary rocks consist of mineral particles (mud, sand, clay) formed from the breakdown of older rocks. In general, sedimentary rocks are less resistant to **weathering** and **erosion** than igneous rocks. Some, like mudstone, are so weak that they are easily broken by hand. Limestone, chalk and coal differ from other sedimentary rocks, because they are the fossilised remains of ancient plants and animals. Sedimentary rocks are most easily recognised because:

- They occur in layers, known as **strata** or beds.
- There are sharp boundaries or **bedding planes** between individual rock layers (Fig. 2.2).

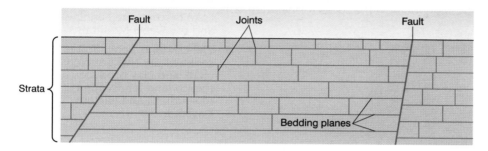

Figure. 2.2
Joints and bedding planes in sedimentary rocks

METAMORPHIC ROCKS

Metamorphic rocks have been altered either by intense heat or intense pressure or both. For example, limestone rock in contact with molten granite may be baked or **metamorphosed** into marble. Alternatively, intense pressure can metamorphose a sedimentary rock, such as mudstone, into slate.

Table 2.1	Some common rock types	
ROCK GROUP	ROCK TYPE	FORMATION
Igneous	**Basalt**	Runny lava erupted at the surface from a volcano or fissure.
	Granite	Magma intruded into the Earth's crust.
Sedimentary	**Sandstone**	Sand-sized particles either compressed or cemented together.
	Limestone	Accumulation of shells and skeletons of tiny sea creatures (e.g. coral) on the sea floor.
	Coal	Fossilised remains of trees and other plants.
Metamorphic	**Marble**	Limestone altered by heat and/or pressure.
	Slate	Shale, clay and volcanic ash altered by great pressure.

2.3 ROCKS AND RELIEF

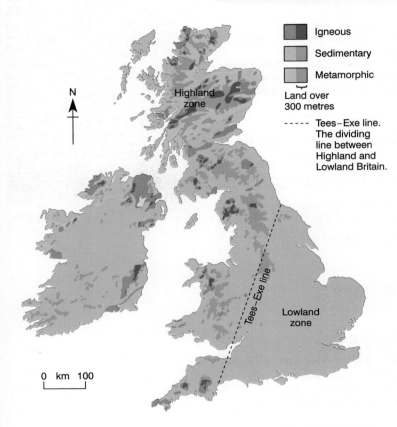

Igneous

Sedimentary

Metamorphic

Land over
300 metres

- - - - Tees–Exe line.
The dividing
line between
Highland and
Lowland Britain.

Highland
zone

Lowland
zone

Tees–Exe line

0   km   100

The distribution of igneous, sedimentary and metamorphic rocks has a strong influence on relief in the British Isles (Fig. 2.3). An imaginary line from the mouths of the rivers Tees and Exe divides Britain into two relief zones:

- The Highland Zone. Hard rocks, resistant to **weathering** and **erosion** dominate the north and west. They form uplands such as the Scottish Highlands, the Lake District, the Pennines and the Welsh Mountains.

- The Lowland Zone. Softer, sedimentary rocks such as chalk and clay produce the lowland landscapes of southern and eastern England.

Figure 2.3
Distribution of major rock groups in the British Isles and relief

2.4 WEATHERING

Although some rocks are very hard they are weakened by **joints**, **faults** and bedding planes (Fig. 2.2). The forces of weathering and erosion affect these weak areas the most.

Rocks which crop out at or near the Earth's surface undergo changes of heat and moisture. The effect of these changes causes rocks to disintegrate. We call this process weathering. There are two main types of weathering:

- Physical weathering – when rocks break down into smaller particles.
- Chemical weathering – when chemical processes alter the minerals in rocks and cause them to disintegrate.

PHYSICAL WEATHERING

In high latitudes and high mountains most physical weathering is by **freeze-thaw**. This happens in four stages:

- Water seeps into joints and cracks in rocks.
- Temperatures drop below freezing, turning the water into ice.
- Freezing causes the water to expand, putting enormous pressure on the surrounding rock.
- If the pressure is great enough the rock eventually splits apart.

Physical weathering by freeze-thaw creates two important landforms: **screes** and **blockfields**. If freeze-thaw occurs on a well-jointed cliff face, small rock fragments broken off by the frost roll downslope where they accumulate as **scree** (Fig. 2.4). On flatter surfaces, especially where rock joints are widely spaced, freeze-thaw breaks up the rock into massive boulders to form **blockfields**.

Plants can also contribute to physical weathering. Tree roots, for example, can grow into rocks, widening joints and loosening blocks. If a tree topples over in a gale, its roots can lever out great chunks of rock.

Insolation weathering occurs in hot deserts where rocks are exposed to the sun's powerful rays during the day, then cool rapidly at night. This type of weathering involves the following processes:

- Intense sunlight causes rock surfaces to heat up to 60 °C, and above.
- Different minerals in the rock expand at different rates.
- This leads to stress, weakening the rocks and causing the outer rock layers to peel away.

This 'onion-peel' weathering (**exfoliation**) often produces boulders and rock outcrops with smooth rounded shapes.

Figure 2.4 *Scree slope at Cronkley Scar, County Durham*

CHEMICAL WEATHERING

Chemical weathering covers a wide range of complex chemical reactions. Most of these reactions require moisture and heat, so chemical weathering is most effective in hot, wet climates, such as those found near the Equator. Chemical weathering is least effective in dry, desert conditions and in cold climates.

Three common forms of chemical weathering are **solution**, **oxidation** and **hydration**:

- Solution occurs when rock minerals such as calcite (in limestone) dissolve in rainwater.
- Oxidation occurs when minerals react with oxygen.
- Hydration occurs when minerals absorb water.

All of these processes lead to the chemical alteration of rocks and their subsequent break down.

Check yourself

QUESTIONS

Q1 What is the difference between a mineral and a rock?

Q2 Which of the following are rocks?

limestone, olivine, sandstone, chalk, quartz, granite

Q3 What are the names of the three main groups of rocks?

Q4 Name the two main types of weathering.

Q5 What type of weathering is more likely to occur in the hot, wet regions along the Equator?

Q6 Explain the difference between solution, oxidation and hydration in the context of minerals.

ANSWERS

A1 A mineral is a single chemical substance; a rock is usually made up of a number of different minerals.

A2 Limestone, sandstone, chalk and granite.

A3 Igneous, sedimentary, metamorphic.

A4 Physical weathering, chemical weathering.

A5 Chemical weathering.

A6 Solution is when the minerals in a rock dissolve in water, whereas hydration takes place when the minerals absorb water. Oxidation is the result of a chemical reaction between the minerals and oxygen.

TUTORIALS

T1 *It is important that you understand the difference between a mineral and a rock because the way rocks break down and influence the scenery depends on the minerals found in them.*

T2 *The rocks that are most likely to be tested in your GCSE exam are limestone, chalk, granite and clay.*

T3 *Make sure that you read the question carefully. It asks for groups of rocks, not names of different types of rock.*

T4 *Always check to see whether a question like this is asking for the main types of weathering, or the different types of physical and chemical weathering.*

T5 *Both heat and moisture help to produce chemical weathering reactions.*

T6 *Although these are separate types of chemical weathering, in many cases all three will be taking place at the same time. Carbonation, which is a very important form of chemical weathering in limestone areas, is described in the section on the Yorkshire Dales (p. 23).*

2.5 ROCKS AND LANDSCAPES

Granite, limestone, chalk and clay all have a strong influence on landscape and scenery in the UK.

GRANITE UPLANDS: DARTMOOR

Dartmoor in South-west England is a rugged upland rising to over 600 metres. The upland is made entirely from granite, one of the toughest rocks. The Dartmoor granite is part of a much larger mass (**batholith**) which underlies much of the south-west peninsula. Smaller masses crop out further west at Bodmin Moor, Land's End and the Scillies (Fig. 2.5).

The magma which formed the Dartmoor granite cooled and solidified slowly within the Earth's crust. Gradually, after millions of years of weathering and erosion the overlying rocks were stripped away, exposing the granite at the surface (Fig. 2.6).

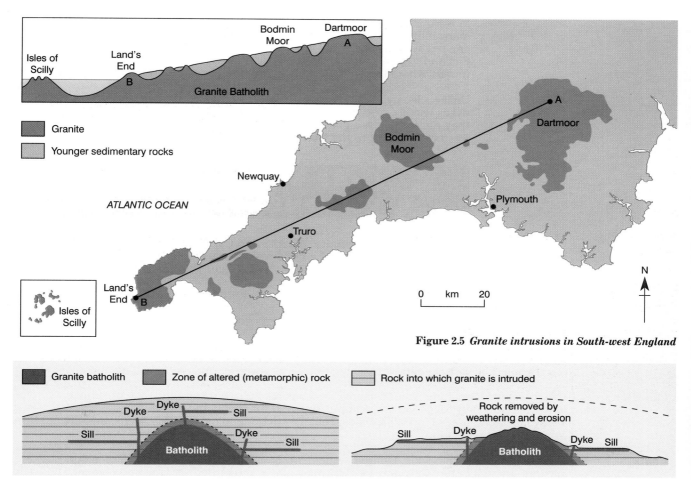

Figure 2.5 *Granite intrusions in South-west England*

Figure 2.6 *Formation of a batholith*

Granite landscapes owe their appearance to the rock's hardness, impermeability and many joints. Thus granite landscapes are often:

● Rugged uplands like Dartmoor and the Cairngorms.

● Poorly drained with large expanses of boggy moorland.

● Deeply dissected into steep valleys by the many surface streams and rivers.

● Dominated by isolated rock outcrops called **tors**.

Tors are probably Dartmoor's most striking landforms. Masses of weathered granite like Hay Tor rise 20 to 30 metres above Dartmoor's surface (Fig. 2.7). They form by deep chemical weathering along the granite's vertical joints.

MINOR IGNEOUS INTRUSIONS

Masses of igneous rock which cool slowly within the Earth's crust are known as **intrusions**. Batholiths such as Dartmoor are large-scale intrusions. But most intrusions are much smaller. These minor intrusions include **sills** and **dykes** (Fig. 2.6).

Sills are horizontal sheets of igneous rock sandwiched between older rocks. Because igneous rocks are generally harder than surrounding rocks they erode more slowly. This means that where sills crop out (e.g. on valley sides) they often form steep slopes. One of the best known sills in the British Isles is the Whin Sill. It has a strong influence on the landscapes of northern England.

Figure 2.7 *Tor on Dartmoor*

21

In Northumberland, the Whin Sill forms a steep ridge which is followed for many miles by Hadrian's Wall (built in Roman times). Where the Whin Sill crosses streams and rivers it creates rock steps and waterfalls. Two of England's most spectacular waterfalls – High Force and Cauldron Snout – have formed where the Whin Sill cuts across the River Tees in the northern Pennines.

Unlike sills, dykes cut across the bedding planes of older rocks. As a result dykes usually crop out vertically, in long narrow bands (Fig. 2.6). Sometimes they run for miles, e.g. the Cleveland Dyke stretches all the way from Mull in western Scotland to the North York Moors.

CASE STUDY: QUARRY DEVELOPMENT ON HARRIS?

Hard rocks such as granite, dolerite and Carboniferous Limestone are important resources for the building industry (Table 2.2). However, these rocks are often found in areas of high scenic value. This can lead to conflict.

Table 2.2	The economic value of rocks
ROCK TYPE	VALUE AND LAND USE
Granite	Upland areas with steep slopes and poor soils. Rough grazing for sheep. Water catchment. Recreation (hill walking, climbing). Quarrying for roadstone, ornamental stone and china clay.
Limestone	Quarrying for roadstone, lime, cement, steelmaking, etc. Thin soils and lack of surface water support only rough grazing and pasture land for sheep and cattle. Many limestone areas (Yorkshire Dales, Peak District, Mendips) are very scenic and are important for recreation.
Chalk	Lack of water and thin soils. Limited settlement. Mainly rough grazing and permanent pasture, though better soils may be cultivated. Chalk is quarried for lime and cement.
Dolerite	Mainly quarried for roadstone. Outcrops of dolerite cover only small areas and therefore have little effect on land use.
Clay	Produces heavy soils suitable for livestock farming, especially dairying and beef. Clay (e.g. Gault Clay and Wealden Clay) is widely quarried to make bricks in many parts of the UK.

In 1993, Redland, a large transnational quarrying company applied for permission to extract an igneous rock (anorthosite) on the island of Harris in the Outer Hebrides (Fig. 2.8). The company planned to develop the largest quarry in Europe, and produce 600 million tonnes of stone chippings for the building industry.

The local council supported Redland's plans. It reasoned that the quarry would bring substantial economic benefits to Harris. Among the benefits were:

- Employment. The quarry would create 100 new jobs. With a total population of just 2,200 and high unemployment on Harris, this was a significant number.
- A halt to depopulation. The quarry would bring money into the island's economy. This would help to slow down out-migration and population decline (between 1951 and 1991 Harris's population fell by 40 per cent).

Environmentalists and most of the islanders opposed the development. They argued that:

- The quarry would be a permanent scar on one of the most beautiful and unspoilt islands in the Outer Hebrides. It would mean the removal of an entire mountain – Roineabhal.
- The proposed site of the quarry was protected as a National Scenic Area.
- The quarry would create a lot of noise and dust.
- The fish and shellfish industries would be at risk from polluted ballast water discharged by 120,000-tonne bulk carriers needed to transport the rock.
- The quarry would harm the island's tourism industry.

In 1995, a public enquiry looked into the issue. Eventually it rejected the proposal. The enquiry concluded that the cost to the environment was simply too great and did not justify the economic benefits.

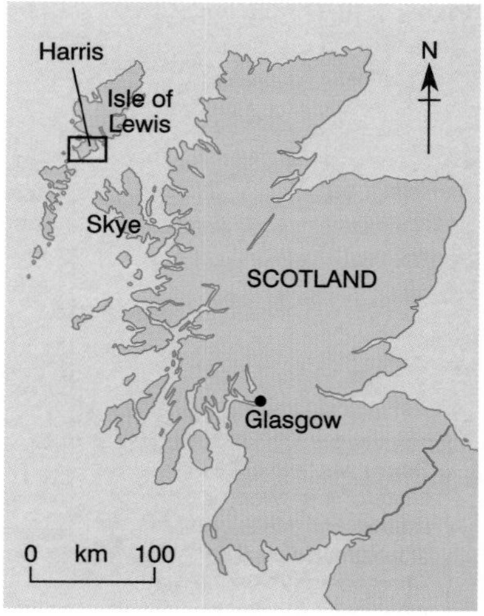

Figure 2.8 *Harris Island, Scotland*

LIMESTONE: THE YORKSHIRE DALES

The largest area of limestone in the UK crops out in the Yorkshire Dales in northern England (Fig. 2.9). This hard Carboniferous Limestone has one distinctive property; it dissolves slowly in rainwater:

- Rain falls through the atmosphere reacting with carbon dioxide gas to form weak (carbonic) acid. The weak acid soaks into the soil.
- The carbonic acid reacts with limestone to form calcium bicarbonate.
- The calcium bicarbonate dissolves in water. The rate of lowering of a limestone surface is around 4 cm per 1,000 years.

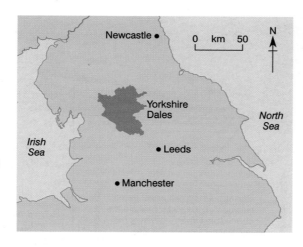

**Figure 2.9
*Yorkshire Dales***

The result of this chemical weathering is a distinctive limestone or **karst scenery** (Fig. 2.10). Its main features are: limestone pavements, scars, dolines and shake holes, swallow/sink holes, and caves.

CHALK: THE SOUTH DOWNS

Chalk is a type of soft limestone. It is also a **porous** rock. Like a sponge, chalk traps water in the tiny air spaces (or pores) between its mineral particles. The rock's porosity explains why there are so few permanent streams and rivers on chalklands.

Figure 2.10 *Formation of karst scenery*

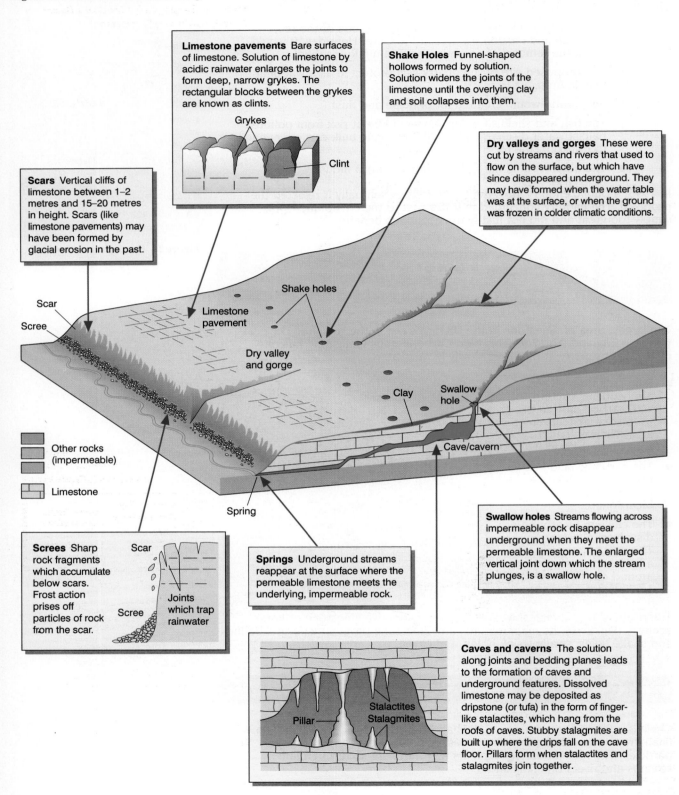

Limestone pavements Bare surfaces of limestone. Solution of limestone by acidic rainwater enlarges the joints to form deep, narrow grykes. The rectangular blocks between the grykes are known as clints.

Grykes

Clint

Shake Holes Funnel-shaped hollows formed by solution. Solution widens the joints of the limestone until the overlying clay and soil collapses into them.

Dry valleys and gorges These were cut by streams and rivers that used to flow on the surface, but which have since disappeared underground. They may have formed when the water table was at the surface, or when the ground was frozen in colder climatic conditions.

Scars Vertical cliffs of limestone between 1–2 metres and 15–20 metres in height. Scars (like limestone pavements) may have been formed by glacial erosion in the past.

Scar

Scree

Shake holes

Limestone pavement

Dry valley and gorge

Clay

Swallow hole

Cave/cavern

Other rocks (impermeable)

Limestone

Spring

Screes Sharp rock fragments which accumulate below scars. Frost action prises off particles of rock from the scar.

Scar

Scree

Joints which trap rainwater

Springs Underground streams reappear at the surface where the permeable limestone meets the underlying, impermeable rock.

Swallow holes Streams flowing across impermeable rock disappear underground when they meet the permeable limestone. The enlarged vertical joint down which the stream plunges, is a swallow hole.

Stalactites
Stalagmites

Pillar

Caves and caverns The solution along joints and bedding planes leads to the formation of caves and underground features. Dissolved limestone may be deposited as dripstone (or tufa) in the form of finger-like stalactites, which hang from the roofs of caves. Stubby stalagmites are built up where the drips fall on the cave floor. Pillars form when stalactites and stalagmites join together.

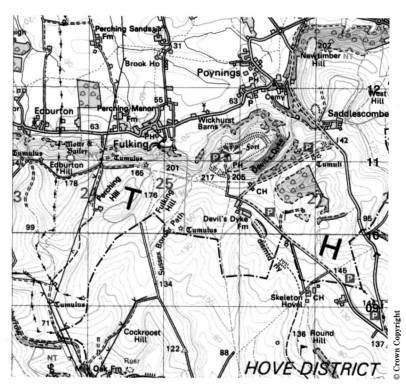

Figure 2.11
Chalk landscape: part of the South Downs (1:50,000 Ordnance Survey map)

© Crown Copyright

Lack of surface water presents a problem for settlement in chalk areas. As a result settlements tend to cluster around wet points such as springs (Fig. 2.11). There are two places where springs commonly occur in chalklands:

- At the foot of steep **scarp slopes** where the chalk rests on impermeable rock such as clay (Fig. 2.12).
- On **dip slopes** where the zone of saturated rock (**water table**) reaches the surface (Fig. 2.12).

Figure 2.12
Water table in chalk escarpment, South Downs

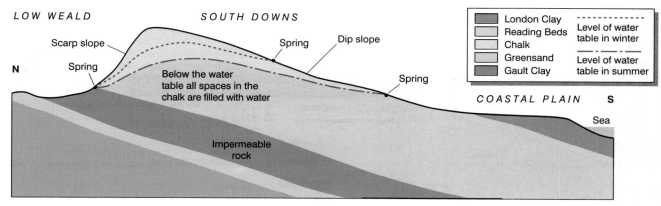

London Clay	- - - - - -
Reading Beds	Level of water
Chalk	table in winter
Greensand	
Gault Clay	Level of water table in summer

The South Downs are a line of chalk hills (an **escarpment**) stretching from Hampshire to Beachy Head near Brighton. Although averaging only 200 metres in height, they are impressive. Most prominent is the steep, north-facing scarp slope which rises abruptly from the Low Weald (Fig. 2.11). Behind the scarp, a gentle dip slope runs down to the Channel coast. In several places the escarpment is cut by the valleys of southward flowing rivers such as the Arun, Ouse and Cuckmere.

Although chalk is a relatively less resistant rock, it often forms bold relief features such as escarpments. There are two reasons for this:

25

- Chalk is often more resistant than its surrounding rocks which are worn down more quickly.
- The absence of streams and rivers (normally the main factors in erosion) in chalkland areas.

The complicated network of dry valleys on the dip slope of the South Downs tells us that rivers and streams were at one time common in chalk areas (Fig. 2.11). These dry valleys formed during the Ice Age when the chalk was permanently frozen, and rivers flowed on the surface during the brief arctic summers.

CLAY

Clay is one of the least resistant of all rocks. Easily weathered and worn down by rivers and glaciers, it often forms extensive lowlands. In northern Britain lowlands such as the Vale of York and the Solway Plains are covered with a thick layer of **till** (boulder clay). This heavy, sticky material was left behind 13,000 years ago as the great ice sheets and glaciers of the last ice age finally melted. The clay found in southern Britain is much older. Sandwiched between more resistant rocks such as chalk and limestone, it often forms broad valleys (vales) like the Vale of Oxford, and the Vale of the White Horse in Wiltshire.

Check yourself

QUESTIONS

Q1 What do permeable and porous rocks have in common?

Q2 What is the main difference between a permeable and a porous rock?

Q3 Name one area where each of the following rock types is found:

granite, limestone, chalk, clay

Q4 Why do limestone areas have both underground streams and dry valleys on the surface?

Q5 Explain the formation of springs.

Q6 Why were villages sited on springs?

REMEMBER! Cover the answers if you want to.

ANSWERS

A1 Both permeable and porous rocks allow water to pass through them.

A2 In a permeable rock the water moves through joints in the rock whereas in a porous rock the water moves through the tiny air spaces or pores.

A3 Granite – Bodmin Moor.

Limestone – Yorkshire Dales.

Chalk – South Downs.

Clay – Vale of the White Horse.

TUTORIAL

T1 This is the main reason for the difference between the underground features in limestone and clay areas.

T2 Carboniferous limestone is a permeable rock which has a particularly well developed system of joints. This is why caves form in this type of rock.

T3 There are other examples in this chapter.

ANSWERS

A4 Limestone at the present time is permeable, so the water does not remain on the surface. During the Ice Age joints in the rock became blocked with ice. This stopped any surface water draining away. Rivers flowed over the surface, carving out valleys. When the underlying rock thawed, the joints became unblocked, allowing the surface water to drain away, and leaving dry valleys.

A5 Springs are formed where underground water comes to the surface. This will happen where water soaks through a porous or permeable rock and meets an impermeable rock, or where the water table reaches the surface.

A6 Springs provided a regular supply of water.

TUTORIAL

T4 *A similar explanation can be given for the dry valleys in chalk areas.*

T5 *The most common area is along the foot of the scarp slope where the chalk meets the clay.*

T6 *These villages had the additional advantage of being above the flood level and would enjoy better soils, formed from a mixture of chalk and clay.*

2.6 FOLDING AND FAULTING

Some landscapes owe their appearance more to folding and faulting than to rock types. Folding and faulting result from massive **tectonic** forces (chapter 1) in the Earth's crust.

FOLDING

Most sedimentary rocks were originally deposited in horizontal layers. Sometimes these rocks lay undisturbed for millions of years. More often, tectonic forces within the crust compress the rocks and fold them into new shapes. Folded sedimentary rocks form the highest mountains ranges in the world including the Himalayas, the Alps, the Andes and the Rockies.

ANTICLINES AND SYNCLINES

If you place a sheet of A4 paper on a flat surface and apply gentle pressure at both ends, a simple arch or upfold will form. Powerful tectonic forces fold rocks in a similar way. We call these simple upfolds **anticlines** (Fig. 2.13).

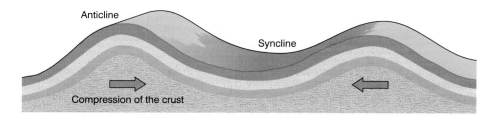

Anticline

Syncline

Compression of the crust

Figure 2.13
Anticlines and synclines

In South-east England, the Weald of Kent and Sussex was once a dome-shaped anticline. However, the forces of weathering and erosion soon got to work. Rivers stripped away the outermost layers of rock, to create an **eroded anticline** (Fig. 2.14). Today, the youngest rocks form the outer rim of the Weald leaving the oldest rocks exposed near the centre. The outer covering of chalk has almost disappeared. Only the inward facing escarpments of the North and South Downs survive (Fig. 2.15).

Figure 2.14
Cross-section of the Weald, an eroded anticline

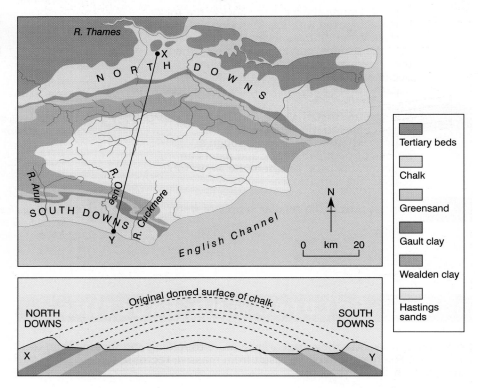

Sometimes, instead of pushing the rocks up, folding creates a downfold or **syncline** (Fig. 2.13). Both London and Paris occupy locations in the centre of shallow synclines.

EXPLAINING FOLDING

How can huge masses of rock crumple to form mountains up to 8 kilometres high? Imagine two continents, separated by a shallow sea, which are slowly moving together. As the continents get closer, the sedimentary rocks on the sea bed arch upwards to form **fold mountains**.

This is how the Himalayas formed. India, transported on the Indo-Australian plate, moved northwards towards Eurasia. The ancient sea separating the two continents narrowed until India collided with Eurasia. The rocks on the sea floor buckled into a concertina of folds, forming the Himalayas.

FAULTING

Tectonic forces don't always cause folding. Some rocks are either too rigid or too brittle to fold. When these rocks are put under pressure they are more likely to break. We call this **faulting**.

Faulting results from both tension and compression in the Earth's crust. Tension occurs when the crust is stretched. This happens at constructive plate margins, where rising magma from the mantle forces plates apart (chapter 1). The most spectacular effect of faulting is the formation of **rift valleys** (Fig. 2.15) such as the East African Rift valley and Thingvellir in Iceland. Outbursts of volcanic activity often accompany the formation of rift valleys.

There are three different types of fault: **normal faults**, **reverse faults** and **tear faults** (Fig. 2.16). Both normal and reverse faults can give rise to steep slopes known as **fault scarps**, and block mountains (**horsts**).

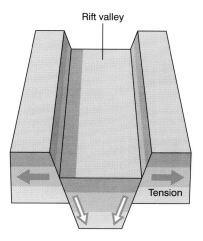

Figure 2.15 *Formation of rift valleys*

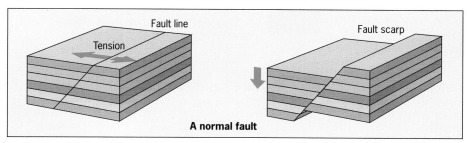

A normal fault

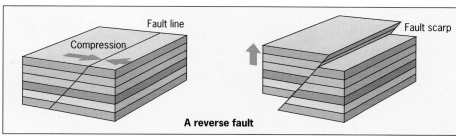

A reverse fault

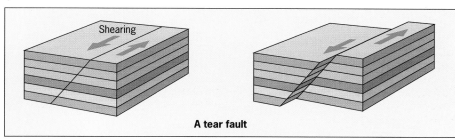

A tear fault

Figure 2.16
Types of fault

Check yourself

QUESTIONS

Q1 Name and locate an example of each of the structures A–C below:

Q2 What is the difference between folding and faulting?

Q3 Why are the oldest rocks found in the central part of the Weald of South-east England?

Q4 What kind of mountains are the Himalayas?

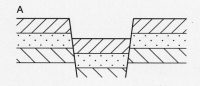

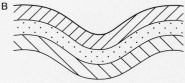

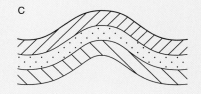

ANSWERS

A1
A Rift Valley, e.g. East Africa.

B Syncline, e.g. London Basin.

C Anticline, e.g. Weald of South East England.

A2
When rocks are subjected to immense pressure from the side they fold, so long as they are not brittle. If they are brittle they crack or fault.

A3
The rocks in the centre of the Weald were the earliest layers of sedimentary rocks to be laid down. The whole area was folded upwards into an anticline. The top layers were eroded away to reveal the oldest rocks at the surface.

A4
Fold mountains.

A5

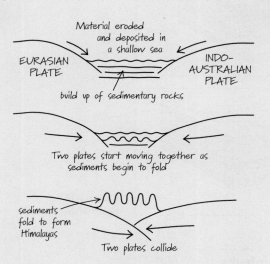

TUTORIAL

T1
Definitions and examples are very common questions in GCSE examinations. Make sure that you know which features are specifically listed in the syllabus and that you remember a good example of each.

T2
Remember that there are three kinds of faults: normal, reverse and tear.

T3
The rocks at the centre of an anticline are stretched when they are folded. This makes them weaker, and therefore more easily eroded.

T4
Other examples are the Alps, the Rockies and the Andes.

T5
There is a difference between a labelled diagram and an annotated diagram. A labelled diagram merely includes single words or phrases labelling the different parts. An annotated diagram includes short descriptions or explanations in the diagram.

EXAMINATION CHECKLIST

The facts and ideas that you should know and understand after studying rocks and landforms are:

- Understand that rocks are made up of a number of different minerals.

- Know that there are three groups of rocks.

- Know that igneous rocks are made from molten magma below the Earth's surface, which solidifies and appears at the surface when the overlying rocks are eroded away.

- Know that metamorphic rocks are rocks that have been changed by heat and pressure.

- Know that sedimentary rocks are either fossilised remains of animals and plants or layers of rocks that have been broken down by weathering or erosion.

- Understand how the two kinds of weathering can break down rocks 'in situ'.

- Understand that granite is an impermeable rock on which tors and boggy marshland develop.

- Understand that limestone is a permeable rock on which karst scenery develops.

- Understand that chalk scenery has a lack of surface drainage with a complex system of dry valleys.

- Understand that clay is found over extensive areas of lowlands and produces soils which are sticky and heavy when wet.

- Understand that pressure on rocks can cause folding and faulting which leads to the formation of anticlines, synclines and rift valleys.

KEY WORDS

These are the keywords. Tick them if you think you know what they mean. Otherwise check on them.

minerals	igneous	sedimentary	metamorphic
magma	lavas	basalt	granite
weathering	erosion	strata	bedding planes
metamorphosed	erosion	joints	faults
freeze-thaw	scree	blockfields	insolation
weathering	exfoliation	solution	oxidation
hydration	batholith	tors	intrusions
sills	dykes	karst scenery	porous
scarp slopes	dip slopes	water table	escarpment
till	tectonic	anticlines	eroded anticline
syncline	fold mountains	faulting	rift valleys
normal faults	reverse faults	tear faults	fault scarps
horsts			

EXAM PRACTICE

Sample Student's Answer and Examiner's Comments

1a) i) *and* **ii)**
The answers are correct.

iii)
He has misunderstood the question. Instead of describing the features, he has dealt with climate, soil factors and weathering. The features of a granite landscape are:

- *rugged uplands* **(1 mark)**
- *large expanses of boggy moorland* **(1 mark)**
- *steep valleys dissected by streams and rivers* **(1 mark)**
- *isolated rock outcrops called tors* **(1 mark)**

The one mark given is for the mention of tors in the final line.

iv)
This question was marked in levels. He does not reach beyond Level 1, because all that he has recognised is the basic link between the granite and areas of low population density. In order to reach the Level 2, which shows clear understanding, he would have to mention that some granite areas (e.g. Penwrith, St. Austell) have a higher population level. Level 3 demands detailed understanding, so a grade A candidate would have to explain that other rock types, like those found on Exmoor, also support low population densities.

---

1 (a) Study Figure 2.5 and the map below showing population density in South-west England.

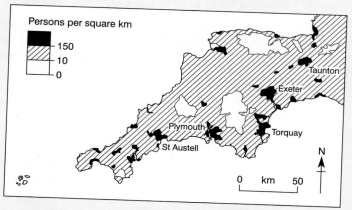

Persons per square km

150
10
0

Taunton
Exeter
Plymouth
Torquay
St Austell

N

0   km   50

(i) What type of rock is granite? (1 mark)

Granite is an igneous rock and it doesn't let water in it.

(ii) Name ONE economic use of granite. (1 mark)

Used in buildings.

(iii) What are the main features of a granite landscape? (4 marks)

The main features of a granite landscape are high rainfall and low fertility. The rocks will not have weathered that much because they only weather when the rainwater gets into their joints and then the water freezes. This will expand the rock by about 10%. I think it will have a low fertility rate. And the landscape may have tors on them.

(iv) Use the maps to describe the relationship between the areas of granite and population density in South-west England. (3 marks)

There is not a high population density where there is an area of granite. For example, Penwrith is a granite area but only has 10 persons per square km. No one lives on Dartmoor where there is granite, and where there is no granite (e.g. areas such as Torquay) 150 people per square km live there. So I think the relationship is that very few people live in granite areas, whereas in non-granite areas there are a lot more people (high population density).

(b) Why do Carboniferous Limestone areas often have large underground drainage systems? (6 marks)

Many limestone areas often have these drainage systems because the limestone is permeable and porous which allows water through. The swallow hole lets surface water through. This makes a cave after a while and a spring is formed with stalagtites and stalagmites. Water gets in through the pavement too.

(c) Choose either a CHALK or LIMESTONE or GRANITE upland area that you have studied.

How has human activity affected the beauty of this area? (4 marks)

Rock type: Limestone.

Area studied: Pennines — Yorkshire.

Effects of human activity:

The Pennines in Yorkshire attract many tourists who enjoy walking and pot-holing. This weakens the structure of the caves underground. More water is being let through the pavements which are being worn away. Many stalagtites and stalagmites have been stolen from the caves and some have been vandalised. The cars and vehicles gradually ruin the landscape.

SEG, 1993

b) This question is testing the candidate's understanding of physical processes and so credit is given for explanation. The candidate has shown only a basic understanding of the permeability of limestone rocks, and so he cannot be awarded more than 1 mark (Level 1). A grade A candidate would have to show a detailed understanding of the carbonation process, and how calcium carbonate reacts with the water, which is really a weak solution of carbonic acid, (worth 5–6 marks).

c) The area of the study chosen is too large to gain a mark. The area must be much more specific, such as the Yorkshire Dales or even a smaller area like Malham. He has tried to relate the effect of tourism to the beauty of the chosen area. He has included clear references to walking, pot-holing and the effect of cars, all of which are problems in limestone areas. This allows the answer to be marked at Level 2 (2 marks given). If the area chosen had been more specific, it would have given the student the opportunity to make more detailed references, and therefore reach Level 3, worth 3–4 marks.

He achieved 10 out of 23 marks which would have been a Grade C. A grade A candidate would have to achieve 15–16 marks.

Questions to Answer

The answer to Question 2 can be found in Chapter 18.

2 a) i) Study the diagram below which shows some of the features of limestone (karst) scenery near Gaping Gill in the Yorkshire Dales National Park.

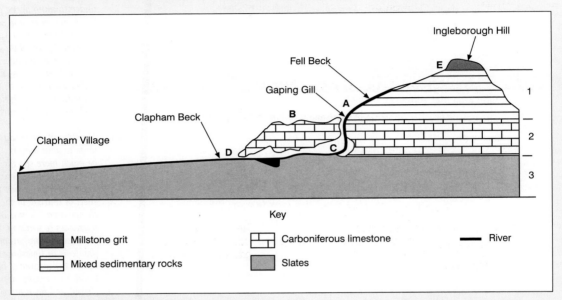

Key

Millstone grit   Carboniferous limestone   —— River

Mixed sedimentary rocks   Slates

   Which of the letters shows where you would find:

   A limestone pavement?

   A swallow hole/sink hole?

   A cavern?   (3)

ii) Describe the course of Fell Beck.   (3)

iii) Describe the formation of Gaping Gill and the course of Fell Beck.   (6)

b) What problems could be caused by large numbers of visitors to Gaping Gill?   (3)

SEG (specimen paper)

3.1 THE WATER CYCLE

Water moves in an endless cycle between the atmosphere and the Earth's surface. At its simplest the **water cycle** consists of a number of stores and flows. The stores, which include the atmosphere, oceans, soils, permeable rocks, lakes and ice sheets hold water for varying lengths of time. Flows transfer water between the various stores. The main flows in the water cycle are precipitation, evaporation and rivers.

3.2 RIVERS AND THE WATER CYCLE

When precipitation reaches the ground it gets into rivers by one of three pathways:

- Over the ground surface.
- Through the soil.
- Through permeable rocks such as chalk and sandstone.

Water running over the surface gets into rivers quickly – often within a few hours. Water flowing through the soil takes longer – up to one or two days. However, this is rapid compared to the rate at which water moves through permeable rocks. Water following this route may take months or even years before it adds to river flow.

3.3 WHAT RIVERS DO

Rivers are channels of water which drain the land surface. They do three main things:

- They erode the land.
- They transport rock particles (sediment) and dissolved minerals produced by **erosion** and **weathering**.
- They deposit the transported material.

In doing these things rivers create new **landforms**. In the uplands these landforms mainly result from erosion. In the lowlands they are formed mainly by the deposition of river sediment.

3.4 DRAINAGE BASINS

Precipitation falling onto the land surface eventually flows into rivers:

- The area drained by a river and its tributaries is called a **drainage basin** or **catchment**.
- The boundaries (**watersheds**) of a drainage basin separate one drainage basin from another.

The River Ure in North Yorkshire drains an area of just over 1,000 square kilometres (Fig. 3.1). Figure 3.1 shows that the River Ure and its tributaries form a tree-like (**dendritic**) drainage pattern. Tiny tributaries such as Fossdale Gill reach to the most distant watersheds. Here on the boggy, peat-covered moors of the North Pennines the River Ure has its **source**. From its source the river flows south-eastwards for nearly 80 km. The River Ure receives two major

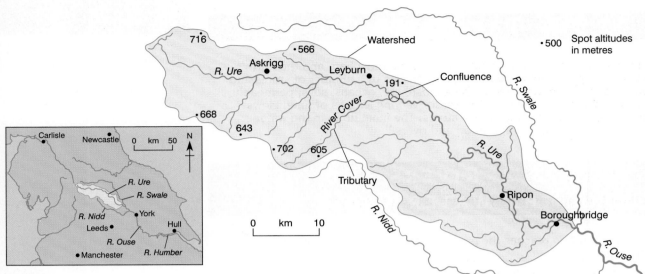

Figure 3.1
The River Ure's drainage basin.

tributaries – the Swale and the Nidd. After its **confluence** with the Nidd it forms the River Ouse, and eventually drains into the Humber **estuary** and the North Sea.

3.5 RIVERS AS LANDSHAPING AGENTS

THE LONG PROFILE

The cross-section of a river, from its source to its mouth, is known as the **long profile** (Fig. 3.2). The long profile is typically concave with a steep gradient in the upper course and a gentler gradient downstream. As we move downstream three changes take place:

- A decrease in the river's gradient.
- An increase in the volume of water (i.e. discharge) in the river.
- An increase in the amount of sediment carried by the river.

These changes affect the river's ability to erode the landscape and transport its sediment **load**. As a result, different processes and different landforms are found in a river's upper, middle and lower courses.

Figure 3.2
Long profile of the River Ure.

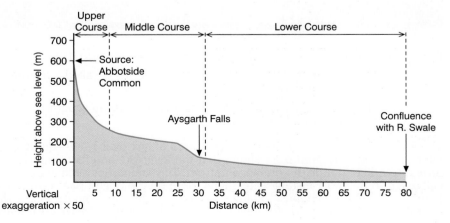

THE UPPER COURSE

Steep slopes dominate the upper course of the River Ure. Much of this area lies between 300 and 600 metres above sea level. The North Pennine hills force moist air from the Atlantic Ocean to rise, drenching the highest areas of the catchment with more than 1500 mm of precipitation a year. In the upper course, three things give the River Ure and its tributaries plenty of energy:

- Slopes with steep gradients.
- High altitude (means water has potential energy).
- Heavy precipitation.

The River Ure and its tributary streams use this energy to:

- Transport water.
- Transport sediment.
- Overcome friction caused by the river's bed and banks.
- Erode the river's bed, banks and valley sides.

EROSION PROCESSES

River erosion is most effective in the upper course. Not only do rivers have lots of energy here but weathering and erosion also produce large quantities of coarse rock fragments. These sediments form most of the river's load (Table 3.1). They are also the river's main erosional tools. After heavy rain these coarse sediments slide and roll along the river bed (Table 3.1).

Table 3.1	The river's load
Bed load	Coarse sediments (boulders, cobbles, pebbles) rolled and dragged along the river bed. This movement is called traction. Smaller, sand-sized particles are bounced along the bed in a process called saltation.
Suspended load	Fine silt and clay particles suspended in the water and transported downstream.
Dissolved load	Rocks which are soluble, such as limestone, are transported in solution. Unlike the bed load and suspended load (which are transported only at high flow), the dissolved load is transported all the time.

All this causes the river to act like a giant grinding machine, cutting vertically into its bed and eroding the land.

Table 3.2	River erosional processes
Abrasion	Coarse sediments (bedload) wear away the bed and banks.
Attrition	The bedload itself is gradually worn down as it is transported (by scraping along the river bed and by collision with other sediments). Sharp edges are removed and sediments become both rounder and smaller.
Hydraulic action	The force of running water alone can erode soft rocks such as clay, sands and gravels. The pressure of water moving into cracks and bedding planes can remove slabs of rocks from the channel bed and sides.
Solution	Rocks such as chalk and limestone can be dissolved by acid river water and transported away in solution.

Check yourself

QUESTIONS

Q1 Why is the term 'water cycle' a useful one to describe the movement of water between the atmosphere and the Earth's surface?

Q2 Draw a simple diagram to show three ways in which a river transports its load.

Q3 Why is a river with a large bed load likely to erode more effectively than a river with a smaller bed load?

Q4 Match the following 'Heads and Tails':

Heads	Tails
A source of a river	is where two rivers join.
A tributary	marks the edge of a drainage basin.
A confluence	is a river which flows into another river.
A watershed	is the start of a river.

REMEMBER! Cover the answers if you want to.

ANSWERS

A1 There is a continuous movement of water from the atmosphere to the Earth's surface (precipitation), across the land (water stored in rivers, seas, etc.) and then back to the atmosphere (evaporation).

A2

A3 The bed load is the largest material a river carries. Unlike the solution and suspension loads, the bed load is in contact with the bed, so it erodes more.

A4 A source of a river is the start of a river.

A tributary is a river which flows into another river.

A confluence is where two rivers join.

A watershed marks the edge of a drainage basin.

TUTORIALS

T1 *Make sure that you use technical terms such as stores, evaporation and precipitation. If you use technical terms effectively you will gain credit in two ways. First, you will gain marks for your geographical knowledge. Second, the examiner can award up to a further 5 per cent for your English. The 'SPaG' mark covers spelling, punctuation, grammar, and technical language.*

T2 *Many questions will ask you to draw diagrams. This is particularly common in physical geography topics. If a question asks for a diagram (or diagrams) then you must use them, as there will be marks for them in the mark scheme. On the other hand, if the question does not ask for diagrams then you can still use them and gain credit. Make sure that your diagrams are clear and well labelled.*

T3 *This is a more difficult question because it is asking you to show your understanding of facts about the transport of a river's load. You need to know about traction and saltation. You also need to show that you can take your answer a stage further, and relate these processes to the erosion of the river's bed. This type of question will be towards the end of a particular section in an exam paper. This is the type of question the grade A and B candidates will be expected to do well at.*

T4 *Make sure that you can define technical terms such as these.*

3.6 LANDFORMS IN THE UPPER COURSE

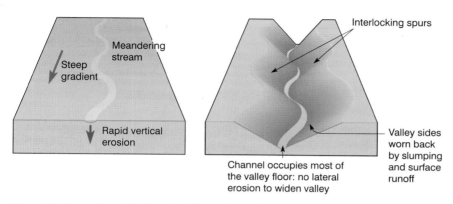

Figure 3.3 *Formation of V-shaped valley and interlocking spurs.*

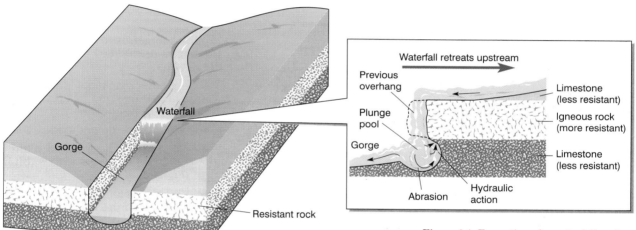

Figure 3.4 *Formation of a waterfall and gorge.*

The main landforms in the upper course are:

- V-shaped valleys.
- Interlocking spurs.
- Pot holes.
- Waterfalls and rapids.

As the river erodes vertically into its bed it cuts deep **V-shaped valleys** (e.g. Fossdale Beck in Figure 3.7). Where a river flows over solid rock (e.g. where a band of hard limestone crosses the River Ure at Aysgarth Falls), pebbles trapped in swirling eddies drill circular **pot holes** and slowly wear away the bed. While the river erodes vertically it often follows a winding course. This gives V-shaped valleys a meandering plan. In such valleys **interlocking spurs** block the view upstream (Fig. 3.3).

Where bands of harder rock cross the channel, **waterfalls** and **rapids** form (Fig. 3.4). Softer rock which crops out at the foot of the waterfall, is attacked by abrasion and hydraulic action (Table 3.2). Slowly the harder rock is undercut until it overhangs and eventually collapses (Fig. 3.4). In this way the waterfall gradually retreats upstream. As it does so it leaves behind a deep narrow gorge (Fig. 3.5).

Figure 3.5 *The gorge downstream from High Force.*

39

3.7 LANDFORMS IN THE MIDDLE COURSE

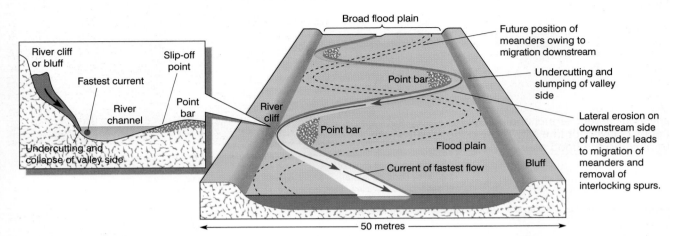

Figure 3.6 *The main features of a river's middle course.*

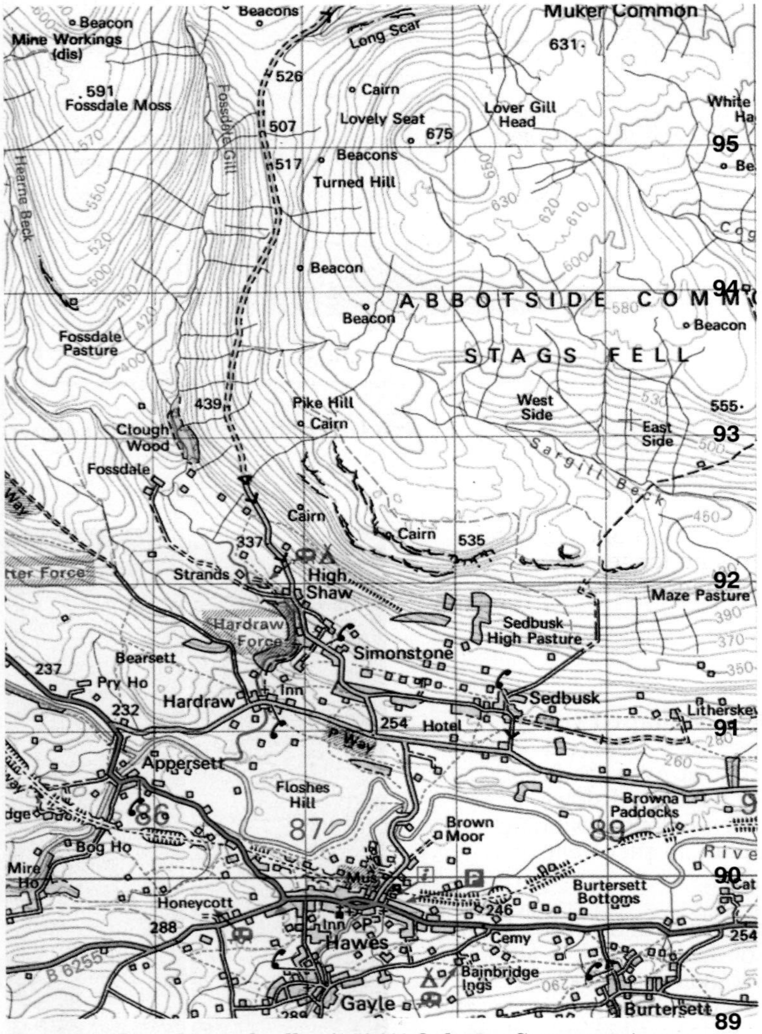

Eight or nine kilometres from its source the River Ure enters its middle course (Fig. 3.2). Here the river has:

- A greater discharge – it drains a larger area and has received many tributaries.

- A greater sediment load.

- A broad, flat floor (**flood plain**) bordered by gentle slopes (**bluffs**) (Fig. 3.6).

- Larger meanders which swing from one side of the valley to the other (Fig. 3.6).

- Steep **river cliffs** where the river erodes the valley sides (Fig. 3.6).

- A gentler gradient.

Why do these changes occur? The answer is that the processes operating in the middle course differ from those in the upper course. With a gentler gradient and more pronounced meanders, **lateral erosion** becomes important. Lateral erosion causes the river to widen its valley. Meandering is the key to understanding the change in valley shape.

In a meander the water flows fastest on the outside of the meander bend (Fig. 3.6). The current undercuts the bank and causes erosion. If the meander is right up against the valley side, this undercutting can result in the collapse of the valley slope. In this way the valley is gradually widened. This is called lateral erosion.

Figure 3.7 *River Ure and valley (1:50,000 Ordnance Survey map).*

© Crown Copyright

Opposite the undercut bank is a lower bank (**slip-off slope**) (Fig. 3.6). Here sediments are deposited to form a **point bar**. Over hundreds of years the meanders slowly change position and move downvalley. As the meanders migrate they remove all traces of interlocking spurs.

The river's wide, flat valley floor is known as a flood plain (Fig. 3.8). It is made up of river sediment (**alluvium**). Alluvium comprises both coarse and fine sediments. Pebbles and gravel accumulate as point bars on the inside of meanders. As meanders migrate across the valley, point bar deposits eventually cover the entire flood plain. Meanwhile, when the river spills out of its channel and across the valley floor it deposits layers of fine silt. These deposits also help to build up the flood plain.

Figure 3.8 *Flood plain of the River Lune in Cumbria.*

3.8 LANDFORMS IN THE LOWER COURSE

The River Ure enters its lower course in the last 30 kilometres or so before it joins the River Ouse. Compared to its middle course the river has:

- An even gentler gradient.
- A larger sediment load which mainly consists of fine silt held in suspension.
- A larger discharge as the river now drains a much larger area.
- A very broad, shallow valley: so broad that the meanders no longer reach from one side of the valley to the other.
- Larger meanders with occasional cut-off (**ox-bow**) lakes.
- Natural embankments called **levées** on each side of the river channel.

OX-BOW LAKES

In a river's lower course the meanders no longer reach from one side of the flood plain to the other. This means that the valley is no longer being widened. Instead, erosion is confined to the river's channel. Ox-bow lakes form (Fig. 3.9) when:

- Meanders loop back on themselves (forming an almost complete circle).
- Lateral erosion cuts through the narrow meander neck and straightens the river's course.
- The old meander is abandoned and left isolated on the flood plain as an ox-bow lake.

LEVÉES

Levées are natural embankments along the sides of rivers' channels. They form because in times of flood there is a sudden loss of energy when the river leaves its channel. As a result the river deposits much of its load immediately beside its channel.

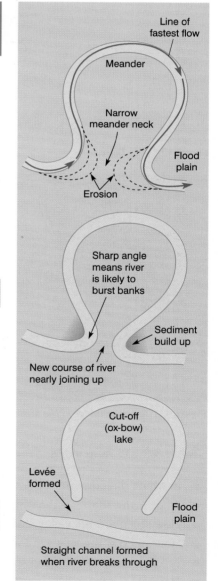

Figure 3.9 *Formation of ox-bow lakes.*

3.9 RIVER MOUTHS

A river mouth is the place where a river meets the sea. There are two types of river mouth: estuaries and deltas.

ESTUARIES

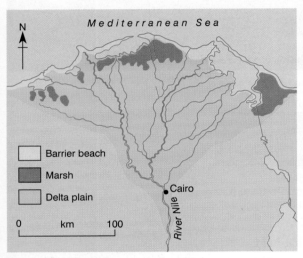

Figure 3.10 *Nile Delta.*

Legend:
- Barrier beach
- Marsh
- Delta plain

0   km   100

Estuaries are funnel-shaped river mouths. They form where strong tidal currents remove the sediment deposited by the river. About 20,000 years ago during the Ice Age, estuaries like the Thames and the Humber were wide, lowland river valleys. Then the Ice Age ended. As the ice sheets and glaciers melted the sea level rose. This flooded the lowland valleys and formed wide, shallow river mouths. Sediments swept in by the tides built-up mud flats and salt marshes, narrowing the river mouths. It is this that gives estuaries their distinctive smooth, funnel shape today.

DELTAS

Not all river mouths are estuaries. Some rivers reach the sea in **deltas**. Deltas form where river mouths become choked with sediment. This causes the main river channel to split up into hundreds of smaller channels or **distributaries**.

Deltas form because river silt is deposited faster than it can be removed by waves and tides. This happens in two circumstances:

- When tides are weak, e.g. in the almost tideless Mediterranean and Black Sea.
- When rivers have very large sediment loads (e.g. Ganges and Brahmaputra rivers in South Asia) so that waves and tides cannot remove all of the silt deposited by the river quickly enough.

There are two common types of delta: **arcuate** and **bird's foot**. The River Nile has a classic triangular-shaped (arcuate) delta (Fig. 3.10) with a smooth, rounded coastline. The Mississippi has a bird's foot delta with a distinctive branch-like appearance (Fig. 3.11).

Table 3.3 is a checklist of important questions you should ask yourself when describing a river and its valley from an OS map.

Figure 3.11 *Satellite image of the Mississippi Delta.*

Table 3.3 OS map skills: describing a river and its valley

- In which direction does the valley run?
- What is the shape of the valley in cross-section?
- How steep are the valley sides?
- How steep is the valley in long profile?
- Are there any interlocking spurs?
- How wide is the valley floor?
- Are there any waterfalls or rapids?
- Is there a flood plain?
- Are there any ox-bow lakes?
- Does the river and/or valley meander?
- Is the valley typical of a river's upper, middle or lower course?

Check yourself

QUESTIONS

Q1 Look at the following diagrams of a typical river's course.

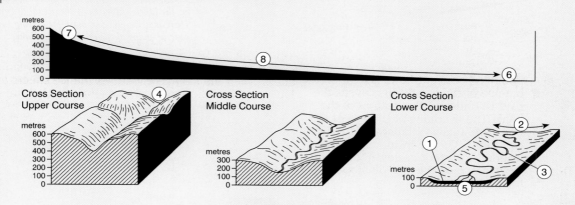

Match each of the labels 1–8 in the diagram to the following list:

deposition; long profile; delta; meander; steepest gradient; slightest gradient; V-shaped valley; widest floodplain.

Q2
i) Draw a labelled cross-section of a river meander to show clearly the differences between the inside and the outside of a river bend.
ii) Explain fully the features you have shown.

Q3 What is the difference between a tributary and a distributary?

Q4 Divide the following features into three lists under the headings of upper course, middle course and lower course:

levées, river cliffs or bluffs, point bars, meanders, waterfalls, interlocking spurs, flood plain, lateral erosion, alluvium, V-shaped valley, ox-bow lakes, deltas, potholes.

REMEMBER! Cover the answers if you want to.

ANSWERS

A1
1 – Deposition; 2 – Widest flood plain;
3 – Meander; 4 – V shaped valley;
5 – Delta; 6 – Slightest gradient;
7 – Steepest gradient; 8 – Long Profile.

TUTORIALS

T1 *This is an idealised picture of a typical river. If you have the chance, study a local river in the field. Look at a number of rivers on Ordnance Survey maps. In the UK rivers are generally too short to show a well developed lower course. The Mississippi in the USA is a very good example of a river which has all the classic features of the lower course.*

ANSWERS

A2 i)

INSIDE   OUTSIDE

DEPOSITION

River cliff

Slip off slope   Point bar

EROSION

ii) The river's current flows fastest on the outside of the bend. This causes the river to undercut the bottom of the bank. The overhang at the top of the bank eventually collapses and a river cliff forms. On the inside of the bend where the current is slower, deposition takes place on the slip-off slope to form a point bar.

A3 A tributary brings water to another river. A distributary takes water away from a river.

A4

Upper Course	Middle course	Lower course
waterfalls	river cliffs or bluffs	deltas
interlocking spurs	point bars	levées
V-shaped valley	lateral erosion	ox-bow lakes
potholes	meanders	flood plain
		alluvium

TUTORIALS

T2 i) *Remember that the cross-section is a view looking either up or down the valley. You may be asked to construct an accurate cross-section from an Ordnance Survey map, or to draw a simple sketch section. Remember that most of the marks will be for the labels rather than the actual drawing. There may be just one mark for getting the general shape of the cross-section right.*

ii) *Watch for the command word. This question asks for explanation, not description.*

T3 *Distributaries are associated with the formation of deltas.*

T4 *These are the key landforms that you are likely to be asked about in a GCSE question on rivers. Make sure that you know what they are. You may be asked to draw or describe them, or explain their formation. It is useful to know an example of each landform too.*

3.10 RIVER REGIMES AND HYDROGRAPHS

RIVER REGIMES

The volume of water flowing down a river in a given time is known as its **discharge**. We usually measure discharge in cubic metres per second (cumecs). Over a year the pattern of discharge for a river is rarely even. These seasonal changes of flow are called the **river's regime**.

River flow in the British Isles shows marked seasonal contrasts. The highest flows normally occur in winter; the lowest in summer. The main reasons for this pattern are seasonal differences in rates of **evaporation**, **transpiration**, and **interception**, and the amount of moisture in the soil (Table 3.4).

Table 3.4	Natural influences on river regimes in the British Isles
Precipitation	Precipitation is fairly evenly distributed throughout the year.
Evaporation	Evaporation is highest in summer so only a small amount of precipitation gets into rivers at this time.
Transpiration	Plants transpire moisture throughout the growing season (between April and September).
Interception	In summer most moisture trapped on leaves and stems is evaporated before it reaches the ground.
Soil moisture	In winter, soils are waterlogged. Precipitation reaching the ground simply runs-off the surface and into rivers.

People can also influence river regimes:

- Dams create reservoirs which even-out river flow (e.g. Aswan High Dam, Egypt, and the River Nile).
- Water abstracted from rivers or from permeable rocks reduce river flow (e.g. River Kennet in Berkshire).
- Afforestation of drainage basins reduces the volume of water that gets into rivers (e.g. Kielder Forest and North Tyne river in Northumberland).
- Water transferred between river basins will both increase and decrease river flow (e.g. water transferred from the River Tyne to the River Tees in North-east England).

STORM HYDROGRAPHS

Storm hydrographs (Fig. 3.12) are concerned with short-term precipitation events lasting a few hours and their effects on river flow:

- Storm **hydrographs** plot precipitation amounts and river discharge at hourly intervals.
- Discharge is made up of **slowflow** and **quickflow**.
- Slowflow is water which comes from permeable rocks and the soil.
- Quickflow is water from recent precipitation events (generally surface flow).
- **Peak discharge** is the maximum river flow.

Figure 3.12 *A Storm hydrograph.*

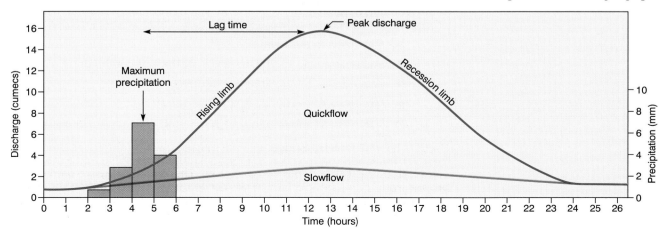

- The **rising limb** of the hydrograph shows the increase in discharge following a period of precipitation.
- The **recession limb** of the hydrograph shows falling discharge.
- The difference in time between maximum precipitation and peak discharge is called the **lag time**.

Table 3.5	Factors influencing the shape of a storm hydrograph
Precipitation characteristics	<ul><li>The amount of precipitation per hour (i.e. intensity). High intensity precipitation is less likely to seep into the soil (and therefore more likely to run off into rivers).</li><li>The total amount of precipitation.</li><li>The type of precipitation. Snow may take days or weeks to melt.</li></ul>
Soil moisture characteristics	<ul><li>If the soil is saturated precipitation will quickly run off into rivers. Drier soils will absorb precipitation. Water will then move slowly through the soil into rivers.</li></ul>
Drainage basin characteristics	<ul><li>Rock type: porous rocks such as chalk and sandstone will store water and release it slowly. Impermeable rocks such as granite and shale will cause rapid run-off.</li><li>Vegetation cover: the denser the vegetation cover, the greater the interception and transpiration. Interception increases evaporation and slows down the movement of water to rivers.</li><li>Slopes: the steeper the slopes the faster the rate of run-off.</li><li>Drainage density: the more streams and rivers that drain an area the faster the run-off.</li><li>Drainage basin shape: near circular drainage basins have higher peak flows than long, narrow drainage basins.</li></ul>

3.11 RIVERS AS HAZARDS

FLOODING ON THE RIVER URE

Flooding is a natural thing for rivers to do, and flood plains are where they do it! But because we build settlements on flood plains, floods are often a major hazard to people and property.

Between 21 and 23 February 1991 the biggest floods for over a century occurred around several North Yorkshire rivers. At the peak of the flood the River Ure at Boroughbridge reached a record flow of 550 cumecs. In the Ure's headwaters nearly 200 mm of rain fell between the 21 and 22 February. However, heavy precipitation was not the only cause of flooding. Other factors included:

- Snowmelt in the Pennines.
- Steep slopes in the higher areas of the Ure catchment.
- Ground which was already saturated.
- Low rates of evaporation and transpiration in winter.
- Low rates of interception by trees and other plants in winter.

Hardest hit was Boroughbridge, a small market town on the River Ure. Here the river breached the town's flood embankments and spilled into the town centre, flooding it to a depth of 1.4 metres. There was extensive damage to property and many people had to be rescued from homes and stranded cars by dinghy (Fig. 3.13).

£2M DEFENCE SCHEME FAILS TO PROTECT TOWN

A FLOOD defence scheme costing £2m built to protect Boroughbridge from a one-in-100-year disaster, failed yesterday – nine years after the town was last inundated to a depth of 1.2 m.

Within 50 minutes of water first pouring over the flood barriers the town was covered with 1.4 m of water.

Angry and sometimes tearful owners immediately demanded an inquiry.

And that was exactly what they were promised by the chairman of Harrogate council's public works committee, Councillor Bob O'Neill, who spent the day in the town.

He said: "We owe it to the people of Boroughbridge. It [the inquiry] will look at all aspects of this calamitous situation and I promise that there will be no whitewash."

After the disaster of 4 January 1982, when more than 100 homes flooded, the River Tutt was diverted out of the centre of Boroughbridge along a relief channel which allowed the water to be pumped into the River Ure upstream of the town.

New brick and earth flood defence barriers were also built to keep the water out of the town even if it reached the 1982 level.

Although the Tutt diversion worked at the weekend the water crept around the north-east corner of Boroughbridge and began pouring over the earth barrier into the car park, spreading along High Street and Fishergate.

Council workmen and volunteers tried to build a wall of sandbags but their efforts were abandoned after 40 minutes because lives were at risk.

The flooding happened so quickly that a car owned by Harrogate council's chief executive, Mr John Lovell, and another owned by a National Rivers Authority official were stranded in Fishergate with only their roofs showing.

Efforts were then turned to rescuing 35 people trapped in their homes.

Many were rescued by a fleet of small dinghies owned by local people before the operation was continued in steel boats provided by the Royal Engineers from Claro Barracks in Ripon.

People were scooped from their upstairs windows using the bucket of a front-loading shovel.

Most people were evacuated to the schoolroom of Boroughbridge Methodist Church, where the WRVS set up an emergency centre.

A reconnaissance by Army helicopter revealed that the River Ure had spread across its flood plain to a width of more than two miles in places.

The helicopter also checked on the safety of occupants on isolated farms. Many traders, including an antique dealer, Mr Richard Wilson, whose shop stands at the lowest point in the High Street, had no chance to move their property to safety.

Mr Wilson, Chairman of Langthorpe parish council, where many homes were flooded said: "People put their trust in the river authority and they have been let down".

Source: *Yorkshire Post*, 1991.

Figure. 3.13
Article from the Yorkshire Post.

FLOOD CONTROL MEASURES

Various methods are used to prevent and control flooding (Fig. 3.14). Flood prevention is the most effective. It includes managing land use within drainage basins to minimise run-off, and building dams to store flood water. Schemes which involve the construction of dams and reservoirs are often multi-purpose. Apart from flood prevention they may also generate hydroelectricity, supply water and provide opportunities for recreation and leisure.

Another approach is flood control. Here the aim is to confine flood waters to the river. This may be achieved by building embankments and relief channels, or by widening, deepening and straightening river channels. But perhaps the simplest solution to the flood problem is to avoid locating settlements on flood plains.

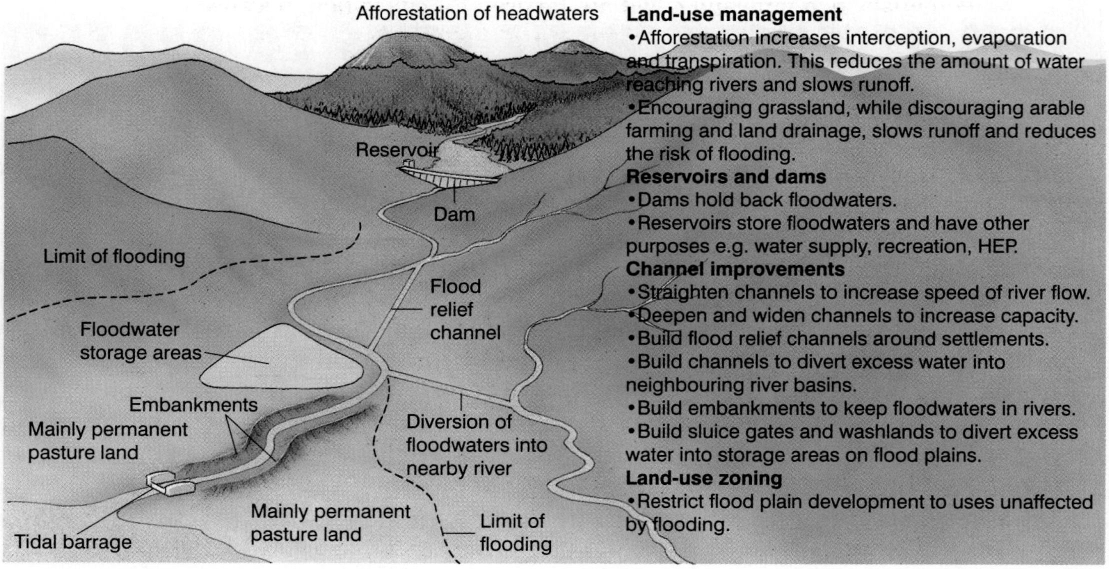

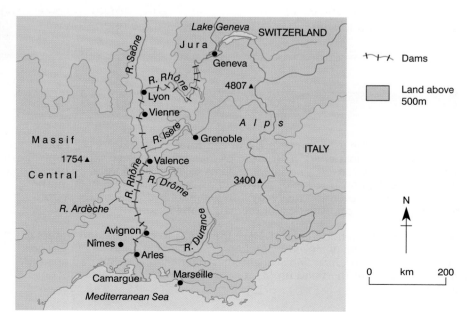

Afforestation of headwaters
Land-use management
•Afforestation increases interception, evaporation and transpiration. This reduces the amount of water reaching rivers and slows runoff.
•Encouraging grassland, while discouraging arable farming and land drainage, slows runoff and reduces the risk of flooding.
Reservoirs and dams
•Dams hold back floodwaters.
•Reservoirs store floodwaters and have other purposes e.g. water supply, recreation, HEP.
Channel improvements
•Straighten channels to increase speed of river flow.
•Deepen and widen channels to increase capacity.
•Build flood relief channels around settlements.
•Build channels to divert excess water into neighbouring river basins.
•Build embankments to keep floodwaters in rivers.
•Build sluice gates and washlands to divert excess water into storage areas on flood plains.
Land-use zoning
•Restrict flood plain development to uses unaffected by flooding.
Reservoir
Dam
Limit of flooding
Flood relief channel
Floodwater storage areas
Embankments
Mainly permanent pasture land
Diversion of floodwaters into nearby river
Mainly permanent pasture land
Limit of flooding
Tidal barrage

Figure 3.14
Flood control and flood prevention methods.

3.12 River Management: Taming the Rhône

The Rhône is one of Europe's largest rivers. Its source is a glacier high up in the Alps in Switzerland. After a journey of 800 km the Rhône reaches the Mediterranean Sea in southern France, where the river forms a large delta known as the Camargue (Fig. 3.15).

Until the mid-twentieth century the Rhône was a wild river. Violent and unpredictable, and fed by powerful meltwater tributaries such as the Durance and Isère, the Rhône was a major hazard to people living along its banks. The untamed Rhône caused three main problems:

- At regular intervals its floods devastated towns such as Arles, Avignon and Vienne.

Figure 3.15
The River Rhône and its principal tributaries.

Lake Geneva
SWITZERLAND
Jura
Geneva
R. Saône
R. Rhône
4807
Lyon
Vienne
Alps
R. Isère
Grenoble
Massif Central
1754
ITALY
Valence
R. Rhône
R. Drôme
3400
R. Ardèche
R. Durance
Avignon
Nîmes
Arles
Camargue
Marseille
Mediterranean Sea
Dams
Land above 500m
N
0 km 200

- Potentially rich farmland could not be used for cultivation, because its flood plain was both poorly drained and at risk from flooding.
- In spring its powerful flood waters hindered navigation, while in summer low flow and shallow water disrupted navigation.

All this changed in 1933 with the creation of the Compagnie Nationale du Rhône (CNR). The CNR's objective was to tame the river and harness its huge potential as a resource. Over the next 50 years the CNR built 17 dams; shipping locks; and canals along the river. These developments transformed the Rhône from a wild river to a series of artificial lakes and canals. Even where the river flowed freely it was confined within a concrete channel. The taming of the Rhône brought many advantages:

- Control of the river by dams meant an end to flooding.
- Security from flooding allowed the flood plain to be used for the intensive cultivation of fruit, vines and arable crops.
- Water taken from the Rhône was used to irrigate crops.
- HEP generated by turbines installed in the dams provided 20 per cent of France's hydroelectricity.
- The evening-out of the river's flow greatly improved navigation.

3.13 LAND USE IN A RIVER BASIN: THE RIVER TEES

The River Tees has its source on Cross Fell, the highest point in the Pennines. Its mouth is a broad estuary on the North Sea coast, over 90 km to the east. If you were to follow the Tees from its source to its mouth you would notice many changes in land use (Fig. 3.16). These changes reflect differences in the resources and opportunities in the three main parts of the river basin: the uplands, the lowlands, and the estuary.

Uplands

Rough pasture and peat-covered moors dominate the upland parts of the Tees basin. Here, population density is low and settlements are widely dispersed. The main economic activities are:

- Hill sheep farming.
- Quarrying.
- Water catchment.
- Recreation and leisure.

Hill sheep farming is the main economic activity. Other types of farming cannot survive in such a harsh environment. Hill farmers face problems of: a short growing season, poor soils and steep slopes. Quarrying is important in Upper Teesdale. A tough igneous rock called dolerite crops out in this part of the dale and makes an ideal roadstone. High precipitation in the Pennines favours water catchment. There are several large reservoirs in the upper dale, built to supply water to the heavy industries on Teesside. Recreation and leisure are important users of the uplands. Large tracts of heather moorland are managed for grouse shooting and the Pennine Way long distance footpath crosses the area. Other attractions include the spectacular waterfalls of High Force and Cauldron Snout.

Lowlands

The lowlands are densely settled and there are market towns and large villages. In the last 20 years some of the villages have attracted Teesside commuters and have grown rapidly. The Tees Lowlands is a prosperous farming region. Its combination of low precipitation, gentle relief and fertile soils allows a mixture of arable livestock farming.

Estuary

Situated at the mouth of the River Tees is densely populated urban area known as Teesside. Teesside, which includes Middlesbrough, Stockton and Hartlepool is a small conurbation of 350,000 people. It is also one of the largest concentrations of heavy industry in the EU. The estuary provides an excellent location for industries such as iron and steel, chemicals, oil refining and nuclear power. Its advantages include:

- Deep water for large ships which supply the heavy industries with raw materials such as iron ore and crude oil.
- Large areas of reclaimed land – ideal for heavy industries which need large amounts of space.
- Offshore winds which disperse industrial pollution away from Teesside and out to sea.
- Water from the river used for cooling and other industrial processes.

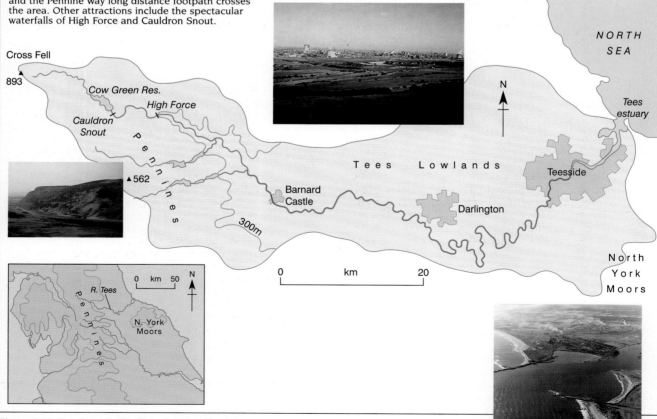

Figure 3.16 *Land use in the Tees drainage basin.*

Check yourself

QUESTIONS

Q1 Study Figure 3.12 and answer the following questions:

i) What was the total rainfall in millimetres?
ii) How many hours did the storm last?
iii) How many hours after the storm did the river reach peak discharge?
iv) Why was there a time lag between the end of the storm and the river reaching peak discharge?

v) If the land near the river was concreted over, how would this affect the lag time?

Q2 Describe the main features of the River Ure and its valley using the Ordnance Survey map extract (Fig. 3.7).

REMEMBER! Cover the answers if you want to.

ANSWERS

A1
i) 15 millimetres.
ii) 4 hours.
iii) 7 hours.
iv) Some of the water did not go directly into the river. Water had to run over the surface to the river. Some water would have soaked into the ground and taken time to move through the soil and rocks.
v) The rainwater would run directly over the surface into the river. The lag time would be shorter.

A2 (The letters refer to the comments in the tutorial section.)

(a) The river runs from west to east. (b) It is slow flowing and is meandering across the valley floor. (c) It comes up against the valley side on the outside of the meanders. The valley has a wide flood plain; about one kilometre in width. (d) The valley sides are quite steep rising 100 metres in less than a kilometre. (e) The gradient of the valley floor is gentle with no major breaks of slope. (f) The valley is typical of the middle course of a river.

TUTORIAL

T1 This type of question, which tests your ability to read a graph and to explain what it shows, is very common. Make sure that you read the graph accurately and use the correct scale. The scale for precipitation is on the right hand side of the graph. Many candidates will use the discharge scale on the left hand side. Always include the units when giving a numerical answer. Part v) is testing your understanding of hydrographs by asking you to consider what would happen in another context.

T2 Notice that the question asks you to describe **both** the river **and** its valley. It is important that you read the questions carefully. Use the series of questions in Table 3.3 to help you answer the question.

a) You can tell this by looking for contour lines that cross the river. Another way is to look at the shape of the confluence, where a tributary joins the main river. (e.g. at 859908). At the point where the tributary joins the main river, it will be dragged in the direction that the main river is flowing.
b) The speed of the river can be deduced from the gentle gradient of the valley floor.
c) Always try to give measurements if possible. They need not be precise, but they will show the examiner that you have some appreciation of scale. Use the grid squares, which are one kilometre in size, as a guide.
d) There is no need to work out accurate gradients. If the contour lines are close together then it is sufficient to say that the land is steep.
e) Major waterfalls are often shown. If they are not, look for a series of contour lines crossing the river.
f) Use all the pieces of evidence you have quoted to state which course of the river it is.

EXAMINATION CHECKLIST

The facts and ideas that you should know and understand after studying rivers are:

- Rivers are part of the endless movement of water known as the water cycle.
- Rivers erode, transport and deposit.
- Rivers can be divided into three parts or courses, each with distinctive profiles and cross sections.
- Rivers transport three types of load.
- There are four types of river erosional processes.
- The upper course of a river has distinctive charactersitics such as V-shaped valleys, interlocking spurs, pot holes and waterfalls.
- The middle course of a river has distinctive characteristics such as meanders, lateral erosion, river cliffs or bluffs, point bars and slip-off slopes.
- The lower course has distinctive characteristics such as a large flood plain, ox-bow lakes, levées, estuaries and deltas.
- A river's regime shows the variations in flow over time, and can be influenced by a number of factors.
- Storm hydrographs show the relationship between precipitation and river discharge.
- Floods are caused in a number of ways.
- A number of control and prevention measures are used to reduce the hazard of flooding.
- Human management of rivers has to be over a whole river basin, such as that of the River Rhône.
- Distinctive types of human land use are found at different positions along a river's course, as shown by the example of the River Tees.
- Ordnance Survey maps can be used to describe the main physical and human features of a river and its valley.

KEY WORDS

These are the keywords. Tick them if you think you know what they mean. Otherwise check on them.

water cycle	erosion	weathering	landforms
drainage basin	catchment	watersheds	dendritic
source	tributaries	confluence	estuary
long profile	load	V-shaped valleys	pot holes
interlocking spurs	waterfalls	rapids	flood plain
bluffs	river cliffs	lateral erosion	slip-off slope
point bar	alluvium	ox-bow lakes	levées
deltas	distributaries	arcuate delta	bird's foot delta
discharge	river regime	evaporation	transpiration
interception	hydrographs	slowflow	quickflow
peak discharge	rising limb	recession limb	lag time

EXAM PRACTICE

Sample Student's Answers and Examiner's Comments

1 Study the figure showing the upper courses of the River Wye and River Severn in Wales.

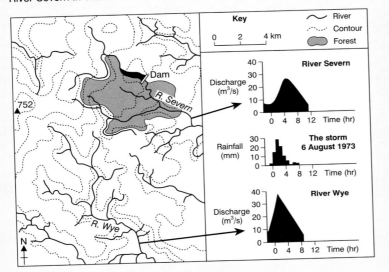

(a) (i) Which river had the higher discharge?   (1 mark)

River Wye.

(ii) Describe how the storm affected the discharge of the two rivers.   (2 marks)

The storm brought high levels of rainfall which increased the discharge. The discharge peaked where the rainfall was highest. The River Severn did not have as high a discharge as the Wye, because it is surrounded by forest which intercepts the rain. This, in turn, spreads the discharge out over a longer period, because rain has to drip off trees into the river.

(iii) From the map, name **one** feature which may have affected the discharge of the River Severn. Explain your choice.   (2 marks)

Name of feature: Forest

Explanation: The trees intercepted the rain which spread the discharge out over a longer period, because the water has to run off the trees into the river.

SEG (specimen paper)

SEG (specimen paper)

EXAMINER'S COMMENTS

This is a Foundation Tier paper and so it is targeted at grades C to G. It is not possible to get higher than a grade C if you are entered for this tier. This means that you have to score very highly in order to reach a grade C. The questions will tend to be straight forward. There will be a number of single-word answers. There will be only one command word in each question. When a question is level marked there are likely to be only two levels, rather than the three found on the higher tier paper.

1a) i)

This is correct. She has read the scale on the hydrographs correctly. Make sure that you read the question carefully. The question does not ask for the height of the discharge. This is the sort of mistake that is easily made, especially at the start of an examination.

ii)

She gives some explanation which would not gain credit as the question says "describe". Two descriptive points are made. "The discharge peaked where the rainfall was highest" and "spreads the discharge out over a longer period". She does not state which river is being referred to. However, the reference to the forest is enough for the examiner to see that the River Severn is the one where the discharge is more spread out. The student should have made it clear which graph is being discussed.

iii)

This question is testing her understanding of factors affecting discharge. There are two credit-worthy points in this answer. These are: the interruption of the rain by the forest, and the fact that it takes time for the water to run off the trees, back into the river.

b) i)

She has used the diagram effectively and makes three separate points. There are two in the first sentence, dealing with the water flowing over the hard rock at the top and then falling into the plunge pool. The third point is to do with the river's load being deposited as a ridge.

ii)

She has not read the question carefully enough. There is enough evidence of understanding the formation of water falls. This allows the answer to reach the top of Level 1, gaining 2 marks. However, her answer does not explain the formation of the gorge by waterfall retreat. The answer cannot therefore reach the highest level, worth 3 marks in this case.

She scored 10 out of the 11 marks available for this part of the question. That would be enough to reach a grade C.

(b) Study the figure, which shows a section through the waterfall at High Force in Upper Teesdale.

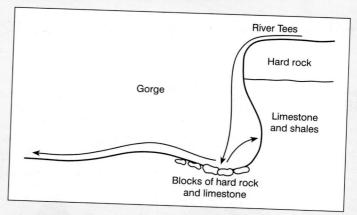

(i) Describe the main features of the waterfall shown in the figure.

(3 marks)

> The river flows over the hard rock at the top and falls into the plunge pool where some water flows downstream, and some splashes back towards the back wall (limestone and shales). Some of the river's load is deposited as a ridge where the water slows down after the plunge pool.

(ii) Explain how the gorge at High Force has been formed.

(3 marks)

> Over millions of years water has flowed over the waterfall at High Force. It may have started as a small waterfall at a fault line but over time the softer rock beneath has been eroded away. The back wall has been eroded by the hydraulic action of the splashback. The lower level of the waterfall will not be eroded much more, because the hard rock is very difficult to erode. The ridge after the plunge road was made by the deposition of material.

Questions to Answer

The answer to Question 2 can be found in Chapter 18.

2 a) Study the field sketch of a meandering river.

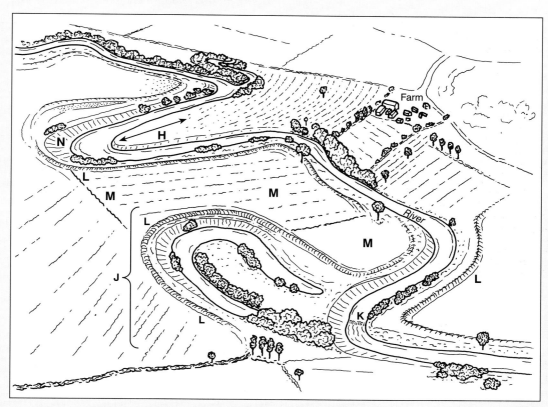

i) Name the features by completing the table below

Letter	Name of feature
H	.... slope
J	....
K	weir
L	flood control embankment
M	....
N	....

(4)

ii) Which way is the river flowing? Give a reason for your answer. (2)

iii) Explain the river processes which have led to the development of landforms H and N. (5)

iv) Explain how the two flood control measures shown attempt to reduce this kind of hazard.

v) State three reasons why river floods generally cause more deaths in LEDCs than in MEDCs? (3)

ULEAC, 1993

CHAPTER 4

GLACIATION

4.1 INTRODUCTION

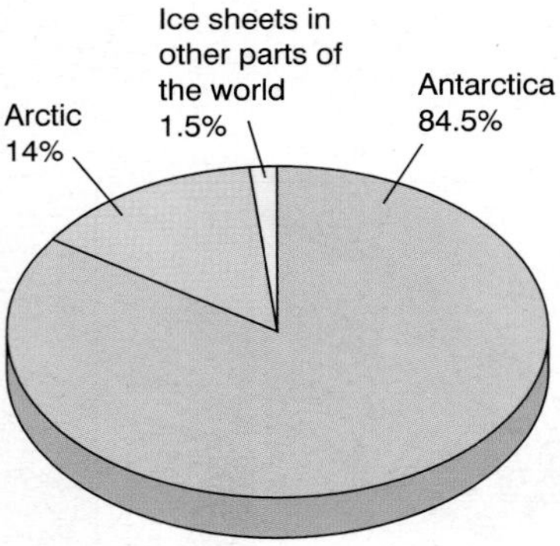

Of all the forces which shape the landscape none has a more dramatic effect than glacier ice. Glaciers are like powerful, earth-moving machines: excavating rocks in the uplands; transporting the rock debris; and finally dumping it in the lowlands. In doing all this glaciers change the landscape.

Ice covers nearly 15 million square kilometres of the Earth's surface. Most of this ice is in the polar regions (Fig. 4.1). However, during the last ice age a vast ice sheet covered the whole of northern Britain. In places ice buried the land to a depth of more than one kilometre.

Then 12,000 years ago the Ice Age ended. A brief cold snap (lasting 1,000 years) saw the return of small glaciers to Britain's uplands. By 10,000 years ago these glaciers had melted too. This was the last occasion that glaciers existed in the British Isles.

Arctic 14%
Ice sheets in other parts of the world 1.5%
Antarctica 84.5%

Figure 4.1
Global distribution of glaciers.

4.2 TYPES OF GLACIER

There are three main types of glacier:

- **Ice sheets** are glaciers on a continental scale. Antarctica is the biggest ice sheet.
- **Ice caps** are mini-ice sheets. They occupy much smaller areas, but like ice sheets they also smother the landscape. The Vatnajökull in Iceland, which is similar in size to Yorkshire, is Europe's largest ice cap.
- **Valley glaciers** are the smallest glaciers. These rivers of ice fill valleys in all of the world's great mountain ranges (Fig. 4.2).

Figure 4.2 *Aletsch valley glacier, Switzerland.*

4.3 GLACIERS AS SYSTEMS

Glacier ice forms in upland areas which lie above the **snowline**. Here snow accumulates faster than it melts. This creates a permanent cover of snow and ice.

Permanent snowfields are the **accumulation zones** for the ice which feeds glaciers (Fig. 4.3). It takes 30 or 40 years for snow to form dense glacier ice. When the ice forms it starts to flow downslope under its own weight. These 'rivers' of ice are called valley glaciers.

If the climate cools or snowfall increases, glaciers will advance. On the other hand, if the climate gets warmer or drier, glaciers are likely to retreat. In the last 150 years most glaciers have been shrinking.

4.4 GLACIER MOVEMENT

Despite being solid and hard, glacier ice flows rather like thick custard. This happens because:

- Individual ice crystals within a glacier slide across each other.
- Meltwater at the base of a glacier lubricates the ice, causing it to slide.

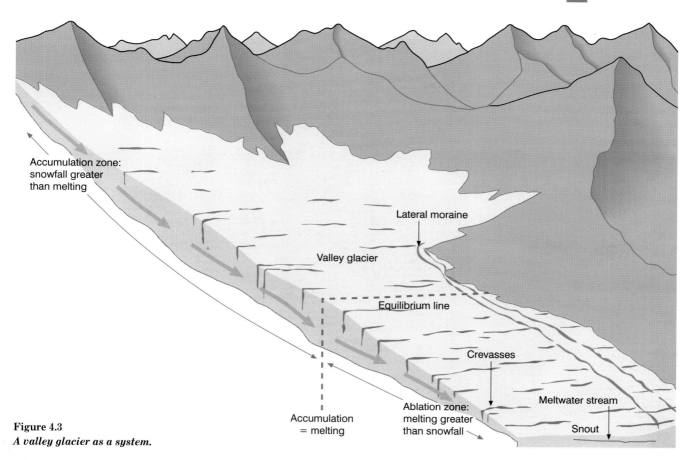

Figure 4.3
A valley glacier as a system.

Glaciers vary in their speed of movement, from 3 metres to 300 metres a year. Their speed depends on:

- Temperatures at the base of the ice: warmer conditions lead to more rapid movement.
- The steepness of the valley down which a glacier flows.
- The amount of ice produced in the accumulation zone.

Different parts of a glacier move at different speeds. One effect of this is to wrinkle the surface of the ice and create giant cracks or **crevasses** (Fig. 4.3).

4.5 CASE STUDY: LANDFORMS OF GLACIATED UPLANDS

The Lake District in Cumbria is a rugged upland made of hard volcanic rocks (Fig. 4.4). During the last two million years ice sheets and glaciers have carved this region into spectacular shapes. The Lake District is a classic glaciated upland. It contains all the major landforms of glacial erosion: corries (cirques), arêtes, glacial troughs, hanging valleys and ribbon lakes.

CORRIES

A **corrie** is a rock basin, surrounded on three sides by steep craggy walls. Blea Water (Fig. 4.5; GR 4410), nestling below the summit of High Street in the eastern Lake District, is one of the largest corries in the British Isles (Fig. 4.6). Today a small circular lake (tarn) fills the Blea Water corrie.

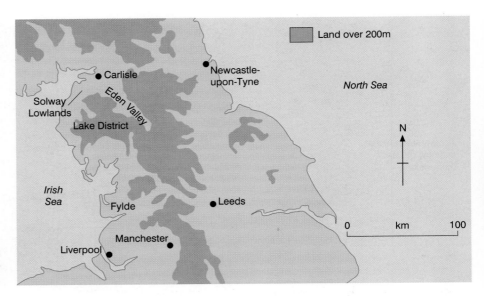

Figure 4.4
*The situation of the Lake District
in northern England.*

Blea Water owes its shape to glacial erosion (Fig. 4.7). This is how it formed:

- During the Ice Age strong westerly winds swept snow from the High Street ridge and piled it up on the eastern slopes.
- Facing ENE, and in shadow for much of the year, the snow beds were protected from melting.
- Over many winters the snow turned to ice and formed a small glacier.
- As the glacier increased in size it began to move downslope.
- As the glacier moved, rock fragments frozen into the ice scraped the sides of the mountain slope. This grinding action is called **abrasion**.
- The glacier also eroded its basin by **quarrying** (plucking). Meltwater at the base of the glacier froze onto rocks. And as the glacier moved forward it dragged or quarried loose blocks from the corrie floor.
- Erosion was less severe at the outlet to the corrie which formed a distinctive 'step' or lip.

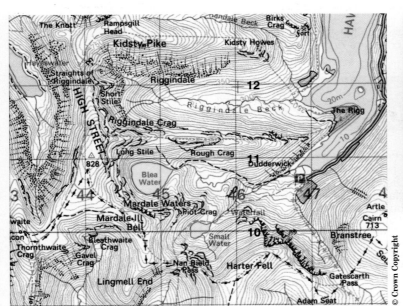

© Crown Copyright

Figure 4.5 *Blea water relief (1:50,000 Ordnance Survey map).*

Figure 4.6 *Blea Water.*

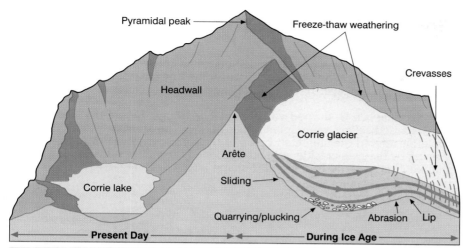

Figure 4.7
Corrie during and after glaciation.

The classic bowl shape of corries is caused by the rotational movement of glacier ice: • Near the centre of the corrie, ice flow is directed downwards to the rock surface. This gives maximum erosion by plucking and abrasion and leads to over-deepening. • Near the lip, the flow is towards the glacier surface. Erosion is less important here. • Plucking causes retreat of the headwall, which is steepened by freeze-thaw weathering.

Glacial erosion did not act alone. Freeze-thaw weathering shattered the rocks on the exposed slopes and helped the corrie eat into the High Street ridge. Meanwhile, these weathered rock fragments fell onto the glacier providing new tools for further abrasion.

ARÊTES

Arêtes are steep ridges which separate glacial valleys or corries. Glacial erosion and freeze-thaw weathering have reduced what were once broad ridges to narrow, knife edges. The ridge between Blea Water and Riggindale (Fig. 4.5; GR 4511, 4611) is an example of an arête.

Figure 4.8
Ice accumulation and glacier movement at the head of Mardale.

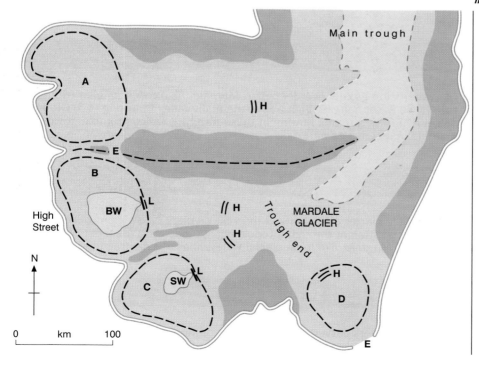

Ice accumulation sources

A Riggindale
B Blea Water
C Small Water
D Gatesgarth

〰️ Shoreline of reservoir

〰️ Shoulder of overdeepening

▨ Trough sides

- - - Ridge or arête

BW Blea Water ⎫ Corie
SW Small Water ⎭ tarns

Ice movement

E Ice smoothed col
H Mouth of hanging valley
L Corrie lip

U-SHAPED VALLEYS

As the Blea Water glacier grew it spilled out of its corrie and flowed downslope (Fig. 4.8). Soon the glacier was joined by ice from the Small Water corrie and from Gatesgarth to form the large Mardale glacier.

Today, Mardale is a **U-shaped valley** or glacial trough. Before the Ice Age most U-shaped valleys were upland river valleys. The Mardale glacier completely altered the shape and plan of the former river valley. Abrasion and quarrying by the glacier widened and deepened the valley, transforming its old V-shaped cross section to a broad U-shape (Fig. 4.9).

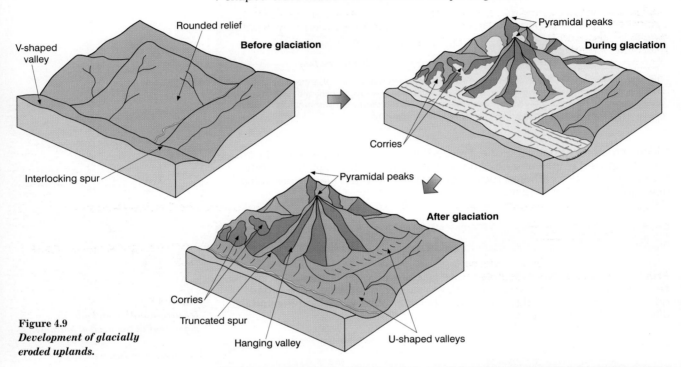

Figure 4.9
Development of glacially eroded uplands.

HANGING VALLEYS

Glacial erosion greatly overdeepened Mardale. As a result smaller tributary valleys were left hanging high above the main valley floor (Fig. 4.5; GR 4612, 482117). Today, streams flowing in these **hanging valleys** tumble down to Mardale in a series of waterfalls.

TRUNCATED SPURS

The Mardale glacier also changed the valley's plan. Like a giant bulldozer the glacier sliced straight through interlocking spurs leaving them cut off or **truncated**. Mardale, like most glacial valleys, has a very straight plan (Fig. 4.9).

RIBBON LAKES

In places, glaciers carved out rock basins on floors of glacial troughs. This happened when erosion increased because of:

- a steepening of the valley's gradient;

- the main glacier being joined by a tributary glacier;
- an outcrop of weaker rock.

After the Ice Age these rock basins flooded to form long, narrow **ribbon lakes**. Haweswater, in Mardale, is a ribbon lake although it has been greatly enlarged by a human-made dam at its northern end. Ribbon lakes can also form where glacial deposits build a natural barrier across a glacial trough.

ROCHES MOUTONNÉES

Roches moutonnées (translation: 'rock sheep') are small outcrops of rock smoothed and steepened by glacier erosion. A smooth gentle slope scoured by glacial abrasion faces up-valley. The down-valley slope, shaped by quarrying, is much steeper.

Check yourself

QUESTIONS

Q1 Name an example of each of the following:
i) ice sheet.
ii) ice cap.

Q2 What is the difference between a valley glacier and an ice sheet?

Q3 Use Figure 4.7 to list three features of a corrie.

Q4 State three ways in which a valley changes after glaciation.

REMEMBER! Cover the answers if you want to.

ANSWERS

A1 i) Antarctica.
ii) Vatnajökull (Iceland).

A2 A valley glacier is confined to a valley. An ice sheet covers a complete area. Valley glaciers are found in highland areas, ice sheets tend to cover lowland areas.

A3 Circular shape, steep back wall (head wall), rock lip at front.

A4 Changes to a U-shape, becomes deeper, becomes straighter.

TUTORIALS

T1 Try to remember one example of each for your exam. Remember not to confuse the Arctic and Antarctica. The Arctic ice is around the North Pole and covers the Arctic Ocean. There is a large land mass under Antarctica which is the area around the South Pole.

T2 The effect of ice in highland areas is sometimes called valley glaciation. This emphasises that the main effect of ice erosion and deposition is in the valleys. The peaks were not covered by ice and so the main effect on these higher areas is from frost shattering. Areas like Antarctica show the effect of continental glaciation, which is an alternative name for lowland glaciation. The word continental gives a better indication of the scale involved.

T3 The term 'armchair shape' is often used. This describes the circular nature of a corrie with its steep slopes on three sides.

T4 The remains of the former valley can be seen on the tops of the valley sides, e.g. truncated spurs, hanging valleys.

4.6 LANDFORMS OF GLACIATED LOWLANDS

Glaciers and ice sheets transport massive amounts of rock debris. This debris comes from two sources:

- Glacial erosion, by abrasion and quarrying (plucking).
- Rockfalls from steep valley slopes, caused by freeze-thaw weathering and rock avalanching.

BOULDER CLAY

Eventually glaciers and ice sheets dump the rock debris they carry. We refer to this material as **boulder clay** (till). Boulder clay is easy to recognise by its unsorted appearance: a random mixture of boulders, rocks, sand and clay.

Most glacial deposition takes place in the lowlands. In North-west England ice sheets from the Lake District blanketed the surrounding lowlands with thick layers of boulder clay known as **ground moraine**. Today, **till plains** like the Solway Lowlands and the Fylde are important areas for livestock farming.

MORAINES

Boulder clay often forms small mounds and ridges which we call moraines (Fig. 4.10):

- **Lateral moraines** form along the sides of glaciers, and are caused by weathering and rockfalls from valley slopes. If a glacier shrinks and retreats up its valley lateral moraines are left as low ridges along the valley side (Fig. 4.11).

- **Medial moraines** form when two valley glaciers meet, and their lateral moraines join together.

- **Terminal moraines** are ridges of till deposited at the front of an ice sheet or glacier. Terminal moraines left by valley glaciers usually form low ridges which stretch from one side of a glacial valley to the other (Fig. 4.10).

- **Drumlins** are low rounded hills made of moraine. In cross-section they look like half-an-egg. They often occur in large numbers and their streamlined shape suggests they were formed by moving ice. Large swarms of drumlins occur in the Eden Valley, between the Lake District and the North Pennines.

- **Erratics** are rocks transported by ice and deposited in completely different geological areas. These rocks stand out as being 'foreign'. For instance, granite erratics from Shap, on the eastern edge of the Lake District, can be found as far away as Cheshire and the Tees Lowlands.

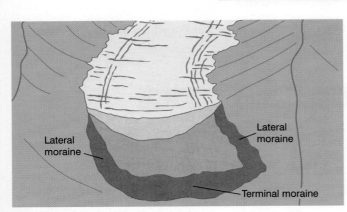

Figure 4.10 *Glacial moraines.*

Figure 4.11 *Lateral moraines, Thorsmark, Iceland.*

MELTWATER DEPOSITS

Powerful meltwater streams and rivers flow beneath ice sheets and glaciers.
They transport huge loads of sand, gravel and boulders. When deposited
these sediments create several distinctive landforms including eskers, kames
and outwash plains (Fig. 4.12).

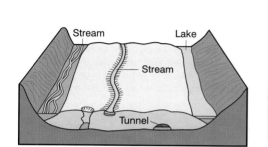

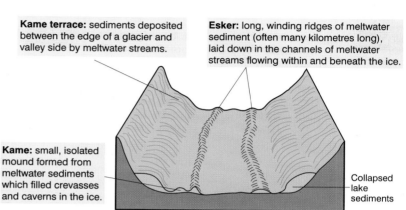

Kame terrace: sediments deposited between the edge of a glacier and valley side by meltwater streams.

Esker: long, winding ridges of meltwater sediment (often many kilometres long), laid down in the channels of meltwater streams flowing within and beneath the ice.

Kame: small, isolated mound formed from meltwater sediments which filled crevasses and caverns in the ice.

Figure 4.12 *Meltwater deposits.*

Check yourself

QUESTIONS

Q1 How do glacial deposits (moraines) differ from river deposits?

Q2 Study the map of Denmark
  i)   What evidence is there that Eastern Jutland and the islands were once covered by ice?
  ii) How was the low range of hills in central Jutland formed?
  iii) Why is Western Jutland known as an outwash plain?

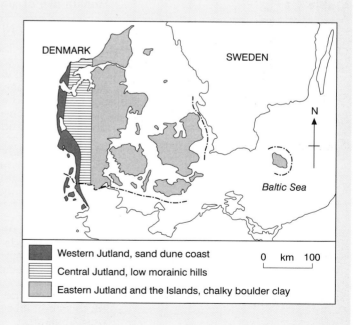

Western Jutland, sand dune coast
Central Jutland, low morainic hills
Eastern Jutland and the Islands, chalky boulder clay

ANSWERS

A1 Glacial deposits are unsorted. Rivers grade or sort their material.

A2
i) The area is covered with boulder clay, which was the ground moraine carried underneath the ice.
ii) They were formed from the material pushed in front of the ice.
iii) The sand deposits were 'washed out' from the terminal moraine by the melt water streams.

TUTORIALS

T1 *This means that in an area where there are moraines there is a great variety of deposits. These will range from very fine sediment, through sands and gravels, and up to large boulders and rocks, some weighing several tonnes.*

T2
i) *This area is very similar to the Fylde Lowlands (see section 4.12). Dairy farming is important here, but it is based on arable crops rather than grass.*
ii) *The terminal moraine marks the furthest point reached by the ice. In this case it had moved south from Norway and Sweden. The alternative name for a terminal moraine is an end moraine.*
iii) *This is evidence that water grades its material. The sand deposits have been sorted out from the mixture of deposits which make up the terminal moraine.*

4.7 THE HUMAN USE OF GLACIATED UPLANDS

Glaciated uplands provide opportunities and impose limits on human activities (Table 4.1). On the one hand their spectacular scenery, landforms and snow

Table 4.1	Human use of glaciated uplands
TYPE OF USE	DESCRIPTION AND EXAMPLES
Recreation and tourism	Spectacular glacial landforms (e.g. cirques, arêtes, U-shaped valleys, hanging valleys, waterfalls, ribbon lakes, etc.) provide opportunities for sight-seeing, walking, rock climbing, etc. Winter tourism in the Alps and Scotland is based on skiing. Summer tourism centres on sight-seeing and water-based activities on the many ribbon lakes. Many glaciated uplands in the UK, Europe and North America are protected as national parks.
Hydroelectric power (HEP)	Glaciated uplands are important for HEP in France, Switzerland, Austria and Norway. Glaciated landforms assist HEP, e.g. U-shaped valleys and hanging valleys create high 'heads' of water. Ribbon lakes are natural storage reservoirs.
Farming	Steep slopes, a cold and damp climate, and thin soils severely limit farming. Only extensive livestock farming (hill sheep) is found in the glaciated uplands of the British Isles.
Water catchment	Heavy relief precipitation, deep glacial lakes for water storage and low population densities provide ideal conditions for water catchment. In the English Lake District, Haweswater and Thirlmere (both ribbon lakes) provide water for towns and cities in North-west England.

make them increasingly popular for recreation and tourism, as well as being ideal for hydroelectric power and water catchment. On the other hand, the harsh climate, thin soils and rugged relief of glaciated uplands offer limited scope for agriculture.

4.8 FARMING IN GLACIATED UPLANDS: THE LAKE DISTRICT

Harsh physical conditions restrict the scope for farming in glaciated uplands. The problems faced by farmers in the Lake District are typical:

- Large areas above 500 metres.
- Steep, rocky slopes.
- Thin, acidic soils which are often poorly drained.
- A growing season which lasts for less than 6 months on the fells.
- A cold, cloudy and damp climate – annual precipitation above 2,000 mm on the western fells.

The physical environment sets limits to what farmers can do. Hill sheep farming is one of the few options. Farms are sited in the valleys where there is shelter and where deeper soils support good quality pasture for hay and silage. Hardy sheep breeds, like the Herdwick and Swaledale, graze the surrounding fells for most of the year. Hill sheep farming has a number of features:

- It is a low input-low output enterprise. Poor quality grazing on the fells means that stocking densities are low.
- Sheep are brought off the fell for lambing in the spring; shearing and dipping in the summer; and for the sale of lambs to lowland farms in the autumn.
- Hill sheep farming is barely profitable, i.e. it is a marginal enterprise.
- Without subsidies from the European Union's Common Agricultural Policy (a fixed annual payment for each ewe) most hill farmers would not survive.
- The long-term future of hill farming is in doubt. Many hill farmers rely increasingly on conservation grants. They receive money to look after the landscape – repair walls, manage hedgerows and farm less intensively in order to conserve wildlife.

4.9 HYDROELECTRIC POWER IN NORWAY

Three-quarters of Norway's energy consumption and all of its electricity is supplied by HEP (Fig. 4.13). The conditions for HEP generation are especially favourable in southern Norway:

- The high plateau (fjell) supports a small ice cap and valley glaciers.
- Precipitation exceeds 2,000 mm a year in many parts of the plateau.
- There are numerous ribbon lakes and corrie lakes which provide natural water storage.
- Glacial erosion has created over deepened glacial troughs and hanging valleys. The result is large vertical differences in height and lots of potential for HEP production.

Figure 4.13
HEP production in Norway.

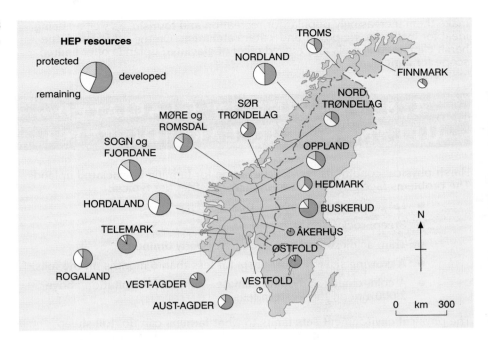

- Powerful meltwater streams drain the ice cap and glaciers of the plateau.
- Southern Norway is the most densely populated part of the country. It includes the four largest cities: Oslo, Bergen, Stavanger and Trondheim. This means that the main region of demand for electricity is also the main region producing electricity.

4.10 SKIING IN THE CAIRNGORMS

Commercial skiing in the British Isles is confined to the Highlands of Scotland. Only in Scotland are the mountains high enough to give a reliable snow cover in winter.

Scotland's first ski resort opened in the Cairngorms in 1961. Since then skiing in Scotland has become big business. In 1995, there were five ski resorts which between them attracted nearly 500,000 people (Fig. 4.14). Skiing is important to the economy of the Scottish Highlands. It creates around 3,000 jobs and is worth £30 million a year.

Cairn Gorm is Scotland's oldest and most popular skiing centre (Fig. 4.15). Skiing began at Coire Cas in 1961 when a new access road from Aviemore through Glen More to Coire Cas was built. A second centre at nearby Coire na Ciste followed in 1974. Cairn Gorm has been highly successful. It has over 50 km of downhill runs and attracts 200,000 skiers a year.

Aviemore, located 15 kilometres from Coire Cas, has grown to be the main resort for Cairn Gorm. During the 1960s and 1970s a range of services and facilities, including hotels, guest houses, chalets, a swimming pool and a new shopping centre were provided for tourists.

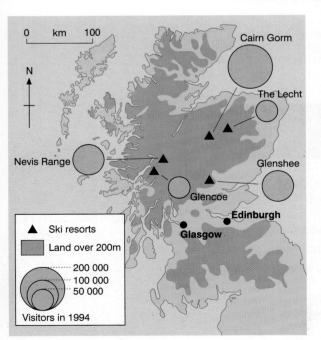

Figure 4.14 *Skiing in Scotland.*

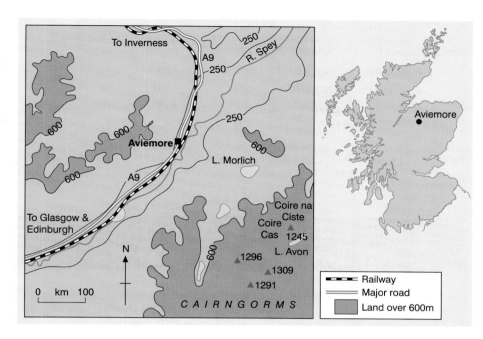

Figure 4.15
Aviemore and the Cairngorms.

As a result, Aviemore became one of the few all-year-round resorts in the UK. While winter visitors flock to the ski slopes, summer visitors come to roam the hills and ancient pine forests, and admire the scenery and wildlife.

4.11 CASE STUDY: ENVIRONMENTAL CONFLICT IN THE CAIRNGORMS

Glaciated uplands such as the Cairngorms are under pressure from the huge growth in tourism and recreation in the last 40 years. Hill walkers, climbers, mountain bikers and skiers compete to use the uplands. The Cairngorms is a unique environment:

- At 1,100 metres it is the highest plateau in the British Isles.

- It has many spectacular glacial landforms: corries, arêtes, glacial troughs, moraines, etc.

- It supports a tundra-like vegetation and is home to some rare plants (e.g. alpine saxifrage) and birds (e.g. ptarmigan, snow bunting, etc.).

The Cairngorms is recognised as an important conservation area; protected both as a National Scenic Area and a National Nature Reserve. Despite its status, protection is not guaranteed. In recent years the main threat to the area has come from the proposed expansion of skiing around Coire Cas. Skiing already has a considerable, if localised impact on the environment (Fig. 4.16):

- It causes erosion on hillsides, leaving ugly scars which are visible in summer.

- It creates unsightly access roads, bulldozed tracts and car parks.

- Chair lifts, ski tows and snow fences straggle the ski slopes.

Figure 4.16 *Coire Cas – skiing and the environment.*

So far, conservationsists have managed to stop further development. However, the developers have the support of local people and the local council. Skiing brings a number of advantages:

- It brings money into the the local economy.
- It creates jobs for local people.
- By providing more local employment it reduces out-migration from the area.

However, if tourism and recreation are to be sustainable and not degrade the upland environment, careful management is vital. This means that a balance between the interests of conservation, developers and local people has to be found.

4.12 FARMING IN GLACIATED LOWLANDS

The Fylde in West Lancashire is a glaciated lowland. During the last ice age, ice sheets moving south from the Lake District plastered the region with a thick layer of boulder clay. These glacial deposits form the basis of an intensive dairy industry (Fig. 4.17):

- The boulder clay weathers to give heavy but fertile soils.
- The damp, mild climate of North-west England, supports lush pasture.
- The mild climate allows a long growing season (275 days a year) so that cattle can graze outside from April to October.
- Farmers make silage from the rich pastures for winter feed.
- There is a huge market for fresh milk on the Fylde's doorstep in Greater Manchester and Merseyside.

Check yourself

QUESTIONS

Q1 Name a location in a glaciated area for each of the following types of human activity:

i) HEP.
ii) Water storage.
iii) Winter sports.

Q2 For each location give one reason why glaciation has helped this human activity in your chosen area.

REMEMBER! Cover the answers if you want to.

ANSWERS

TUTORIALS

| **A1** | i) | HEP – Norway; ii) Water storage – Lake District; iii) Winter sports – Cairngorms. |

A2	i)	Ribbon and corrie lakes act as natural reservoirs. Fast-flowing water falls down the steep sides of a glacial trough from a hanging valley.
	ii)	Creation of reservoirs in natural lakes. Possibility of flooding glacial troughs.
	iii)	Plenty of steep slopes.

T1 *There are other examples but it is best to know one example that you can write about in depth.*

T2 *Notice that the question asks for glaciated features. There are other features which are important, but are not the direct result of glaciation, e.g. the high precipitation in glaciated highland areas is very important for HEP production and for the building of storage reservoirs.*

EXAMINATION CHECKLIST

The facts and ideas that you should know and understand after studying glaciation are:

- The different forms that ice takes.
- The characteristic landforms found in glaciated highland areas.
- What corries, arêtes, hanging valleys and glacial troughs look like.
- How corries, arêtes, hanging valleys and glacial troughs are formed.
- The different forms of glacial deposits.
- How river and glacial deposits differ.
- Why glaciated highlands provide opportunities for HEP, water storage and tourism.
- Case studies to illustrate these forms of human activities in glaciated highland areas.
- That these human activities bring both advantages and disadvantages to an area.

KEY WORDS

These are the keywords. Tick them if you think you know what they mean. Otherwise check on them.

ice sheets	ice caps	valley glaciers
snowline	accumulation zones	crevasses
corrie	abrasion	quarrying
arêtes	U-shaped valley	hanging valleys
truncated	ribbon lakes	boulder clay
ground moraine	till plains	moraines
lateral moraines	medial moraines	terminal moraines
drumlins	erratics	sustainable

EXAM PRACTICE

Sample Student's Answers and Examiner's Comments

(Note: When this question was given in an examination the candidates had a photograph as well as the field sketch.)

1a) i)
This is correct. Notice that she had to make a positive choice of two from three suggested words. The examiner does this to cut down the chance of the candidate getting the answers correct by guesswork.

ii)
She gains both marks. The first mark is in the first sentence. The second mark is for the elaboration in the rest of the answer. In this case the elaboration is a description of the different types of moraine with appropriate examples. One example would have been enough to gain the second mark. This second mark could have been gained by noting one feature of moraines, such as their unsorted nature.

1 (a) Study the field sketch of a glaciated mountain landscape.

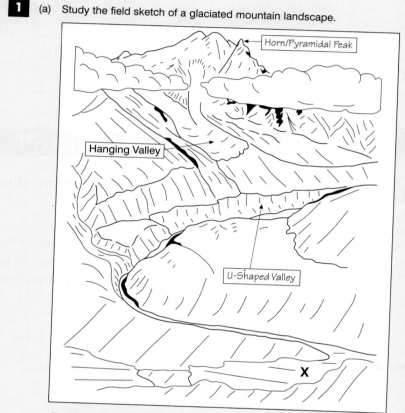

(i) Complete the boxes by using two of the following terms:
(2 marks)

HORN (PYRAMIDAL PEAK)   U-SHAPED VALLEY   CORRIE

(ii) What is a moraine?
(2 marks)

A moraine is a glacial deposit. There are four main types of moraines – lateral moraine (this collects at the side of the glacier and is formed by freeze-thaw action), medial moraine (formed by the joining of two tributary glaciers), terminal moraine (at the front of the ice mass) and englacial moraine (within the glacier).

(iii) Describe the main features of a hanging valley such as that shown. (4 marks)

A hanging valley is a continuous U-shaped depression in the side of a U-shaped valley. It was formed by a small tributary glacier joining the main valley glacier. It has a river running through it and culminates in a waterfall running down the steep valley sides. The waterfall occurs because of the action of the main valley glacier – originally, it was a river valley with interlocking spurs/hills. These were truncated by the glacier, leaving steep valley sides.

(iv) What are the advantages of the location of village X marked in the Figure? (3 marks)

Village X is located in an alluvial fan – alluvium is a glacial deposit that is very fertile and (as can be seen from the photograph) is used for crop growing. There is a good water supply near the village and it is sheltered by the mountains around it (it lies in the valley) and by the coniferous forests surrounding it.

SEG, 1993

a) **iii)**
*She gives a very full answer, but only gains three out of the possible four marks. This is because much of it is explanation rather than the description required by the question. The question allows her to use her factual knowledge. Watch out for the term "such as".
If it is not used in the question, the information has to come from the stimulus material provided; in this case the field sketch (or photograph).
The first two marks are for the position of the hanging valley on the side of the U-shaped valley or glacial trough, and for the tributary glacier joining the main glacier. The third mark came from the reference to the river falling into the main valley via a waterfall. She got this from the photograph rather than the sketch. However, it is a characteristic feature of many hanging valleys and would have gained a mark even if it were not present in this particular example.*

iv)
This question tests her understanding of the relationship between the physical and human geography of glaciated highland areas. She may have studied settlement as part of her GCSE course. If this were the case, then it would be an advantage. However, the knowledge of another geographical topic is not essential. The first mark comes from her study of alluvial fans. The recognition of the importance of water supply and shelter comes from careful analysis of the field sketch and the photograph.

She gained 10 out of a possible 11 marks and would have gained a grade A in this part of the question.

Questions to Answer

The answer to Question 2 can be found in Chapter 18.

2 a) i) Study Figure 4.5 and the simplified contour map below of part of the same area.

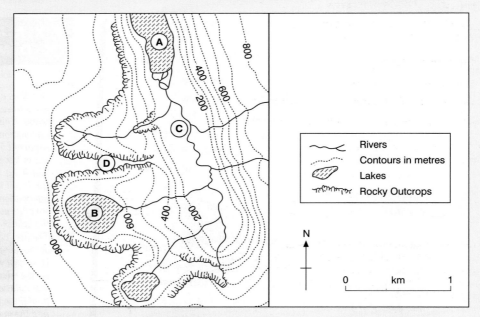

Use both maps to complete the table. Use the correct words from the following list:

Riggindale Crag   glacial trough   ribbon lake   arete   Blea Water

	GLACIAL FEATURE	EXAMPLE
A	....	Haweswater
B	Corrie	....
C	....	
D	....	....

(5 marks)

ii) Describe and explain the differences in shape between the western and eastern sides of the valley shown on the contour map.　(4 marks)

b) Explain why some people live in glaciated highland areas despite steep slopes, poor communications and the cold.　(3 marks)

WJEC, 1983

5.1 THE COASTAL SYSTEM

The coast is the narrow zone where the land meets the sea. We can understand the coastline better if we think of it as a system. The coastal system consists of:

- energy inputs from waves, tides and winds;
- coastal landforms, e.g. cliffs, beaches, etc. These are the outputs of the system.

Waves, tides and winds do three things:

- they erode the coastline.
- they transport pebbles, sand and mud.
- they deposit these sediments elsewhere.

In doing this waves, tides and winds create coastal landforms by erosion and deposition.

5.2 WAVES

Sea waves are movements of energy through the water caused by the wind. As the wind blows across the sea, friction between the wind and the sea's surface causes turbulence. Downward gusts press down on the sea surface to form wave troughs. Upward air movements have the opposite effect allowing the surface to rise to form wave crests (Fig. 5.1).

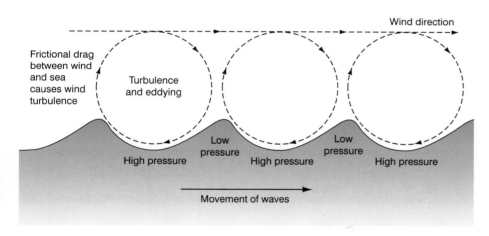

Figure 5.1
Formation of waves

If you watch a wave travelling across the sea's surface, it is easy to think that the water is moving forward. In fact what you are seeing is a movement of energy. The water particles have no real forward movement: they simply follow a circular orbit (Fig. 5.2). However, when waves reach the coast things start to change. In shallow water waves:

- 'feel' the sea bed and slow down;
- increase in height;
- eventually become unstable and break.

As waves break they surge up the beach as **swash**. Then with their energy spent, the water particles drain down the beach as **backwash**. Low energy or **constructive waves** move sand on-shore and build up steep beaches. In stormy conditions powerful **destructive waves** transport sand off-shore to create flat beaches.

Figure 5.2
Waves in shallow water

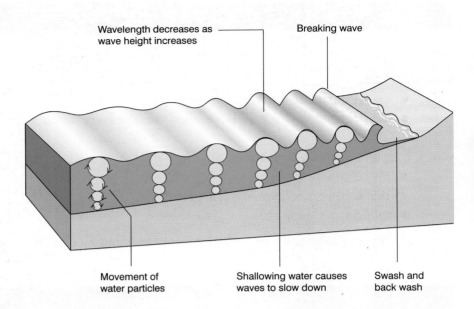

Wavelength decreases as wave height increases

Breaking wave

Movement of water particles

Shallowing water causes waves to slow down

Swash and back wash

The amount of energy in waves depends on their height. Four factors determine wave height and energy:

- Wind speed. When it is very windy, damaging storm waves crash against the coastline.

- Wind duration. The wind does not have to be strong to generate large waves. A moderate wind blowing for several hours can generate large waves.

- Fetch. Fetch is the distance of open sea over which the wind blows. Where the fetch is very long, as on coast of North Cornwall, very large waves can occur. On more sheltered coasts such as the Irish Sea, where the fetch is short, waves are smaller.

- Offshore gradient. Along gently sloping coastlines waves break a long way from the shore. By the time they reach the shore they contain little energy.

5.3 COASTAL LANDFORMS IN SOUTH DEVON AND DORSET

The coastline of southern England, between Start Point in Devon and the Isle of Purbeck in Dorset, has some of the most spectacular coastal scenery in the British Isles (Fig. 5.3). The appearance of the coast owes much to the rocks and relief of the area. The hard metamorphic rocks at Start Point and tough limestones at Berry Head form rugged **headlands**. Where less resistant rocks meet the coast, the sea has eroded broad **bays** such as Lyme Bay and Worbarrow Bay in Dorset. Much of the Devon and Dorset coastline is upland. Erosion of these upland coasts creates dramatic **cliffs** like Golden Cap in Dorset, the highest on the south coast.

Rocks and relief are not the only influences on coastal scenery. Wave energy along the south coast is high: waves approaching from the south-west have a fetch of several thousand kilometres. Such powerful waves erode the more exposed stretches of coast and form features such as cliffs, **stacks** and **wave-cut (or shore) platforms**. Elsewhere, in sheltered bays and estuaries, waves transport and deposit sediment to form sand and shingle beaches, and **salt marshes**.

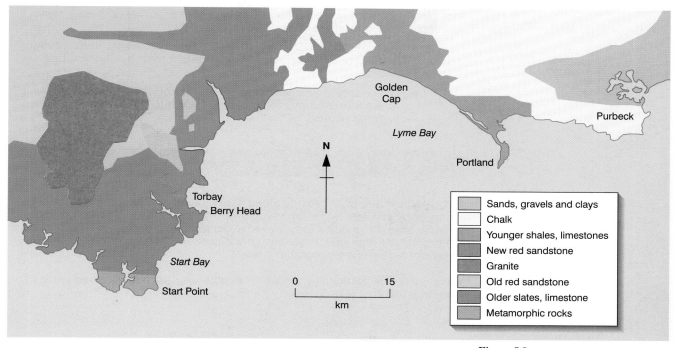

Figure 5.3
Coastline of south Devon and Dorset

5.4 EROSIONAL PROCESSES AND LANDFORMS

Wave erosion (Table 5.1) gives rise to a number of distinctive coastal landforms. The main erosional landforms are: cliffs, caves, arches, stacks and wave-cut (or shore) platforms.

Table 5.1	Processes of wave erosion
Abrasion/corrasion	Sand and shingle carried by waves scour and grind the rocks along the coastline.
Hydraulic action	The pounding effect of water on the coastline during storms. Even the hardest rocks can break up as they are loosened along joints and bedding planes.
Corrosion/solution	The dissolving of rocks by sea water.
Attrition	The wearing away and rounding of sediments (to form sand and shingle) by abrasion and by rubbing against each other.

In addition to wave erosion, weathering also attacks rocks on the coast. Salt spray, alternate wetting and drying, and the activities of tiny sea creatures such as limpets and other shellfish, cause rocks to break down.

CLIFFS

Cliffs are common features on upland coasts. Along these coasts abrasion cuts a notch at the base of cliffs. Eventually this undermines the cliffs which collapse and retreat inland. The rate of retreat depends on rock strength. Cliffs made from weaker rocks like the shales of Lyme Bay retreat rapidly. Those made of harder rocks like the slates at Start Point show few signs of erosion.

Most sea cliffs have steep profiles. This is because the waves quickly remove any rocks eroded from the cliffs:

- Vertical profiles develop where the rocks are either horizontally bedded or dipping inland. These cliffs retreat by undercutting and collapse.
- Lower angled profiles occur where the rocks dip seawards. Rocks loosened by erosion easily slide into the sea along the bedding planes.

CAVES, ARCHES AND STACKS

Caves form at the base of cliffs along joints, faults and bedding planes enlarged by erosion. Some caves are linked to the cliff top by a vertical shaft or **blow hole**. Blow holes form where rocks have collapsed into a cave along a major joint. At high tide, in stormy conditions, spectacular jets of water can spray onto cliff tops through blow holes.

Wave erosion is particularly strong on headlands. It produces a sequence of erosional features (Fig. 5.4):

Figure 5.4
Erosional landforms on an upland coast

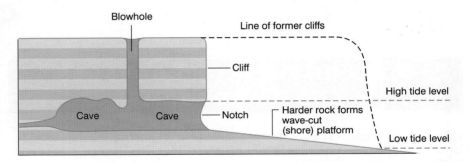

- Caves develop on opposite sides of a headland.
- Further erosion causes the caves to meet and form a **natural arch**, e.g. Durdle Door on the Dorset coast is carved out of limestone.
- Eventually erosion and weathering leads to the collapse of natural arches leaving behind isolated rock pinnacles or **stacks**, e.g. Old Harry Rocks in East Dorset.
- As the cliffs recede inland and the waves destroy arches and stacks they leave behind wave-cut (or shore) platforms (Fig. 5.5). Wave-cut platforms are the roots of older cliffs; scoured and quarried by the waves at high tide; and weathered when exposed at low tide.

Figure 5.5
Stages in the formation of wave-cut (shore) platforms

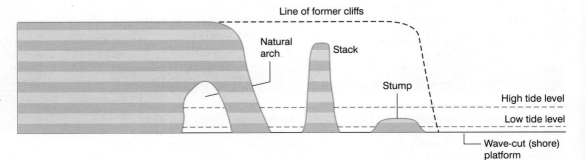

5.5 TYPES OF COASTLINE

The south and east coasts of Purbeck in Dorset are made of the same rock types: limestone, clay and chalk (Fig. 5.6). But in plan, the two coasts are very different. Apart from a few bays, the south coast has a regular outline. In contrast, the east coast comprises a series of headlands and bays. The reason for this difference is the alignment of the main rock outcrops in relation to the coast:

- Along the south coast of Purbeck the rocks run parallel to the coast. This means that a single rock type – limestone – dominates the coast and gives it a smooth outline. Such coasts are known as 'Pacific' or accordant coastlines.

- In east Purbeck the same rocks crop out at right angles to the coast. Here waves have eroded the weaker clays and gravels to form bays like Studland and Swanage. The more resistant limestone and chalk form headlands such as Peverill Point and Durlston Head. East Purbeck is an 'Atlantic' or discordant coastline.

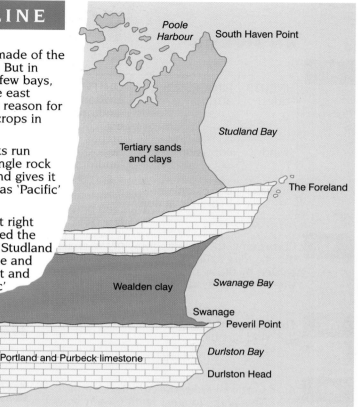

Figure 5.6 *Geology of Isle of Purbeck*

Check yourself

QUESTIONS

Q1 Complete the following systems diagram using words from the list:

Tides, attrition, depositional, wind, corrasion, hydraulic action, erosional, corrosion, waves.

INPUTS	PROCESSES	OUTPUTS
....	....	.... landforms, e.g. cliffs arches
....	....	.... landforms, e.g. beaches
....	....	
	....	

Q2 What is the difference between corrasion and corrosion?

Q3 What is the fetch of a wave?

Q4 i) Give two reasons why Cornwall is regularly hit by powerful waves.
ii) With the help of the section on granite in Chapter 1, explain why Lands End in West Cornwall is able to withstand these powerful waves.

ANSWERS

A1

INPUTS	PROCESSES	OUTPUTS
tides	attrition	erosional landforms, e.g. cliffs arches
wind	corrasion	depositional landforms, e.g. beaches
waves	corrosion hydraulic action	

A2 Corrasion is the wearing away of the coast by the scouring action of the sand and shingle carried by the sea's waves. Corrosion occurs when the sea dissolves rocks.

A3 The fetch is the length of sea over which the wind has blown.

A4
i) Cornwall faces the Atlantic Ocean. This is the longest fetch for any waves approaching the British Isles.
ii) Land's End is made of granite which is a very resistant rock. It therefore takes a very long time to erode, despite being attacked by powerful waves.

TUTORIALS

T1 The systems diagram is a very useful way of summarising cause and effect in geography. This form of diagram can be used in many areas of physical and human geography. You should also be able to a draw systems diagram for a river and a glacier.

T2 These two words are very easily confused. To help you remember the difference between the two, in the word 'corrosion' the -rosion part has an 'o' like solution, whereas in the word 'corrasion the -rasion part has an 'a' like abrasion.

T3 The fetch is the main influence on a wave's strength. A gentler wind blowing over a long fetch will produce a more powerful wave than a strong wind which has blown only over a short fetch.

T4
i) There are over 4,000 kilometres of fetch from the coast of Brazil to Cornwall.
ii) It is also worth noting that the prevailing winds over the British Isles come from the south west and so blow over the long fetch of the Atlantic Ocean.

5.6 DEPOSITIONAL LANDFORMS

Depositional landforms are most common on lowland coasts. Beaches are the most common depositional landforms.

BEACHES

Beaches are accumulations of sand and shingle deposited by waves and currents. Some of this sediment comes from cliff erosion but most is brought down to the coast by rivers. There are several kinds of beach: **spits**, **tombolos**, **barrier beaches** and **bayhead beaches**.

SPITS

- Spits are beaches joined to the coast at just one end.
- At their seaward end shingle ridges form a series of recurves or hooks.
- Spits often develop across river mouths or where there are abrupt changes in the direction of the coastline.
- Spits form by a process called **longshore drift** (Fig. 5.7).

Dawlish Warren (Fig. 5.8), at the mouth of the River Exe, is the only spit on the south coast between Start Point and Purbeck. Dawlish Warren owes its growth to dominant south-westerly waves which have driven sand and shingle across the Exe estuary. The recurves or hooks at the spit's seaward end mark stages in its growth. They also tell us that Dawlish Warren has grown by longshore drift. Tucked away behind spits are quiet backwaters. Waves cannot reach these areas. This allows tidal currents to deposit fine silt and build-up **mud flats** and **salt marshes**.

Figure 5.7 *Longshore drift*

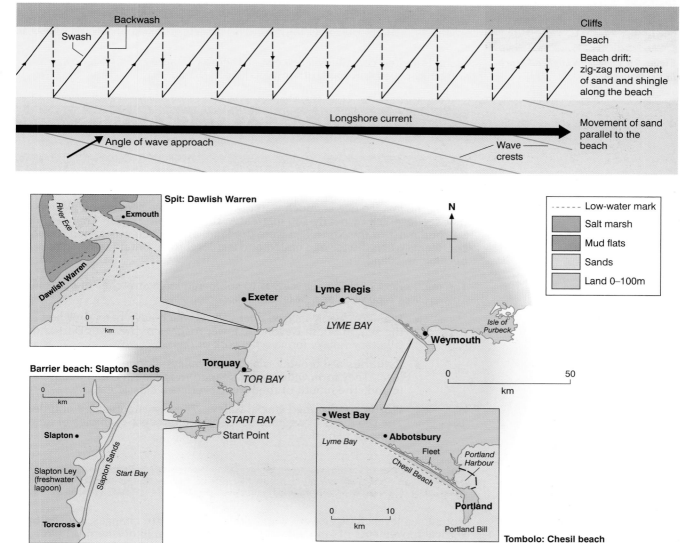

Figure 5.8 *Depositional landforms on the coast of South Devon and Dorset*

TOMBOLOS

A tombolo is a beach which joins an island to the mainland. Chesil Beach, linking mainland Dorset with the Isle of Portland (Fig. 5.8) is a classic tombolo. Unlike Dawlish Warren, Chesil did not form by longshore drift. Thousands of years ago when the sea level was much lower, Chesil was a shingle bar out in the English Channel. Then as the ice age ended and sea level rose, the waves gradually rolled the shingle bar onshore. Eventually (around 6,000 years ago) Chesil reached its present position.

BARRIER BEACHES

Barrier beaches are long and narrow and extend across a bay. Often a lagoon forms on the landward side of the beach. Slapton Sands in South Devon is a barrier beach (Fig. 5.8). It is thought that Slapton Sands formed in a similar way to Chesil.

BAYHEAD BEACHES

Figure 5.9 *Cove with bayhead beach in South Devon*

Along indented coastlines, crescent-shaped bayhead beaches occupy sheltered coves, bays and other inlets (Fig. 5.9).

5.7 SEA LEVEL CHANGES

SUBMERGED COASTS

During the last ice age so much water was frozen in ice sheets and glaciers, that sea level fell by nearly 140 metres. At this time the English Channel, Irish Sea and most of the North Sea were dry land, and Britain was joined to the continent. When the ice age ended and sea level rose, Britain once again became an island.

The main effect of rising sea level is to submerge large stretches of coastline. This creates a number of new landforms, such as:

- **Rias** are deeply incised river valleys which have been drowned by the sea. In South Devon the lower reaches of the River Dart and its tributary valleys forms a network of rias.
- **Estuaries** are broad lowland river valleys, flooded by rising sea level. They form wide funnel-shaped river mouths, which narrow inland. The mouth of the River Severn is a classic estuary.
- **Fjords** are drowned glacial valleys. They are steep-sided and deep. The sea lochs of western Scotland are the best examples of fjords in the British Isles.

EMERGENT COASTS

Not all sea level changes were worldwide. Some relative changes, caused by vertical movements of land, affected only small areas. In northern Britain these movements formed **raised beaches**:

- During the Ice Age huge masses of ice loaded northern Scotland.

- The ice was so thick and heavy that it pushed down on the land surface, lowering it by hundreds of metres.

- As the ice melted, the land began to rise again. It is still rising today.

- Ancient beaches, cliffs, caves and shore platforms have been lifted out of the sea. This is called **isostatic uplift**.

Today, raised beaches, ten metres or so above modern sea level, are common around the coast of western Scotland (Fig. 5.10).

Figure 5.10 *Raised beach on the south coast of Arran, Scotland*

Table 5.2 OS Map skills: describing a coastline and its landforms

- In which direction does the coastline run?
- How high is the coastline? Is it an upland or lowland coastline?
- Is the coastline smooth or is it indented with headlands, bays and coves?
- Does the coastline show any evidence of submergence, e.g. rias, fjords, estuaries?
- Are there any erosional landforms such as cliffs, stacks, wave-cut (shore) platforms?
- Are there any beaches, e.g. bayhead beaches, spits, tombolos, barrier beaches, etc.?
- Are there any areas of sand dunes, mud flats, sand flats or salt marshes?
- Is there any evidence that coastal erosion (e.g. groynes) or coastal flooding (e.g. tidal embankments) is a problem in the area?

Check yourself

Q1
i)   What is longshore drift?
ii)   Why does the swash of a wave approach the beach at an angle?
iii) Why does the backwash run straight back down the beach?

Q2   Study the sketch of a section of coast.

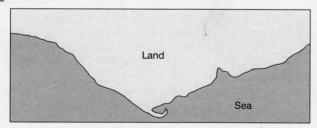

i)   Copy the sketch and label the spit.
ii)   Mark and label each of the following: swash; backwash; prevailing winds; direction of longshore drift.

Q3 Describe the section of coastline shown in the Ordnance Survey map.

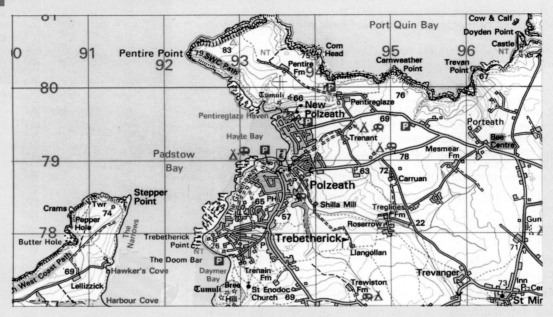

REMEMBER! Cover the answers if you want to.

ANSWERS

A1

i) Longshore drift is the zig-zag movement of sand and shingle along a coast.

ii) The swash follows the direction of wave approach.

iii) The backwash is influenced by gravity and so runs straight back out to sea.

TUTORIALS

T1

i) *This is a very common question in Geography GCSE examinations. It is the type of question that is best answered by means of a labelled or annotated diagram.*

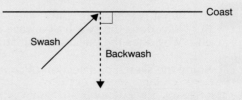

ii) *Because the prevailing winds across the British Isles are from the south west, the waves (and swash) will approach the south coast of England from this direction.*

iii) *Make sure that your diagram is drawn accurately with the backwash at right angles to the coast. Very often students show the backwash at 45° to the coast.*

A2

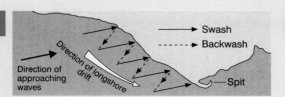

T2 *Spits have the characteristic curved end. Hurst Castle spit in Hampshire grew out into the Solent towards the Isle of Wight.*

ANSWERS

A3 The coast lines run approximately from south west to north east. The general trend is interrupted by a large inlet and the headland of Pentire Point. The coastline is an upland coastline with steep drops of around 80 metres from the flat plateau surface down to the sea. In addition to Padstow Bay there are two other bays: Hayle Bay and Port Quin Bay. The area between Stepper Point and Trebetherick Point is a broad entrance to an estuary (of the River Camel). Erosion has resulted in the formation of cliffs for example at 910785. Pepper Hole and Butter Hole in squares 9077 and 9078 could be either caves or blow holes. The Cow and Calf at 966809 are stacks. Sand has been deposited in Daymer Bay and Hayle Bay, part of which is only visible at low tide.

TUTORIALS

T3 *In answering this question you need to show that you have written a logical answer. The checklist of questions in Table 5.2 will help you with this. The questions provide a framework to the answer and show you what to look for in the OS map extract. Here is an opportunity for you to build up some simple contour patterns of coastal features. If any of the check list questions are not relevant to the particular map extract just ignore them.*

5.8 MANAGING COASTAL EROSION: HOLDERNESS

Nowhere in Europe is coastal erosion more rapid than at Holderness in East Yorkshire. Here, between Flamborough Head and Spurn Point (Fig. 5.11) an average of two metres of cliff are lost to the North Sea every year. Locally, rates of erosion are even higher: waves can take giant bites – up to 10 or 20 metres at a time – from the coast.

CAUSES OF EROSION

The battle between land and sea at Holderness has been going on for thousands of years. Since Roman times over 30 villages have disappeared into the North Sea. There are several reasons why erosion at Holderness is so rapid:

- The coast is made of soft glacial till (boulder clay).
- The coast has little protection from waves from the north-east. These waves have a long fetch and are very powerful.
- There are no sandy beaches to absorb wave energy and protect the cliffs. This is because the cliffs are made of fine clay which is transported away or held in suspension.
- Longshore drift carries what little sand there is along the coast to Spurn Point, a spit at the mouth of the Humber.

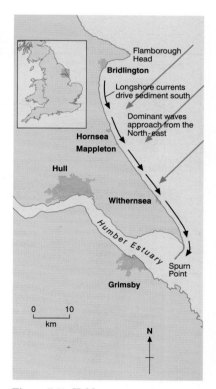

Figure 5.11 *Holderness coast*

TACKLING THE EROSION PROBLEM

The Holderness coast is dotted with settlements. Most are isolated farms, but there are also villages (e.g. Atwick and Mappleton) and small towns such as Hornsea and Withernsea (Fig. 5.11). Coastal erosion directly threatens some of these settlements. Without protection many will fall into the sea.

A variety of measures have been used to protect the coast from erosion (Fig. 5.12). Hornsea and Withernsea have both sea walls and groynes, while at Mappleton both armour blocks and groynes protect the cliffs.

Responsibility for sea defences at Holderness rests with the local district councils. Their policy is to defend the larger settlements, but do nothing to stop erosion elsewhere. They are against protecting the entire coastline because:

- It is very expensive.
- Most of the land at risk is farmland. Farmland has limited value, and makes protection hard to justify.
- Cliff erosion at Holderness adds 2.5 million square metres of mud to the North Sea every year. Currents carry this mud south to the Humber estuary and to the coast of Lincolnshire. There it builds mud flats and salt marshes which protect these low lying coasts from flooding by the sea.

Thus, stopping erosion at Holderness could create an even bigger flooding problem elsewhere. As nearly 500,000 people live around the Humber estuary this threat needs to be treated seriously.

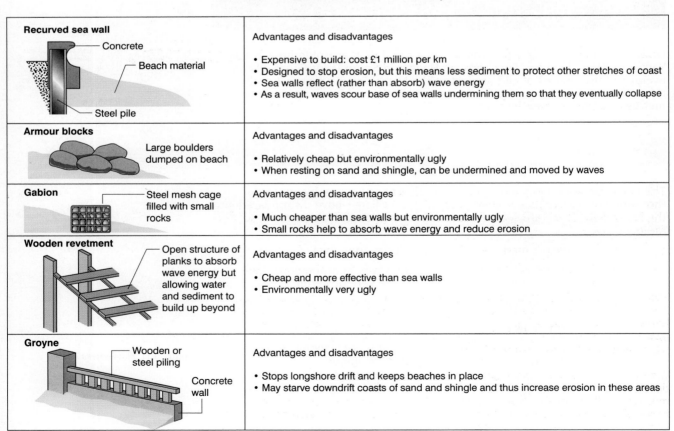

Recurved sea wall — Concrete, Beach material, Steel pile	Advantages and disadvantages
	• Expensive to build: cost £1 million per km • Designed to stop erosion, but this means less sediment to protect other stretches of coast • Sea walls reflect (rather than absorb) wave energy • As a result, waves scour base of sea walls undermining them so that they eventually collapse
Armour blocks — Large boulders dumped on beach	Advantages and disadvantages • Relatively cheap but environmentally ugly • When resting on sand and shingle, can be undermined and moved by waves
Gabion — Steel mesh cage filled with small rocks	Advantages and disadvantages • Much cheaper than sea walls but environmentally ugly • Small rocks help to absorb wave energy and reduce erosion
Wooden revetment — Open structure of planks to absorb wave energy but allowing water and sediment to build up beyond	Advantages and disadvantages • Cheap and more effective than sea walls • Environmentally very ugly
Groyne — Wooden or steel piling, Concrete wall	Advantages and disadvantages • Stops longshore drift and keeps beaches in place • May starve downdrift coasts of sand and shingle and thus increase erosion in these areas

Figure 5.12 *Methods of coastal protection*

MANAGED RETREAT

Coastal protection is an important issue not just in East Yorkshire and Lincolnshire, but along most of the coast of South-east Britain. Because of the enormous costs of maintaining coastal defences, a policy called managed retreat has been introduced (Fig. 5.13). The policy means that some sea walls and tidal embankments will not be maintained, allowing farmland to be flooded by the sea. However, the sea, through deposition will eventually build its own natural barriers – mud flats, salt marshes and beaches – which will stop flooding and erosion. In turn, these create valuable new marshland habitats for plants and birds.

With global warming likely to cause a rise in sea level of at least half a metre in the next 50 years, the cost of maintaining coastal defences will be too high. Thus in areas of low population density there is probably little alternative to the managed retreat policy.

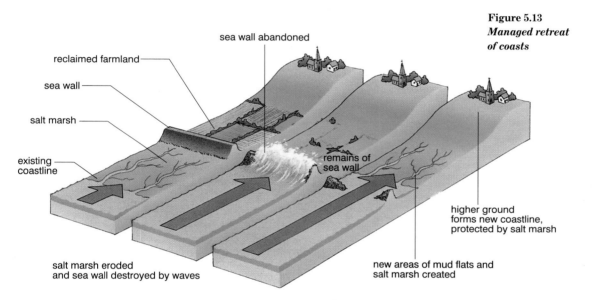

Figure 5.13
Managed retreat of coasts

5.9 CASE STUDY: TOURISM AND COASTAL MANAGEMENT AT STUDLAND BAY, DORSET

Studland Bay in East Dorset is a lowland coastline of sand dunes and shallow seas (Fig. 5.14). The sand dunes run parallel to the coast and are important habitats for a number of reptiles, including snakes, slow worms and sand lizards. The National Trust and English Nature own much of the coast, part of which is protected as a Nature Reserve.

With its sandy beaches, safe bathing and dunes, Studland is a popular destination for visitors. Over one million tourists visit the area every year making Studland one of the most popular beaches on the south coast. However, large numbers of visitors put great pressure on the environment. The sand dunes are a particularly vulnerable and fragile environment. Trampling by visitors destroys the vegetation cover; exposes the dunes to wind erosion; and threatens important wildlife habitats. Tourism causes other problems: litter; pollution of sea water by sun oil; and the pollution of bathing beaches by the large number of pleasure boats which moor in the bay.

Studland can only survive these pressures through careful planning. English Nature and the National Trust have a management plan which aims to protect the environment and make tourism sustainable. Management involves:

- Re-planting marram grass on dunes damaged by trampling; and putting up barriers to prevent access while the grass grows.
- Waymarking trails to keep visitors to footpaths and away from sensitive areas.
- Organised litter collection and warden patrols.
- Providing amenities for tourists – parking, toilets, shops, showers, etc. – at Knoll Beach, away from the most sensitive areas.
- Not allowing water skiing within 200 metres of the beach and banning jet skis altogether.
- Building gabions (Fig. 5.12) to protect some areas of dunes and beach from wave erosion.

Figure 5.14
Studland Bay and South Haven Peninsula

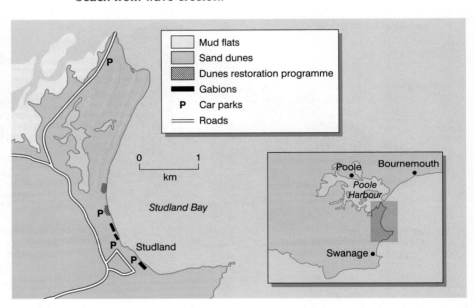

Legend:
- Mud flats
- Sand dunes
- Dunes restoration programme
- Gabions
- P Car parks
- Roads

Studland Bay
Studland

Poole
Poole Harbour
Bournemouth
Swanage

Check yourself

QUESTIONS

Q1 Study Figure 5.11.

i) Suggest why Flamborough Head is different from the rest of the Yorkshire Coast.

ii) What is Spurn Head?

iii) Why does the end of Spurn Head turn inwards towards the Humber Estuary?

Q2 Which of the reasons given in Section 5.8 for the rapid erosion of the Holderness coast do you consider the most important?

QUESTIONS

Q3 Correctly match the following 'heads and tails':

A gabion	is a series of piles built up at right angles to the coast
A groyne	consists of a series of large boulders dumped on the beach
An armour block	is very expensive to build
A recurved sea wall	is a steel mesh cage filled with rocks

Q4 Study the following diagram.

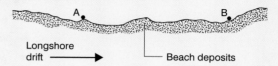

A and B are both coastal villages. A groyne is to be built between the two villages.

i) Which village is likely to benefit from the groyne?

ii) Draw a diagram to show the coastline a few years after the groyne has been built.

REMEMBER! Cover the answers if you want to.

ANSWERS

A1
i) It is made from a more resistant rock (i.e. chalk) than the rest of the coast.
ii) A spit.
iii) Waves entering the Humber estuary have turned the end of Spurn Head back on itself.

A2 The coast is made of soft glacial till which is easily eroded.

A3

A gabion	is a steel mesh cage filled with rocks
A groyne	is a series of piles built up at right angles to the coast
An armour block	consists of a series of large boulders dumped on the beach
A recurved sea wall	is very expensive to build

A4
i) Village A is likely to benefit most.

ii)
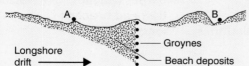

TUTORIALS

T1
i) *The situation on the Yorkshire coast is very similiar to that on the Dorset coast discussed in this chapter. Flamborough Head is made of chalk, so it is has been left as a headland when the less resistant glacial till has been eroded back.*

ii) *Notice that Spurn Head has developed across a river mouth. This is one of the two situations mentioned in the text where spits develop.*

iii) *Spurn Head has a single shingle ridge forming a recurve or hook.*

T2 *There is no one reason which is most important. They all contribute to the rapid erosion along the Holderness coast. In this type of question it is sufficient just to give a possible reason.*

T3 *Questions on the human response to coastal erosion are very common in GCSE examinations.*

T4 *This shows that human modifications on one part of a coast can have a negative effect on another part. This must be recognised when suggesting a management plan for any particular coastline.*

EXAMINATION CHECKLIST

The facts and ideas that you should know and understand after studying coastal landforms are:

- Waves, tides and winds erode, transport and deposit.
- Waves are a transformation of the surface of the sea.
- Wind speed, wind duration, the length of the fetch and offshore gradient all affect the energy of waves.
- There are four main processes of wave erosion.
- The direction of the dip of the rock affects the steepness of the cliffs.
- Differential erosion leads to the formation of headlands, bays and coves.
- The erosion of headlands leads to the formation of caves, arches and stacks.
- The retreat of cliffs landwards leads to the formation of wave-cut platforms.
- The coast of Dorset is a classic area for landforms formed by the action of the sea.
- Discordant and accordant coastlines reflect the structure of the rocks.
- Beaches, spits, tombolos and beaches are features of coastal deposition.
- The rise and fall of sea level has led to the formation of particular landforms around the coast.
- There are a number of methods of coastal protection.
- Coastal management in one part of the coast may have bad effects on another part of the coast.
- Tourism in coastal areas requires careful management.
- Holderness and Dorset are coastal areas with specific problems which require different solutions and management plans.

KEY WORDS

These are the key words. Tick them if you think you know what they mean. Otherwise check on them.

swash	blow hole	mud flats
backwash	natural arch	salt marshes
constructive waves	stacks	rias
destructive waves	spits	estuaries
headlands	tombolo	fjords
bays	barrier beaches	raised beaches
cliffs	bayhead beaches	isostatic uplift
wave-cut (shore) platforms	longshore drift	

EXAM PRACTICE

Sample Student's Answer and Examiner's Comments

1 (a) Study the photograph of spit at Dawlish Warren in Devon.

(i) Describe the physical features of the spit at Dawlish Warren
(4 marks)

A headland sticks out from the coastline as it turns the corner. The coastline also has a large spit with grass, etc. growing on it. The water on the inside of the spit is shallower because of deposition. There are lots of fields and a settlement just on and just off the spit. There is sea on one side of the spit and the river mouth on the other.

(ii) Explain how spits such as Dawlish Warren are formed. (6 marks)

The spit has been formed by deposition. It could have been formed in two different ways:
1. The longshore drift carries the sediment up the beach until it hits another solid wall of water, e.g. a river. This makes it deposit all its sediment there. The river also brings down sediment. The new spit then starts building out from the land into the sea, until it gets too big and starts to turn back in again, or joins on to an island to form a tombolo.
2. Exactly the same way but instead of the river it meets a different direction of longshore drift.

(iii) Choose either a COASTAL AREA or RIVER VALLEY that you have studied. How has human activity affected the beauty of this area?
(4 marks)

Type of area: Coastal area
Area studied: Cocklawburn to Spittal Point (Berwick)
Effects of human activity: Humans have affected this area by mining for salt and for limestone. Pollution is also a big problem. Every day, litter can be found on the beaches and prom. Humans built a prom to protect Spittal against the sea and have commercialised Spittal as a tourist spot. Groynes have been built to keep the sand on Spittal and big stone cages have been erected to stop the sea intruding into Spittal.

SEG, 1997

Questions to Answer

The answer to Question 2 can be found in Chapter 18.

2 Study the field sketch which shows parts of the Quantock Hills and the north coast of Somerset.

   i)   Name the coastal features A–D by copying and completing the table:

(4 marks)

Letter	Name of landform
A	....
B	....
C	....
D	....

   ii)   Study the incomplete cross-section X to Y marked on the field sketch. There is evidence of rapid cliff erosion. Describe the processes which cause cliff recession.

(6 marks)

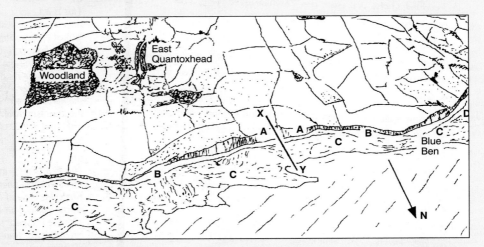

   iii)   How might this part of the coast suffer as a result of an influx of tourists? (3 marks)

   iv)   Suggest two ways in which tourism could be managed without damaging the environment. (2 marks)

LEAG, 1993

6.1 WEATHER AND CLIMATE

Weather and climate concern factors such as temperature, precipitation, wind speed, wind direction, sunshine, cloudiness, pressure, etc. But weather and climate do not mean the same thing:

- Weather is the temperature, precipitation, sunshine, etc. today and in the next few days.
- Climate is the seasonal *pattern* of weather we can expect on the basis of past records extending over at least 30 years.

CLIMATE GRAPHS

We can summarise the main features of a place's climate by using climate graphs. Climate graphs plot the mean monthly temperatures as a line graph, and the mean monthly precipitation as a bar graph (Figs. 6.1 and 6.2).

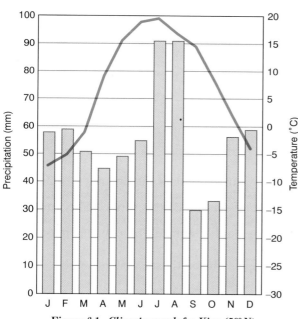

Figure 6.1 *Climate graph for Kiev (50°N)*

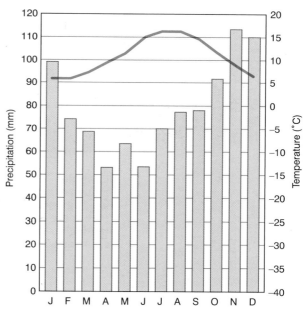

Figure 6.2 *Climate graph for Plymouth (50°N)*

6.2 THE GLOBAL CLIMATE

Large parts of the world have similar seasonal patterns of temperature and precipitation. We can therefore define broad climate regions such as the desert of central Australia, and the tundra of northern Canada (Fig. 6.3). At the global scale four main factors affect climate: latitude; altitude; distance from the sea; and prevailing winds.

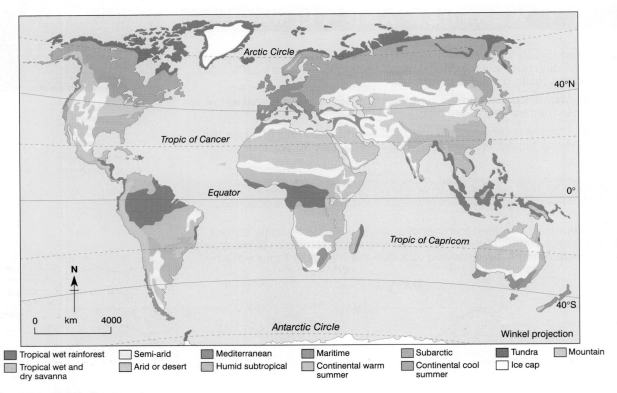

Figure 6.3 *Global climate regions*

Tropical wet rainforest | Semi-arid | Mediterranean | Maritime | Subarctic | Tundra | Mountain
Tropical wet and dry savanna | Arid or desert | Humid subtropical | Continental warm summer | Continental cool summer | Ice cap

LATITUDE

Latitude – the position of a place north or south of the Equator – is the major influence on climate. This is because latitude determines the height and intensity of the sun's rays as they arrive at the Earth's surface. The simple rule is that the higher the sun is in the sky, the more concentrated are its rays, and the higher the temperature is at the Earth's surface (Fig. 6.4). Figure 6.4 explains why:

- Temperatures in the tropics exceed those in middle and high latitudes.

- Temperatures in summer are higher than in winter.

Figure 6.4
Latitude and solar radiation

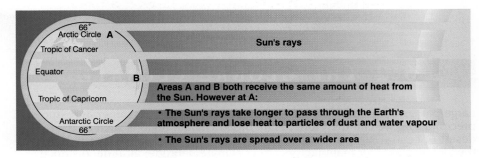

Latitude also affects temperatures by influencing day length. Day length does not vary much around the Equator. However, as latitude increases day length increases in summer and shortens in winter. In the British Isles during the winter day length is short and nights are long. Fewer hours of sunshine contribute to lower temperatures. Further north, inside the Arctic Circle (66.5°N) the winter days become so short that for several weeks the sun does not rise at all. There is, however, some compensation in summer when there are 24 hours of daylight.

ALTITUDE

Temperatures fall on average by 6.5°C for every 1,000 metres of altitude. This gives high, mountainous areas distinctive climates. At 5,000 metres above sea-level it is so cold that glaciers can exist on the Equator (e.g. in the Andes and in Kenya and Tanzania). Figure 6.5 explains why temperatures decrease with altitude.

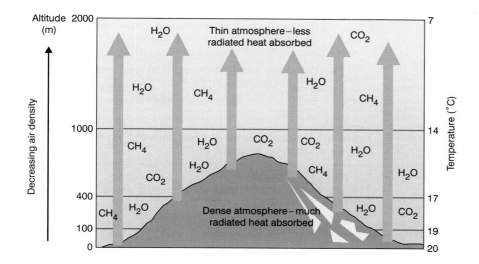

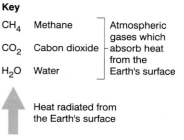

Figure 6.5
Relationship between altitude and temperature

Key

CH_4	Methane	Atmospheric gases which absorb heat from the Earth's surface
CO_2	Cabon dioxide	
H_2O	Water	

Heat radiated from the Earth's surface

DISTANCE FROM THE SEA

Distance from the sea has a strong effect on climate. Land and sea respond differently to temperature. The land heats up quickly but also loses heat quickly. In contrast the sea heats up and cools down much more slowly. The reasons for this are:

- The sea is a liquid and water heated at the surface can circulate to a greater depth.

- The land is a solid and is heated to a depth of no more than 30 cm.

- Water needs to absorb more heat than most other common substances before its temperature rises. However, this means that as it cools it gives out large amounts of heat.

The global distribution of land and sea gives rise to **continental** and **oceanic climates**.

- In the centre of huge landmasses, such as Asia and North America, the sea has little effect on climate. The result is a continental climate. Such climates have extreme temperature ranges. Winter temperatures are severe, but summers are surprisingly warm (Fig. 6.1).

- Near the coast, the sea has a moderating effect on temperature. Because the sea is slow to lose heat in winter, temperatures during the winter are mild. In summer, when the sea is slow to heat up, temperatures remain modest. Therefore places near the sea often have a fairly narrow range of temperature (Fig. 6.2).

- Most precipitation comes from moisture evaporated from the oceans. Places on the coast will be wetter and more humid than those in continental interiors (compare Figs 6.1 and 6.2).

PREVAILING WINDS

Prevailing winds are the winds which blow most often. In the British Isles the prevailing winds are westerlies. Around the tropics the prevailing winds are the North-east (NE) and South-east (SE) trade winds (Fig. 6.6). Prevailing winds influence temperature and precipitation in two ways:

- On-shore winds (from sea to land) spread the influence of the sea onto the land. This means a relatively small difference in temperature between the warmest and coldest months (Table 6.1); greater humidity and greater precipitation.

- Off-shore winds (from land to sea) give rise to a more extreme temperature range (Table 6.1), and lower humidity and precipitation.

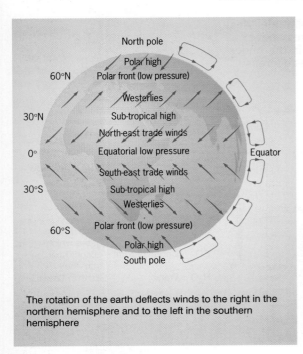

The rotation of the earth deflects winds to the right in the northern hemisphere and to the left in the southern hemisphere

Figure 6.6 *Global winds*

Table 6.1 Temperatures at Plymouth (50°N) and St John's, eastern Canada (47°N)

	Plymouth (on-shore westerlies)	St John's (off-shore westerlies)
January	6°C	–5°C
July	17°C	15.5°C

The influence of prevailing winds does depend on other factors. For instance, coastal mountain ranges can prevent prevailing winds penetrating far inland. This happens in Canada, where the Rockies block the westerlies and prevent mild air from the Pacific Ocean reaching the interior. In contrast, in western Europe where there are no major mountain barriers to the westerly winds, mild oceanic air can easily penetrate into eastern Europe.

In some parts of the world there is a seasonal change in wind flow. This often gives a wet and a dry season. In South Asia the South-west monsoon winds blow from the Indian Ocean for half of the year. The winds bring heavy precipitation to India between June and September. For the rest of the year the winds blow off-shore (i.e. north-east) and cause drought conditions. In winter, the Mediterranean experiences westerly winds. These bring unsettled, wet weather, but in summer they move northwards and the Mediterranean becomes hot and dry.

6.3 THE CLIMATE OF THE BRITISH ISLES

The British Isles are situated on the western edge of the huge Eurasian land mass. To the west there are 5,000 kilometres of open sea, and on three days out of every four, the winds blow from this direction. The result: the British Isles have a mild, damp oceanic climate.

TEMPERATURE

The relatively high latitude of the British Isles (50°N to 60°N) means that the sun is not powerful enough to produce more than modest average temperatures. However, the range of latitude is large enough to have some influence on temperature. The Isles of Scilly (50°N) in the far south-west have an average annual temperature of 11.9°C. This compares with 7.5°C in the Shetland Isles, which are 10 degrees of latitude further north.

WINTER TEMPERATURES

The most remarkable feature of temperatures in the British Isles is their mildness in winter. We can thank the Atlantic Ocean, and the prevailing on-shore westerlies for this. The ocean, slow to cool in winter, keeps the temperatures in the British Isles well above the average for the latitude. The ocean's warming influence is strongest in the west (Fig. 6.7).

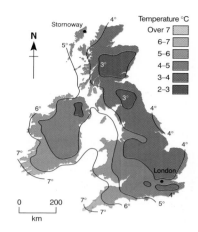

Figure 6.7 *January temperatures in the British Isles*

SUMMER TEMPERATURES

Throughout the summer the ocean stays cooler than the land, keeping temperatures below average for the latitude. In summer, latitude dominates temperatures and **isotherms** (lines joining points of equal temperature) run from east to west (Fig. 6.8). Therefore the warmest areas are in the south (London averages 18°C in July) and the coldest (which may not reach 14°C) are in the far north.

THE NORTH ATLANTIC DRIFT

The mild winters of the British Isles are not only caused by the nearness of the Atlantic Ocean, and the on-shore westerly winds. A warm ocean current, driven by the prevailing westerlies, brings tropical water from the Caribbean to northern Europe. The influence of this warm North Atlantic Drift is felt far to the north of the British Isles. The North Atlantic Drift keeps the coasts of Iceland and northern Norway (71°N) ice-free in winter.

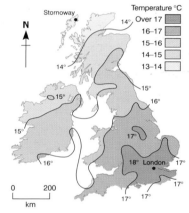

Figure 6.8 *July temperatures in the British Isles*

PRECIPITATION

In the British Isles mean annual precipitation is high and evenly spread throughout the year. Unlike South Asia and the Mediterranean, there is no wet or dry season. The distribution of precipitation in the British Isles, however, is uneven (Fig. 6.9). The driest regions in the South-east have only 600 mm of precipitation a year. Compare this with the mountains of the north and west, which may have more than 5,000 mm. Reasons for this include:

- The prevailing westerlies pick up moisture from the Atlantic Ocean. As this moist air rises over the western mountains of the British Isles the air cools and sheds large amounts of precipitation (Fig. 6.10). We call this **relief or orographic precipitation**.

- In the eastern lowlands there is less precipitation. In the east the air is drier for two reasons: (1) because so much moisture has been precipitated in the uplands; (2) because the moist air warms up as it descends from the mountains, evaporating the clouds, reducing precipitation and creating a **rain shadow** (Fig. 6.10).

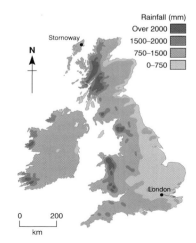

Figure 6.9 *Distribution of precipitation in the British Isles*

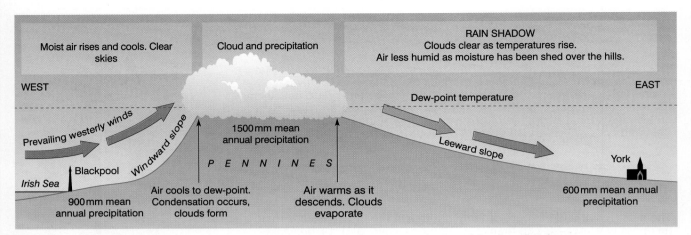

Figure 6.10 *Relief precipitation*

Most precipitation in the British Isles comes from mid-latitude storms or depressions. However, in eastern England thunderstorms contribute significant amounts of **convectional precipitation** (Fig. 6.11). In summer the sun heats the ground, causing warm air to rise in a column or convection current. As the air rises and cools it forms towering cumulo-nimbus clouds. These clouds bring thunder and very heavy showers of rain and hail.

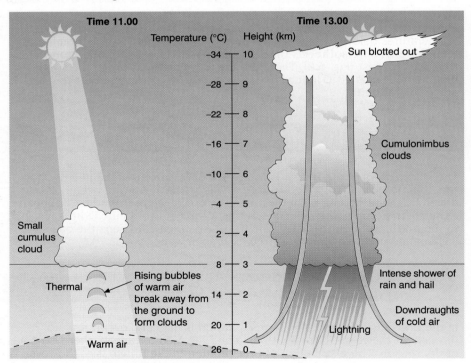

Figure 6.11 *Convectional precipitation and thunderstorms*

Check yourself

QUESTIONS

Q1 Write one sentence to explain the difference between climate and weather.

Q2 Study Figure 6.2.

i) What is the temperature of the warmest month?
ii) What is the temperature of the coldest month?
iv) Which month is the wettest?
v) Describe the pattern of the precipitation.

Q3 Explain how you can tell from figures 6.1 and 6.2 that Kiev is a long way from the sea and Plymouth is on the coast.

Q4 Study the map of the British isles below, and those areas with a precipitation greater than 800 mm (Fig. 6.9). Explain:

i) why the isotherms in January tend to run from north to south;
ii) why the isotherms in July tend to run from west to east;
iii) why the west is wetter than the east.

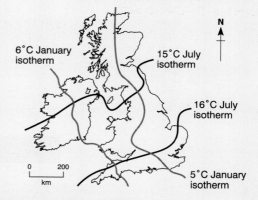

6°C January isotherm
15°C July isotherm
16°C July isotherm
5°C January isotherm
N
0   200
km

REMEMBER! Cover the answers if you want to.

ANSWERS

A1 Climate is the average of the weather.

A2
i) 16°C. ii) 5°C. iii) November.
iv) 52 mm.
v) There is precipitation all the year around. The wettest season is the winter, and November has the highest rainfall. The spring and early summer is the driest period but there is an increase in precipitation in May.

A3 The range of temperature in Kiev is 27°C compared to only 11°C in Plymouth. The average temperature does not drop below freezing in Plymouth, whereas in Kiev the average temperature is below freezing for four months of the year. The total precipitation in Kiev is lower than in Plymouth. Kiev has a summer maximum. In Plymouth winter is the wettest season.

TUTORIALS

T1 *It is often said that the British Isles have no climate only weather. This is because the weather changes frequently and it is difficult to say what the average conditions are. In equatorial regions the weather conditions do not vary from day to day so it is possible, perhaps, to say that these places have no weather only climate!*

T2
i)–iv) In any question where you have to give a numerical answer make sure that you always give the units, if there are any.
v) You will often be asked to describe patterns in a set of figures, a graph or a distribution map. Remember this: first, describe the general pattern; then refer to any specific features in the pattern; and finally point to any exceptions.

T3 *Kiev has a continental climate. The modifying influence of the ocean on Plymouth gives the town a maritime climate. The latitude is the same for both places. Their relative altitudes may also affect their temperature and precipitation.*

ANSWERS

A4

i) The west is warmer than the east. This is because the temperatures in the west are kept up by the warming influence of the ocean. The Atlantic Ocean is particularly warm because of the North Atlantic Drift. The east is under the influence of the cold landmass of Eurasia.

ii) The north is cooler than the south because the Sun is at a lower angle in the sky.

iii) The prevailing winds are from the south-west and they bring moisture from the Atlantic Ocean to the west of the British isles. By the time, the winds reach the eastern part of the Isles they have lost a lot of this moisture.

TUTORIALS

T4

i) *This shows that the influence of the ocean is greater in winter.*

ii) *The ocean's influence is cancelled out by the effect of latitude in the summer.*

iii) *The higher land in the west of the British Isles is also important. The mountains force the moist winds to rise, producing precipitation. The east of the country is said to be in a 'rain shadow'. The mountains in the west shelter the east from the rain-bearing winds.*

6.4 WEATHER CHARTS

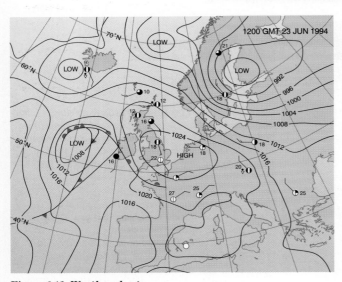

Figure 6.12 *Weather chart*

Weather charts are used to summarise the current weather over the British Isles, or over larger areas such as western Europe and the North Atlantic (Fig. 6.12). The charts are essential for weather forecasting. **Isobars** are the most important feature on weather charts.

- Isobars are lines which join places of equal atmospheric pressure.

- Atmospheric pressure is measured in millibars (mb). The average pressure at sea level is 1013 mb.

- Areas of low pressure (**depressions**) and high pressure (**anticyclones**) are shown by circular patterns of isobars.

- Closely packed isobars indicate strong winds. Widely spaced isobars indicate light winds or calm conditions.

- Isobars indicate wind direction because surface winds blow more or less parallel to the isobars, from areas of high pressure to areas of low pressure.

Weather charts provide other information about current weather – temperature, precipitation, cloud cover, wind direction and wind speed – at selected weather stations. This information is shown on weather charts as a series of distinctive symbols (Fig. 6.13).

6.5 DEPRESSIONS AND ANTICYCLONES

DEPRESSIONS

On most days either depressions or anticyclones dominate the weather in the British Isles:

- Depressions are large areas of low pressure in middle and high latitudes (Fig. 6.14).

- Most depressions move rapidly from west to east taking just 3 or 4 days to cross the Atlantic.

- Depressions bring mild and changeable weather: stormy periods of cloud and rain are followed by spells of bright and sunny weather.

- The cloudy and wet conditions brought by depressions form along boundaries known as **fronts**.

- There are three main types of front: warm, cold and occluded.

- Fronts separate warm air from cold air.

- Air rises along a front. As it rises air cools to form thick cloud and precipitation.

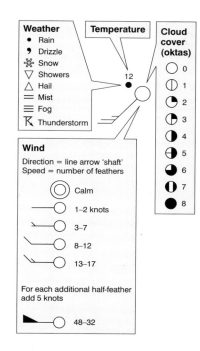

Figure 6.13 *Weather chart symbols*

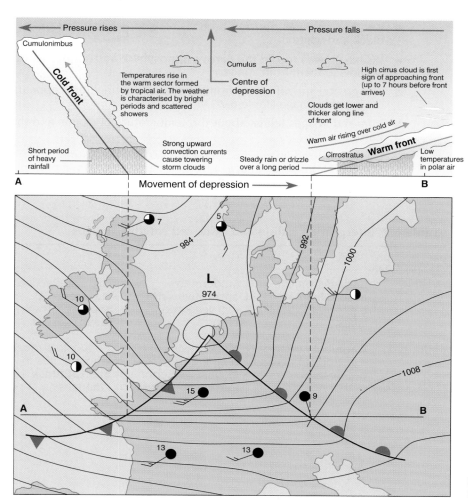

Figure 6.14
Weather conditions in a depression

ANTICYCLONES

Anticyclones are more or less the opposite of depressions.

- They are areas of high pressure.
- They bring spells of calm, dry and settled weather.
- In summer, they often bring warm, sunny conditions, with temperatures well above average.
- Winter anticyclones bring below average temperatures, and night-time frost is common.
- Sunshine amounts vary, especially in winter. Some winter anticyclones bring bright, clear weather. Others produce overcast or foggy conditions. Overcast and foggy weather lasting for several days is known as 'anticyclonic gloom'.
- Air moves downwards towards the Earth's surface in anticyclones. This movement prevents thick cloud (and heavy precipitation) from forming.

6.6 SATELLITE IMAGES

Weather forecasters rely on satellite images as well as weather charts for their forecasts.

- Weather satellites transmit both visible and infra-red images in black and white.
- Visible images record the Earth's atmosphere and surface as we would see them from space.
- The greater the reflection from a surface, the brighter it appears on a visible image (Table 6.2).
- Infra-red images tell us about the temperature of clouds and the Earth's surface.
- On an infra-red image the darker the surface the warmer it is (Table 6.2). Infra-red images give weather forecasters important information about the height of clouds, and the temperatures of land and sea surfaces.

Figure 6.15 *When seen from space the fronts in a depression form swirling bands of cloud, like a giant catherine wheel. Behind the fronts shower clouds have a mottled appearance, with each individual cumulus cloud standing out as a tiny parcel.*

Table 6.2 Interpreting visible and infra-red satellite images

	Black	Grey	White
Visible	Surfaces which absorb light, e.g. oceans, seas, lakes.	Moderately absorptive surfaces, e.g. vegetation, crops.	Highly reflective surfaces, e.g. snow, ice, thick cloud, deserts.
Infra-red	Warm/hot surfaces, e.g. tropical oceans, hot deserts.	Moderate temperatures: low clouds; western Europe in winter.	Cool/cold surfaces: land and sea in high latitudes; high clouds.

Check yourself

REMEMBER! Cover the answers if you want to.

QUESTIONS

Q1 Draw an annotated sketch to describe the weather associated with the passage of a depression.

Q2 Why does rain occur along a front?

Q3 Why do winds blow into a depression and out of an anticyclone?

Q4 Why is the weather associated with a depression more changeable than the weather associated with an anticyclone over the British Isles?

ANSWERS

A1 For this question you should aim to redraw the top part of Figure 6.14 including the features and annotations shown.

A2 Rain occurs along a front because warm air is forced to rise over cold air. The warm air in the warm sector contains moisture in the form of water vapour. As the air rises it cools and the water vapour condenses to form precipitation.

A3 Winds are movements of air from high to low pressure. A depression is an area of low pressure so winds will blow towards its centre. Anticyclones are areas of high pressure, so the opposite happens: the winds blow out from the centre.

A4 A depression moves across the British Isles from the North Atlantic, bringing a sequence of three different air masses: it starts with cold air, then changes to warm air, before being replaced again by cold air. When an anticyclone develops it tends to stay put for a while, giving a period of settled weather.

TUTORIALS

T1 In the GCSE examination you are most likely to be asked to describe the weather associated with the passage of a depression. If you are able to do this using an annotated diagram like Figure 6.14 you are likely to score well.

T2 All rain is formed as a result of air rising, cooling and the water vapour in the air condensing. Air rises in one of three ways: where the air is forced to rise over mountains; where the heating of the ground in summer causes convection currents (section 6.3),; and where warm air moves above cold air along a front.

T3 In the case of the anticyclone there is frequently little or no air movement. The isobars are widely spaced indicating a gentle pressure gradient and so calm conditions. What winds there are will blow in a clockwise movement around the anticyclone in the northern hemisphere. Stronger winds are associated with a depression, particularly towards its centre where the pressure is lowest. In the northern hemisphere the winds will blow anti-clockwise into a depression.

T4 Anticyclones frequently take up blocking positions where they stop depressions crossing the British Isles. When an anticyclone forms over the British Isles the depressions moving across the North Atlantic are forced to the north or the south. Blocking can lead to drought conditions in the British Isles because most rainfall comes from depressions. Blocking was responsible for the very dry summers of 1975 and 1976.

6.7 WEATHER HAZARDS

Extreme weather conditions present serious hazards to people. Every year floods, storms and droughts cause massive damage to property, crops and livestock, and loss of life. The impact of extreme weather conditions is greatest in the poorest countries.

TROPICAL CYCLONES

Tropical cyclones are violent storms in South Asia generated over warm tropical seas such as the Indian Ocean. Similar storms in the Caribbean and USA are called **hurricanes**; and in East and South-east Asia they are known as **typhoons**.

- Tropical cyclones, like mid-latitude depressions, are areas of intense low pressure.
- Very strong winds, cloud and heavy precipitation rotate around tropical cyclones. Wind speeds may exceed 150 km/h and can cause immense damage.
- Over the sea the winds pile up the water into enormous waves or **surges** which may flood low-lying coastal areas.
- Tropical cyclones usually develop over the oceans in late summer and early autumn when the surface water is at its warmest (at least 27°C).
- High temperatures result in the rapid evaporation of sea water.
- As the water vapour rises it cools, condenses and releases huge amounts of heat. This heat provides the energy to power tropical storms.
- When over a land mass, and cut-off from their energy supply, tropical cyclones quickly blow themselves out.

The 1991 Bangladesh cyclone disaster

Bangladesh is one of the world's most densely populated and poorest countries. Around 122 million people live in Bangladesh, in an area barely half the size of the UK.

Situated at the head of the Bay of Bengal, most of Bangladesh is on a delta formed by the Ganges, Brahmaputra and Meghna rivers (Fig. 6.16). About 80 per cent of the country is less than 1.5 metres above sea level. Every year the rivers flood half the country to a depth of 30 cm. The floods last for several months and cause great disruption. However, these annual floods are small compared to the catastrophic floods which accompany tropical cyclones. In 1970, a tropical cyclone and tidal surge hit Bangladesh, killing more than 450,000 people there.

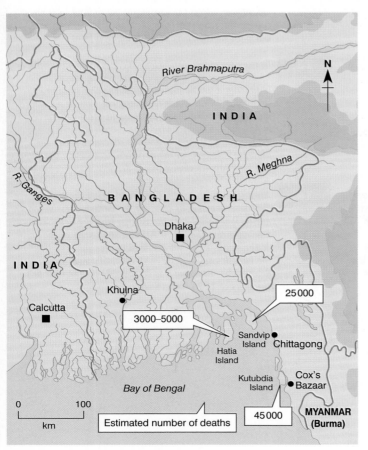

Figure 6.16
Bangladesh: effects of 1991 cyclone disaster

In 1991, a tropical cyclone caused a similar disaster along Bangladesh's south-east coast and delta region:

- Winds faster than 200 km/h whipped up a 7-metre high tidal wave.

- The tidal wave overwhelmed the coastal districts killing 125,000 people.

- Crops, livestock, roads, bridges and electricity pylons were destroyed.

- Salt water contaminated farmland, and drinking water supplies were polluted.

- The Bangladesh government estimated the damage at £1 billion.

Where natural disasters hit hardest

In 1992, hurricane Andrew devastated the coast of Florida in the USA. It was one of the most powerful storms on record. And yet it killed fewer than 30 people. Natural disasters such as tropical cyclones hit poor countries such as Bangladesh hardest. There are several reasons for this.

- Because people are poor and the country is so densely populated, millions of people are forced to live in areas vulnerable to tidal surges from tropical cyclones.

- Evacuation and emergency relief measures are inadequate. Meanwhile, poorly developed transport systems often make it difficult to get what relief is available to remote areas.

- If Bangladesh were better-off it could build dykes to protect the areas most at risk from flooding. It could also give people radios so that they could receive early warning of floods; and build storm shelters to protect those who cannot be evacuated.

DROUGHT IN ANDALUCIA

In 1994 and 1995, Andalucia in southern Spain (Fig. 6.17) suffered its worst drought in living memory. Andalucia has a Mediterranean climate. Its summers are hot and dry, and it relies on winter depressions from the Atlantic Ocean for most of its precipitation. In 1994 and 1995, the winter rains failed. By May 1995 reservoirs were down to just 10 per cent of their capacity. The drought cost Spain nearly £3 billion in lost farm production. Outputs of wheat and crops, such as rice and cotton, which depend on irrigation, were badly affected. Many farmers faced ruin.

However, the drought in Andalucia was not caused only by unusually low precipitation. This part of Spain is used to droughts. The difference this time was the huge rise in demand for water over the last 30 years.

Figure 6.17 *Location map for Andalucia, Spain*

- New crops based on irrigation have replaced traditional drought-resistant crops such as vines and olives. Today, agriculture uses 80 per cent of water in the region.

- The massive growth of tourism along the southern coast of Spain, especially in the Costa del Sol, consumes water.

- The development of golf courses which rely on irrigation and can consume as much water as a village.

- Water is lost through leaky irrigation canals and pipes.

The Spanish government responded by placing limits on water use. Some towns in Andalucia were without water for 10 hours a day. Farmers received some compensation for crop losses from the European Union.

The Spanish government also has long-term plans to tackle drought in Andalucia. It wants to encourage farmers to grow crops which need less water. The government is also planning to build a water grid to transfer surplus water from regions of northern Spain to the drier south. So far this scheme has proved unpopular and has brought angry protests from water-rich regions.

Check yourself

QUESTIONS

Q1 What is the difference between a typhoon, a hurricane and a cyclone?

Q2 Why are the effects of natural disasters (e.g. cyclones) greater in LEDCs such as Bangladesh compared to MEDCs such as the USA?

Q3 Andalucia, in southern Spain, lies between 36°N and 38°N. Use Figure 6.6 to explain how the prevailing winds normally cause winter rain and summmer drought in Andalucia.

Q4 Why has the growth of tourism in southern Spain worsened the effect of the recent drought?

REMEMBER! Cover the answers if you want to.

ANSWERS

A1 These tropical storms are found in different parts of the world. Typhoons are found in East and South-east Asia; hurricanes are a feature of the climate in the south-east of the USA and the Caribbean islands; and cyclones are found in South Asia, particularly in the Indian sub-continent.

A2 In LEDCs a greater proportion of the population works in agriculture, which means the food supply can be disrupted. Weather forecasting is often inaccurate and the infrastructure is less able to cope with disasters.

A3 During the summer Spain is under the influence of high pressure and the North-east trade winds which blow off shore (i.e. from land to sea). In the winter the westerlies blow on shore bringing rain.

A4 The increased number of people using water.

TUTORIALS

T1 *These storms are all tropical low-pressure systems. In other words the equivalent of the depressions in temperate latitudes.*

T2 *In this question you need to consider both the short-term and long-term effects. LEDCs are less able to get emergency aid to people. In the long-term they have little money available, or technological know-how, to restore the infrastructure and remedy the effects of a disaster. For MEDCs the opposite is generally true.*

T3 *This part of Spain has different prevailing winds in the summer and winter seasons because of the movement of pressure and wind belts. In the northern summer the winds move north with the passage of the overhead sun to the Tropic of Cancer. In the winter, the sun is overhead at the Tropic of Capricorn in the southern hemisphere, so the winds move south. In the British Isles this movement does not have the same effect, because the region stays in the westerly wind belt all year around.*

T4 *The situation is made even worse by the largely seasonal nature of tourism. The height of the tourist season is at the same time as the height of the drought.*

EXAMINATION CHECKLIST

The facts and ideas that you should know and understand after studying weather and climate are:

- The difference between weather and climate.
- The climate of a place is influenced by its latitude, altitude, distance from the sea, and prevailing winds.
- The main features of the temperature and precipitation of the British Isles.
- The factors causing this pattern of temperature and precipitation.
- The three ways in which precipitation can form.
- The representation of anticyclones and depressions on a weather chart.
- The weather associated with anticyclones and depressions.
- The importance of satellite images in weather forecasting.
- The causes of short-term hazards such as tropical cyclones, hurricanes and typhoons.
- The cause and effects of cyclones in LEDCS, e.g. Bangladesh.
- The cause and effects of the drought in Andalucia, southern Spain.

KEY WORDS

These are the key words. Tick them if you think you know what they mean. Otherwise check on them.

continental climate	isobars	hurricanes
oceanic climate	depressions	typhoons
isotherms	anticyclones	surges
relief precipitation	fronts	
rain shadow	tropical cyclones	
convectional precipitation		

EXAM PRACTICE

Sample Student's Answer and Examiner's Comments

EXAMINER'S COMMENTS

a) i)
All three parts are correctly labelled. This has all the features of a typical depression. The warm front is seen approaching the British Isles. The front has not reached the Bay of Biscay and Northern Spain.

ii)
This is correct.
She has given more than is required for the one mark. She also states that there are two fronts in a depression.

iii)
She shows clear understanding of why there is rain along a front. The first mark is for stating that warm air rises, and the second mark for stating that the cooling of the air results in condensation. There are credit worthy points for mentioning the lower density of the warm air, and that condensation eventually leads to the formation of rain.

1 (a) Study the satellite image showing a weather system moving eastwards towards the British Isles.

(i) Add the following labels. The first one has been done for you.

(3 marks)

CENTRE OF DEPRESSION
CLOUDS ALONG THE FRONT
AREA OF SCATTERED SHOWERS
AREA OF CLEAR SKIES

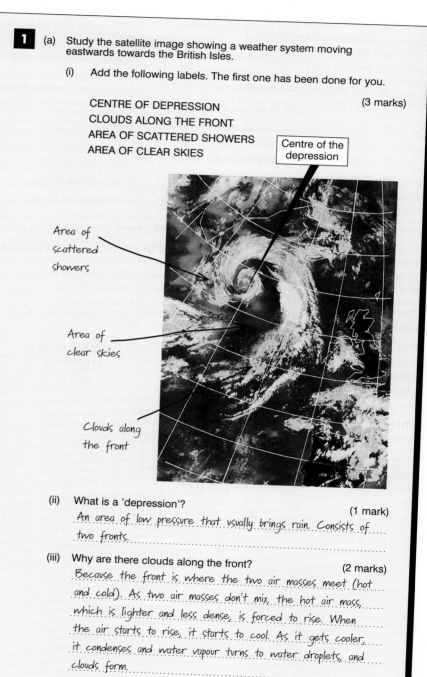

Centre of the depression

Area of scattered showers

Area of clear skies

Clouds along the front

(ii) What is a 'depression'? (1 mark)
An area of low pressure that usually brings rain. Consists of two fronts.

(iii) Why are there clouds along the front? (2 marks)
Because the front is where the two air masses meet (hot and cold). As two air masses don't mix, the hot air mass, which is lighter and less dense, is forced to rise. When the air starts to rise, it starts to cool. As it gets cooler, it condenses and water vapour turns to water droplets, and clouds form.

iv)
This is correct.

v)
The answer has been point marked. She reaches full marks at the end of the third sentence. There are around another nine credit worthy points in this answer.

This is an outstanding answer and gains full marks.

(iv)   What units are used to measure atmospheric pressure?
(1 mark)

Millibars.

(v)   The weather system took about 24 hours to move eastwards and cross the British Isles. Briefly describe the sequence of weather that would be experienced in the southern half of Britain over such a period.
(4 marks)

The first sign of a warm front approaching would be high, thin clouds (cirrus). The cloud would get lower and thicker (stratus). As the warm front passes the winds would get stronger and the temperature would rise. Then there would be a long period of heavy rain from (nimbostratus) clouds. The weather in the warm sector is less predictable, probably light showers, drizzle or weak sunshine. The weather at the cold front is more extreme. Very heavy rain from cumulonimbus clouds, possible hail and thunder. The rain lasts for a shorter duration than at the warm front. Heavy rain dies out to heavy showers, where increasingly longer sunny intervals break through.

SEG, 1997

Questions to Answer

The answer to Question 2 can be found in Chapter 18.

2   Study Figure 6.12.

i)   What kind of weather system is affecting England?   (1 mark)

ii)   What kind of front is crossing South-west Ireland?   (1 mark)

iii)   State four facts about the weather in South-east England.   (4 marks)

iv)   Why is it raining in Northern Ireland?   (2 marks)

v)   By the 24 June 1994, the cold front was lying along the east coast of England. Explain what the weather conditions were likely to be on 24 June 1994.   (6 marks)

7.1 THE ECOSYSTEM CONCEPT

At a global scale, climate, vegetation and soil have similar distributions. This is because they each form part of an natural interrelated system called an **ecosystem**:

- Ecosystems consist of living organisms (plants, animals, decomposers) and the physical environment (non-living features such as rocks, climate, soil, water, atmosphere, etc.) (Fig. 7.1).

Figure 7.1

Ecosystems: the physical environment and living things.

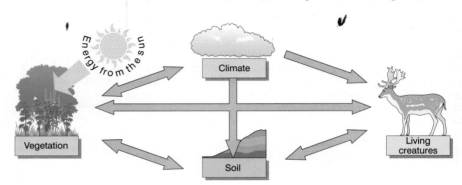

- Plants, animals and decomposers are linked to each other, and to the physical environment by complex flows of energy and materials (Fig. 7.2).

Figure 7.2

Energy and nutrient flows in a heath ecosystem.

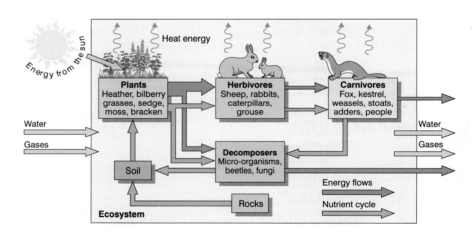

7.2 ENERGY FLOWS

Ecosystems are powered by sunlight (Fig. 7.2). Within ecosystems, energy transfers from plants to animals along **food chains** and **food webs**. These pathways usually have a number of different levels called **trophic levels** (Fig. 7.3):

Trophic level 1

- Green plants or **primary producers**. These trap the sun's energy which combines with carbon dioxide from the air and water to produce sugars and oxygen. This process is called **photosynthesis**. The sugars are converted to starches in the plants, which act as an energy store. Primary producers are the source of energy for most living things in ecosystems.

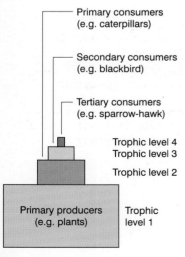

Figure 7.3 *Trophic levels.*

Trophic level 2

- Animals which feed directly on plants are **herbivores** or **primary consumers**. They range in size from aphids to elephants.

Trophic level 3

- **Carnivores** (meat-eating animals) or **secondary consumers**. Like herbivores, carnivores are a very varied group. They include many insects, insect-eating birds such as blue tits, and powerful predators such as lions and wolves.

At the end of all food chains are decomposer organisms such as fungi and bacteria.

At each trophic level in the food chain there is a reduction in the biological mass (**biomass**). The biomass of plants is much greater than animals, and there are many more herbivores than carnivores. The reduction in biomass is because when consumers eat animals or plants from lower trophic levels, biomass is shed as waste, and energy stores are transferred to the surroundings as heat, e.g. through respiration (Fig. 7.2).

7.3 NUTRIENT CYCLES

Ecosystems cycle mineral nutrients such as nitrogen, phosphorus, potassium and calcium. The nutrient cycle consists of a number of stages:

- Weathering of rocks releases mineral nutrients into the soil.
- Plants take up these mineral nutrients through their roots.
- Herbivores eat plants and carnivores eat herbivores so that the nutrients transfer along the food chain.
- Eventually when the plants and animals die, bacteria and fungi in the soil decompose them to release the nutrients. The nutrients are recycled within the ecosystem.

Check yourself

QUESTIONS

Q1 What is an ecosystem?

Q2 What is a trophic level?

Q3 Redraw Figure 7.2 as a food chain adding the following labels:

primary producers, primary consumers, secondary consumers.

Q4 Arrange the following into a food web. Draw arrows to show the energy flows:

beech tree, beetle, caterpillar, field mouse, grass, kestrel, owl, sparrow, vole, worm

Q5 Why is there a reduction in the number of individuals in each successive trophic level?

ANSWERS

A1 Living and non-living things and the relationship between them.

A2 A level or stage in a food chain, containing similar types of living organisms.

A3

Primary Producer	Primary Consumer	Secondary Consumer
Plants →	Rabbit →	Fox

Decomposers
Bacteria

A4

Kestrel, Owl, Field Mouse, Sparrow, Caterpillar, Grass, Beech Tree, Beetle, Worms, Voles

A5 There is less energy from one trophic level to the next, higher trophic level.

TUTORIALS

T1 *The main non-living parts of ecosystems are climate, soil and the rock type or geology. The animals and plants are the living parts of an ecosystem. Remember that a diagram can show the relationship between the different parts of the ecosystem more easily than a written description. All the different parts of an ecosystem are interlinked (Fig. 7.1). This means that changing one part of the ecosystem will have an effect on the other parts.*

T2 *Remember that decomposer organisms are at the bottom of the trophic levels.*

T3 *There are rarely more than four or five food trophic levels in a food chain. This is because of the energy reduction from one trophic level to the next. Humans are often at the top of a food chain.*

T4 *Even the simplest ecosystems have an enormous feeding complexity, e.g. a pond. Many parts of the food web are food for more than one organism. Remember that energy flows from the organism that is eaten to the organism that is doing the eating. Make sure you draw in energy arrows correctly to show this. Space out your diagram so that the lines/arrows don't cross too often.*

T5 *There is not a steady decline in the number of individuals from one trophic level to the next. One whale can eats millions and millions of microscopic plants and animals!*

7.4 TROPICAL RAINFOREST

At the global scale there are several major vegetation systems (Fig. 7.4). These are called **biomes**. The tropical rainforest is one such biome. Others include tundra, steppe and desert. Confined to the equatorial lowlands, tropical rainforests extend across South America (Amazonia), central Africa (Zaire Basin), and South-east Asia (Indonesia and Malaysia).

The rainforests have enormous biomass and biodiversity. A typical hectare of rainforest may contain 5,000 trees and have a biomass of 11,000 tonnes. Such is the diversity of life in the rainforest that 90 per cent of the world's plant and animal species are found there. Tall forest trees dominate the rainforest ecosystem (Fig. 7.5). They fix the sun's energy and affect the environment of all other life forms.

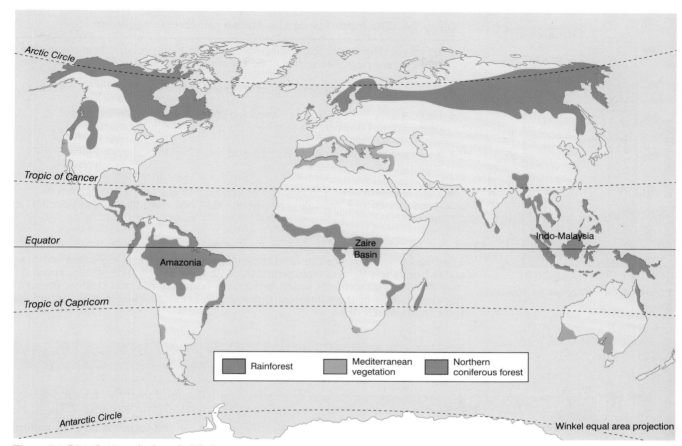

Figure 7.4 *Distribution of selected global ecosystems.*

Figure 7.5
*Tropical rainforest,
Cape Tribulation, Australia.*

The equatorial lowland climate provides ideal conditions for plant growth and decomposition (Fig. 7.6):

- An annual rainfall ranging from 1,500 to 5,000 mm.

- Constant temperatures averaging between 25°C and 30°C all year.

- A growing season which lasts all year.

111

Figure 7.6

| Manaus, Brazil |
| 3°08'S, |
| 60°01'W |
| Altitude 44m |

Figure 7.6 *Climate graph for Manaus, Brazil.*

Table 7.1 The influence of climate on rainforest vegetation

- Trees are deciduous: high temperatures and high precipitation mean that plants grow new leaves and shed them all year round.

- Trees have thick, leathery leaves to protect them against intense sunlight.

- Leaves have drip tips which shed moisture quickly following daily convectional downpours.

- Trees are tall and shallow rooted and have buttress roots to give extra support.

- High temperatures and high humidity lead to the rapid breakdown of dead plants and animals. This means that recycling of nutrients occurs quickly.

The trees also influence the rainforest climate. Like giant pumps they extract water from the soil, and transpire it through their leaves. The water vapour they release forms clouds which bring daily convectional rain storms. Present day destruction of the rainforest threatens to break this water cycle and make the climate much drier.

FOREST LAYERS

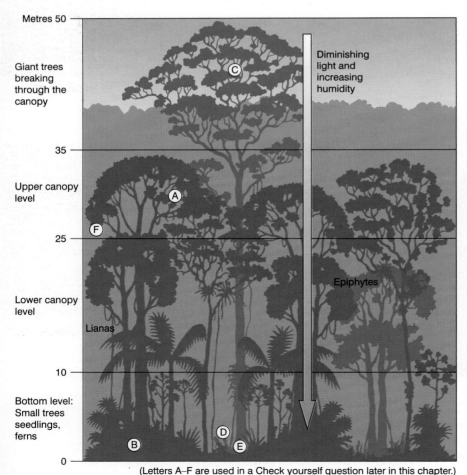

(Letters A–F are used in a Check yourself question later in this chapter.)

The rainforest has a well defined vertical structure (Fig. 7.7):

- In the topmost layer or canopy of the forest intense sunlight assists plant growth in the form of leaves, flowers and fruits. The canopy provides a rich food source which attracts huge numbers of insects, mammals (e.g. monkeys, bats) and birds.

- Mosses and climbing plants (e.g lianas) festoon the forest trees. Many have aerial roots and obtain their nutrients from rainwater.

- Below the canopy giant trees cast a dense shade, so that ground vegetation is sparse and consists mainly of flowering plants, grasses and ferns.

Figure 7.7
Structure of the rainforest.

RAINFOREST SOILS

Soils are a mixture of mineral and organic matter. The typical soils of the rainforest are shallow and acidic (Fig. 7.8). Iron oxides stain the top layers (or horizons) red.

The luxuriant rainforest vegetation suggests that the soils are rich and fertile. In fact, the rainforest soils are among the poorest in the world. There are two reasons for this:

- The soils are very old. Having been weathered for thousands of years they contain few plant nutrients.
- Heavy rainfall quickly washes away any nutrients which are not taken up by the roots of the trees.

Despite its infertile soils, the rainforest survives because of its rapid and efficient nutrient cycle. Plant and animal remains soon decay in the warm, humid climate. And shallow-rooted trees quickly absorb the nutrients released by decomposition. Few nutrients are lost from the nutrient cycle, but at any one time the soil contains only a small store of nutrients. Most nutrients are stored in the vegetation, particularly in the stems of the forest trees.

7.5 LOGGING IN THE SARAWAK RAINFOREST

Sarawak lies on the northern tip of the island of Borneo in Malaysia. (Fig. 7.9). Around 70 per cent of the Sarawak region is covered with primary (virgin) tropical rainforest.

ECONOMIC BENEFITS OF LOGGING

Rising demand for tropical hardwoods, especially in Pacific Rim countries has led to a huge increase in commercial logging in Sarawak. Logging has brought important economic benefits to the region:

- jobs for local people;
- timber exports which support the regional economy;
- export earnings which help to improve local services and provide essential infrastructure (roads, schools, healthcare, etc.).

ENVIRONMENTAL EFFECTS

Although logging does not involve clear felling, it has none the less caused considerable harm to Sarawak's natural environment:

- Because of the rainforest's biodiversity, only a few trees per hectare are commercially valuable hardwoods. Also, extracting these trees is difficult. On average for every tree that is extracted five others are badly damaged.
- The use of tractors and bulldozers causes environmental damage through road building and dragging timber along skid trails.
- Heavy machinery churns up the soil. This leads to soil erosion; the silting of rivers and destruction of fisheries; and an increase in the risk of flooding.

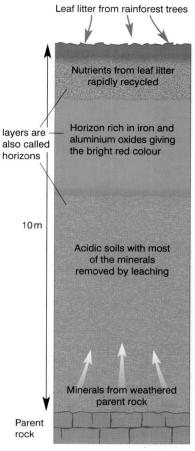

Figure 7.8 *Rainforest soil profile.*

Figure 7.9 *Location map for Sarawak.*

113

- Forest destruction threatens the traditional subsistence life of cultivators such as the Iban and Penan tribes.

- Removing trees and damaging others affects the food web. Some animals have to migrate or die, thereby reducing biodiversity.

SUSTAINABILITY

Between 1963 and 1986, 30 per cent of Sarawak's total forest area was logged. Ideally, any logging operation should be **sustainable**. For example, if a hectare of forest grows one cubic metre of new wood in a year, then to protect the forest resource, no more than this amount should be harvested annually. Present rates of logging are unsustainable. Unless action is taken Sarawak's rainforests will have disappeared by 2020.

The Malaysian government has introduced rules to achieve sustainable yields:

- Loggers must extract no more than 10 to 20 per cent of timber from any one concession area.

- When operations have finished the logged zone must be left to recover for between 25 and 40 years.

So far these rules have been largely ignored. The government has made little effort to enforce them. In future, sustainability might be achieved by changing the industry from the export of raw logs to the processing of timber into veneers and plywood. These products have greater added value; they create more jobs; and the work means that fewer trees have to be felled.

Transporting felled trees by helicopter, though more costly than conventional logging, would help to reduce damage to the rainforests.

Table 7.2 The value of tropical rainforests

- Rainforests are the major source of tropical hardwood timber such as teak, rosewood and mahogany.

- Timber exports are vital to the economies of many LEDCs.

- At least a quarter of all pharmaceutical products come from rainforest plants. Many plants have properties which one day may be of enormous benefit in drugs for the treatment of human diseases, such as cancer.

- The rainforest trees play a vital role in the global ecosystem. They absorb carbon dioxide from the atmosphere and release oxygen. Rainforest destruction causes more carbon dioxide to build up in the atmosphere. As a result, deforestation contributes to global warming and the greenhouse effect.

- The rainforest is a beautiful and diverse natural system. We should preserve it both for aesthetic reasons and for future generations.

Check yourself

QUESTIONS

Q1 Study Figure 7.6.
i) State two features of the temperature in Manaus.
ii) Describe the pattern of the precipitation.

Q2 Study Figure 7.7. Match the letters in Figure 7.7 to the correct phrases in the following list:

not much undergrowth, buttress roots, forest giants(emergents), leaves with drip tips, crowns spread to form a canopy, dense undergrowth in clearings.

Q3 Explain why there is less plant life at ground level in the rainforest compared with the upper levels.

Q4 Explain why the tropical rainforests look like they are 'evergreen'.

Q5 State one reason why the destruction of the tropical rainforest in Sarawak will have:
i) local economic and environmental effects
ii) an effect at a global scale.

REMEMBER! Cover the answers if you want to.

ANSWERS

A1
i) The temperature remains steady at about 28°C.
ii) There is precipitation in all seasons with the wettest period being in the summer months of December to May. The driest season lasts from June to November. The wettest month is March, with over 260 mm.

A2 D, E, C, F, A, B.

A3 The light is dim on the forest floor, so there is little plant and animal life there. There is plenty of light in the upper levels which encourages wildlife.

A4 There are no definite seasons in equatorial areas, so that different trees shed their leaves at different times. At any one time there will be some trees in full leaf.

A5
i) If all the timber is destroyed, the amount of money in the local economy will fall. The environment will be harmed by machines cutting up the soil. Many rare species of plants and animals will become extinct.
ii) The loss of rainforests means that more carbon dioxide accumulates in the atmosphere, because there are fewer plants to photosynthesise the gas. This leads to global warming.

TUTORIALS

T1
i) *Try to include geographical terms, such as range of temperature.*
ii) *Identify the general, specific and exception(s) in this description.*

T2 *Make sure that you know these rainforest characteristics. This information is regularly asked for in a GCSE Geography examination. The question might ask you to draw a labelled diagram.*

T3 *The great variations in different parts of the tropical rainforest ecosystem explains why there is such a great biodiversity.*

T4 *The seasons do not vary because the sun always remains high in the sky. Look back at the section on weather and climate on p.92. Rainforest trees are actually deciduous, not evergreen.*

T5 *Make sure that you remember the difference between the greenhouse effect and global warming. Many candidates seem to think that these, along with ozone depletion, are the same thing. They are explained more fully in Chapter 15.*

7.6 MEDITERRANEAN VEGETATION

Mediterranean vegetation is widely distributed. In addition to the Mediterranean Basin it occurs in California, Chile, South Africa, and South and Western Australia (Fig. 7.4). All of these areas have a similar climate (Fig. 7.10):

- Summers are hot and dry with average temperatures ranging from 20°C to 30°C.

- Winters are mild and wet with temperatures averaging between 8°C and 12°C.

- The main feature of the Mediterranean climate is the summer drought.

Figure 7.10
Climate graph for Mallorca (39°N), Spain.

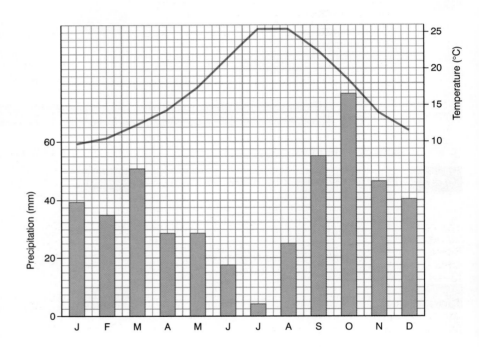

VEGETATION

Figure 7.11
Garrigue vegetation, Minorca (39°N).

Thousands of years ago a rich forest of oak, pine and cypress trees covered much of Mediterranean Europe. Forest clearance for farming, intensive grazing and firing means that few areas of original forest remain today. In its place there is a type of vegetation called garrigue, which is dominated by shrubs and small trees (Fig. 7.11). Typical plants of the garrigue include cistus, gorse, heather, rosemary and lavender. The Mediterranean vegetation owes its character as much to human influence as it does to natural factors such as climate and soil.

PLANT ADAPTATION TO THE MEDITERRANEAN CLIMATE

To survive in the Mediterranean climate plants must overcome the problem of drought. Plants have responded in two ways: some plants are drought resistant; others are drought evading. Drought resistant species have certain characteristics:

- Long roots to tap underground water supplies, e.g. vines, almond trees.
- Thick, waxy leaves to reduce water loss by transpiration.
- Bulbs and tubers which survive the summer after the plant has flowered in the spring, e.g. asphodel.
- Water storage within the plant tissue (succulents), e.g. prickly pear cacti.
- Plants which can close their stomata (pores) to reduce water loss; or roll their leaves to trap humidity, e.g. marram grass.

Some plants, such as annual grasses, evade the drought by dying down in summer and surviving as seeds.

7.7 NORTHERN CONIFEROUS FOREST

The northern coniferous forest stretches in a great belt around the northern hemisphere. It extends from Scandinavia, through Siberia and across the Bering Straits into Alaska, Canada and the USA (Fig. 7.4). A handful of tree species – mainly conifers such as pine, spruce, fir and larch – dominate the forest (Fig. 7.12).

The northern coniferous forest is the world's main source of softwood timber and wood pulp. In North America and Scandinavia timber products are leading exports and the forests are managed on a sustainable basis.

Figure 7.12 *Coniferous (pine) forest with fern carpet.*

CLIMATE

- The northern coniferous forest belt extends through high latitudes (50°N to the Arctic Circle) and the continental interiors of North America and Asia.
- For several months a year temperatures are below freezing and the growing season is short (Fig. 7.13).
- The brief growing season and the low temperatures are compensated partly by long hours of daylight in summer.
- The cold climate means that humidity and precipitation are low. Most precipitation falls as rain in summer (Fig. 7.13). In winter there is a light covering of snow.
- A lot of precipitation is locked up as ice and snow, so it is not available to plants.

Figure 7.13
Climate graph for Inari (69°N), Finland.

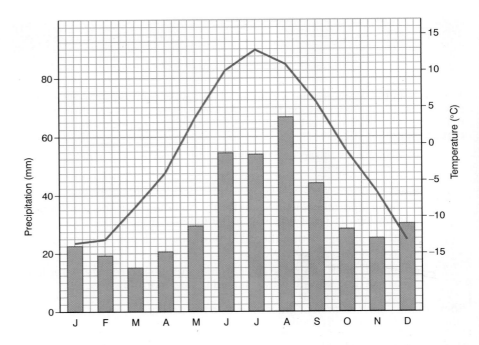

Table 7.3 Climatic contrasts in Finland

	No. of months with average temperature below 0 °C	No. of months with average temperature above 0 °C
Helsinki (60°N)	4	5
Inari (69°N)	7	3

ADAPTATIONS OF THE FOREST TO CLIMATE

Compared to the rainforest, the coniferous forest has little biodiversity. There are relatively few plant and animal species, and the total biomass is small.

The severe climate explains the lack of biodiversity. Few species have adapted to the freezing temperatures and short growing season. Although some broad-leaved trees, such as birch and aspen, thrive in high latitudes, it is conifers such as pine and spruce which have been most successful. Conifers have several advantages:

- Conifers keep their leaves all year around. This allows them to photosynthesise as soon as air temperatures rise above a daily average of 6 °C. This gives conifers a head start over deciduous trees which need time to grow new leaves each spring.

- Conifers have needle-shaped leaves which reduce moisture loss.

- Conifers have a conical (Christmas tree) shape which helps them to shed snow easily in winter.

The coniferous forest has a simple structure: a canopy of forest trees; a ground layer of bilberry and cowberry; and a carpet of lichens and mosses on the forest floor. Typical forest herbivores include insects, moose, beaver, squirrels and a variety of seed-eating birds (e.g. crossbills). Carnivores include lynx, wolves, owls, pine martens and bears.

SOILS

- The typical soils of the coniferous forest are podsols (Fig.7.14).

- Podsols are shallow and acidic and have little or no agricultural value.

- Rainwater washes minerals and humus through the soil (leaching), which leaves the upper horizons bleached and sandy.

- Because of their acidity podsols contain few earthworms. As a result there is little mixing of the different soils layers, and horizons are sharply defined.

- Low temperatures mean that conifer needles on the surface take many years to decompose. Hence the soil contains little humus.

7.8 CONIFEROUS FORESTS IN FINLAND

Finland's coniferous forests are its most important natural resource (Fig. 7.15). Softwood timber and timber products, such as wood pulp and paper, account for 8 per cent of the country's gross national product (GNP). Unlike Sarawak, Finland's forest industries are conservation-minded. Since the end of the nineteenth century Finland's forests have been exploited at a sustainable rate. Also, Finland aims to preserve the forest's biodiversity, and protect its rivers and atmosphere from pollution caused by timber processing industries.

Although re-planting concentrates on the commercially valuable conifers, deciduous trees such as birch, aspen and willow are planted too. Logged areas are usually less than 2 ha, and thinning is preferred to clear felling. Each year about 2 per cent of the total forest area is cut down and then re-planted.

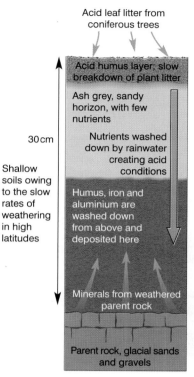

Figure 7.14 *Podsol soil profile.*

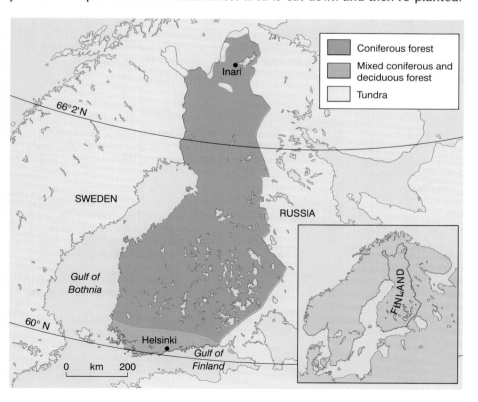

Figure 7.15
Finland's natural vegetation.

Soils are poor and regeneration takes many years (60 years in the south, 120 years in the far north). Chemical fertilisers speed up growth rates but they damage the environment and are used sparingly.

Finland has also tried to reduce the environmental impact of wood processing industries such as pulp and paper making. Less water is used in manufacturing processes now and waste products are treated before being discharged into rivers.

Check yourself

QUESTIONS

Q1 Explain the different ways in which coniferous and Mediterranean vegetation has to withstand seasonal drought.

Q2 What is a podsol?

Q3 What is leaching?

Q4
i) What is sustainability?
ii) Why is Sarawak's timber industry not sustainable?
iii) How has Finland organised its timber industry to ensure sustainability?

REMEMBER! Cover the answers if you want to.

ANSWERS

A1 In areas of Mediterranean vegetation the plants have long roots to tap underground water supplies. The thick waxy leaves reduce water loss by transpiration. Water is stored within the plant tissue and the plants are capable of closing their pores to reduce water loss.

The needles on pine trees in the coniferous forest ecosystem have a small surface area and are leathery. This reduces water loss through transpiration.

A2 Podsols are soils that develop under coniferous forests.

A3 Leaching is the washing out of the minerals and the humus from soils by rainwater.

A4
i) Sustainability is maintaining the ecosystem by not removing more than is replaced.
ii) More than 30% of Sarawak's total forest was destroyed up to 1986 without any similar amount of tree planting to replace trees removed for timber.
iii) There is a policy of reafforestation in Finland. This means that there is an on-going programme of tree planting. This ensures timber resources for the future.

TUTORIALS

T1 *Questions on ecosystems are very likely to ask you to explain how the vegetation has adapted to climate. Plants need warmth and moisture to survive and grow. If either are missing during a particular season the plants must devise ways of overcoming the problem. If the climate changes rapidly, the plants will not have time to adapt and there will be a change of vegetation.*

T2&3 *You need to understand technical terms such as these. Make sure that you can show your understanding by writing precise definitions.*

T4
i) *Sustainability is a very difficult concept to understand. It is probably easiest to think in terms of actual resources.*
ii) *Remember that the Malaysian government has now introduced new laws which aim to maintain the availability of timber resources in Sarawak.*
iii) *The Finnish timber industry illustrates the wider aspects of sustainability. The importance of protecting the environment is recognised.*

EXAMINATION CHECKLIST

The facts and ideas that you should know and understand after studying ecosystems are:

- An ecosystem comprises living and non-living things and the relationships between them.
- Ecosystems are powered by sunlight.
- There is movement of energy and nutrients through food chains in the ecosystem.
- There are a number of trophic levels in a food chain.
- The equatorial rainforest is an example of a large-scale ecosystem (or biome).
- The vegetation in a rainforest has adapted to the hot and humid conditions near the Equator.
- There is a definite structure to the rainforest.
- The unique biodiversity of the rainforest can easily be destroyed.
- Sustainable management strategies are required, if the rainforest ecosystem is to survive.
- The Mediterranean vegetation has evolved in order to survive summer drought.
- The coniferous forests have adapted in order to survive severe climatic conditions in winter.
- The Finnish timber industry is an example of the sustainable exploitation of an ecosystem.

KEY WORDS

These are the key words. Tick them if you think you know what they mean. Otherwise check on them.

ecosystem	photosynthesis	biomass
food chains	herbivores	biomes
food webs	primary consumers	sustainable
trophic levels	carnivores	podsols
primary producers	secondary consumers	

EXAM PRACTICE

Sample Student's Answer and Examiner's Comments

EXAMINER'S COMMENTS

a) i)
She has made two credit worthy points. She recognises the general distribution around the Equator, and the areas of rainforest in South-east Asia. However, the rest of the answer is too generalised. South America and Africa are continents, so to gain further credit, she would have to narrow these down to the Amazon and Zaire basins. She could also have given the latitudinal extent. Mentioning the lack of rainforests in the higher areas of the Andes, East Africa, and central areas of the South-east Asian islands of Malaysia and Indonesia would have gained credit too.

ii)
She has not used the left scale accurately. The correct answer is within the range 300–310 mm. She has recognised that all numerical answers must have units in order to gain credit.

iii)
She does not understand the reasons for high annual rainfall in the Equatorial regions. The only credit worthy point is the reference to evapotranspiration. A good answer would have included details on convectional precipitation. The intense heat causes warm air containing water vapour to rise. The water vapour then cools to form rain.

1 (a) Study the information about the Equatorial rainforests in the diagram.

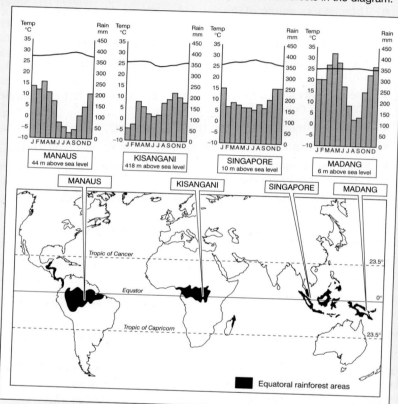

MANAUS
44 m above sea level

KISANGANI
418 m above sea level

SINGAPORE
10 m above sea level

MADANG
6 m above sea level

Equatoral rainforest areas

(i) Describe the distribution of the equatorial rainforest areas. **(3 marks)**

They all seem to be near to the Equator. Some are in the northern hemisphere and others in the southern hemisphere. They are in a warm climate. They are in South America, Africa and South-east Asia.

(ii) What is the average rainfall in Madang in January? **(1 mark)**

350mm

(iii) Why do equatorial rainforests have a high annual rainfall? **(3 marks)**

There are many trees which evapotranspirate, drawing a lot of water from the soils. This then falls again, as rain. The weather is very warm, causing very low pressure; and clouds are high, so that rain is produced.

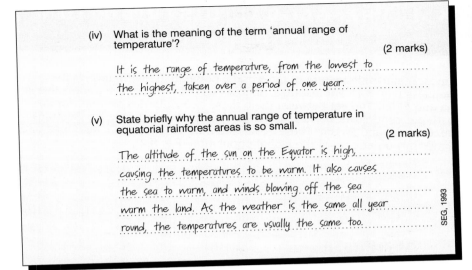

(iv) What is the meaning of the term 'annual range of temperature'?

(2 marks)

It is the range of temperature, from the lowest to the highest, taken over a period of one year.

(v) State briefly why the annual range of temperature in equatorial rainforest areas is so small.

(2 marks)

The altitude of the sun on the Equator is high, causing the temperatures to be warm. It also causes the sea to warm, and winds blowing off the sea warm the land. As the weather is the same all year round, the temperatures are usually the same too.

SEG, 1993

EXAMINER'S COMMENTS

a) iv)
She has not recognised that there are two parts to this question. The definition needs to explain 'annual' as well as 'range of temperature'. One mark is given for her understanding that the range is the difference between the highest and lowest temperatures.

v)
She shows complete understanding here. The marks are for the first part of the first sentence and for the second sentence. Marks would also have been given for mentioning the concentration of the sun's rays and the constant length of daylight throughout the year.

She gained 6 marks out of a possible 11 which is of Grade C standard.

Questions to Answer

The answer to Question 2 can be found in Chapter 18.

2 **a)** **i)**   Why are rainforest areas described as 'equatorial'? (1 mark)

ii)   State two characteristics of the temperatures in equatorial rainforest areas. (2 marks)

iii)   State two characteristics of the precipitation in equatorial rainforest areas. (2 marks)

b) **i)**   What is the meaning of the term 'ecosystem'? (2 marks)

ii)   A single rainforest tree can support 5,000 species. How are equatorial rainforests able to support so many living things? (2 marks)

c)   Study the diagram showing the rate of deforestation in the equatorial rainforest areas. Comment on the information shown. (6 marks)

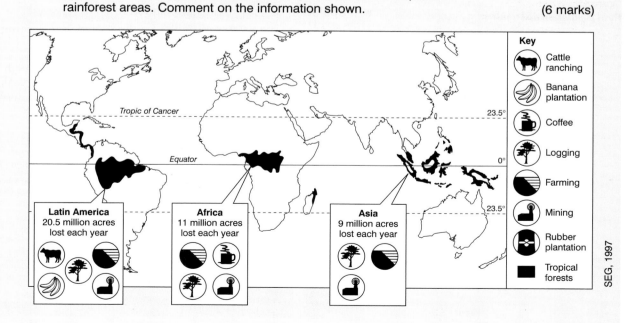

8.1 THE GLOBAL DISTRIBUTION OF POPULATION

The most remarkable feature of the world's population distribution is its unevenness (Fig. 8.1). For instance, almost two out of every five people live in China and India. And yet between them these two countries account for less than 10 per cent of the world's land area. At the other extreme are Australia, Brazil, Canada, and Russia. These cover one third of the world's land area and yet have only 6 per cent of the global population (Fig. 8.2).

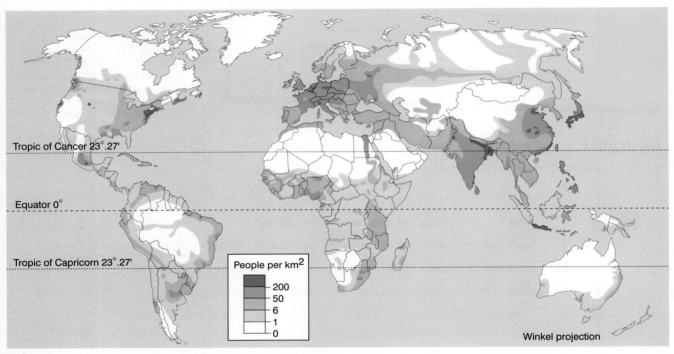

Figure 8.1
World population distribution.

- **Population density** relates population to area.
- Average population density is the total population in a country or region divided by its area (usually in people/km²).

While countries such as Bangladesh and Singapore have extremely high population densities, there are vast areas of the world which are virtually uninhabited. In fact, the average population density of the planet is quite low; even excluding Antarctica it is still only 43 people/km².

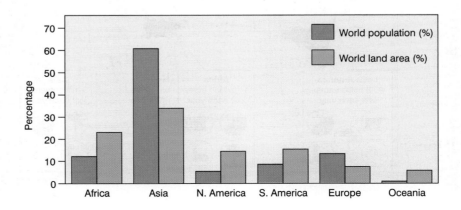

Figure 8.2
Population distribution and land area.

EXPLAINING THE GLOBAL DISTRIBUTION OF POPULATION

At the global scale physical factors such as climate, relief, vegetation and soil, determine the broad pattern of population distribution (Table 8.1). Large empty or sparsely populated areas usually indicate a physical environment unfavourable to settlement. In contrast densely populated areas suggest a favourable combination of physical resources which attracts economic activities and settlement.

Figure 8.3
High mountains are hostile to human settlement too.

Table 8.1	Global population distribution: the influence of physical factors	
	Favourable	**Unfavourable**
Climate	• In humid, tropical areas such as South and South-east Asia, high temperatures and high precipitation make it possible to grow two or three crops a year. Wet rice cultivation supports the highest rural population densities in the world. Other regions with favourable climates for agriculture include western Europe, the Mediterranean, central and eastern USA, eastern China and the seasonally wet tropical areas of Africa and Latin America.	• Large parts of continents are too dry to support many people. The world's hot deserts (e.g. Sahara, Arabian, Australian) have insufficient precipitation for cultivation. Even temperate deserts such as the Gobi in central Asia, are just as dry. • In high latitudes low temperatures rather than lack of rainfall deter settlement. In Antarctica and Greenland ice sheets cover an area equal to North America. No-one lives permanently in these icy areas. • The climates of the tundra and coniferous forest in Alaska, Canada and Siberia are less extreme than the polar regions. None the less population densities are sparse. Low temperatures and a short growing season make cultivation impossible. Only small groups of hunters and nomadic herders (e.g. the Sami in Lapland) have adapted to these conditions.
Relief	• Within the tropics, mountainous areas often have more favourable climates for agriculture than the lowlands, e.g. in Ethiopia. In contrast to the scorched lowlands, there is enough precipitation to allow cultivation. Also, the highlands have fewer insect-borne diseases such as malaria and yellow fever.	• Outside the tropics mountain ranges such as the Himalayas (Fig. 8.3), Rockies, and Alps are too cold to attract large populations. Even where temperatures are high enough for farming, steep slopes and poor soils often make cultivation impossible.
Soil	• Fertile soils and water for irrigation encourage high population densities. The highest rural densities in the world are found on the rich alluvial soils of the Nile, Ganges–Brahmaputra, Mekong and other deltas.	• Infertile soils like those of the tropical rainforests attract few settlers. Shifting cultivation, which supports population densities of just 1 or 2 people/km^2, is the only sustainable agriculture in rainforests.
Vegetation		• Inaccessible rainforest and tropical diseases account for the very low densities in Amazonia, the Zaire Basin and much of Indo-Malaysia.

Figure 8.4
Areas of limited opportunity for settlement.

However, physical factors alone cannot explain the global distribution of population. Economic, technological and historical factors also exert a powerful influence (Table 8.2).

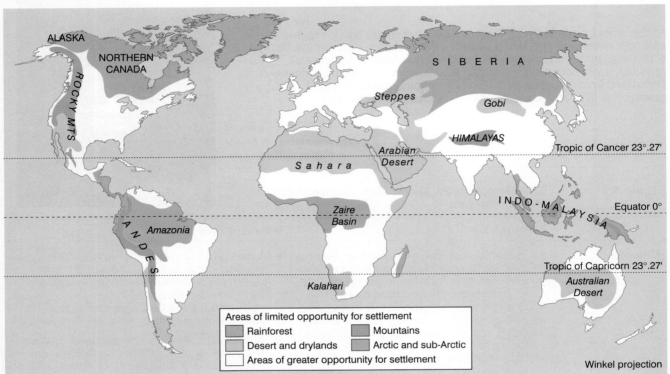

Table 8.2	Global population distribution: the influence of human factors
Economic activities	● Agriculture: because this uses land as a resource it takes a large area to support a farming community. This usually results in moderate to low population densities. ● Industry and services: these activities rely on materials, energy and trade brought in from elsewhere. They use land for location, not production. The world's greatest concentrations of population (western Europe, the Pacific coast of Japan, and the north-east and south-west USA) are urban centres based on industry, services and trade.
Human resources	● MEDCs are rich in human resources: high technology, and an educated, highly skilled workforce. Countries such as Japan, Singapore and Taiwan support high density, urban populations. In contrast, most LEDCs depend on low technology and have poorly educated, underskilled workforces. Their populations are mainly rural and have much lower densities.
Natural resources	● Natural resources such as energy, timber and minerals often have only a localised impact on population densities. Primary activities such as mining, quarrying, forestry, etc. employ relatively few people. Also, many LEDCs (e.g. Brazil, Congo, etc.) with immense natural resources often lack the necessary capital, skills and technology to exploit them.
Historical factors	● The regions of highest density tend to be those that have been longest settled. The high densities in much of India, eastern China and Europe reflect civilisations which go back thousands of years. Compare this with North and South America, Africa and Oceania, which until a few hundred years ago had only small populations (e.g. the Aborigines in Australia; the Indians in North America).

Check yourself

QUESTIONS

Q1 What is population density?

Q2 Complete the following table:

Country	Population (millions)	Area (km²)	Population density (persons per km²)
Bangladesh	112.5	143,995	872
Canada	26.3	9,976,139	
China	1122.4	9,596,961	116
India		3,287,590	254
UK	57.1		233

(1991 figures)

Q3 Study Figure 8.3. State three reasons why this area is so sparsely populated.

Q4 Use Table 8.2 to suggest why some parts of desert areas may support higher population densities.

Q5 Choose a densely populated urban area known to you. Write down three reasons why so many people live the area.

REMEMBER! Cover the answers if you want to.

ANSWERS

A1 The number of people per unit area.

A2 Population density of Canada is 3 per km². Population of India 835 million Area of UK is 245,064 km².

A3 The altitude of the area is very high, so that the climate is bleak and exposed. The steep slopes also make settlement difficult.

TUTORIALS

T1 An easy way to remember this is by the formula:

$$\text{Density} = \frac{\text{Population}}{\text{Area}}$$

T2 These examples show that population density is a useful measure when comparing countries. The great variation in the population densities of Canada and Bangladesh tell us a great deal about the two countries.

T3 These are only a few of the possible answers. Other disadvantages include the lack of soil depth; and the remoteness and inaccessibility of mountainous areas. If you have studied a particular mountainous area as a case study, give as many detailed facts as you can. Look back at Chapter 6 to remind you how (and why) temperature decreases with altitude.

ANSWERS

A4 The existence of natural resources such as oil can lead to the development of densely populated areas in a desert. Irrigated farmland also helps to support a much denser population. Oases also support settlement.

A5 Possible answers are that the urban area you have chosen is an industrial centre, a source of mineral wealth, a focus of communication, or a port.

TUTORIALS

T4 *Oil is the reason for higher population density in parts of the Middle East. In places such as Saudi Arabia the wealth generated from the oil has allowed settlements to overcome the lack of rain. Desalinisation of sea water is one method of producing fresh water. Irrigation from the Nile has allowed the development of high-density population along the side of the river. The Nile delta in Egypt supports some of the highest population densities in the world.*

T5 *This type of question allows you to use detailed knowledge of your local town or city. Remember that you will probably know more about your local urban area than the examiner, so don't forget to state the obvious.*

8.2 WORLD POPULATION GROWTH

The world's population is growing rapidly:

- Every day the global population grows by another 225,000. That's more than 82 million people a year; equal to the entire population of Nigeria in 1997.

- This rapid population growth is comparatively new (Table 8.3). Humanity reached its first billion in the early 1800s. Today, the global population stands at 6 billion.

- Population growth will continue until well into the twenty-first century. The latest estimates suggest that the world population will stabilise somewhere between 8 and 12 billion by 2050.

- Approximately 95 per cent of population growth in 1997 was in LEDCs. Since 1950 there has been a huge increase in the world's population living in poorer countries (Table 8.4). This trend will continue in future (Fig. 8.5).

Figure 8.5
Forecast of world population distribution (millions) in 2025.

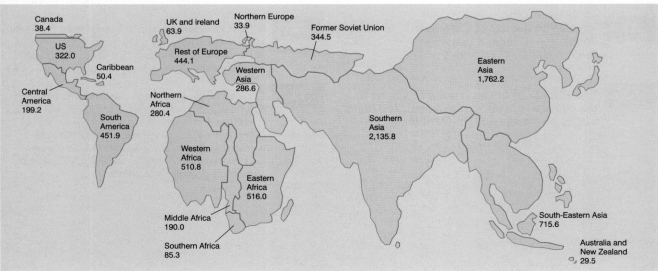

Canada 38.4
US 322.0
Caribbean 50.4
Central America 199.2
South America 451.9
UK and ireland 63.9
Northern Europe 33.9
Rest of Europe 444.1
Former Soviet Union 344.5
Western Asia 286.6
Northern Africa 280.4
Western Africa 510.8
Eastern Africa 516.0
Middle Africa 190.0
Southern Africa 85.3
Southern Asia 2,135.8
Eastern Asia 1,762.2
South-Eastern Asia 715.6
Australia and New Zealand 29.5

Table 8.3	World population growth: 1804–1998	
DATE	BILLIONS	YEARS TAKEN TO ADD 1 BILLION
1804	1	
1927	2	123
1960	3	33
1974	4	14
1987	5	13
1998	6	11

Table 8.4	Changing distribution of the world's population	
Date	MEDCs (millions)	LEDCs (millions)
1950	806	1713
1994	1182	4448
2025	1243	7050

8.3 HOW DOES POPULATION GROW?

- Population change within a country, city or region equates to:

  (Number of births) − (number of deaths) +/− (migration).

- At a global scale the population grows when the number of births exceeds the number of deaths.

- It is usual to state the number of births and deaths per 1000 of the population. The number of births per 1000 people is known as the **crude birth rate** (CBR), and the number of deaths per 1000 people, the **crude death rate** (CDR).

- The difference between the crude birth rate and the crude death rate is the **natural increase** of a population. It is usually expressed as a percentage per year:

$$\text{Natural increase (\%)} = \frac{\text{Crude birth rate} - \text{crude death rate}}{10}$$

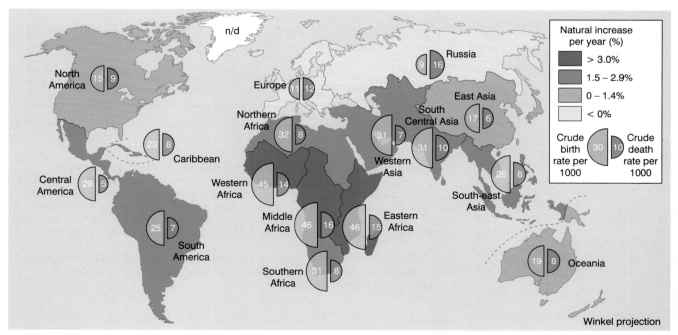

Figure 8.6 *Variations in birth rates, death rates and natural increase rates, 1994.*

For example, in 1995 the world's crude birth rate was 24 per 1000 and the crude death rate was 9 per 1000. This gave a natural increase of 15 per 1000 or 1.5 per cent (dividing 15 by 10).

Globally, there are huge contrasts in birth rates, death rates and rates of natural increase (Fig. 8.6):

- Birth rates are highest in LEDCs, averaging 28 per 1000 in 1995, compared with just 12 per 1000 in the MEDCs. The highest birth rates (50 per 1000) were in Africa, south of the Sahara Desert.

- Death rates vary more than birth rates. Some LEDCs (mainly in sub-Saharan Africa) continue to have high death rates (above 20 per 1000). Others such as Mexico and Costa Rica, with higher standards of living and very youthful populations have death rates of just 4 or 5 per 1000.

- In most MEDCs death rates are fairly steady at around 10 per 1000.

8.4 THE DEMOGRAPHIC TRANSITION

The **demographic transition** describes what has happened to birth and death rates in today's MEDCs since 1800. As its name suggests, the demographic transition is a gradual process. It has four stages (Fig. 8.7).

Figure 8.7
The demographic transition.

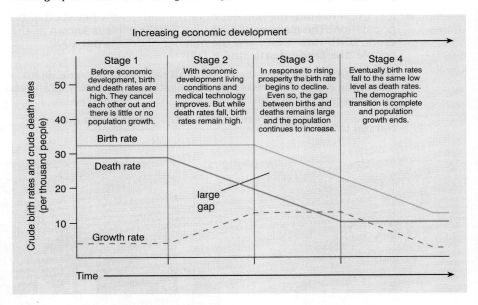

It seems unlikely that today's LEDCs will follow the same demographic transition as today's MEDCs. Birth rates are currently falling everywhere in the LEDCs. However, falling birth rates are not a result of economic development and rising standards of living. Instead they reflect the growing acceptance of family planning and the use of contraception. In MEDCs contraceptives were neither widely available nor widely accepted until the twentieth century.

Economic development is just one factor which causes population change. Other important influences include social, religious, political and environmental factors (Table 8.5).

Table 8.5	Reasons for variations in birth and death rates
Age structure	• A high proportion of women of reproductive age (15–49) increases the birth rate. • A high proportion of old people increases the death rate.
Diet, housing, living conditions	• A balanced diet and sufficient food intake lower death rates, especially among children. • Good housing conditions with adequate sanitation and clean water lower death rates. • Improvements in living standards mean that more children survive. This may help to lower birth rates.
Medicine, healthcare	• The availability of medicines, hospitals and doctors reduce death rates.
Family planning and contraception	• Birth rates in LEDCs are often high because women do not have access to family planning services. • Where family planning is available birth rates often fall rapidly. • Family planning is more readily available in towns and cities than in the countryside.
Economic conditions	• In rural areas in LEDCs children are often an economic asset. They do farm work at an early age. This makes large families sensible for food production. • In urban areas children are an economic burden. As a result birth rates in LEDCs are lower in urban areas than in rural areas. • In MEDCs children spend at least ten or eleven years in full-time education. They are supported by their parents during this time, so there is little economic advantage to large families.
Social and religious factors	• The education and status of women has an important influence on birth rates in LEDCs. • The more educated and the higher the status of women, the fewer children they have. • Religion (or superstition) may forbid contraception (e.g. Catholicism). • Children may be seen as 'god-given'. • In some societies women marry in their early teens, thus increasing the chance of larger families.
Political factors	• Governments may adopt policies either to encourage or to discourage births. Governments can encourage population growth by banning abortion or the sale of contraceptives, or by awarding financial benefits for children. • Currently, most governments in LEDCs have policies aimed at reducing population growth through family planning.

POPULATION CHANGE IN INDIA

By the turn of the century India will become the second country in the world (after China) to have a population of one billion. India's huge population is largely a result of rapid and sustained growth in the last 40 years.

Until the early twentieth century, India's birth and death rates were roughly the same and its population grew only slowly. Then, as health services improved, its CDR fell dramatically: from 45 in 1941 to just 9.9 in 1991. This caused rapid population growth. Thanks to better health care, better education and family planning, the CBR also fell during this period. However, its decline was nowhere near as fast as the fall in the CDR.

Despite this, India's CDR cannot fall much lower, so in future its population growth rate should start to slow down. Already in some parts of the country,

131

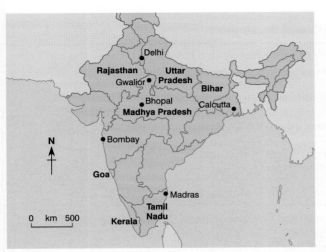

Figure 8.8
Location map, India.

notably Goa, Kerala and Tamil Nadu (Fig. 8.8), the birth rate is below **replacement level** (the rate which is needed to replace both parents). However, this has not happened in other regions. The four poorest states – Uttar Pradesh, Bihar, Madhya Pradesh and Rajasthan – which account for 40 per cent of India's total population, have made only limited progress. Even so, some **family planning** projects in these states have succeeded. In Bhopal and Gwaloir (Madhya Pradesh) birth rates have fallen where children have been immunised (thus reducing infant mortality) and where mothers have received some education. Despite this, India's population will only level out (at around 1.45 billion) some time in the mid-twenty first century.

Check yourself

QUESTIONS

Q1 Why are birth and death rates expressed as rates per 1000?

Q2 Use Figure 8.6 to work out the percentage natural increase of population per year in the following parts of the world:

Eastern Africa
Europe
South America
Russia.

Q3 Study the following figures for the birth and death rates per thousand, in England and Wales between 1721–2001.

	1721	1741	1761	1781	1801	1821	1841	1861	1881	1901	1921	1941	1961	1981	2001
Birth rate	31	34	35	36	35	33	30	30	33	30	22	15	17	13	13
Death rate	31	35	30	25	20	22	21	21	20	17	15	12	10	12	11

i)   Plot a graph like Figure 8.7 for the birth rates and death rates on the same axes.
ii) Draw vertical lines to divide the period 1721–2001 into the four shorter periods of the demographic transition model.
iii) Shade the part of the graph which represents the natural increase in population.

Q4 Explain the following reasons given in Table 8.5 for variations in birth and death rates:

i)   "Improvements in living standards which lower death rates mean that more children survive. This may help to lower birth rates."
ii) "The more educated and the higher the status of women the fewer children they have."

QUESTIONS

Q5 Use the information on India (pp. 131–132) to answer the following:

i) Which stage of the demographic transition model does India appear to be in?

ii) What evidence is there that India's population might follow a similar pattern to that of England and Wales. (The pattern for England and Wales is shown in the graph you drew for question 3.)

REMEMBER! Cover the answers if you want to.

ANSWERS

A1 This is because of the need to compare like for like.

A2 Eastern Africa +3.1%
Europe −0.1%
South America +2.1%
Russia −0.7%

A3 i)

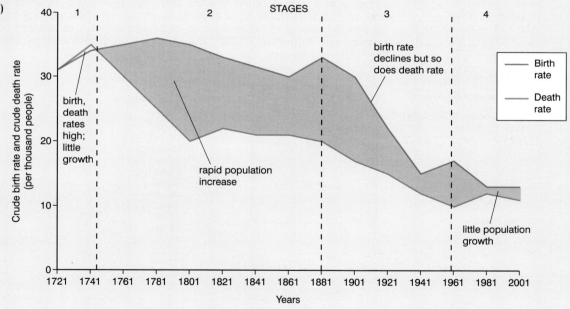

ii) See graph in part i).
iii) See graph in part i).

TUTORIALS

T1 *It would be unrealistic to compare the total number of births in a country such as China (large population) with the total number of births in, say, the UK (much smaller population).*

T2 *Remember the formula for working out natural increase.*

T3 *This shows that the demographic transition model can give an over simplified picture. The situation in England and Wales does not fit exactly. There is no precise date when countries move from one stage to another.*

ANSWERS

A4 i) In LEDCs women have many children because many children die in infancy. They feel that by giving birth to a greater number of children there will be more chance that some will survive.

ii) The more educated a woman is the more aware she is of family planning options, and indeed career options.

A5 i) It appears to be moving from Stage 3 to Stage 4.

ii) The birth and death rates are declining, so the natural increase is likely to fall. This is typical of the final stage which England and Wales entered in the 1950–60s.

TUTORIALS

T4 *Children in LEDCs are still seen as an economic asset, because they can do farming work.*

T5 *The decline in the death rate in India has been greater than the corresponding stage in the demographic transition for England and Wales. This means that the population growth has been more rapid, so India will take longer to reach Stage 4 when population increase slows.*

8.5 AGE–SEX STRUCTURE

The age–sex structure of a population can be shown in a special type of graph called a **population pyramid** (Fig. 8.9). Three factors control the shape of any population pyramid: births, deaths and migrations. At a national scale births and deaths are usually most important. However, when we look at population pyramids for smaller areas such as cities and regions, **migration** becomes increasingly important. LEDCs and MEDCs have population pyramids with very different shapes.

Figure 8.9
Population pyramid for Nigeria.

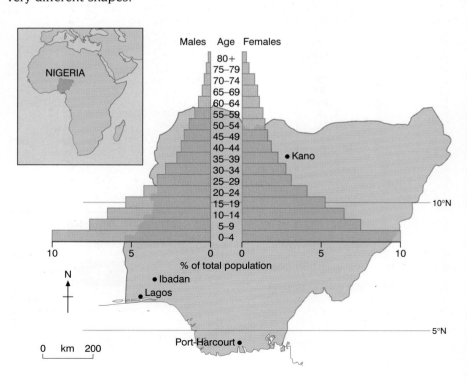

NIGERIA'S POPULATION PYRAMID

Nigeria is a LEDC in West Africa. Its population pyramid (Fig. 8.9) has three features which are typical of poorer countries: a very broad base; steeply tapering sides; and a narrow top (or apex).

- The pyramid's broad base tells us that the country has a large proportion of children. In fact, nearly half of Nigeria's population is less than 15 years old. Such a youthful population results from a very high CBR. In 1995, the CBR was 44 and on average each woman could expect to give birth to a total of 6.5 children. Large families reflect the low status of women; early marriage (half of all Nigerian women marry by the age of 17); lack of education; and the small proportion of adults who use modern family planning methods (6 per cent).

- The steeply tapering sides show that the CDR is high, especially for young children. Although rapid progress has been achieved in reducing mortality, poor sanitation, inadequate diets and parasitic infections still mean that one in every 10 infants die before their first birthday.

- **Life expectancy** improved from 37 years to 53 years between 1960 and 1995. Even so, these relatively short life expectancies mean that the proportion of old people is quite small. This explains why the population pyramid has a narrow apex.

The combination of high CBR and falling CDR has resulted in very rapid population growth in Nigeria over the last 50 years. With a current growth rate of around 3 per cent, Nigeria's population will double within 25 years.

SWEDEN'S POPULATION PYRAMID

Sweden, one of the world's richest countries, is at the opposite end of the development scale to Nigeria. This shows in its population pyramid (Fig. 8.10) which has two distinguishing features: a narrow base and straight sides.

Figure 8.10
Population pyramid for Sweden.

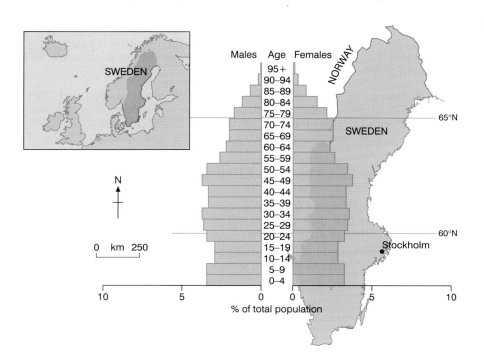

- Only 18 per cent of Sweden's population is under 15 years of age, so its population pyramid has a narrow base. On average Swedish women have only two children. The average age of mothers when they have their first child is 27 years. Unlike in Nigeria, contraception is universal in Sweden. Also, excellent medical care and high standards of living mean that the infant death rate is low.

- Death rates are high only in extreme old age. This accounts for the pyramid's straight-sided appearance. On average a Swedish woman can expect to live for 81 years; and a Swedish man for 76 years. At the 1995 natural increase rate it would take nearly 1,000 years for Swedes to double their population!

8.6 PROBLEMS OF POPULATION CHANGE

Changes in the size of a population or in its age structure often lead to serious problems. In most LEDCs the scale of population growth is itself a major problem. Overwhelmed by rising population, many governments cannot meet even the most basic needs of their people, e.g. food and water. Most governments recognise the need for slower population growth; fewer have the means to do much about it.

Changes in age structure most often give rise to the problem of **age dependency**. Children and old people depend on the economic support of the adult working population. If the percentage of children or the aged increases more resources have to be found to pay for schools, healthcare, pensions, and so on. Increasing age dependency is a problem which affects both rich and poor countries.

RESPONDING TO POPULATION CHANGE IN BANGLADESH

Bangladesh, in South Asia, is one of the world's poorest countries. In 1995, its average GNP per person was just US$180. About 90 per cent of Bangladesh's 122 million people are rural dwellers and work in farming. The farms are tiny, averaging less than one hectare. One third of farm workers are labourers who own no land at all.

Despite its poverty Bangladesh's population doubled between 1965 and 1998 (Fig. 8.11). Since 1975 the Bangladeshi government has tried to slow the rate of growth by promoting family planning. Its family planning programme includes:

- Laws which have raised the age of marriage to 18 for women and 21 for men.

- Support for full-time area health workers who provide a contraception service.

- Better healthcare for mothers and their babies – only when women are sure that their children will survive will they limit their families to just two or three children.

- Improving women's education. Studies have shown that the higher the level of literacy among women the fewer children they have.

These policies have had some success. In 1981, only 18 per cent of adults practised family planning, but by 1995 this figure was nearly 45 per cent. As a result the average number of children born to each woman fell from 6 in

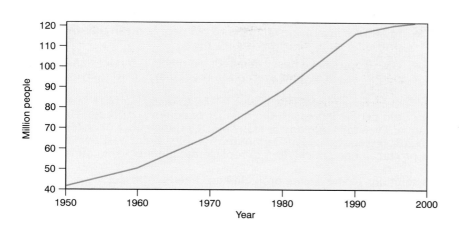

Figure 8.11
Population growth in Bangladesh.

1981 to 4.3 in 1995. However, some obstacles to the acceptance of family planning remain:

- Islam is the dominant religion and many women are governed by purdah. This means that they cannot leave home without permission and must cover themselves when they do so. This means that it is often difficult for health workers to contact women.

- Despite government legislation, early marriage is still common. Girls often marry by the age of 13 and have their first baby within a year.

THE GREYING OF THE WORLD'S POPULATION

Higher living standards and better healthcare has meant that people are living longer. Today, the average life expectancy exceeds 73 years in North America, Europe and Oceania, and is rising quickly throughout the economically developing world. By 2025, nearly one in five of the world's population will be aged 65 and over. This so-called greying of the world's population is most advanced in the richer countries of the developed world (Fig. 8.12).

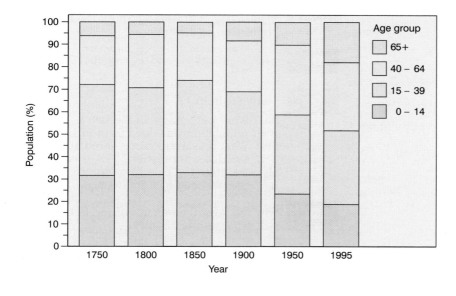

Figure 8.12
Sweden's changing age structure.

Ageing causes problems, because old people are consumers not producers:

- In MEDCs increasing numbers of old people mean that the cost of providing state pensions is growing.
- Old people make heavy demands on medical services and very old people (aged 80 and over) often require expensive nursing care.

The problem of ageing in MEDCs is also linked to declining birth rates. As the number of old people increases, the number of adults in work remains largely the same, or even falls. Already in many MEDCs the number of children born is well below replacement level. Japan for example, in the past two decades, has not produced enough children to replace the parents' generation.

Various solutions to the ageing problem have been proposed:

- Increase the workforce, either by encouraging the immigration of young adults from poorer countries, or by giving financial rewards to couples who have more children.
- Raise the age of retirement so that old people remain in work, continue to pay taxes, and receive pensions for a shorter period.
- Make those in work pay higher taxes.
- Abolish state pensions and make people pay towards their own private pension.

Check yourself

QUESTIONS

Q1 What does a population pyramid show?

Q2 Study the following sketch of a population pyramid.

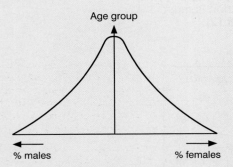

i) Is the sketch typical of the population in an LEDC or a MEDC?
ii) Give one reason for your answer.

Q3 Draw sketches to show the population pyramids of the following:
i) A country with a low birth rate and a low death rate.
ii) A country which experienced a major war 20 years ago when many men were killed.
iii) A country with an ageing population.

Q4 What does the population pyramid for Nigeria (Fig. 8.9) suggest about the future population of the country?

Q5 What is meant by 'age dependency'?

Q6 Study Figure 8.12.
i) What percentage of Sweden's population was aged 0–14 in 1750?
ii) What age group represented 20% of Sweden's population?
iii) Describe the changing pattern of people aged 65+ in Sweden.

Q7 Why are governments interested in the age structure of their country.

ANSWERS

A1 It shows the population structure of a country. It also shows the percentage or number of people in each age group. The percentages of males and females are usually shown as well.

A2 i) LEDC.
ii) The broad base shows that the country has a high proportion of young people. It is a country where the birth rate is still high.

A3

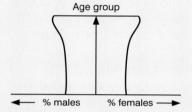

Age group

◄— % males   % females —►

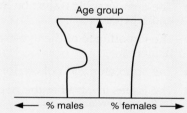

Age group

◄— % males   % females —►

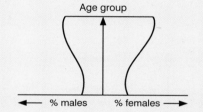

Age group

◄— % males   % females —►

A4 As an LEDC Nigeria has a very young population. A high percentage of its population are under 15. In the near future there will be a large number of potential mothers. This is likely to mean that the birth rate will stay high.

A5 This term refers to children and old people who, because of their age, are not able to contribute to the economic life of the country. They are dependent on others, namely people of working age.

A6 i) 32%
ii) 40–64
iii) The percentage of people aged 65+ in Sweden has been increasing since about 1900. In 1900, the percentage was less than 10% but by 1995 it had risen to about 18%. There was a slight decline in 1850.

A7 The higher the proportion of young people the greater the cost of providing school places. A country with a large proportion of old people will exert a greater pressure on health and welfare services.

TUTORIALS

T1 *The population pyramid is a kind of bar graph. The only difference is that the main axis is vertical rather than horizontal.*

T2 *In an examination you would not be expected to draw an accurate age–sex pyramid. A sketch would be sufficient.*

T3 *Think about the shape of the population pyramid for countries during each stage of the demographic transition model.*

T4 *The timescale for population growth in a particular country is very difficult to predict. It is assumed that the population in LEDCs will follow the same pattern as the MEDCs. The time it will take is harder to be certain of.*

T5 *The combined percentages of children and aged is sometimes called the 'dependency ratio'.*

T6 *i) & ii) Charts like Figure 8.12 are called proportional or divided bar graphs. They are useful for showing more than one type of information in one graph. Remember to read values from the base line of each subdivision. A frequent error is to read only the top of the subdivision.*

iii) Remember to refer to the general, specific and exception when describing any pattern or trend.

T7 *This is a very common question at GCSE. It often leads on to issues associated with an ageing or greying population.*

EXAMINATION CHECKLIST

The facts and ideas that you should know and understand after studying population are:

- There is an uneven global distribution of population.
- Physical factors (relief, climate, soil, vegetation, resources) influence the global distribution of population.
- Human factors (political, social, economic, historical) influence the global distribution of population.
- The present and future population growth.
- The changing distribution of the world's population.
- The relationship between birth rates and death rates, and the rate of natural increase.
- The factors influencing birth rates and death rates.
- The demographic transition model and its relationship to LEDCs and MEDCs.
- The importance of the age–structure of populations in future planning.
- The strategies and polices for managing population growth.
- The issues involved in the population geography of Bangladesh, India and Sweden.
- The correct use of line graphs and divided (proportional) bar graphs.

KEY WORDS

These are the key words. Tick them if you think you know what they mean. Otherwise check on them.

population density	demographic transition	replacement level
crude birth rate	migration	family planning
crude death rate	life expectancy	population pyramid
natural increase	age dependency	

EXAM PRACTICE

Sample Student's Answer and Examiner's Comments

1 (a) Study the table showing information on the number of babies born to each woman and life expectancy in eight LEDCs for 1981 and 1992.

ARE YOUR CHILDREN BAD FOR YOU?

The fewer children you have, the longer you are likely to live. Too many children may drain your health as well as your pocket.

Countries	1981		1992	
	A	**B**	**A**	**B**
Bangladesh	6.4	48	4.8	53
Morocco	6.9	57	4.4	63
El Salvador	5.6	63	3.2	66
Vietnam	5.1	63	3.9	64
Egypt	4.8	57	4.2	61
India	4.8	52	3.9	60
Brazil	4.0	64	2.8	66
Colombia	3.7	63	2.7	69

Column **A**: Average number of babies born to each woman.

Column **B**: Life expectancy at birth (in years)

(i) What is the meaning of the term 'Life expectancy at birth'? (1 mark)

'Life expectancy at birth' — the time that the child is likely to live for in relation to the world's stage of development at that time.

(ii) Which of the countries shown had the longest life expectancy in 1992? (1 mark)

Colombia.

(iii) Which of the countries shown had the greatest improvement in life expectancy between 1981 and 1992? (1 mark)

India.

EXAMINER'S COMMENTS

a) **i)**
This is correct.
The mark is given for the statement 'the time that the child is likely to live'. The last part of the sentence is irrelevant, but does not lose her any marks. Remember that GCSEs are positively marked, so it is better to write something than nothing.

ii)
This is correct.

iii)
This is correct.
Make sure that you read information from the table carefully. This part is a little more difficult than part ii), as it involves a calculation too.

EXAMINER'S COMMENTS

iv)
These are both correct.
Notice that the command word is 'state'. There is no need for any description or explanation.

v)
Her answer reaches Level 2 as there is evidence of clear understanding. She reaches Level 2 in the final part of the answer, where she points out that the greater the number of children a woman has, the less money she has to spend on medicine and clothing.
There are credit worthy statements in the first two sentences:
'pregnancy can affect the health of a woman' and 'there may not be the level of aid to treat the woman'. These are both Level 1 statements showing basic understanding.

She gained 7 out of a possible 9 marks in this question. Typically, these sections would be at the start of a question as they are fairly straightforward. An A or B grade candidate should score well in these sections.

(iv) State two factors that have helped to reduce the average number of babies born to each woman in LEDCs. (2 marks)

Increased contraception.

Education about birth control.

(v) The information in the table states that 'The fewer children you have, the longer you are likely to live.'
Why is there a link between the number of children born to each woman and life expectancy in LEDCs? (4 marks)

The figure refers to the draining of health and wealth. Pregnancy can affect the health of a woman, and in LEDCs there may not be the level of aid to treat the woman. So her life expectancy may drop. Another factor is money. If a mother has to support a lot of children then the amount of money she earns will be divided, and so sacrifices in living standards have to be made. If this happens then money will not be made the best use of, in terms of medical aid, clothing, food, etc. This all contributes to life expectancy.

SEG, 1996

142

Questions to Answer
The answer to Question 2 can be found in Chapter 18.

2 Study the four population pyramids. They have been drawn from the following population studies:

A city in an MEDC like Los Angeles
A MEDC like India
Migrants to a city in an LEDC like Calcutta from the surrounding countryside
A village in a rural area like the Ganges delta 800 m from Calcutta. (8)

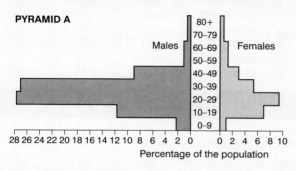

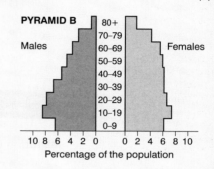

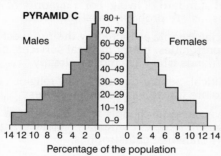

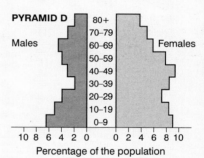

For each pyramid state which population it represents.
Give a reason for each answer.

NEAB, 1993

143

9.1 DEFINING MIGRATION

Migration is a movement of people which involves a permanent or semi-permanent change of residence. It has a number of characteristics:

- Migration is usually over some distance, at least from one region to another.

- When migration occurs between countries (i.e. international migration) we describe it as either **immigration** (migrants coming into a country) or **emigration** (migrants leaving a country).

- Migration varies in direction. Within LEDCs most migration is from rural to urban areas. Within MEDCs migration is generally in the opposite direction – from urban to rural areas.

- Migration can be forced or voluntary. People forced to migrate owing to political persecution or environmental disasters are called **refugees.**

9.2 REASONS FOR MIGRATION

Migration occurs for many different reasons.

- Economic: people wanting to improve their job prospects, income and standard of living. For a majority of migrants economic reasons are probably most important.

- Social: people attracted by the prospect of better educational opportunities, better medical services, or the desire to join family or friends who have moved already.

- Political: people threatened by religious or political persecution who are forced to flee for their lives.

- Environmental: people whose lives have been disrupted by drought, famine, epidemics, volcanic eruptions and other environmental catastrophes.

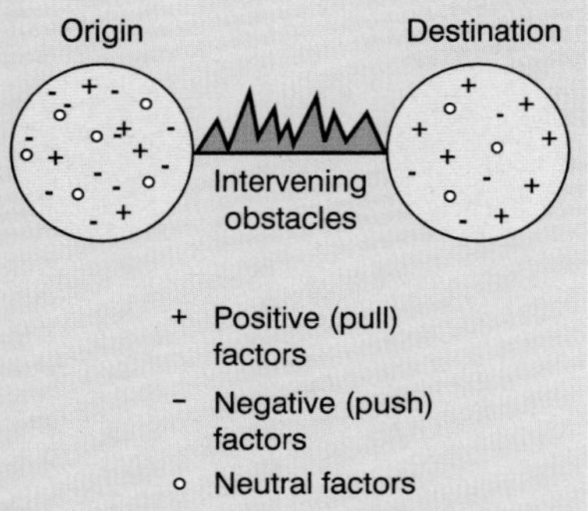

PUSH AND PULL FACTORS

Origin   Destination

Intervening obstacles

+ Positive (pull) factors

- Negative (push) factors

o Neutral factors

Figure 9.1 *Lee's model of migration.*

We divide the reasons for migration into two groups of factors: **push factors** and **pull factors.**

- Push factors are the disadvantages within an area which cause people to leave (e.g. lack of jobs, few educational opportunities, religious persecution, etc.).

- Pull factors are the advantages which attract migrants to a particular destination. Most pull factors are the opposite of push factors (i.e. available jobs, good educational opportunities, religious tolerance, etc.).

Many potential migrants, however, ignore both push and pull factors and decide not to move. Often family ties are just too strong for people to move away. Many obstacles stand in the way of migrants (Fig. 9.1). These include lack of transport, the cost of moving, and the difficulty of crossing political borders.

Table 9.1   Rural–urban migration in the developing world: push and pull factors

Push factors from countryside	Pull to towns and cities
• Land shortage owing to inheritance laws, sub-division of land and population pressure. • Unemployment in agriculture. • Poverty and crop failure. • Debts in rural areas, especially among tenant farmers. • Natural disasters. • Poor medical facilities. • Lack of educational opportunities. • Poor transport, housing, water, electricity and sewage disposal. • Traditional way of life with limited social facilities for young people.	• Prospects of a higher standard of living. • More job opportunities in industry and services. • Higher wages in urban jobs. • Less interest on loans. • Fewer natural disasters. • Better medical facilities, clinics and hospitals. • Greater number and better quality of schools. • Prospect of better services. • Attraction of the bright lights of the city. Media, entertainment, television and radio are all more accessible.

9.3 RURAL–URBAN MIGRATION IN A LEDC

Peru is the fourth largest country in South America. In 1995, its population was 24 million, and increasing rapidly. However, its average population density is low: only 18 per km^2.

Peru consists of three main regions (Fig. 9.2):

- The desert along the Pacific coast.
- The Andes mountains.
- The hills and rainforest-covered lowlands of the east.

Peru's population is distributed unevenly between these regions. Just over half of the county's population lives in the coastal desert region. Most are in the capital city, Lima. The Andes mountains are home to around one third of the population; the rest occupy the sparsely populated eastern region.

Most migration in Peru is from the countryside to the towns. This **rural–urban migration** has caused rapid **urbanisation** (chapter 11). By 1995, nearly three in every four people in Peru were urban dwellers, compared to just one in three in 1950. Lima has been the main attraction for migrants.

CAUSES OF RURAL–URBAN MIGRATION

A combination of push and pull factors explains rural–urban migration in Peru:

- Living conditions in the countryside are desperate (Fig. 9.3). (push)

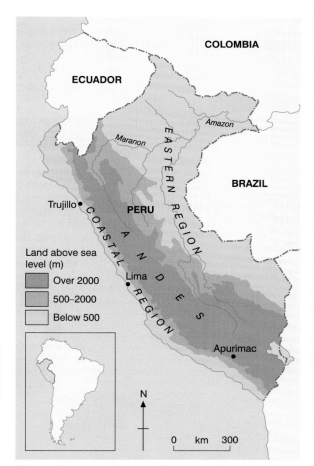

Figure 9.2 *Peru: principal cities and regions*

145

Figure 9.3 The living conditions for these Iquitos indians in Peru are quite basic.

- Rural households in Peru are three times more likely to be poor than urban households. (push)
- Infant mortality is twice as high in rural areas than in urban areas. (push)
- Malnutrition is more common in the countryside. (push)
- Wages are higher in the towns and cities, and jobs are easier to find. (pull)
- If migrants don't succeed in finding paid employment in the city, they can get by on self-help, e.g. washing cars, running errands, re-cycling waste materials, etc. (pull)

One-third of Lima's inhabitants live in squalid shanty towns. Yet despite the lack of decent housing, essential services (e.g. clean water, electricity, sewerage systems, etc.) and jobs, migrants continue to pour into Lima. Most are farmers and farm labourers from poor regions like the Andes (Fig. 9.2). Also, while most migrants to the cities remain poor, few want to return to the countryside (Table 9.2).

Table 9.2 Reasons for migrating from the countryside to urban areas in Peru

Reason	% giving reason
To earn more money	37
To join family	23
No work in villages	10
Work available in towns	9
Dislike of village life	9
Poverty	7
To pay for education	5

9.4 SELECTIVENESS OF MIGRATION

Migration is a selective process. Young adults are most likely to migrate. In Peru, most migrants are aged between 15 and 40. In general, migrants tend to be better educated and have more skills than non-migrants. In Latin America most migrants are women (Fig. 9.4). Compared to rural areas, towns and cities offer women a wider range of jobs, particularly in domestic service, office cleaning, shops and street selling. However, in most of Africa and South Asia different traditions and cultures have resulted in the opposite trend. Here, men are more likely to migrate than women.

Figure 9.4
Age–sex profiles of net migration for Mexico City.

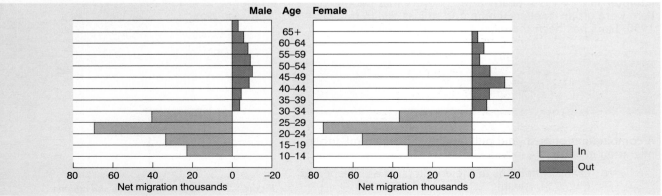

9.5 EFFECTS OF RURAL–URBAN MIGRATION

Rural–urban migration creates advantages as well as disadvantages for both urban and rural areas. For urban areas:

- Migrants provide industry and commerce with a young and cheap workforce.

- Large-scale in-migration can put enormous strains on services. This may result in housing shortages, a lack of basic services, and insufficient jobs. For millions of people in the developing world, urban migration simply means exchanging rural poverty for urban poverty.

The selectiveness of rural–urban migration often creates problems in the countryside. In particular a shortage of young adults may lead to:

- A fall in the rural birth rate.

- A decline in food production, which supports urban as well as rural populations.

The effect of this loss of young adults is made worse by the fact that these migrants tend to be better educated and more 'go-ahead' than non-migrants. Even so, rural areas can also benefit from out-migration:

- Migrants working in towns and cities often send money back to relatives in rural areas.

- In some LEDCs, rural–urban migration may reduce the pressure of population on soil and water resources. This has happened in Peru, especially in the Andes and the coastal plain regions.

- Migrants returning may bring back new skills.

Check yourself

QUESTIONS

Q1 What is migration?

Q2 Study the following descriptions of migrants. For each one, decide whether the reason for migration was economic, social, environmental or political:

Most of the inhabitants of Tristan da Cunha, an island in the Atlantic, moved to Britain following the eruption of a volcano.

Following intertribal warfare many ethnic Hutus left their homelands in Rwanda for the neighbouring country of Zaire (Democratic Republic of the Congo).

In the 1950s, London Transport recuited many West Indians to work on the buses and underground. This followed advertisments placed in the local Caribbean newspapers.

Mrs Garbett, an eighty-year-old grandmother, has just taken her first flight. She is joining her son and daughter-in-law in New Zealand.

Q3 Look at Figure 9.2. Use Lee's model of migration (Fig. 9.1) to explain why relatively few people from Peru's eastern region migrate to Lima.

QUESTIONS

Q4 Read the following passage:

Calcutta is the largest city in India, with a population of over 12 million. It was formerly the capital of India. It still retains important administrative functions for North-east India. The city is sited on the Hooghly River and is an important port, as well as having a wide industrial base. Calcutta is one of the fastest growing cities in the world.

The surrounding states of Orissa, West Bengal and Bihar are still predominantly rural areas based on subsistence agriculture. Over 75% of the farmers have less than two hectares of land, which is not sufficient to support a family. Many farmers have built up a large rural debt. Agriculture in India is very dependent on the monsoon rains which frequently fail. These areas are poorly provided with medical and welfare services.

Calcutta lies to the west of Bangladesh, one of the most densely populated countries in the world. Bangladesh covers the low-lying delta of the Ganges and Brahmaputra rivers, which although very fertile, is very prone to flooding. This area, at the head of the Bay of Bengal, is frequently hit by severe tropical storms called cyclones.

Use the information in the passage to make a list of the push and pull factors which help to explain the rapid population increase in Calcutta.

Q5 Draw a pie graph to illustrate the figures in Table 9.2

REMEMBER! Cover the answers if you want to.

ANSWERS

A1 The movement of people which involves a permanent or semi-permanent change of residence.

A2 Environmental; political/social; economic; social.

A3 The mountainous Andean region acts as a barrier between the inland eastern region and the coast.

TUTORIALS

T1 *The important part of the definition is the 'change of residence'. It is not sufficient to say that people move. This could mean commuters who travel to work each day.*

T2 *It is not always possible to put the reasons for migration into single categories. Migrants often have many reasons for moving. A person may migrate to find a job, but other reasons, such as where family members live, may determine where they look for work.*

T3 *The obstacles in Lee's model may not be physical ones. Crossing political boundaries is often difficult and reduces the amount of international migration (section 9.7). Another version of Lee's model includes opportunities as well as obstacles. Studies of migration have shown that many migrants move in a series of stages often over quite short distances. For example in Peru, migrants may move to a town in their local area first, and then to Lima later on.*

ANSWERS

A4 **Push Factors**

Surrounding states are predominantly rural areas based on subsistence agriculture.

75% of the farmers have less than two hectares of land; less than the minimum required to support a family.

Many farmers have a large rural debt.

The rural areas have poor medical and welfare services.

The Monsoon rains frequently fail.

Bangladesh is one of the most densely populated countries in the world.

The delta area is very prone to flooding.

The Bay of Bengal is prone to cyclones.

Pull factors

Calcutta has a larger population, so it is likely to have a larger range of facilities and services.

The city's administrative functions could provide jobs.

The industrial base is a potential source of employment.

The port area of the city is a potential source of employment.

A5

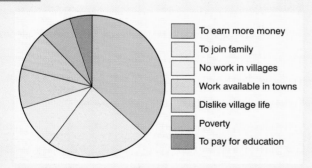

- To earn more money
- To join family
- No work in villages
- Work available in towns
- Dislike village life
- Poverty
- To pay for education

TUTORIALS

T4 *These reasons are similiar for many rapidly growing cities in LEDCs. This answer gives you an idea of the level of detail that you should be aiming to remember, if you are studying another city as a case study.*

T5 *Pie graphs are one of four types of graphs that you may be asked to draw or complete in a GCSE examination. Remember that figures have to be in percentages if you use them to draw a pie chart. Don't forget to include a key for pie charts.*

9.6 MIGRATION WITHIN THE UK

Regional differences in population growth in the UK are largely caused by migration (Fig. 9.5). During the 1980s and 1990s two trends dominated population change in the UK:

- Rural counties such as Cambridgeshire and Buckinghamshire grew rapidly.

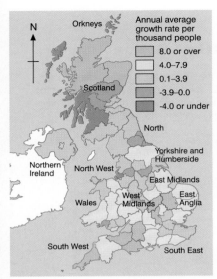

Figure 9.5 *Population change in the UK, 1981–93.*

- The populations of urban counties (**conurbations**) such as Merseyside and Strathclyde declined.

In the rural counties which experienced rapid population growth, more people moved in than moved out. These counties experienced a **net migrational gain**. The conurbations experienced a **net migrational loss** which resulted in population decline.

NORTH–SOUTH SHIFT

Two separate migration flows account for the pattern of population change in Figure 9.5:

- The gradual movement of population from North to South.
- The urban–rural shift of population or **counterurbanisation.**

For most of the twentieth century the South has been more prosperous than the North. Until the 1970s the prosperity of northern England, Scotland and Northern Ireland depended on heavy industries such as coal, steel, shipbuilding and textiles. These industries fell into decline (Fig. 9.6). The result was above average levels of unemployment in northern Britain. Meanwhile new jobs in the fast-growing service sector and high-tech industries were to be found in the South. This combination of push and pull factors caused a net movement of population from North to South (Fig. 9.7).

Figure 9.6 *Derelict industrial area in northern Britain.*

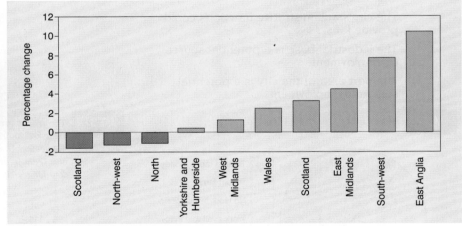

Figure 9.7 *Population change by region, 1981–91.*

COUNTERURBANISATION

Counterurbanisation describes the movement of people out of conurbations and large cities to smaller urban centres and rural areas. While all metropolitan counties (i.e. conurbations) in the UK declined in population between 1981 and 1991, the more rural counties of southern Britain, stretching in a broad belt from Cornwall to Lincolnshire, grew rapidly (Fig. 9.5). Several factors explain this counterurbanisation:

- For many people, small towns and rural areas offer a better quality of life (Fig. 9.8). Among the advantages are less pollution, less traffic congestion and lower levels of crime.

- Improved transport links (e.g. motorways), increased private car ownership, and rising incomes meant that many more people could afford to live in rural areas and small towns, but commute into large towns and cities.

- Increasing numbers of retired people are moving to environmentally attractive areas such as the south coast of England and East Anglia. Thanks to occupational pensions and home ownership many more people can afford to move when they retire.

Most counterurbanisation results from short-distance migration by commuters who want to live within an hour's travel time of their work place. However, some people have moved away from big cities to live and work in smaller towns. And a few have moved even further afield to remote, rural areas such as central Wales and northern Scotland. Computers, fax machines, electronic mail, etc. have allowed many people to work from remote locations.

Figure 9.8 *Lewes, East Sussex.*

Check yourself

QUESTIONS

Q1 Study Figure 9.5. With the aid of an atlas:
  i)   Name two counties with a population growth greater than 8 per 1,000.
  ii) Name one region with a population decline of 4,000 or under.
  iii) Describe the pattern of population change in the UK between 1981–1993.

Q2
  i) Plot the following figures which show the rate of population change in different types of areas in England and Wales.

Villages	+11%
Semi-rural areas	+8%
Resorts and retirement areas	+7%
New Towns	+4%
Industrial towns	+4%
Small market towns	+8%
Small cities	−0.5%
Large cities	−2%
Conurbations	−8%
London	−7%

  ii) Suggest reasons for the different rates of growth.
  iii) Between 1971 and 1981, London's population declined by 10%. Suggest why the decline is now less marked.

ANSWERS

A1

i) Cornwall, Somerset, Dorset, Wiltshire, Northamptonshire, Cambridgeshire, Buckinghamshire. (any two)

ii) Strathclyde, Western Isles.

iii) With the exception of the Highlands the main areas of population growth are in Southern England. Central Scotland has had a significant population loss. North Yorkshire is the area with the biggest population increase in the North of England. The industrial regions of West Yorkshire, Greater Manchester and Merseyside have all seen a decline in population, along with the West Midlands and West Glamorgan in West Wales. The eastern part of South Wales, the Bristol area and Greater London have experienced only small population growth. West Wales, the English–Welsh border area, and East Anglia have grown between 4 to 7.9 per thousand. Similiar growth rates are seen in Devon, South Central England and the coast of South-east England. There are three areas of very high population growth: Cornwall; the eastern part of South-west England and the area north of London.

A2

i)

```
                          -8  -6  -4  -2   0   2   4   6   8  10  12
       London       |====================|
   Conurbations  |=======================|
  Large cities            |===|
  Small cities               |=|
                    Small market towns  |==========|
                    Industrial towns  |=====|
                    New Towns  |=====|
                    Resorts and retirement areas  |========|
                    Semi-rural areas  |========|
                    Villages  |==========|
                         -8  -6  -4  -2   0   2   4   6   8  10  12
                         Loss        Percentage        Gain
```

ii) The population growth in the villages and semi-rural areas was the result of the increasing mobility of the population. More people commute to work. The ageing population meant that a significant number of people moved into retirement areas, often near the coast. In general, the larger settlements lost population as people moved out. The New Towns continued to receive overspill population from the large conurbations, such as London.

iii) Fewer people are moving out. There has been a tendency for some people to move back into towns.

TUTORIALS

T1 *Sometimes you may be given a special atlas in a GCSE examination. You must make full use of it, e.g. by giving detailed locations. If you do not know the names of individual counties use as precise a location as possible. Make sure that you use geographical terms. You will not gain credit if you write about the top, bottom, right or left of the map. Use standard compass directions.*

T2

i) *A bar graph or histogram should be used for these figures because they are non-continuous data. Although the figures are given as percentages, do not use them to draw a pie chart because they do not add up to 100%.*

ii) *The figures illustrate the general population drift from urban areas. This has been a feature of the UK's population since the 1960s. You should try to take as wide a view as possible in any explanation that you give. The greater availability of cars and the improvements in public transport are very important factors. Another development is the increasing number of people, who because of technological advances, can work from home. The change in the population structure of the country also plays a part.*

iii) *The people moving back into cities are young couples with no children. They like to be near the city centre for both work and entertainment. They do not need open spaces quite as much, as they do not have children. They can afford to pay higher city prices too. Many move into former working class, inner city areas, close to the Central Business District. This process is called gentrification.*

9.7 INTERNATIONAL MIGRATION

Around 70 million people migrate between countries each year. We refer to these population movements as **international migration.** This type of migration is less common than internal population movements such as rural–urban and urban–rural migration. There are two reasons for this:

- The distances involved are longer.
- Political controls make it difficult for migrants to move freely between countries.

MIGRATION FROM MEXICO TO THE USA

The border between the USA and Mexico is not just an international frontier. It is also a boundary where the economically developed world meets the economically developing world. Given the economic contrasts that exist on either side of the US–Mexican border it is hardly surprising that the USA is an irresistible attraction to millions of poor Mexicans (Fig. 9.9). At least one million Mexicans cross into the USA every year, most of them illegally. Those illegal immigrants who are caught – 850,000 in 1995 – are deported to Mexico. Mexican immigrants are unwelcome in the USA where they are seen as seen as a drain on the US economy.

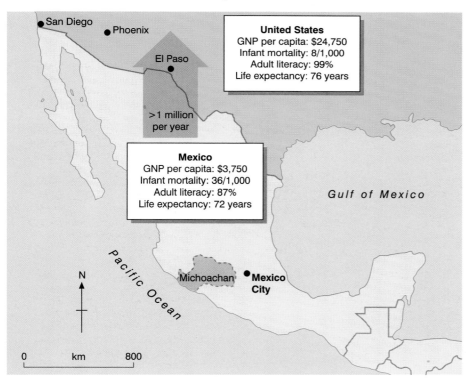

Figure 9.9
Migration into the USA from Mexico.

The causes and effects of this international migration can be seen in central Mexico. Here 15 per cent of Mexican migrants to the USA come from Michoachan state. The effects of emigration in the rural areas of Michoachan have been severe:

- In some places massive emigration has led to **depopulation.** The village of Santa Ines in North-west Michoachan lost two-thirds of its population between 1985 and 1995.

153

- The people emigrating were not that badly off, but wanted to improve their quality of life. Pull factors were more important than push factors.
- At one time only the men migrated, and when they had made enough money they returned home. Now the men stay in the USA.
- Women now outnumber men in rural areas and the women have problems finding suitable marriage partners.
- Young adults tend to migrate, leaving ageing communities behind. With fewer children these communities will gradually die out.

The only benefit Michoachan state gets from emigration is the money sent home by migrants.

9.8 REFUGEE MOVEMENTS

People who are forced to migrate because of persecution, wars and environmental disasters are known as refugees (Table 9.3):

- In the mid-1990s the UN estimated that there were 50 million refugees in the world, half of whom had been forced to leave their country (Fig 9.10).
- About 85 per cent of the world's refugees live in LEDCs.

Figure 9.10
Global movement of political refugees.

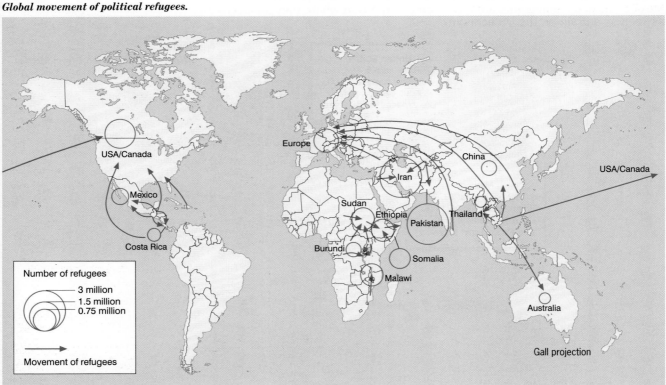

Table 9.3   Factors responsible for creating refugees

Wars	Most refugees are victims of war and civil war, ethnic and religious tensions, and collapsed states. Of the world's 30 armed conflicts in 1995, 12 were in Asia, 6 in Africa, 6 in the Middle East, 3 in Europe and 3 in the Americas.
Food security	Rapid population growth and wars which divert efforts away from food production have created food shortages in many LEDCs. In the Horn of Africa about half the population do not have adequate food supplies; 22 million people require food aid.
Natural disasters	About 130 million people a year are affected by natural disasters such as hurricanes, landslides, floods, droughts, earthquakes and volcanic eruptions. On average, natural disasters kill 140,000 people a year and make 5 million people homeless.
Public works	Projects such as dam building displace 10 million people a year, often with little or no compensation.
Unemployment	In China, lack of employment in rural areas has caused millions of people to migrate to towns and cities. Some of these migrants are now being forced to go back to the countryside.

POLITICAL REFUGEES IN LEBANON

In 1996, 400,000 people in southern Lebanon suddenly found themselves homeless. Caught up in the fighting between the Israeli army and Hezbollah (Arab freedom group) they were forced to flee their homes. Early in 1996, Israel declared southern Lebanon a security zone (Fig. 9.11) and issued a deadline for the people to leave. Thousands fled from the small towns and villages in the security zone. Meanwhile, the nearby town of Tyre with a population of 200,000 was completely evacuated. Most refugees fled to the coastal town of Sidon and found shelter in overcrowded refugee camps. A desperate situation arose with aid organisations appealing to the international community for help to provide the refugees with food, blankets and money.

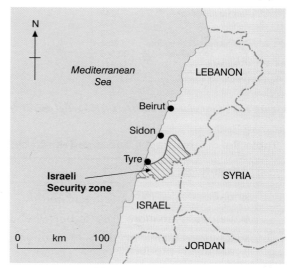

Figure 9.11   *Israeli security zone in the Lebanon.*

ENVIRONMENTAL REFUGEES

Today's 23 million political refugees are outnumbered by environmental refugees, who have been displaced by disasters such as drought, flooding and famine (Fig. 9.12). Most environmental refugees are in Africa and China (Fig. 9.13). Their numbers are likely to increase in future. For example, rising sea levels caused by global warming could make up to 150 million people homeless in Bangladesh, Egypt, China and India within the next 50 years.

Few countries welcome large influxes of refugees. This is especially true in the LEDCs. The governments of LEDCs struggle to provide their own populations with even the most basic needs. However, for MEDCs refugees can bring more advantages than disadvantages (Table 9.4).

Figure 9.12   *Refugees of the Sudan floods, Khartoum*

155

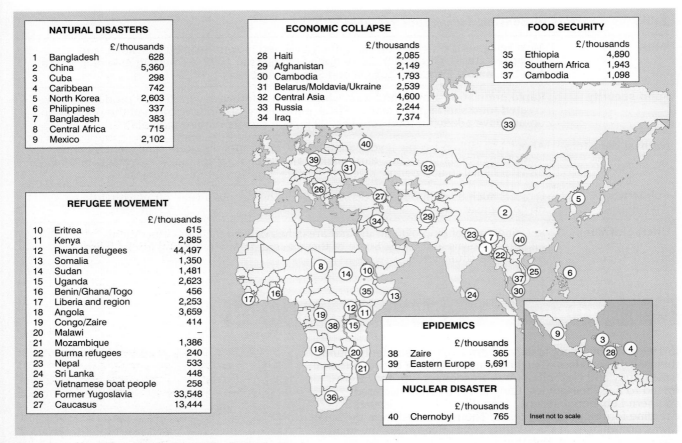

Figure 9.13 *Cost of world disasters (1995 relief operations)*

Within the figure:

NATURAL DISASTERS

		£/thousands
1	Bangladesh	628
2	China	5,360
3	Cuba	298
4	Caribbean	742
5	North Korea	2,603
6	Philippines	337
7	Bangladesh	383
8	Central Africa	715
9	Mexico	2,102

ECONOMIC COLLAPSE

		£/thousands
28	Haiti	2,085
29	Afghanistan	2,149
30	Cambodia	1,793
31	Belarus/Moldavia/Ukraine	2,539
32	Central Asia	4,600
33	Russia	2,244
34	Iraq	7,374

FOOD SECURITY

		£/thousands
35	Ethiopia	4,890
36	Southern Africa	1,943
37	Cambodia	1,098

REFUGEE MOVEMENT

		£/thousands
10	Eritrea	615
11	Kenya	2,885
12	Rwanda refugees	44,497
13	Somalia	1,350
14	Sudan	1,481
15	Uganda	2,623
16	Benin/Ghana/Togo	456
17	Liberia and region	2,253
18	Angola	3,659
19	Congo/Zaire	414
20	Malawi	–
21	Mozambique	1,386
22	Burma refugees	240
23	Nepal	533
24	Sri Lanka	448
25	Vietnamese boat people	258
26	Former Yugoslavia	33,548
27	Caucasus	13,444

EPIDEMICS

		£/thousands
38	Zaire	365
39	Eastern Europe	5,691

NUCLEAR DISASTER

		£/thousands
40	Chernobyl	765

Inset not to scale

Table 9.4 **Advantages and disadvantages of refugee movements from LEDCs to MEDCs**

	Advantages	Disadvantages
Receiving countries	• Refugees usually better educated. • Refugees are more likely to be self-employed. • Refugees mainly aged 20–45. Economically they are highly productive. • Refugees are often more mobile than the native population and are more willing to move around to find jobs. • Because they are mainly young and skilled, refugees pay more in taxes than they receive in benefits (e.g. unemployment benefit). • Because refugees are mainly young adults they make fewer demands on the healthcare system.	• Refugees usually young. Their children are more likely to make more demands on schools and hospitals. • Conflict between native population and refugees. Native people may think that refugees have 'stolen' their jobs.
Sending countries	• May reduce population pressure on limited resources of land, water, etc. • Refugees send money back.	• Unbalanced age structure in rural areas, with fewer young adults and children. This has a negative effect on the rural economy. Future of rural communities threatened. • Unbalanced ratios of males and females. • Sending countries lose their better educated and more skilled people.

Check yourself

QUESTIONS

Q1 What is international migration?

Q2 Look at Figure 9.9. Use the statistics to explain why so many people migrate from Mexico to the USA.

Q3 Between 1985 and 1995 the village of Santa Ines in Mexico suffered depopulation.

i) What is depopulation?
ii) Use information in this chapter to sketch two age–sex pyramids which show how the population structure of Santa Ines changed between 1985 and 1995.

Q4 i) What is a refugee?
ii) What are the political and economic factors which produce refugees?

REMEMBER! Cover the answers if you want to.

ANSWERS

A1 Where people move across international boundaries to settle in another country.

A2 The GNP per capita shows that the USA is much wealthier than Mexico. Better medical facilities in the USA help to reduce infant mortality, and extend life expectancy. In the USA there is a more developed education system.

A3 i) The movement of people out of an area so that the population declines.
ii)

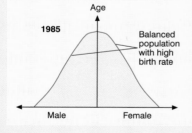

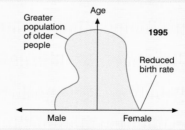

A4 i) Someone who is forced to migrate rather than migrate by choice.
ii) The political reasons are usually to do with disagreement on the government's policies. There may be religious differences or differences of opinion on ethnic or tribal conflicts. Economic factors largely occur as a result of natural disasters which destroy peoples' chances of earning a living.

TUTORIALS

T1 *As with all migrations, it is important to emphasise that the movement involves a permanent or semi-permanent change of residence. Simply crossing an international boundary does not mean migration.*

T2 *Here you are being asked to turn figures into words. The various measures of development which can be used to compare countries are covered in greater depth in chapter 13.*

T3 i) *Depopulation normally results from a movement of people out of an area.*
ii) *If you have difficulty with this look at population pyramids in chapter 8.*

T4 i) *It is important that you emphasise the forced nature of the movement.*
ii) *You could use topical information to help you answer this question. Try to keep yourself up to date with what is happening locally, nationally and internationally. News programmes are a good way of doing this.*

EXAMINATION CHECKLIST

The facts and ideas you should know and understand after studying migration are:

- Migration is a movement of people that involves a permanent or semi-permanent change of residence.
- The difference between immigration and emigration.
- There are economic, social, political and environmental reasons for migration.
- Push and pull factors can be used to explain migration.
- Migration is having a major effect on the distribution of population in Peru.
- Migration affects both rural and urban areas.
- Migration happens within MEDCs such as the UK.
- International migration takes place across political boundaries.
- Refugees are forced to migrate and for a variety of reasons.
- There are advantages and disadvantages of emigration and immigration to both the sending and receiving countries.
- The correct use of pie diagrams.

Key words

These are the key words. Tick them if you think you know what they mean. Otherwise check on them.

immigration	rural–urban migration	counterurbanisation
emigration	urbanisation	international migration
refugees	conurbation	depopulation
push factors	net migrational gain	
pull factors	net migrational loss	

EXAM PRACTICE

Sample Student's Answer and Examiner's Comments.

This question was taken only by candidates who were aiming for a Grade A or B. There are few short-answer questions and the candidates had to write longer answers in their own words.

1 (a) Study the diagram which shows regional population changes in France from 1982–1990. Answer the questions which follow.

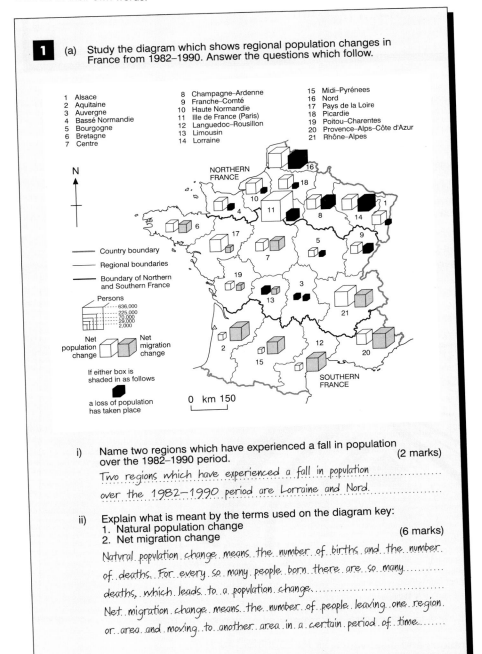

1 Alsace
2 Aquitaine
3 Auvergne
4 Bassé Normandie
5 Bourgogne
6 Bretagne
7 Centre
8 Champagne–Ardenne
9 Franche–Comté
10 Haute Normandie
11 Ille de France (Paris)
12 Languedoc–Rousillon
13 Limousin
14 Lorraine
15 Midi–Pyrénées
16 Nord
17 Pays de la Loire
18 Picardie
19 Poitou–Charentes
20 Provence–Alps–Côte d'Azur
21 Rhône–Alpes

NORTHERN FRANCE

N

—— Country boundary
—— Regional boundaries
—— Boundary of Northern and Southern France

Persons
636,000
225,000
70,000
29,000
2,000

Net population change   Net migration change

If either box is shaded in as follows

a loss of population has taken place

0 km 150

SOUTHERN FRANCE

i) Name two regions which have experienced a fall in population over the 1982–1990 period. (2 marks)

Two regions which have experienced a fall in population over the 1982–1990 period are Lorraine and Nord.

ii) Explain what is meant by the terms used on the diagram key:
1. Natural population change
2. Net migration change (6 marks)

Natural population change means the number of births and the number of deaths. For every so many people born there are so many deaths, which leads to a population change.
Net migration change means the number of people leaving one region or area and moving to another area in a certain period of time.

a) i)
He gets only one correct – Lorraine. The diagram is very complicated and needs careful examination. At first it might appear that many regions have experienced a fall in population. However, natural population change and migration change are shown separately. There are only three regions – Auvergne, Limousin and Lorraine – where migration is greater than natural change.

ii)
He reaches Level 2. He shows clear understanding of the meaning of the two terms. However, his definition of natural change is not precise, because he does not emphasise that the change is because of differences between the birth and death rates. His definition of population change is better and shows a fair level of understanding. He achieved 3 out of 4 marks available at Level 2.

To reach Level 3, worth 5–6 marks, he needed to make more use of appropriate geographical terms. For example, net migration change is the difference between immigration and emigration.

iii)

He reaches the top of Level 2, gaining 4 marks. The answer shows some understanding, but he uses sweeping statements such as "mainly in the North of France" and "there is more net migration taking place in the South of France". The last sentence shows understanding.

A Level 3 answer would be something like: "France is sub-divided into 21 regions. Two boxes in each region – one for natural change and one for migration change – are drawn in proportion to the number of people they represent. Any population gain or loss over the period 1982–1990 is illustrated. The total population change for each region can be worked out by comparing these two boxes.

iii) Describe and explain what the figure is attempting to show.   (6 marks)

> The figure is attempting to show the population changes throughout the different regions of France between 1982–1990. It is also showing that there has been a loss in population, mainly in the North of France, and that there is more net migration taking place in the South of France. The diagram is also showing the differences in the natural population change in the different regions of France.

NISEAC, 1993

Questions to Answer

The answer to Question 2 can be found in Chapter 18.

This question is taken from a higher tier paper for which candidates can achieve only Grades A* to D.

2 Study the map which shows the migration of people to West Germany from other parts of Europe and North Africa in the 1980s.

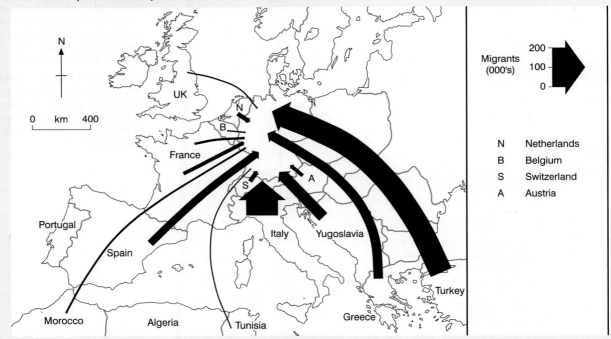

SEG (specimen paper)

i) Describe the pattern of migration to West Germany as shown on the map.   (4 marks)

ii) What are the advantages and disadvantages for countries, such as Germany, that have encouraged large numbers of immigrants to live there?   (7 marks)

10.1 RURAL AND URBAN SETTLEMENTS

We divide settlements into two basic types: rural and urban. There is no simple definition of a rural or urban settlement. However, there are a number of clear differences between rural settlements (villages, hamlets and isolated farms) and urban settlements (conurbations, cities and towns):

- Rural settlements are smaller than urban settlements (both in population size and size of built-up area).
- Rural settlements have fewer services such as shops, schools, public transport, etc.
- Rural settlements have a lower population density.
- Rural settlements have a larger percentage of their workforce in rural activities such as farming, forestry, quarrying, etc.

10.2 RURAL SETTLEMENT PATTERNS

Rural settlement patterns are characterised by two things:

- the distribution and density of settlement;
- the types of settlement which make up the pattern.

DISTRIBUTION AND DENSITY

The distribution of settlement across a region may be regular or irregular. In a regular settlement pattern the settlements are more or less evenly spaced. This type of pattern suggests that the physical conditions for farming (soils, water supply, drainage, relief, etc.) are much the same everywhere. Regular settlement patterns are often found in glaciated lowland landscapes like East Anglia.

In reality, regular settlement patterns are uncommon. This is because in most regions resources are unevenly distributed. Settlements tend to cluster in areas with more favourable resources. In the less favoured areas settlements exist either at very low densities or are absent altogether.

NUCLEATION AND DISPERSION

The basic unit of all rural settlement patterns is the farm. A farm is an agricultural workshop which cannot be separated from the land it relies on. Sometimes farms cluster together to form villages and hamlets. If most people in a region live in villages (rather than hamlets or small farms) we say that the settlement pattern is **nucleated** (Figs. 10.1 and 10.2).

Nucleated settlement patterns are often found:

- in places where peasants farmed co-operatively during the Middle Ages, under the feudal system (e.g. in the English Midlands);
- where water is scarce and is available only at specific **wet-point sites** such as springs, e.g. spring lines in chalklands at the foot of scarp slopes;

- in poorly drained and flood-prone areas, where settlement was confined to **dry-point sites,** e.g. on river terraces above flood plains.

Settlement patterns dominated by isolated farms and small hamlets are described as **dispersed** (Figs. 10.1 and 10.3). Dispersed settlement is typical of regions where the agricultural land is poor (e.g. North Pennines), because each farm needs a lot of land to be profitable.

However, nucleation and dispersal patterns are the extremes. In reality, many settlement patterns are a mixture of isolated farms, hamlets, and villages (Fig. 10.1).

Figure 10.1
Nucleated and dispersed settlement patterns.

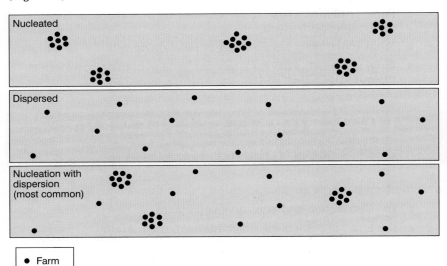

Nucleated

Dispersed

Nucleation with dispersion (most common)

• Farm

Figure 10.2 *Nucleated settlement pattern in Thornham, Norfolk.*

Figure 10.3 *Dispersed settlement pattern around Haverhill, Suffolk.*

10.3 CASE STUDY: RURAL SETTLEMENT PATTERNS IN BRITAIN

In chapter 2 we saw that the Tees–Exe line divides Britain into two contrasting regions of geology and relief: the Highland Zone; and the Lowland Zone. This division has influenced settlement patterns in Britain:

- High density, nucleated settlement patterns dominate the Lowland Zone.

- Lower density, dispersed patterns are more common in the Highland Zone.

LOWLAND ZONE: THE SOUTH DOWNS

The map extract in chapter 2 (Fig. 2.11) covers part of the South Downs (a chalk upland) and an adjacent lowland in southern Britain. The main features of the settlement pattern in this area are:

- uneven distribution;

- very low density settlement, especially on the South Downs;

- high density settlement on the lowland at the foot of the steep, north-facing slope of the Downs;

- strongly nucleated settlement, with most people living in villages such as Poynings, Fulking and Edburton.

Figure 10.4 *Factors influencing the sites and distribution of settlement.*

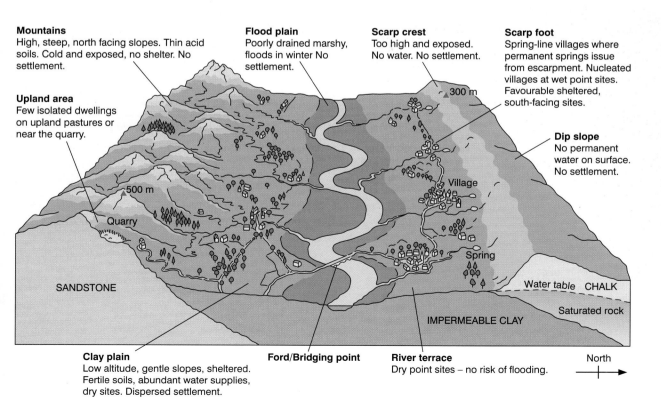

Mountains
High, steep, north facing slopes. Thin acid soils. Cold and exposed, no shelter. No settlement.

Upland area
Few isolated dwellings on upland pastures or near the quarry.

Flood plain
Poorly drained marshy, floods in winter No settlement.

Scarp crest
Too high and exposed. No water. No settlement.

Scarp foot
Spring-line villages where permanent springs issue from escarpment. Nucleated villages at wet point sites. Favourable sheltered, south-facing sites.

Dip slope
No permanent water on surface. No settlement.

300 m

Village

Spring

Water table CHALK

Saturated rock

500 m

Quarry

SANDSTONE

IMPERMEABLE CLAY

Clay plain
Low altitude, gentle slopes, sheltered. Fertile soils, abundant water supplies, dry sites. Dispersed settlement.

Ford/Bridging point

River terrace
Dry point sites – no risk of flooding.

North

The map provides some clues to explain this pattern:

- The lack of surface streams and rivers on the chalk Downs probably accounts for the absence of settlement there. Chalk is a porous rock (chapter 2), so rain quickly soaks into the ground. This means that there is a lack of water supply.

- Most settlements have concentrated at sites where water is available. Springs emerge from the base of the scarp slope, and it is at these wet-point sites that villages exist. We call these villages **spring-line settlements** (Fig. 10.4).

HIGHLAND ZONE: WENSLEYDALE

Figure 3.7 (p. 40) shows a very different settlement pattern. Wensleydale is a broad Pennine valley in North Yorkshire, surrounded by moorlands rising to 600 metres. The settlement pattern in Wensleydale has the following features:

- an uneven distribution;
- few settlements above 300 metres;
- few settlements on the flood plain of the River Ure;
- concentrated settlement above the flood plain but below 300 metres;
- apart from the small town of Hawes, a dispersed pattern characterised by isolated farms and hamlets.

Figure 3.8 suggests that physical geography has had a strong influence on Wensleydale's settlement pattern. Areas above 300 metres have attracted little settlement as the slopes are often steep; the climate is cold and wet; and the soils are shallow and acidic.

Probably the best land for farming is on the flood plain, but this area carries a flood risk. Therefore settlement clings to the lower valley slopes; above the flood plain, but below the high moorlands. Here the land is quite sheltered; well drained; and free from any flood risk. Also, morainic deposits on the valley sides support relatively deep and fertile soils.

Table 10.1 OS map skills: analysing rural settlement patterns

- Do most people live in villages, hamlets or isolated farms?
- Is the settlement pattern nucleated, dispersed or a mixture of both?
- Is the overall density of settlement high, medium or low?
- Where are the main concentrations of settlement?
- Where are the areas of sparsest settlement?
- How do any of the following factors influence the settlement pattern: water supply, slopes, altitude, drainage, flood risk?

Check yourself

QUESTIONS

Q1 What is a wet-point site?

Q2 What is a dry-point site?

Q3 State whether a settlement is likely to be on a wet-point or a dry-point site in each of the following areas:

a) an upland area made of permeable limestone;

b) a lowland river valley where the main rock is impermeable clay.

Q4 Study the cross-section through the Severn Vale and the Cotswolds near Gloucester (below). Make a list of advantages and disadvantages for settlements at each site.

Q5 With the help of the cross-section here and information on limestone in Chapter 2 suggest why the Cotswolds is an area of sparse, dispersed rural settlement.

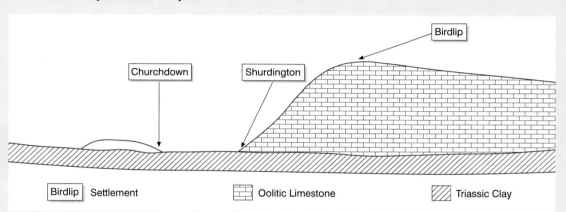

| Birdlip | Settlement | Oolitic Limestone | Triassic Clay |

REMEMBER! Cover the answers if you want to.

ANSWERS

A1 A wet-point site is a wet place in an otherwise dry area.

A2 A dry-point site is a dry in an otherwise wet area.

A3
a) a wet-point site
b) a dry-point site

TUTORIALS

T1&2 *These terms are frequently misunderstood in GCSE examinations. Remember that dry-point sites are found in wet areas and wet-point sites in dry areas. Settlers looking for a site in a wet, marshy area would look for a place that was slightly higher and therefore drier. Alternatively, an oasis is an obvious place to settle in a desert. Wet-point settlements in the UK are found in the permeable limestone and chalk areas (see chapter 2).*

T3 *Here you are being tested on your understanding of geographical terms, i.e. wet-point and dry-point sites. This is a little harder than the straight definitions asked for in questions 1 and 2.*

ANSWERS

A4

Churchdown
Advantage: Near flat land suitable for farming.
Disadvantage: Liable to flood.

Shurdington
Advantage: On a spring providing fresh water.
Disadvantage: On the side of an escarpment.

Birdlip
Advantage: Not liable to flood.
Disadvantage: Far from a source of water.

A5 The Cotswolds is an upland area, so its climate is likely to be more extreme than in the lowlands. It is a farming area so its settlement is likely to be sparse and rural. The permeable limestone rock means that there is little surface water. Therefore, settlement will be concentrated around sources of water. It is an example of a dispersed settlement.

TUTORIALS

T4 *Churchdown is on the side of a small hill so it is less likely to flood. Shurdington is a classic spring line settlement. As well as having the spring as a source of water, the village is sited where limestone soil and clay soil mix. The limestone makes the soil drain more easily.*

T5 *Notice that there are three key words in this question: sparse, rural and dispersed. In your answer you must explain why the settlement has each of these characteristics.*

10.4 SETTLEMENT CHARACTERISTICS

The study of individual settlements focuses on four characteristics: site, situation, shape and function.

SITE

Figure 10.5
Site and situation of settlements.

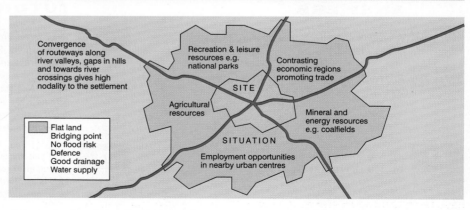

Site is the land on which a settlement is built (Fig. 10.5). In the British Isles most settlements have occupied their present site for at least 1,000 years. Early settlers were looking for water supply, fuel, farming land, shelter/defence, etc. Ideal sites therefore tended to be:

- flat or gently sloping;
- well drained (not marshy);
- free from any risk of flooding;
- close to a permanent water supply;
- sheltered from strong winds.

The site of Barnard Castle in County Durham (Fig. 10.6) has several of these features. Some larger settlements have sites which were selected mainly for strategic reasons. Barnard Castle, for example, controlled an important bridging point on the River Tees. The town also occupies a defensive site, elevated above the surrounding countryside, and protected on two sides by the river.

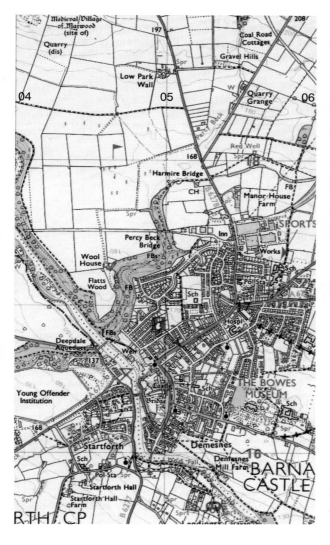

Figure 10.6
Barnard Castle, County Durham
(1:25,000 Ordnance Survey map).

Figure 10.7 *Aerial photo of Barnard Castle, County Durham.*

SITUATION

Situation describes the position of a settlement in relation to locational influences beyond its site (Fig. 10.5). In Anglo Saxon times a village may have been located to give easy access to good arable land and woodland. At a larger scale, towns may grow and prosper from a favourable situation. Physical geography has created the following favourable situations for settlement growth:

- a lowest bridging point before a river widens out into its estuary;
- the convergence of several valleys;
- a gap in a range of hills.

These situations make settlements easily accessible from the surrounding region which encourages their development as markets and trade centres.

SHAPE

Shape (or form) refers to the plan outline of a settlement's built-up area. Settlements may be linear (ribbon-like), rectangular, circular or even star-shaped. Both positive and negative factors influence the shape of settlements. Positive factors (e.g. transport routes and flat land) encourage growth; negative factors (e.g. planning controls and flood-prone valleys) limit growth.

Table 10.2   Explaining settlement shape (GRs refer to Figure 10.6)

FACTORS	DESCRIPTION
Transport routes	Major roads and railways encourage development owing to the access they provide. Infrastructure such as water, gas, electricity and telephone also follow roads. The effect is to give settlements a linear shape (ribbon development), e.g along the A67 (GR 0416).
Slopes	Steep slopes make farming and building difficult, e.g. Black Beck valley (GR0417). Unless land is in short supply, people avoid building on steep slopes. Gentler slopes encourage building (GR 0516).
Flood plains	Rivers spill onto flood plains during times of high flow. Settlements often avoid flood plains altogether, though cases of regular flood damage to buildings shows that this is not always true.
Coastlines	Resorts are often linear as they follow the coastline, e.g. Blackpool. The long, narrow shape maximises tourists' and residents' access to the coast. Coastlines also set limits on the seaward growth of settlements.
Planning controls	Although not marked on OS maps, green belts (chapter 11) place strict controls on urban growth. There may be an abrupt boundary between built-up areas and green belts. Some settlements such as new towns (chapter 11) have been planned from scratch.

FUNCTION

We refer to the economic and social activities and housing areas in settlements as functions (Table 10.3). Normally, the larger the settlement the more functions there are. Sometimes we describe a settlement by its main function. For example, London is a capital city, Felixstowe is a port, Scunthorpe is a steel-making town, and Brighton is a seaside resort.

Table 10.3 **Large urban settlements: functions shown on OS map and aerial photograph (Figs. 10.6 and 10.7)**

Residential	Housing types and ages of housing (pre-1870, 1870–1914, inter-war, post-war). Housing types include: detached, semi-detached, terraces, flats, caravans, etc. The oldest housing is usually located nearest the centre.
Industrial	Manufacturing industry: mills, factories, works, etc. Sometimes large complexes, such as oil refineries and steel works, are named. Industrial estates on edge-of-town sites near ring roads and motorways.
Commercial	Shops, wholesaling, warehousing, etc. are found in all large settlements. Often they are concentrated near the town centre (or central business district, CBD). They are not specifically named on maps whereas new edge-of-town shopping centres (retail parks, superstores) are more obvious.
Administrative	County, district, and local council offices; courts and prisons are sometimes named. Town Halls are marked on 1:50,000 maps.
Social/Environmental	Hospitals, schools, colleges, churches, services, cemeteries, crematoria, water and sewage works.
Recreational	Golf courses, sports centres, tourist information, offices and attractions. Occasionally, theatres and public houses are shown.
Transport	Airports, train and bus stations, ports, ferries, harbours, roads, railways, footpaths, canals.

Check yourself

QUESTIONS

Q1 What is the difference between the site and situation of a settlement?

Q2 Study the sketch map of an imaginary village.

i) Describe the site and situation of the village.

ii) List four advantages of the site. Choose the advantages from the following list: Built on a river mouth making a good harbour site; near flat land suitable for farming; near a source of wood for building and fuel; the wood is on steep land unsuitable for building; on a small river providing a source of fresh water.

iii) State two further advantages of the site.

iv) How might the function of this village have changed over the years?

Q3 Draw a simple sketch map to show the advantages of the situation of a large town or city known to you.

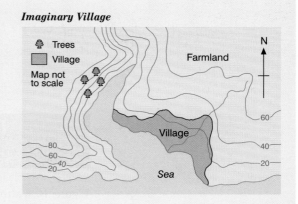

Imaginary Village

Trees
Village
Map not to scale
N
Farmland
60
Village
40
20
80
60
40
20
Sea

ANSWERS

A1 The site is the actual land on which a settlement is built. The situation is the location of the site in relation to the surrounding location.

A2
i) The village is built on gently sloping land where a small river enters a river estuary.
ii) On a small river providing a source of fresh water.
Near flat land suitable for farming.
Near a source of wood for building and fuel.
Built on a river mouth making a good harbour site.
iii) Other possible advantages are:
The village is in a valley and therefore sheltered. It is not sited directly on the coast, so it is sheltered from strong sea winds. The village is built on a slope and so above the danger of flooding.
iv) This village would have started out as a fishing village. This function may continue, but the village is likely to become an important tourist centre.

A3 A possible map may look like this:

Advantages of town's situation

TUTORIALS

T1 *These two are often confused by students. If the question is based on an Ordnance Survey extract then it is most likely to be concerned with the site of a settlement.*

T2
i) *Remember to describe only the land on which the village is built. The site of a settlement is almost always described in terms of physical geography. Situation may have some reference to human factors.*
ii) and iii) *The descriptions using the word "on" are advantages of the village's site. The word "near" involves descriptions of the situation.*
iv) *In the past, most villages were based on agriculture and most of their inhabitants worked on the land. Modern functions of villages include tourism and commuting. Commuting is where people live in a village but travel elsewhere to work. These villages are sometimes called dormitory or commuter settlements.*

T3 *This is an opportunity to make use of detailed knowledge. Remember to include annotations rather than just labels in your sketch. Include a title, north point, key, and some indication of scale. State if the map is not drawn to scale.*

10.5 SETTLEMENTS AS SERVICE CENTRES

Figure 10.8 shows an idealised settlement pattern. Each settlement is a service centre (or **central place**) which supplies goods and services to its own population and to people living in its surrounding **trade area** (or sphere of influence).

This orderly pattern of settlement would only be found in a simplified world where:

- the area occupied by settlement is a plain;
- climate and soils are the same everywhere;

- the population is evenly distributed;
- all areas are equally accessible;
- people always travel to the nearest centre for goods and services.

SETTLEMENT HIERARCHIES

In the idealised settlement pattern in Figure 10.8 as settlement **order** (or size) increases the number of settlements of each order decreases. We call this a settlement **hierarchy.** Two important ideas help to explain settlement hierarchies: **threshold** and **range.**

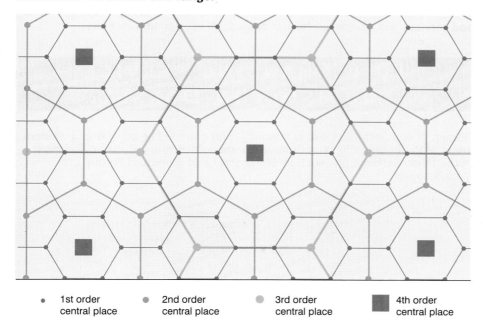

- 1st order central place
- 2nd order central place
- 3rd order central place
- 4th order central place

Figure 10.8
Settlement pattern according to central place theory.

THRESHOLD

Each service in a settlement (e.g. a shop) requires a minimum number of customers to make it profitable. This is known as the service's threshold population. Some services, such as small food shops, have low thresholds. These shops sell **convenience goods.** People buy convenience goods (or services) like food frequently. Over a year people can spend a large amount of money on convenience goods. This means that small post offices in villages and hamlets can make a profit by serving just a few hundred people (Fig. 10.9).

In contrast, people buy **comparison goods** such as clothes and electrical equipment less often. Their total spending on these items in a year is likely to be less than for food. Comparison goods stores such as Marks & Spencer and Dixons require a high threshold population, so they must locate in large towns or cities.

Because few services can survive on low thresholds, only a handful of low-order services locate in villages and hamlets. Towns and cities can support a much greater range and number of services. In this way a hierarchy of central places builds up.

Figure 10.9 *Thropton, Northumberland. A low-order, central place.*

171

RANGE

The distance people travel to buy particular goods or services is known as the range. Range, together with threshold, helps to explain the spacing of settlements. Because people need convenience goods (and services) frequently they travel only short distances to buy them. These goods and services must be available locally. As a result settlements supplying convenience goods and services only will be closely spaced. Close spacing also occurs because the small threshold populations supporting these settlements are usually found within a small area.

Similar arguments apply to comparison goods and services. Because these services have larger thresholds and ranges, they have larger trade areas. Therefore it follows that towns and cities which provide comparison goods and services will be spaced further apart than villages and hamlets.

10.6 CHANGING SERVICE PROVISION IN DORSET

Dorset, in southern England, is a mainly rural county. The central and western areas of the county (Fig. 10.10) have few manufacturing industries and most of the larger settlements, such as Dorchester and Blandford Forum, are market towns.

Figure 10.10
Distribution of service centres in Dorset.

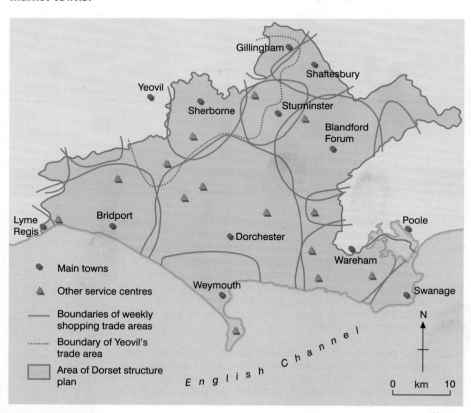

The shopping centres of many British market towns have declined steadily in the last 25 years. In Dorset, Blandford Forum, Wareham and Sherborne have all lost retail floorspace since 1971 (Figs. 10.11). The main reason for this trend is competition from large food superstores and retail warehouses in the larger towns Weymouth, Poole and Yeovil.

10.7 RURAL SERVICE DECLINE

While many market towns have experienced declining trade, it is the smallest service centres in the remoter rural areas, which have been hardest hit. Today, almost two in every five villages in England and Wales have no permanent shop; half have no primary school; and nearly three-quarters have no daily bus service.

There are several reasons for this:

- In some areas population decline has meant there are too few people to support local services. Employment in agriculture for example has fallen continuously in the last 30 years, and between 1993 and 2000 another 100,000 jobs are likely to disappear.

- Lack of public transport and poor roads often make commuting from remote areas difficult (thus encouraging out-migration and discouraging in-migration). At the same time poor transport links discourage businesses from locating in remote rural areas.

- Ageing populations in rural areas mean fewer children, and little demand for village schools.

- Rising car ownership allows people to travel to larger centres offering more choice. This means they no longer use local services, which decline.

In Dorset, these problems have led to much of the county being classed by the government as a Rural Development Area (RDA). RDAs (Fig. 10.12) receive government grants aimed at creating jobs (in tourism and small businesses) and keeping villages alive.

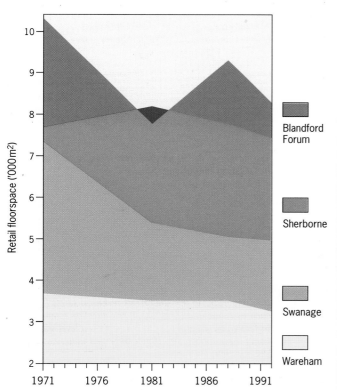

Figure 10.11 *Changing retail floorspace for Dorset towns.*

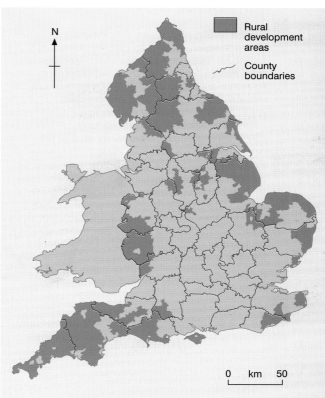

Figure 10.12 *Rural development areas in England and Wales.*

Check yourself

QUESTIONS

Q1 What are the meanings of the following terms:

trade area; settlement hierarchy?

Q2 Explain the difference between:

range and threshold; comparison and convenience goods and services.

Q3 How do the range and threshold of convenience and comparison goods differ?

Q4 Four new shops have opened on a new housing estate on the edge of a town. They are occupied by a newsagent, a hairdesser, a fashion boutique and a video hire store.

i) Which shop is likely to be the least successful?

ii) Explain your answer.

Q5 Why have many shops which opened on new housing estates or in villages in recent years had to close?

REMEMBER! Cover the answers if you want to.

ANSWERS

A1 Trade area is the area served by a settlement.

A settlement hierarchy is when settlements are ranked in order of size or importance.

A2 Range is the maximum distance a customer is prepared to travel to obtain goods or services. The threshold is the minimum area that has to be served by a supplier in order to make a profit. Convenience goods are usually low in value and are bought regularly. Comparison goods are more expensive and are bought infrequently, often after comparing quality and price.

A3 Convenience goods are bought regularly so people are not prepared to travel very far to buy them. The range is therefore quite small. The threshold is also small because the supplier can rely on a high turnover of goods. Comparison goods are expensive and are bought infrequently. People will travel longer distances to places which offer a greater variety. Suppliers have to serve a large area in order to make enough profit.

A4 i) Fashion boutique.

ii) It is unlikely that there will be enough customers buying expensive clothes on a suburban housing estate.

A5 People are more mobile because of car ownership and other transport. They can travel longer distances into city centres.

TUTORIALS

T1 *An alternative name for a trade area is a sphere of influence. There are different ways of classifying settlements into a hierarchy. Population size is the most common way. Other criteria are the number and range of services.*

T2 *A good's range is the maximum size of its trade area whereas its threshold is the minimum size.*

T3 *Testing knowledge of geographical terms is very common in GCSE examinations.*

T4&5 *It is important to use the correct technical terms here, such as range and threshold. If the question is marked in levels you are unlikely to reach the top level without using these terms; even if you show you understand the question.*

EXAMINATION CHECKLIST

The facts and ideas you should know and understand after studying settlement patterns are:

- The differences between rural and urban settlements.
- The different patterns of rural settlement, i.e. nucleated and dispersed.
- The reasons for dispersed and nucleated settlement patterns.
- The difference between the settlement patterns in Highland and Lowland Britain.
- How to describe a settlement pattern from an Ordnance Survey map extract.
- The location, form and function of settlements.
- The difference between the site and situation of a settlement.
- The reasons for the decline of rural services.
- The concepts of hierarchy, and threshold and range of trade area.

Key words

These are the key words. Tick them if you think you know what they mean. Otherwise check on them.

nucleated settlement	central place
wet-point site	trade area
dry-point site	settlement order
spring-line settlements	settlement hierarchy
site	threshold
situation	range
shape	convenience goods
function	comparison goods

EXAM PRACTICE

Sample Student's Answer and Examiner's Comments

EXAMINER'S COMMENTS

i) This is correct.
The answer must be taken from the diagram.

ii)
She has written a full definition and gains full marks. The first mark is given for the comment "large cities or towns are expanding so greatly that they merge together". The second mark is given for the comment "made of several different places". Her answer could have gained her two further marks for her understanding of the fact that a conurbation is made of several settlements merging, and the example given.

iii)
She has interpreted the diagram accurately. She recognises that in a hierarchy there are a large number of the smaller settlements, but as you move up the hierarchy the number of settlements decreases. The two marks are awarded for the final sentence.

This is a harder question as the examiner is testing the understanding of a hierarchy. The first two parts of the question were testing knowledge.

iv)
She makes three credit worthy points and shows a good understanding of the relationship between the size of a settlement and the number of services provided. There is a mark for each of the first three sentences. She did not make use of technical terms such as range and threshold. Use of these terms would have improved her SPaG mark.

She gained full marks on these questions which would have been an A grade in this part of the examination.

---

1 a) Study the diagram which shows a hierarchy of settlements, ranked according to population size.

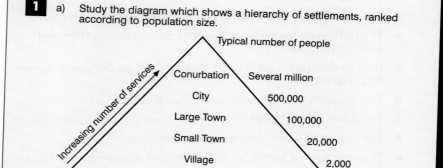

	Typical number of people
Conurbation	Several million
City	500,000
Large Town	100,000
Small Town	20,000
Village	2,000
Hamlet	100
Isolated Farms and Buildings	One family

Increasing number of services

i) Use the diagram to state the number of people in a small town (1 mark)

20,000 people

ii) What is the meaning of the term "conurbation"? (2 marks)

A conurbation is where large cities or towns are expanding so greatly that they merge together forming one large area of buildings, which is made of several different places. Development causes the original areas to expand and one area "runs" into another, e.g. Birmingham, Wolverhampton and Walsall in the West Midlands.

iii) Why is the diagram in the shape of a triangle, with a large base and a narrow point? (2 marks)

Settlement hierarchy shows the order and frequency of settlements according to their size. The ratio of conurbation to an area increases as the area gets smaller, therefore the largest conurbation is at the top-most point of the triangle, and several isolated farms and buildings, being much more frequent, produce a wide base.

iv) Explain why there is a relationship between the size of a settlement and the number of services provided. (3 marks)

If a settlement is small with a small population the services provided will be there only for the population of the area/settlement. The sphere of influence will be elsewhere and the population will be prepared to travel elsewhere for other shops and services. If the settlement is large it will need to provide a greater amount and range of services to satisfy the population. Money will be wasted on a great number of services that will be used only by the settlement's population.

SEG, 1995

Questions to Answer

The answer to Question 2 can be found in Chapter 18.

2   Study Figures 10.6 and 10.7.

i)   Which way was the camera facing when the photograph was taken?

ii)   Look at the following sketch map based on the air photograph.

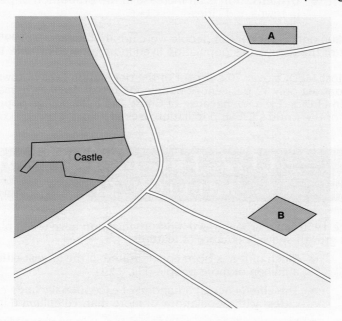

a)   What is the building marked A?

b)   What is the building marked B?

iii)   Use the map and the photograph to describe the advantages of the site of the castle in Barnard Castle.

iv)   What effect has the River Tees had on the layout of the town of Barnard Castle?

v)   Where is the oldest part of Barnard Castle?

vi)   State two reasons for your answer to part v)

vii)   Suggest the likely functions of Barnard Castle.

CHAPTER 11

URBAN SETTLEMENT

11.1 URBANISATION AND URBAN GROWTH

Table 11.1 Proportion of urban dwellers by continent, 1995

CONTINENT	%
North America	79.1
Europe	75.5
Latin America	75
Oceania	73.5
Asia	33.3
Africa	33.2

At a global scale towns and cities are expanding rapidly. An increasing percentage of people live in urban areas.

- **Urban growth** is the physical expansion of towns and cities.
- **Urbanisation** is an increase in the proportion of people living in towns and cities.

In 1800 only 5 per cent of people were urban dwellers. By 1995 over 45 per cent of the the world's population lived in urban areas (Table 11.1).

In most MEDCs over 70 per cent of the population lives in towns and cities. In contrast only 33 per cent of people are urban dwellers in many African and Asian LEDCs. Even so, because of China and India's huge populations, nearly half of the world's urban population lives in Asia.

11.2 THE GROWTH OF MILLION CITIES

Since 1950 rapid urban growth and urbanisation have taken place in LEDCs. This growth shows a number of features:

- Much of it has been concentrated in the largest cities with a million or more people (Fig. 11.1).
- The emergence of a handful of exceptionally large cities (**mega cities**) with populations of more than 10 million (Fig. 11.2).
- In some countries **primate cities**, several times bigger than the second largest city, dominate, e.g. Mexico City, Buenos Aires.

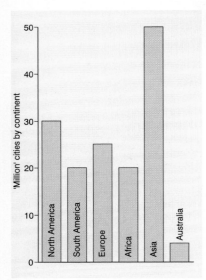

Figure 11.1 *Number of million cities by continent, 1995.*

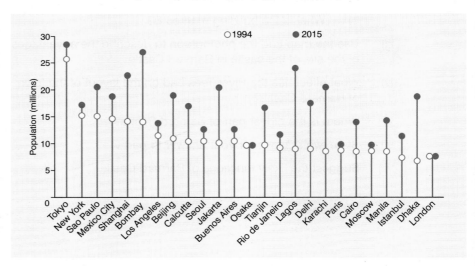

Figure 11.2
Growth of the world's largest cities, 1994–2015.

Table 11.2 Distribution of million cities and mega cities, 1997

	MILLION CITIES	MEGA CITIES
MEDCs	106	3
LEDCs	179	9

11.3 CAUSES OF URBANISATION AND URBAN GROWTH

Urban populations grow in two ways:

- through natural increase (chapter 8);
- through migration (chapter 9).

Rural–urban migration is the main reason for urbanisation and urban growth (see section 9.3). Push factors relating to rural poverty (section 9.3) are the principal cause of rural–urban migration in LEDCs.

11.4 COUNTER URBANISATION IN MEDCs

In MEDCs, urbanisation has largely ended. Major cities such as London, Paris and New York are not expected to show much population growth in future (Fig. 11.2). In MEDCs migration now tends to be in favour of people moving out of cities, to smaller towns and rural areas. We call this process counter-urbanisation (section 9.6). It often leads to population decline in large cities.

Check yourself

QUESTIONS

Q1 Explain the difference between 'urban growth' and 'urbanisation'.

Q2 Study Figure 11.2.
- i) What was the population of New York in 1994?
- ii) What is the estimated population of Sao Paulo in 2015?
- iii) How many of the cities are not in LEDCs?
- iv) Why are cities in LEDCs growing so rapidly?

REMEMBER! Cover the answers if you want to.

ANSWERS

A1 Urban growth is the physical expansion of cities. Urbanisation is the increase in the proportion of people living in towns and cities.

TUTORIALS

T1 *Urban growth is expressed in terms of area, such as square kilometres. Urbanisation is given as a percentage. You are more likely to be asked to explain the term urban growth in an examination.*

ANSWERS

A2
i) 16 million
ii) 21 million
iii) 8
iv) There is a higher expectation of employment in cities than in rural areas. The profits from farming can be very poor, because of damaged soils. Also, natural disasters can ruin crops or homes. Urban areas have better welfare and social facilities. Many rural dwellers follow other members of their families who have already moved to cities. Natural increase is very high in cities.

TUTORIALS

T2
i) and ii)   Make sure that you add 'millions' to your answers. Just writing 16 or 21 is the wrong answer!

iii)   Read the question carefully. Examiners do not write questions in the negative form very often (note the use of the word 'not' in the question).

iv)   It is possible to answer this question using just 'pull' factors. However, it is just as important to emphasise 'push' factors. This does not mean you should list the straight opposites of the pull factors. The rapid decline in death rates in cities in LEDCs while birth rates remain high explains the high rates of natural increase.

The twin effects of migration and natural increase means that urban growth in LEDCs today is much faster than it was in MEDCs.

11.5 LAND USE PATTERNS: CITIES IN MEDCs

The distribution of land use – shops, offices, housing and industry – within cities often forms distinctive spatial patterns (Fig. 11.3). Often housing areas form concentric rings or zones around the city centre. Industries can form wedge-shaped sectors which radiate from the centre along important roads or railways. Elsewhere there may be smaller rectangular-shaped areas of land use, occupied by industrial estates, office parks, retail parks, housing developments, etc.

Figure 11.3
Land use patterns in Southampton.

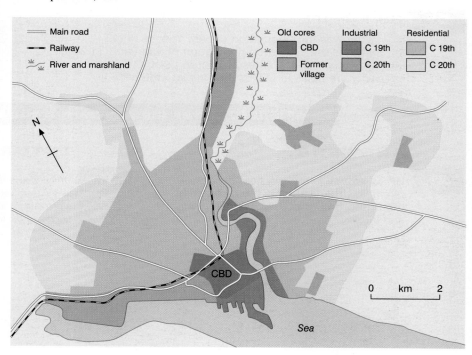

CASE STUDY: SOUTHAMPTON

Southampton is a medium-sized city in southern England (Fig. 11.4). Its natural harbour allowed port activities to flourish. When railways linked Southampton to London in 1850, Southampton became the outport for the capital's trans-Atlantic liner traffic.

Rapid population growth after 1850 led to a massive expansion of the city. The city grew outwards from its commercial core to form ring-like, zonal housing patterns. Trade and industry sectors grew around the waterfront and inland along the Itchen Valley (Fig. 11.3).

Figure 11.4
Centre of Southampton
(1:50,000 Ordnance Survey map)

Figure 11.5 *Inner city housing, Southampton.*

Table 11.3 Land use patterns in a typical British city

The central business district (CBD)
- Shops, offices and entertainment dominate the CBD (Fig. 11.3).
- There are many important public buildings, e.g. town hall, cathedral, museums, etc.
- Limited space and high demand results in high-density, tall buildings. High rents are affordable only by shops and offices. Little housing or industry.
- Roads and public transport converge here making it easily accessible.

The inner city

Rapid population growth between 1850 and 1914 added a zone of high-density housing around the centre, called the inner city (Fig. 11.5). For much of the nineteenth century, people had to live close to work because of poor transport. The result was:
- high-density terrace housing laid out on a simple grid pattern;
- by the mid-twentieth century many terrace houses became slums;
- the replacement of terrace housing, in and after the 1960s, by modern terraces and high-rise flats (urban renewal).

The outer suburbs
- Housing mainly comprises detached and semi-detached dwellings of lower density. Housing built since 1914. Houses are more spacious with gardens (Fig. 11.6).
- Urban growth after 1914 sometimes swallowed-up existing villages, e.g. Weston in Southampton.
- There are open spaces such as parks and school playing fields.
- Many manufacturing, service and distribution firms locate in industrial estates and business parks on edge-of-town sites. These sites offer better access to ring roads and motorways; large, purpose-built, single-storey factories and sheds; storage and parking areas; cheap land. Recently, retailing has moved here, with retail parks and superstores locating along major routeways.

Rural–urban fringe
- The countryside immediately surrounding the city is known as the rural–urban fringe.
- The demand for services and recreation often gives this zone a distinctive land use, e.g. golf courses, sewage works, crematoria, hospitals, market gardening, garden centres, horse livery.
- Countryside here is often green belt land.

The commuter zone

Many middle and high income families have moved out of cities into surrounding villages in the last 50 years..

Figure 11.6 *Housing in the suburbs of West Nottingham.*

Table 11.4   OS map skills: describing urban land use

- Has the city expanded equally in all directions to give a roughly circular shape?
- Have coastlines, valleys, steep slopes, etc. hindered expansion in some directions?
- What functions indicate the location of the CBD?
- Which major routeways converge on the CBD?
- Is there evidence of terrace housing, with uniform grid-iron street patterns surrounding the CBD?
- Is there evidence of twentieth century housing estates, with street patterns forming crescents, cul-de-sacs, etc. in the outer suburbs?
- Are there any distinctive zones of housing?
- How does the density of urban development vary from the CBD to the outer suburbs?
- Where are the main areas of industrial land use in the city?
- Are any industrial areas located on waterfronts, in valleys, along major roads or railways?
- Do any industrial land uses form recognisable sectors or areas?
- Are there any typical rural-urban land uses in the countryside around the edge of the city?
- Is there any evidence of a) villages which have been swamped by urban growth, b) commuter villages within the rural-urban fringe?

11.6 SOCIAL PATTERNS: CITIES IN MEDCs

Where people live in a city depends on four factors: income; family status; ethnic status; and distribution of housing types.

Income

Better-off people have the widest choice. Usually they opt for larger houses, in a pleasant area with access to good schools, shops and other services. Poorer people may have to live in sub-standard housing, where overcrowding, poor services, and crime are serious problems.

Family status

Family status refers to the composition of households, for example a single adult; a couple without children; a couple with young children, etc. This often influences where people live. Changes in family size are a common reason for people moving house, e.g. when a couple have children.

Ethnicity

Many western cities have large ethnic minority groups. In the UK, most ethnic minorities are from South Asia and the Caribbean. Large numbers of immigrants from these areas settled in British cities in the 1960s and 1970s. Often ethnic minority groups are concentrated in particular parts of the city. There are several reasons for this ethnic segregation:

- people prefer to live close to those who share their culture and language;
- local services such as temples, mosques and ethnic food shops develop in these areas;
- members of ethnic groups feel safer within these areas;
- in cities such as Birmingham, Bradford and Leicester, South Asian minorities are often attracted to the inner city because of its affordable terrace housing.

11.7 URBAN PROBLEMS AND PLANNING IN MEDCS

As cities grow their demand for space and resources for housing, transport and jobs increases. Often these demands cannot be met immediately, which results in urban problems.

CASE STUDY: PARIS

Paris has a population of 10.3 million. It is the largest city in Europe. Paris is an ancient city, going back more than 2000 years. Located at an easy crossing point on the River Seine and at the centre of the fertile Paris Basin, it had advantages of both site and situation.

Rapid population growth, an ageing housing stock and an inadequate transport system created a desperate situation in Paris by the mid-twentieth century. However, in the last 40 years the city's planners have worked hard to solve these problems.

Housing: The grands énsembles

After the Second World War Paris had an acute housing problem. The city was overcrowded. Densities in central Paris averaged 35,000 people per km^2; and the population was growing rapidly. Shanty towns appeared in some places.

City planners responded by building high-rise blocks or grands énsembles, in the outer suburbs. In Mantes-la-Jolie, 35 kilometres west of Paris, 6,000 mainly high-rise flats were built in the 1960s. The families who moved there worked at the nearby Renault and Peugeot car factories. As in the UK, the tower blocks soon proved unpopular:

- Re-housing people broke up tight-knit communities from the inner city.
- Often tower blocks were poorly built, expensive to heat and suffered from poor sound insulation.
- They were unsuitable both for young families with children, and old people.
- Vandalism and crime was difficult to control.
- The flats were poorly served by public transport and local services.

During the 1970s the white population of the grands énsembles was replaced by immigrants from West Africa, Tunisia, North Africa and Turkey. With their larger families the tower blocks proved even less suitable.

Planning the growth of Paris

By 1960 it became clear that the capital's problems could not be solved piecemeal. Planners developed a master plan for the entire Paris region (Fig. 11.7). Its main theme was decentralisation. People and jobs were to be moved out of central Paris; and there would be massive investment in new transport systems.

The master plan assumed that the city's population would continue to grow, so the planners proposed:

- two parallel growth corridors running south-east to north-west on either side of the Seine Valley (Fig. 11.7);
- building eight new towns within these corridors;
- a new express metro system (RER) linking the centre of Paris to the new towns;
- an inner ring road (boulevard périphérique).

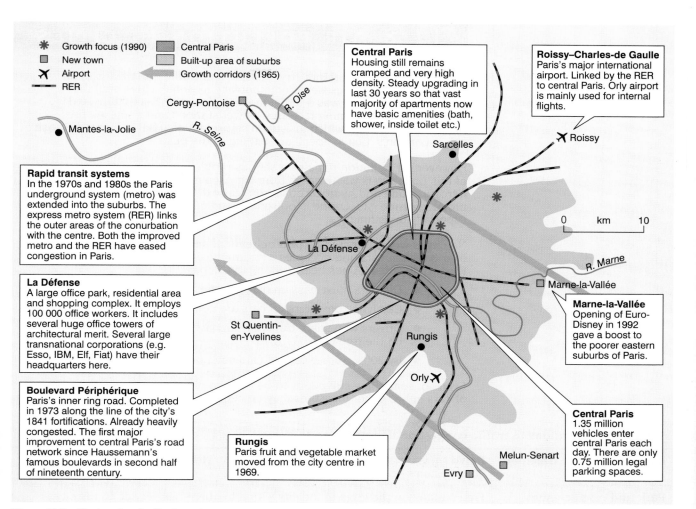

Growth focus (1990) **Central Paris**
□ New town   Built-up area of suburbs
✈ Airport   ⬅ Growth corridors (1965)
━━ RER

Central Paris
Housing still remains cramped and very high density. Steady upgrading in last 30 years so that vast majority of apartments now have basic amenities (bath, shower, inside toilet etc.)

Roissy–Charles-de Gaulle
Paris's major international airport. Linked by the RER to central Paris. Orly airport is mainly used for internal flights.

Rapid transit systems
In the 1970s and 1980s the Paris underground system (metro) was extended into the suburbs. The express metro system (RER) links the outer areas of the conurbation with the centre. Both the improved metro and the RER have eased congestion in Paris.

La Défense
A large office park, residential area and shopping complex. It employs 100 000 office workers. It includes several huge office towers of architectural merit. Several large transnational corporations (e.g. Esso, IBM, Elf, Fiat) have their headquarters here.

Boulevard Périphérique
Paris's inner ring road. Completed in 1973 along the line of the city's 1841 fortifications. Already heavily congested. The first major improvement to central Paris's road network since Haussemann's famous boulevards in second half of nineteenth century.

Rungis
Paris fruit and vegetable market moved from the city centre in 1969.

Marne-la-Vallée
Opening of Euro-Disney in 1992 gave a boost to the poorer eastern suburbs of Paris.

Central Paris
1.35 million vehicles enter central Paris each day. There are only 0.75 million legal parking spaces.

Figure 11.7 *Master plan for Paris region.*

Between 1965 and 1990 population growth in Paris began to slow down. This led to changes to the original plan:

- More emphasis was placed on improving facilities within the city by designating **growth poles.** (Fig. 11.8).
- The number of new towns was reduced to five.
- Greater protection was given to countryside around Paris.
- Five giant poles of urban development in the suburbs were proposed, including universities, hospitals and cultural centres.

New towns: Cergy-Pontoise

Cergy-Pontoise new town lies at the western end of the northern development corridor (Fig. 11.7). Since 1968 the town has grown rapidly. Thousands of Parisians have moved to the new town which offers a pleasant environment, low-density housing, and excellent communications with the capital. There are around 65,000 jobs in the town, mainly in the service sector. Cergy is the administrative centre of the Val d'Oise departement. Although there are excellent rail links to central Paris on the RER, only a small proportion of the working population commute to the capital.

Figure 11.8 *New offices, housing, shops and other services cluster in La Défense, Paris.*

11.8 AIR POLLUTION IN CITIES

Large concentrations of industry, housing and traffic often leads to air pollution. Winter smogs were commonplace in British cities until the mid-1950s. The smog was a lethal mixture of soot and sulphuric acid produced by coal burning factories, power stations and domestic fires. Thanks to legislation which insists on smokeless coal being burnt in British cities, London's 'pea soupers' are a thing of the past.

However, air pollution remains a serious problem in cities. The main cause of this pollution is waste gases from car exhausts. On still, sunny days nitrogen oxide and hydrocarbons from car exhausts react with sunlight to produce ozone gas. Ozone is poisonous and can cause breathing difficulties, especially in asthmatics.

No city is worse affected by **photochemical smog** than Los Angeles. LA has over 8 million cars and occupies a natural basin which traps pollutants. For two decades LA has been fighting the smog.

- Old cars must pass an exhaust emission test.
- Catalytic converters on cars are compulsory.
- Drivers who share transport are given access to a clear lane on the freeways.
- By 2003, 10 per cent of cars must be electric.

Even so, something still needs to be done to reduce the growing number of cars in LA. Other measures may be needed (Table 11.5).

Table 11.5   Solutions to traffic congestion and pollution in cities

Improving public transport	Rapid transit systems, e.g. Tyne–Wear Metro in Newcastle-upon-Tyne. Tram systems, e.g. Metrolink in Manchester.
Park and ride schemes	Free parking on the edge of the city with a frequent bus service to the city centre, e.g. in Oxford.
Bus lanes/cycle lanes	Priority given to buses at rush hour. Dedicated cycle lanes, e.g. Leeds.
Parking	Increase cost of parking. Reduce amount of parking space, e.g. Birmingham.
Road charging	Automated computer systems charge motorists for journeys into city centres, e.g. Leicester.

Check yourself

QUESTIONS

Use Figure 11.4 to answer questions 1 and 2.

Q1
i) Write a description of grid square 4211.
ii) Which of the following urban zones does your description in part i) best fit: CBD, Inner City, Outer Suburbs?
iii) State a four figure grid reference for part of the inner city.
iv) Name one feature of your chosen square that suggests it is part of the inner city.
v) How does square 4413 differ from your chosen square?
vi) In which urban zone of Southampton is the area covered by square 4413?

QUESTIONS

Q2
i) How have physical features affected the growth and development of Southampton?
ii) What evidence on the map suggests that the traffic using the port of Southampton may be changing?
iii) Describe the pattern of main roads in the Southampton area.

Q3 Study the following table.

Pollution in selected megacities.

City	Sulphur dioxide	Dust and smoke	Lead	Carbon monoxide	Nitrogen dioxide
Beijing	●	●	○	—	○
Bombay	○	●	○	○	○
Jakarta	○	●	◐	◐	○
London	○	○	○	◐	○
Mexico City	●	●	◐	●	◐
New York	○	○	○	◐	○
Sao Paulo	○	◐	○	◐	◐
Shanghai	○	●	—	—	—
Tokyo	○	○	—	○	○

Source: adapted from *The Economist*, 1994.
● high pollution ◐ moderate to heavy
○ low — no data

i) Which city suffers the most pollution?
ii) Which type of pollutant causes the most widespread pollution?
iii) State two likely causes of the pollution listed.
iv) For each of your answers in iii) suggest how the causes could be reduced.

.... **REMEMBER! Cover the answers if you want to.** ....

ANSWERS

A1
i) There is no obvious pattern to the roads. The main roads all focus on this square. There are a number of churches, a museum and a college.
ii) CBD.
iii) 4212.
iv) The rectangular pattern of the streets.
v) The street pattern in square 4413 is less ordered, with crescents and cul-de-sacs.
vi) Outer suburbs.

TUTORIALS

T1
i) *Try to include more than just single features such as churches and museums. The examiner is asking you to describe the overall landscape in that particular square. The reason behind this is to help you with your answer to part ii) which tests your understanding.*
ii) *The fact that this square is a focus of communications suggests that it is part of Southampton's CBD. The position of the inner ring road is also a clue to the whereabouts of the CBD. Its position suggests that the CBD extends into part of squares 4112 and 4212. The Civic Centre is another clue.*
iii) *The street pattern is significant here, and so too is the position of the square in relation to the CBD.*
iv) *Look for high-density, straight streets when trying to locate inner city areas.*
v) *Notice the lower density of the built-up area.*
vi) *The suburbs are on the edge of the built-up areas and represent the most recent urban areas to be built.*

ANSWERS

A2

i) Southampton stands between the Rivers Test and Itchen. This gives the city a long waterfront, ideal for the development of docks and marinas. However, the water could have restricted the growth of the city to the area between the rivers, until the River Itchen was bridged. The city therefore grew northwards first. Later, new outer suburbs would have developed west and east along the River Test. There does not seem to be a danger of regular flooding as the city has been built right up to the water's edge. The only area of open space is Southampton Common to the north-west of the map extract in square 4114. The industrial areas are along the banks of the River Test, near the docks.

ii) The existence of a marina in square 4310, suggests that pleasure craft are now using the port as well as large passenger liners.

iii) The main roads converge towards the city centre. There have been new developments to help ease traffic flow: there are a number of dual carriageways, and an inner ring road around the CBD. Two bridges across the River Itchen have improved access from the east of the city. The two main access points to the city are from the west, and the north-east.

A3

i) Mexico City.
ii) Dust and smoke.
iii) Possible answers include industrial pollution and car exhaust fumes.
iv) Filters fitted to chimneys to reduce the amount of industrial pollution. Possible solutions to traffic pollution include those listed in Table 11.5.

TUTORIALS

T2

i) *Physical features are water and relief features. In Southampton's case water features are the most significant. However, relief can play an important part too. Steep upland areas can be left undeveloped. Sometimes more expensive housing is found in higher areas because of the view.*

ii) *The examiner is testing more than just your ability to describe the map. This question is testing your map interpretation skills too.*

iii) *Sometimes the examiner will test your drawing skills in this type of question by asking you to produce a sketch map showing the main roads.*

T3

i) *and* ii) *Make sure that you read the table carefully. In these types of question it is very easy to make a careless slip.*

iii) *and* iv) *Although these questions do not ask for actual examples, it is better to give some if you can.*

11.9 URBAN LAND USE IN LEDCs

Cities in LEDCs have very different land use and social patterns to those in MEDCs. This reflects their different history, traditions and economic conditions. Contrasts between cities within LEDCs are also strong. Even so, there is a general model (Fig. 11.9) which applies to these cities:

- A CBD dominated by modern administrative and commercial activities. Many cities in Latin America, e.g. Mexico City, have a grid-like street plan with high-class housing areas built for colonial administrators. Traditional markets, bazaars, mosques, temples, etc. often occupy separate areas within the CBD.

- Modern high-rise apartments are found close to the CBD. They are home to the better-off and their location gives easy access to services and employment in the CBD. Areas of squatter housing (shanty towns) develop on vacant plots close to the CBD. Many people living in shanty towns work in informal service activities, e.g. street trading, washing cars, etc. (Fig. 11.10).

- Generally the quality of housing decreases with distance from the city centre. The ring of mature suburbs often comprises informal housing which has been upgraded to include basic amenities, e.g. water and electricity.

- Rapid urban growth in the late twentieth century led to a huge expansion of built-up areas. Much of this growth consists of shanty towns on the edge of the city. Initially these settlements, self-built by in-migrants, lack even the most basic amenities.

- Commercial and industrial areas often radiate in sectors from the city centre. They follow major roads and railways. Some are dominated by modern factories and warehouses; others by small workshops set up by the inhabitants of nearby shanty towns (e.g. Mathare Valley in Nairobi).

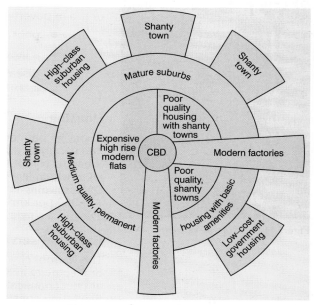

Figure 11.9 *Model structure of a city in a LEDC.*

Figure 11.10 *Shanty towns overlook wealthier areas of Rio, Brazil.*

11.10 URBAN PROBLEMS AND PLANNING IN LEDCs

Cities in LEDCs are growing at an alarming rate. Many cities are unable to provide adequate housing, services and jobs for their inhabitants. Poverty has often meant that environmental concerns have taken second place to economic development.

CASE STUDY: NAIROBI

Nairobi is Kenya's capital and largest city. Like other large African cities its population growth in recent years has been rapid. By 1995 its population was

1.5 million – a fourfold increase in 30 years. This growth resulted from a combination of rural–urban migration and natural increase.

Kibera shanty town

Kibera, Nairobi's largest shanty town (Fig. 11.11), shows all the symptoms of urban poverty in LEDCs:

- poor, inadequate and overcrowded accommodation;
- a lack of essential services;
- disease and high rates of mortality, especially among children;
- lack of paid employment.

Housing

About 55 per cent of Nairobi's population lives in shanty towns (Fig. 11.12). The supply of affordable housing in cities has not matched population growth. Kibera is Nairobi's largest shanty town. It has a population of nearly 250,000 all of whom live in shacks made from mud, whattle and corrugated iron. Overcrowding in Kibera is a major problem. The average population density is 110,000 per km^2. In a typical household there may be four or five people living in a single room.

Essential services

The Nairobi city authority does not provide roads, sewerage, drainage, water or electricity in Kibera. Most people have to buy water from tanks (or kiosks) at uneconomical prices. Others draw water from the polluted Nairobi Dam. Sanitation consists of pit latrines which may be shared by up to 500 people. Human excreta litters the settlement and is a major health hazard, particularly in the rainy season. There is no official refuse collection. All these factors cause high rates of mortality. Diarrhoea associated with poor sanitation and diseased water is a major cause of death among children.

Figure 11.11 *Kibera, Nairobi.*

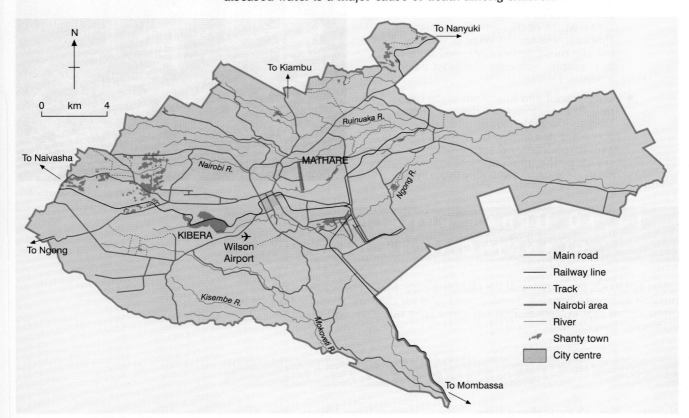

Figure 11.12 *Distribution of shanty towns in Nairobi.*

Education and employment

There are just 20 clinics (set up by non-government and community organisations) and 5 primary schools in Kibera. Average class sizes are 50–60. One-third of children receive no education beyond primary school.

Around two in five people have paid employment mainly as casual labourers, watchmen, servants, cleaners, etc. There is no unemployment benefit, so people without paid jobs have to rely on self-help. Of these about one third of the self-employed (mainly women) cultivate small plots of land. The rest have small business interests, e.g. trading food, cigarettes, fuel, and water. However, there is a wide range of more productive activities. These include metal working, machinery repair, carpentry, construction and shoe making. Earnings are usually very low. Most households rely on children earning money too.

UPGRADING POOR HOUSING

Initially, shanty towns are little more than clusters of shacks. However, as their inhabitants become better-off they improve their homes. This upgrading process may result in shanty towns eventually becoming mature suburbs.

Today, most city authorities have a positive attitude towards shanty towns. They help with upgrading and provide low-cost housing schemes for the poor. Typical responses include:

- Authorities grant squatters legal tenure so that they are more likely to upgrade their homes.

- Site and service projects are set up. Households are given a plot, served by roads, electricity and a water supply. Building a house is the responsibility of the household. Cheap loans and low-cost building materials may be available.

- Core housing schemes are set up. Similar to site and service projects, households are given a plot and one-room core 'house'.

11.11 POLLUTION IN CITIES IN LEDCs

Air pollution is a major problem in many cities in LEDCs. Many industrialising countries, such as China and India, depend heavily on coal as a fuel. Coal burning power stations and factories cause dense smogs in China's capital, Beijing. The problem is so bad that 'oxygen bars' have been opened up!

Mexico City is one of the most polluted cities in the world. It is claimed that two million people there suffer from air pollution related diseases. On 17 March 1992 all school children under 14 years of age were ordered to stay at home because air pollution had reached record levels. The following week the Mayor declared a 28-day state of environmental emergency. Pollution in Mexico City is made worse by the city's high altitude, because cold air traps pollutants. Pollution comes from a variety of sources:

- deforestation and erosion of land around the city creates dust;

- exhaust fumes from cars;

- heavy industries such as oil refining;

- inadequate refuse and sewage disposal.

Check yourself

EXAMINATION CHECKLIST

The facts and ideas you should know and understand after studying urban settlement are:

- The difference between urban growth and urbanisation.
- The growth and location of 'million' cities.
- The causes of urbanisation and urban growth.
- Counterurbanisation in MEDCs.
- Land use in a city in a MEDC.
- How to describe and interpret urban land use from an Ordnance Survey map extract.
- Urban planning and/or problems in cities in MEDCs.
- The case study on urban planning in Paris.
- Urban land use in a city in a LEDC.
- The case study on shanty towns in Nairobi.
- The problems associated with shanty towns and some solutions.

Key words

These are the key words. Tick them if you think you know what they mean. Otherwise check on them.

growth	mega cities	growth poles
urbanisation	primate cities	photochemical smog

EXAM PRACTICE

Sample Student's Answer and Examiner's Comments.

EXAMINER'S COMMENTS

i) and ii) His answers are correct. Extracting information from a table is a very common form of question at GCSE. Beware of making careless slips. Part i) is straightforward but part ii) demands more thought, partly because it is in the negative form. Notice the emphasis of the word 'not'. Part ii) is also testing interpretation and understanding. He recognised that the size of the population had no direct effect on the inhabitants' lives.

iii)

He gained one mark in this section for saying that places with a lot of money usually have a good quality of life. The word 'usually' is important here. He would not have gained credit if he had left it out. An abundance of money does not necessarily guarantee a good quality of life. Always be careful not to make sweeping statements. Qualify your answers if necessary with an appropriate example. The other two reasons given are incorrect. The effect of weather on food production and population do not really affect the quality of life in cities.

He recognised that with three marks available in this section, it is unlikely to be level marked.

---

1 Study the figure showing information on the quality of life in the world's ten largest cities.

	Population (millions)	Murders per 100,000	% of income spent on food	Persons per room	% of houses with water/ electricity	Tele- phones per 100 people	% of children secondary school	Infant deaths per 1,000 live births	Noise levels (1–10)	Traffic flow mph in rush hour	Quality of life score
Tokyo	28.7	1.4	18	0.9	100	44	97	6	4	28.0	81
Mexico City	19.4	27.8	41	1.9	94	6	62	36	6	8.0	38
New York	17.4	12.8	16	0.5	99	56	95	10	8	8.7	70
Sao Paulo	17.2	26.0	50	0.8	100	16	67	37	6	15.0	50
Osaka	16.8	1.7	18	0.8	98	42	97	5	4	22.4	81
Seoul	15.8	1.2	34	2.0	100	22	90	12	7	13.8	58
Moscow	13.2	7.0	33	1.3	100	39	100	20	6	31.5	64
Bombay	12.9	3.2	57	4.2	85	5	49	59	5	10.4	35
Calcutta	12.8	1.1	60	3.0	57	2	49	46	4	13.3	34
Buenos Aires	12.4	7.6	40	1.3	86	14	51	21	3	29.8	55

i) Which of the ten cities shown has the lowest quality of life score?

Calcutta (1 mark)

ii) Which column of information does NOT provide information on the quality of life in the world's ten largest cities?

Population (1 mark)

iii) Why does the quality of life between large cities vary so much? (3 marks)

Weather may be a reason why quality of life is bad, because the growing of food may be hampered if the weather is bad. With insufficient food, the quality of life drops. In another city though, food may not be a problem. Money is another reason why quality of life varies. Places with large amounts of money usually have a good quality of life. The population is another reason. Two cities may have equal amounts of money but one may have a greater population, so the amount of money per person is less. With less money, the quality of life probably falls. These are just three reasons why the quality of life varies.

iv)

He gained 4 out the possible 8 marks. His answer was Level 2, because he showed clear understanding. He referred to two improvements, in two different areas. First 'redeveloping the inner city areas so that people with more money may live there, improving the quality of life'. Second, he gives an example from a LEDC, i.e. Brazil. The last two sentences are also of Level 2 standard.

He reached the top of Level 2 because he referred to a particular place. However, he did not show detailed understanding. To reach Level 3 he would have to give details of a particular improvement scheme in an inner city area, e.g. Paris (see section 11.7). The question clearly states that reference should be made to 'places you have studied'.

There is a lot of irrelevant material in his answer, but he does not lose marks for this. However, by writing irrelevant things down, he may have lost valuable time.

In this section of the paper the candidate scored 7 out of a possible 13 marks which would have been a Grade C standard.

---

iv) 'Planners try to improve the quality of life in large cities.' Comment on this statement, with reference to places you have studied.

(8 marks)

In many places, the quality of life in large cities is not very good. The people who work in the cities (the people with the most money) tend to live outside of the city. As the city grows, out to where they live, they move further out, so they are not living in the city. The people with less money then move into these houses, which are, by this time, quite old. Planners try to improve the quality of the housing, by redeveloping the inner city areas so that people with more money may live there, improving the quality of life. They also build outer city council estates where the people who do not have enough money to buy their own houses live. They tend to have a lower quality of life, as they do not have much money. By planning these estates, out of the city, the people with a lower quality of life, live outside the city, improving the quality of life in the city. In places like Brazil, people who have very little money, tend to build their own shelters ('favelas') on the city edge in the hope of finding work in the city. This lowers the quality of life in the city, so the planners upgrade the favelas in the hope of improving the quality of life in the city. I would agree with this statement.

SEG, 1993

Questions to Answer

The answer to Question 2 can be found in Chapter 18.

2

a) i) Study the figure. There is a relationship between land value and distance from city centre. State this relationship.

ii) Give one reason for this relationship (4 marks)

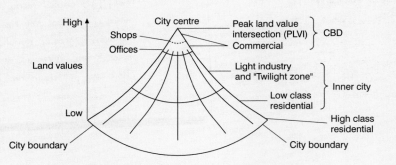

b) The actual pattern of urban zones is likely to be different from this model. For any city in a MEDC you have studied, describe the pattern of urban zones. Give reasons for the pattern you describe. A diagram may help your answer. (6 marks)

London, 1993

CHAPTER 12

AGRICULTURE

12.1 WHAT IS AGRICULTURE?

Agriculture is 'the control and use of plants and animals for the production of food, fibre and raw materials for industry'. Agriculture differs from other economic activities because:

- it relies heavily on the climate, soil, and the life cycles of plants and animals;
- it uses around 37 per cent of the Earth's surface, and is the greatest source of employment worldwide.

12.2 AGRICULTURAL SYSTEMS

A useful way of studying agriculture is to think of it as a system (Fig. 12.1) with inputs and outputs. Agricultural systems occur at different scales (e.g. countries, regions and farms) and can be either ecosystems (see chapter 7) or economic systems. A farm is a simplified ecosystem. Farms differ from natural ecosystems because:

- they concentrate on only those plants and animals which are useful to the farmer;
- they are not self-sustaining: crops and livestock leaving the farm remove nutrients from the system.

As an economic system a farm's input costs are labour, seed, fertiliser, pesticides, machinery, etc. Its outputs are the products it sells. The difference between inputs and outputs is the farmer's profit.

Figure 12.1 *The farm system.*

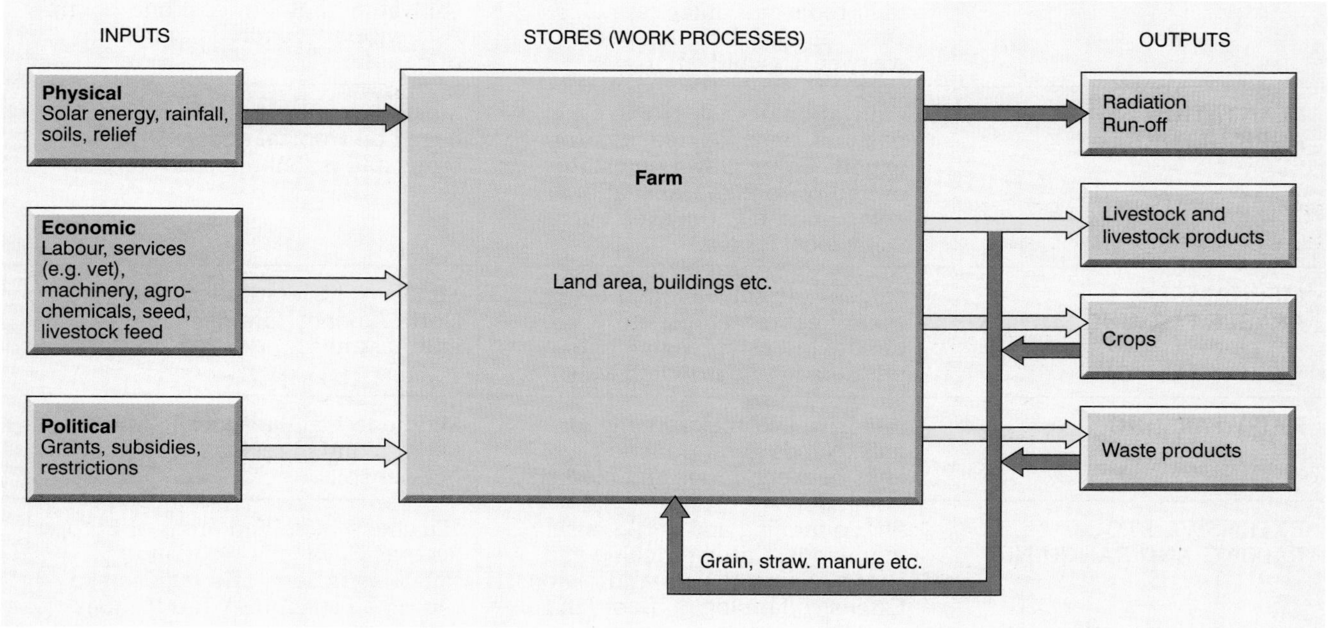

12.3 TYPES OF AGRICULTURE

We describe agriculture in one of three ways: by the dominant **enterprise**; by the intensity of production; and by the extent to which farming is for cash.

FARMING ENTERPRISES

The dominant enterprise refers to the crop(s) a farm produces (Table 12.1), e.g. dairy farms specialise in milk production; arable farms in cereals and root crops.

Table 12.1 Major world agricultural systems

TYPE	FEATURES	EXAMPLES
SHIFTING CULTIVATION	Temporary cultivation of small plots cleared in the rainforest. Simple technology, e.g. axes, hoes. Low population density. Plots are abandoned after harvest.	Tribal groups in rainforests of Amazonia, Central and West Africa and South-east Asia.
NOMADIC PASTORALISM	Constant movement of pastoralists and livestock in search of pasture and water. A response to meagre environment resources. Cattle kept in wetter areas. Sheep, goats and camels in drier parts. Extensive use of land.	Semi-arid areas such as fringes of the Sahara and Arabian deserts. Also movements between uplands and lowlands known as transhumance, e.g. Zagros mountains in Iran.
PEASANT AGRICULTURE	Sedentary cultivation around permanent settlements. High population density. Farmers may be tenants, sharecroppers or owner occupiers. They may own their tools and other capital. Often highly labour intensive, e.g. wet rice cultivation.	Easily the most important type of farming in LEDCs. Found throughout Asia, Africa and Latin America. May be dry farming (based on direct rainfall) or irrigation farming. Wet rice cultivation in South-east and South Asia support hundreds of millions of people.
PLANTATION AGRICULTURE	Cultivation of cash crops, e.g. palm oil, bananas, tea, etc. for export. Crops grown on estates owned by foreign transnational companies, e.g. Unilever, but using local labour.	Most plantation agriculture is based on tropical and sub-tropical crops and is found in LEDCs.
MECHANISED ARABLE FARMING	Large-scale cultivation of cereals, sugar beet, potatoes, etc. Capital intensive. High inputs per person of agro-chemicals.	Middle to high latitudes in North America (prairies), Europe and Australia.
DAIRY FARMING	Intensive livestock farming for milk. Needs good transport links between farms and markets.	Middle to high latitudes in MEDCs. Often found in regions of rainfall and heavier soils.
EXTENSIVE STOCK RAISING AND RANCHING	Sheep farming and cattle raising in uplands. Cattle ranching and sheep raising in semi-arid regions. Extensive farming on poor land with low outputs per hectare.	Hill sheep in upland areas of Europe such as Highlands, Scotland. Ranching in semi-arid regions like the High Plains, USA and Pampas, Argentina.

FARMING INTENSITY

The intensity of production concerns the actual farming methods. Intensive farming involves high inputs of labour, agro-chemicals, machinery, etc. per hectare (ha), with high outputs or yields per hectare, e.g. wet rice cultivation in South-east Asia (Fig. 12.2). Extensive farming is the opposite where low inputs per hectare give low outputs per hectare, e.g. hill sheep farming, cattle ranching.

COMMERCIAL AND NON-COMMERCIAL FARMING

Figure 12.2 *Intensive rice farming in Bali, Indonesia.*

In MEDCs nearly all farming is commercial and farmers grow crops and rear livestock for profit. In LEDCs non-commercial agriculture remains important. Farmers and their families grow crops mainly for their own consumption. Excess food may be sold at local markets. This self-sufficient farming is called **subsistence** agriculture.

12.4 DISTRIBUTION OF AGRICULTURE IN ENGLAND AND WALES

In England and Wales the geographical distribution of agriculture has a simple pattern (Fig. 12.3).

- Arable farming, growing crops such as wheat, barley, oil seed, sugar beet and potatoes, dominates the east.

- Dairy and beef cattle farming dominates western areas.

- Hill sheep farming dominates the upland areas of the North and West.

This pattern reflects differences in climate, soils and relief:

- In eastern and South-east England low precipitation and warm summers favour arable crops.

- In the west precipitation is too high for most arable crops but is ideal for grass, and therefore rearing sheep and cattle.

- The harsh physical environment of the uplands is suitable only for sheep farming and cattle rearing.

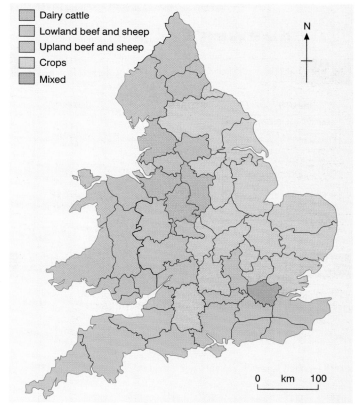

Dairy cattle
Lowland beef and sheep
Upland beef and sheep
Crops
Mixed

N

0 km 100

Figure 12.3 *Distribution of farming types in England and Wales, 1995*

197

Check yourself

QUESTIONS

Q1 With the aid of Figure 12.1 draw a systems diagram to show the main features of a typical arable farm.

Q2 Read the following paragraph:

Canada is a very important cereal producing country. Wheat is one of its main cereal crops and is grown by farmers using an extensive system of production. Outputs from the farms are huge because of the large cultivated area rather than because lots of money is spent on fertilisers and labour. These commercial farms sell much of their grain to markets overseas where it is ground into flour for making bread.

i) Wheat is a cereal crop. Which two of the following are also cereal crops?

Barley   Potatoes   Apples   Maize   Peas

ii) Output per worker is high, but output per area of farmland is fairly low in Canada. Which word in the paragraph describes this type of farming?

iii) Canadian wheat farmers produce huge amounts of grain for the market. Which word used in the paragraph describes this type of farming?

iv) Which type of world farming system describes Canadian wheat farming (use Table 12.1)?

Q3 Study Figure 6.9 (p. 95) and the map on p. 97 showing details of climate and relief in the British Isles.

i) Write a description of the climate in the South-west.

ii) Explain how the two maps can help to explain the farming pattern in Figure 12.3.

REMEMBER! Cover the answers if you want to.

ANSWERS

A1

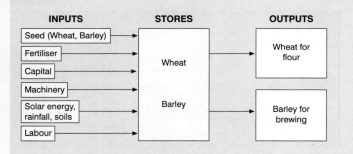

INPUTS → STORES → OUTPUTS

Seed (Wheat, Barley), Fertiliser, Capital, Machinery, Solar energy, rainfall, soils, Labour → Wheat, Barley → Wheat for flour, Barley for brewing

A2
i) Barley and maize.
ii) Extensive.
iii) Commercial.
iv) Mechanised arable farming.

TUTORIALS

T1 *A systems diagram is useful at a variety of scales. Systems diagrams can be drawn to represent the agriculture in a region, an area or even at a national or international scale.*

T2
i) *Other cereals grown in MEDCs include oats and rye. In LEDCs the most important cereals are rice and millet.*

ii) and iii) *Make sure that you understand these terms and the terms 'intensive' and 'subsistence' too. They are frequently asked in GCSE examinations. Intensive is the term that candidates frequently get wrong as they often think only in terms of the outputs. The high inputs are just as important.*

iv) *There are many different classifications of farming. You may find slightly different terms in other books.*

ANSWERS

A3 i) Wetter than 800 mm. Summers warmer then 15°C. Winters warmer than 6°C.

ii) The wet conditions in the west of England and Wales are good for grass, so these areas are suitable for livestock. The high relief in Wales means that farming centres around rough grazing of sheep on the hills, and fattening of cattle on the lower slopes. In the South-west of England, mild winters allow grass to grow all year, thus reducing the need for expensive fodder. The low relief means that there is a greater concentration of dairy rather than beef cattle. High rainfall is also important for dairy farming in North-west England. Eastern England is dominated by arable farming. The low eastern relief and flat land suits the use of machinery. Rainfall is low and there is plenty of sunshine for crops.

TUTORIALS

T3 i) *If you had difficulty with this question turn back to chapter 6. Look at which side of an isotherm the South-west lies and decide whether the temperature will be higher or lower than that particular isotherm. Adjacent isotherms should tell you which direction temperatures are going.*

ii) *Arable farming dominates south and east of the Tees–Exe line (p. 18, Figure 2.3), whereas to the north and west pastoral farming is more important. Remember that the pattern of farming in the British Isles is not only a reflection of physical factors, but of human factors too, e.g.quotas set by the EU.*

12.5 CASE STUDIES: FARMING SYSTEMS

SHIFTING CULTIVATION

Shifting cultivation is the traditional method of farming in the tropical rainforest (Fig. 12.4). It is a form of subsistence agriculture, often combined with hunting and gathering.

Figure 12.4 *Shifting cultivation is practised by the Penan people in Sarawak, South-east Asia.*

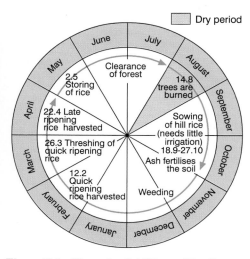

Figure 12.5 *The cycle of shifting cultivation.*

The main obstacle to farming in the rainforest is poor soils. Shifting cultivators, such as the Iban, get around this problem by making temporary forest clearings (Fig. 12.5). Initially rice yields are good. However, cropping and heavy rainfall soon reduce soil fertility, and weeds become a problem. After two years, the Iban make fresh clearings.

Shifting cultivation is **sustainable** agriculture. Providing the intervals between cultivation are long enough it does no long-term damage to the environment.

NOMADIC HERDING

Nomadic herding is a response to an environment which is too harsh for permanent cultivation. Nomadic herding is found in some sub-Arctic areas and high mountain ranges, but mostly it is found on the fringes of tropical deserts, e.g. southern Mauritania in West Africa. This is a semi-arid area where rainfall averages only 100 to 250 mm and is unpredictable. The nomadic farmers:

- keep cattle, camels, sheep and goats;
- are constantly on the move in search of water and pasture, apart from longer stays at summer and winter encampments;
- follow the seasonal rains moving northwards between July and October, and spending winter in the south;
- visit the same wells and pastures each year. A typical annual cycle might involve a journey of 800 kilometres.

Small supplies of water and pasture mean that a large area is needed to support each animal. Thus, output per hectare is small. The nomads exchange livestock products for things they cannot produce themselves with settled village cultivators. Like shifting cultivation, nomadic herding is also a sustainable farming system. It is a type of subsistence farming too.

COMMERCIAL ARABLE FARMING

Grange Farm in North Lincolnshire is situated in the arable core of eastern England (Fig. 12.6). The local climate, relief and soils are ideal for most arable crops (Table 12.2).

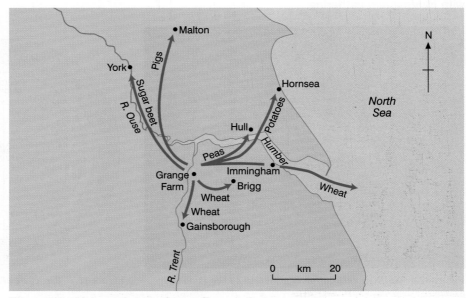

Figure 12.6 *Main markets for Grange Farm products.*

Table 12.2   Grange Farm: physical geography

Altitude (m)	Sea level
Mean July temperature (°C)	16.0
Mean annual precipitation (mm)	600–650
Growing season	March to November
Soils	Rich alluvial soils deposited by the River Trent.

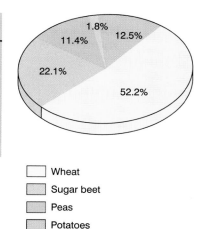

☐ Wheat
☐ Sugar beet
☐ Peas
☐ Potatoes
☐ Set–aside

Figure 12.7 *Land use: Grange Farm.*

Potatoes, sugar beet, wheat and peas are grown on an eight-year cycle or rotation (Fig. 12.7). No one crop is grown in the same field in successive years. This helps to maintain the soil's fertility and to control weeds and pests.

Agribusiness

Grange Farm is typical of arable farming in eastern England. It is:

- part of a large-scale enterprise of 7 farms covering nearly 2,500 ha;
- highly efficient and run on scientific and business principles – it's an **agribusiness;**
- highly mechanised, employing relatively few full-time workers.

Being part of a large business enterprise gives Grange Farm several advantages. The main one is that it can reduce the costs of its inputs. For instance, by buying fertiliser and pesticides (**agro-chemicals**) in bulk. We call these advantages of size **economies of scale.**

Crop yields at Grange Farm are high, partly because of favourable climate and soils, and partly because of high inputs of agro-chemicals and capital equipment, such as tractors, combines, grain driers, etc.

Markets

The choice of crops and methods of cultivation at Grange Farm are affected by EU farming policies and the location of markets. Several crops are grown under contract to large food companies such as Birds Eye and KP (Fig.12.6). Proximity to the farm is vital for Birds Eye, because their peas must be frozen within 40 minutes of picking.

HORTICULTURE IN THE NETHERLANDS

Horticulture is the intensive cultivation of high-value crops such as fruit, vegetables, and flowers. It is a leading branch of agriculture in the Netherlands (Fig. 12.8). Although horticulture occupies only 5 per cent of farmed land there, it accounts for 25 per cent of all Dutch agricultural exports. Its main markets are the EU and North America.

Horticulture is very different from other types of farming:

- it is both labour intensive and capital intensive;
- it relies on high-value crops;
- it relies on advanced technology, and scientific research and advisory services;
- co-operatives provide growers with credit for materials and expensive machinery. They also help to process and market the products.

A feature of Dutch horticulture is regional specialism, e.g. bulbs in Haalem, salad crops in Westland, ornamental trees in Boskoop.

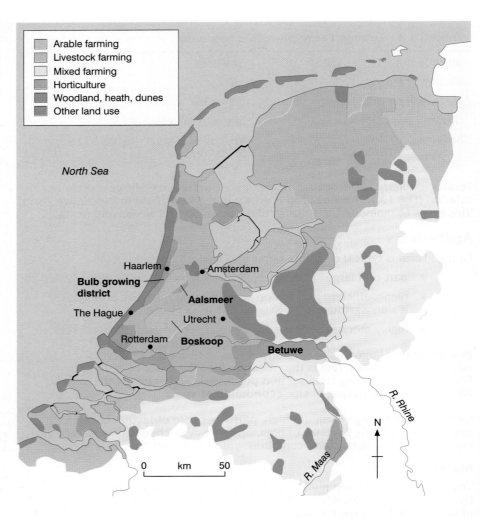

Figure 12.8
Distribution of types of agriculture in the Netherlands.

Arable farming
Livestock farming
Mixed farming
Horticulture
Woodland, heath, dunes
Other land use

North Sea

Haarlem
Amsterdam
Bulb growing district
Aalsmeer
The Hague
Utrecht
Rotterdam **Boskoop**
Betuwe

R. Rhine

N

R. Maas

0   km   50

Check yourself

QUESTIONS

Q1 In Sarawak:

i) Why is agriculture possible all year around?

ii) Why is shifting agriculture sustainable?

iii) Why will it become unsustainable, if there is an increase in population?

Q2 i) Give two reasons why the farmers of Mauritania are nomadic. Use an atlas to help you.

ii) What will happen to the nomads if they increase the number of cattle in their herds?

Q3 i) State one advantage of each of the following physical factors to Grange Farm (see pp. 200–1):

A mean July temperature of 16 °C.

B mean annual precipitation of 600–650 mm.

C rich alluvial soils deposited by the River Trent.

ii) What is an 'agribusiness'?

iii) What are the human factors influencing the agriculture at Grange Farm?

ANSWERS

A1 i) Temperatures and precipitation are high all year.
ii) There is no long-term damage to the environment provided there is time for forest vegetation to regenerate.
iii) An increase in population will shorten the time intervals between cultivation of different areas. The soil will not have time to regenerate.

A2 i) On average, there is less than 250 mm precipitation per year. The annual precipitation is very variable and very seasonal too. This means that there are long periods without any precipitation.
ii) The cattle will eat more pasture, so there will be less pasture per animal in future.

A3 i) A This temperature is quite high for the British Isles, which means that crops should grow well in summer.
B This is quite low for the British Isles. This suggests that the sunshine totals are likely to be higher, which is good for the crops. Also, lower precipitation discourages fungal diseases in crops.
C Rich alluvial soils are light and easily worked. This means that machinery works well. Also, the soils are fertile.
ii) Agribusiness is a highly efficient, large scale type of farming, which is run on scientific and business principles.
iii) Human factors include: large scale use of agro-chemicals and machinery requiring large inputs of capital; the relatively low importance of labour; the influence of political factors such as EU policies; contracts with large food companies.

TUTORIALS

T1 i) *High temperatures and high moisture are ideal growing conditions. These are the conditions in greenhouses.*
ii) *Some research shows that a minimum of 35 years is needed before the vegetation returns to its former condition.*
iii) *This is why there are very few parts of the world where farmers rely entirely on this form of agriculture.*

T2 i) *The unreliability of the precipitation is the greatest problem.*
ii) *This is a major cause of soil erosion and desertification (section 12.12)*

T3 i) A *It is important that crops grow well in summer, because the growing season is relatively short (March to November).*
B *800mm of precipitation is the upper limit for the growth of wheat. The warm summers encourage convectional precipitation, so there is a slight summer maximum of precipitation in eastern England. This is good for bringing grain to maturity just before the autumn harvest.*
C *Look back at chapter 3 to remind yourself about river deposition.*
ii) *You should know this term.*
iii) *These human factors are now more important than physical factors. The application of fertilisers and other chemicals can overcome any problems with soil (although they may create other environmental problems). EU policies are probably the greatest influence on Grange Farm.*

12.6 THE COMMON AGRICULTURAL POLICY (CAP)

The Common Agricultural Policy (CAP) covers the member states of the European Union (EU). Within the EU the CAP has an enormous influence on agriculture (Table 12.3). The crops farmers grow and the success of farming depends as much on the CAP as on environmental conditions.

Table 12.3   Aims of CAP
To ensure:
● a fair standard of living for farmers;
● reasonable prices for consumers;
● adequate food supplies;
● stable food prices;
● increases in productivity through technical progress.

The CAP includes the following measures:

- Intervention buying: to keep prices high the CAP buys produce which does not reach a minimum target price, thus giving farmers a guaranteed market for their crops.
- Grants: in less favoured, upland areas grants are given for each head of livestock to offset the higher costs of production. Grants are also available for farm modernisation, conservation, converting farmland to woodland, and investment in off-land enterprises such as tourism, golf courses, etc.
- Set-aside: farmers are paid not to cultivate or 'set-aside' a proportion of their arable land for at least five years. The land may be left fallow, planted with trees, or put to non-agricultural use. The aim of set-a-side is to reduce food surpluses.

12.7 IMPACT OF THE CAP ON THE ENVIRONMENT

The EU spends nearly half its annual budget on agriculture through the CAP. Although the CAP has been costly to the taxpayer, it has imposed even higher costs on the environment.

- In the UK alone, 377,000 km of hedgerow were destroyed between 1947 and 1990. Large machines needed for arable farming cannot operate efficiently in small fields, so hedgerows were removed to make larger fields (Fig. 12.9).
- Soils have been eroded gradually. Farmers have ploughed land on steep slopes to get EU subsidies for arable crops. The reliance on chemical fertilisers has reduced humus in soils, which helps to bind soil particles together and reduce the risk of erosion.
- Groundwater supplies are contaminated. Nitrates from chemical fertilisers have seeped into underground **aquifers**, threatening people's health. Nitrates encourage the growth of algae and bacteria in streams and rivers. This reduces oxygen levels in the water, killing insects and fish.
- The destruction of habitats (Fig. 12.10) and the use of agro-chemicals have caused serious declines in plant and wildlife. This has reduced **biodiversity**.

Figure 12.9 *The worst effects of the CAP have been felt in intensively farmed arable regions such as eastern England.*

The CAP, by giving subsidies and guaranteeing to buy everything that farmers produce, has encouraged:

- arable farmers to farm more intensively;
- arable farmers to cultivate more land;
- hill farmers to put more sheep on the fells causing overgrazing and soil erosion.

12.8 PROTECTING THE COUNTRYSIDE

Since the late 1980s, the EU has recognised that modern farming needs to be less intensive (Fig. 12.11). There needs to be a balance between the needs of farmers and conservation of the environment (Table 12.4).

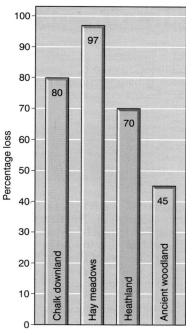

Figure 12.10 *Loss of wildlife habitats in the UK, 1994–5.*

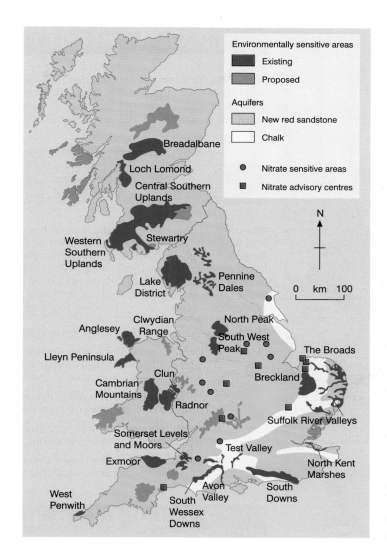

Figure 12.11 *Environmentally sensitive areas in the UK, 1997*

Table 12.4 EU farm policies and the environment

Reductions in output	Environmental policies
• In 1984 milk quotas were introduced to limit production in dairy farming.	• A hedgerow incentive scheme pays farmers to plant new hedges and improve existing ones.
• From 1995, wildlife is set to benefit when large areas of farmland are taken out of production.	• A farm woodland scheme gives annual payments for planting trees on arable and grassland.
• Since 1992 the level of intervention buying has been reduced. Gradually price support per tonne of crop is being replaced by fixed payments per hectare cultivated. This should reduce inputs of fertilisers and pesticides.	• Since 1987, 44 environmentally sensitive areas (ESAs) have been set up (Fig. 12.11). In these areas farmers are paid to farm using traditional methods. In return, farmers receive up to £400 per hectare per year.
	• In some areas farmers are paid compensation by the British government for farming with lower levels of nitrates.
	• Grants are available to farmers who convert farmland to amenities such as golf courses, camp sites, etc.

205

12.9 AGRICULTURAL CHANGE

In the last 40 years major changes have occurred in agriculture in both LEDCs and MEDCs. In LEDCs these changes have been in response to population growth. In MEDCs change has been influenced mostly by government policies. All of these changes have had a significant impact on the environment.

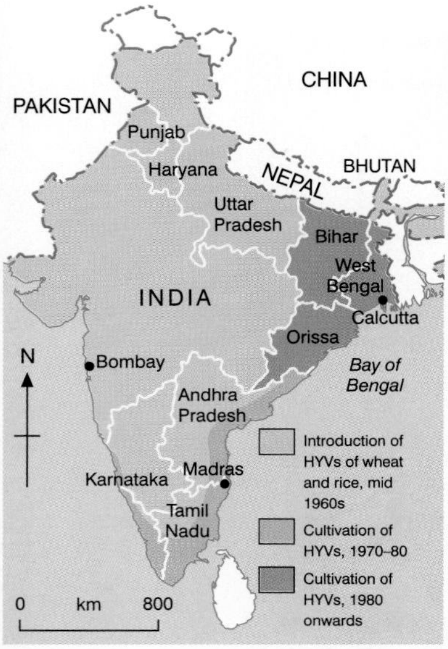

CASE STUDY: THE GREEN REVOLUTION

The development and introduction of high yielding varieties (HYVs) of rice and wheat into many LEDCs is known as the Green Revolution. The Green Revolution led to dramatic increases in food production in much of Asia and Latin America in the 1960s and 1970s. In Punjab and Haryana in northern India (Fig. 12.11) yields of rice and wheat tripled. By the end of the 1960s India was self sufficient in wheat and rice production. Also, the green revolution allowed farmers to use more of their land for other crops.

Despite its successes the Green Revolution has not benefited everyone.

- Even in India the Green Revolution has had little impact in areas such as Uttar Pradesh, Bihar and West Bengal. As a result 300–350 million people in India still have inadequate diets.
- HYVs of rice need regular irrigation but many of the poorest parts of the world depend on rain-fed agriculture.
- HYVs rely on chemical fertilisers and pesticides which many peasant farmers cannot afford.
- To benefit from the Green Revolution, farmers often need credit. This finance is rarely available to small farmers in LEDCs.

Figure 12.12 *The spread of the green revolution in India.*

12.10 LAND DEGRADATION IN LEDCs

Land degradation describes the decline in the quality and productivity of land which is the result of human action. It is a worldwide problem but is most serious in dryland areas in LEDCs. The most common types of land degradation are soil erosion, salt accumulation in soils, and deforestation (Table 12.5).

The fundamental causes of land degradation are population growth and poverty, which force farmers to over exploit the land. The damage to soils can be permanent and may destroy the resources on which production depends.

Table 12.5 Causes of land degradation

Deforestation	Removal of forest and woodland for new farmland, urban development, fuel wood and forestry. Lack of firewood forces farmers to burn dung, a valuable fertiliser.
Overgrazing	Destruction of vegetation cover by animals' grazing and trampling on soils, resulting in soil erosion by wind and water.
Overcultivation	Cultivation of the land without putting back sufficient nutrient fertilisers.
Salinisation	Surface accumulation of salts (and alkalines, e.g. sodium). Caused by over irrigation which leads to rising water tables.

12.12 SOIL EROSION IN THE UK

Soil erosion is the removal of top soil by water and wind faster than it can be replaced by natural processes. It is a worldwide problem. In the UK, soil erosion is most severe in eastern England.

TYPES OF SOIL EROSION

There are two main types of soil erosion: water erosion and wind erosion. Water erosion is the main problem in the UK. Rain runs off the surface of soil carrying with it particles of soil, as well as seeds and fertilisers. As the water runs off the land it erodes channels. The smaller channels can be easily ploughed-out. However, larger channels are more difficult to remove. The problem of water erosion is most severe on steeply sloping fields.

Wind erosion in the UK is a more localised problem. Light, sandy and peaty soils are most at risk, such as those in the Fens in Cambridgeshire and Lincolnshire. The most hazardous time is early spring, when there is little crop cover and soils begin to dry out (Fig. 12.13).

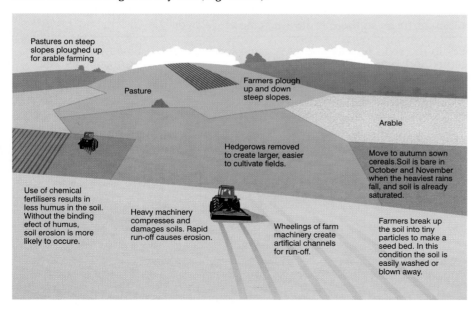

Pastures on steep slopes ploughed up for arable farming

Pasture

Farmers plough up and down steep slopes.

Arable

Hedgerows removed to create larger, easier to cultivate fields.

Move to autumn sown cereals. Soil is bare in October and November when the heaviest rains fall, and soil is already saturated.

Use of chemical fertilisers results in less humus in the soil. Without the binding efect of humus, soil erosion is more likely to occure.

Heavy machinery compresses and damages soils. Rapid run-off causes erosion.

Wheelings of farm machinery create artificial channels for run-off.

Farmers break up the soil into tiny particles to make a seed bed. In this condition the soil is easily washed or blown away.

Figure 12.13
A landscape vulnerable to soil erosion.

CAUSES OF SOIL EROSION

In nature, the soil is usually covered with vegetation. Plants provide a protective cover, against wind and rain, and their roots bind the soil together. Cultivation removes this cover, exposing the soil to erosion (Fig. 12.14).

THE EFFECTS OF SOIL EROSION

Figure 12.14 *Landscape at risk from soil erosion in Glenalmond, Perthshire*

Apart from the loss of soil, soil erosion decreases crop yields and increases the costs of production. Seeds may be washed or blown away; drains may be blocked by eroded soil; and crops may be sand-blasted by the wind. Off the farm, soil erosion increases the silt load of streams and rivers. Muddy waters can cause aquatic plants, insects and fish to disappear.

METHODS OF SOIL CONSERVATION

Farmers can take measures to protect soils from erosion. Some of these measures are listed in Table 12.6.

Table 12.6 Protecting soil from erosion in the UK

Contour ploughing	Ploughing up and down slopes provides channels for rainwater which increases erosion. Ploughing across slopes slows the movement of surface water and reduces erosion.
Use of machinery	Avoid cultivating wet soils with heavy machinery. Tractors compact wet soil, causing more rain to run-off the surface.
Cover crops	Keep fields partly covered with crops or crop residues left after harvest. These slow down the movement of surface water across fields and reduce wind erosion.
Wind breaks	Plant trees and hedges to protect the soil from strong winds. Sensitive crops, such as tomatoes, can be planted in rows between cereals.
Strip cropping	Grow several different crops in strips in the same field. The crops ripen at different times so there is always some crop cover.
Crop rotation	Build-up the soil's fertility and its organic content. Humus binds soil particles together and reduces the risk of erosion. Farmers should use organic as well as chemical fertilisers.
Convert arable to pasture	Pasture provides 100 per cent plant cover.

Check yourself

QUESTIONS

Q1

i) Look at Figure 12.10. What is the greatest loss by any one wildlife habitat?

ii) Why did so many hedgerows disappear between 1947 and 1990?

iii) What feature of the CAP has encouraged farmers to remove so many hedgerows?

iv) What features of Grange Farm (pp. 200–201) show the effects of the CAP?

ANSWERS

A1
i) 97%

ii) To make arable fields bigger. This allows more economic use of machinery and higher food production. The hedgerows are a source of weeds that could damage some crops.

iii) Guaranteed prices for agricultural products.

iv) Grange Farm is a combination of seven individual farms. The single, larger enterprise enjoys economies of scale; 1.8 per cent of the land has been set aside. The high income has been invested in more technology and agro-chemicals rather than labour.

TUTORIALS

T1
i) *A simple question, but one where many candidates make careless slips. The question asks for the amount of loss, not which habitat suffered the loss. Remember to state %.*

ii) *This is a particular problem in large parts of East Anglia.*

iii) *The removal of hedgerows damages the environment, because hedgerows are important habitats for a large number of plants, animals and birds.*

iv) *The CAP has been the main reason for the development of agribusiness.*

EXAMINATION CHECKLIST

The facts and ideas you should know and understand after studying agriculture are:

- A definition of agriculture.
- Why agriculture is the most important form of economic activity.
- The difference between a natural and an agricultural ecosystem.
- The ways in which agriculture can be subdivided into different types.
- The meaning of the terms: intensive, extensive, subsistence, commercial, and sustainable farming.
- How farming at different scales can be viewed as a system.
- An appreciation of the global distribution of agriculture.
- The physical factors influencing farming in the British Isles.
- The distribution of farming types in the British Isles.
- Case studies of shifting agriculture, nomadic herding, arable farming and intensive horticulture.
- Human factors influencing farming.
- Agricultural change in LEDCs and MEDCs.
- The positive and negative effects of the Green Revolution in LEDCs.
- The environmental impact of modern farming practices.
- The causes of soil erosion and possible preventative measures.

Key words

These are the key words. Tick them if you think you know what they mean. Otherwise check on them.

enterprise	agribusiness	aquifers
subsistence	agro-chemicals	biodiversity
sustainable	economies of scale	

EXAM PRACTICE

Sample Student's Answer and Examiner's Comments.

a) He reached Level 2 in this section. There are two distinct command words in the question. He is asked to state one way in which the cycle keeps farmers poor. He quotes the example "little money for improvement, machinery, irrigation and fertilisers". He also needs to explain how this links with other factors to keep the farmer poor. He correctly mentions a lack of profit in the second sentence. In the final sentence he mentions the effect of the low technological status of farmers in LEDCs. However, there is no real attempt to link these two statements together. He therefore gained 2 marks and reached only the bottom of Level 2.

To reach Level 3, he would have needed to give a clear explanation of one way in which the working of the cycle keeps farmers poor, with all links clearly identified. A Level 3 statement might be as follows: "The fact that some of the crop goes to the landowner as rent is a powerful disincentive to production. However hard the farmer works and however much he grows, he will retain only a relatively small amount. This may be just enough to feed his family. Without any surplus cash he is not in a position to improve his position.

b) Again he reaches the top of Level 2, gaining 5 marks. He shows clear understanding of modern agricultural practices and their effects on the environment with references to the removal of hedgerows and increasing use of fertilisers and pesticides.

However, he did not reach Level 3 because he was not specific enough. There are no specific examples or case studies mentioned in his answer. There was one mark available for naming the location of his example. In order to reach Level 3 the details given in his answer had to be specific to the area named. He did not mention an area, so the examiner was unable to tell

1 **a)** Study the diagram which summarises the vicious cycle of poverty in agriculture in developing countries. Answer the questions which follow.

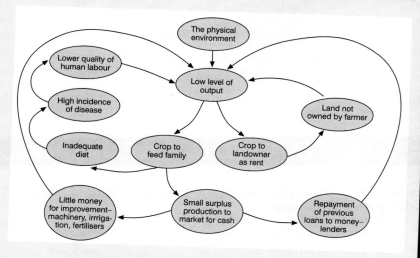

State and explain one way in which the working of the cycle keeps farmers poor. (4)

Little money for improvement, machinery, irrigation and fertilisers. This keeps the farmer poor because what he grows goes towards feeding his family, so he is not able to sell much for profit. Also, not having fertiliser means that crops are poor and small. Having no machinery means that only a small area can be farmed and it is very time consuming.

b) For any part of the world that you have studied, describe how modern agricultural practices, designed to increase productivity, can have harmful effects. (8)

Modern agricultural practices that are designed to increase productivity are having harmful effects on the land and on humans. Trees and hedges are being cleared to create larger fields so that larger crops can be grown. The clearance of hedgerows and trees means that wildlife lose their homes as well as their lives. The soil is not being held together and it is easily washed away and eroded. America is experiencing these problems. When strong winds blow they blow the dry soil away, creating dust storms.

NISEAC, 1993

whether the candidate was showing detailed knowledge and understanding, and therefore unable to award any more marks.

This candidate gained 7 out of the possible 12 marks. This was a higher tier paper aimed at candidates working towards a Grade A or B. This candidate would have gained a Grade C.

Also, many farmers are using harmful pesticides and fertilisers. The pesticides are being eaten by insects such as grubs and caterpillars. In turn birds are eating the insects and dying themselves. Water supplies and rivers are being contaminated by the chemicals in fertilisers. This is destroying the plants and fish that live in the rivers. With chemicals entering rivers directly or via leaching the fish and plants are being starved of oxygen which eventually kills them.

Questions to Answer

The answer to Question 2 can be found in Chapter 18.

2 a) Study Figure 12.3 which shows the types of farming in England and Wales, and the location map here.

i) What is arable farming? (1 mark)

ii) Describe the distribution of arable farming in England and Wales. (3 marks)

iii) State briefly how each of the following climatic factors can help an arable farmer.
A Summer warmth
B Winter frosts. (2 marks)

iv) State two human factors that can also affect arable farming. (2 marks)

v) Explain why some people may disagree with modern methods of arable farming. (3 marks)

b) For a type of farming that you have studied in a LEDC:

i) State briefly the type of farming and its location. (1 mark)

ii) Describe briefly the main features of the type of farming that you have chosen. (3 marks)

iii) Explain why this type of farming occurs in the location that you have studied. (5 marks)

SEG, 1996

INDUSTRY

13.1 TYPES OF ECONOMIC ACTIVITY

We divide economic activities into four main groups: **primary**, **secondary**, **tertiary** and **quaternary**.

- Primary activities produce food and raw materials, e.g. agriculture, fishing, mining.
- Secondary activities cover manufacturing industry.
- Tertiary activities include services such as retailing, tourism, healthcare and transport.
- Quaternary activities involve services which have high levels of decision-making such as administration, finance and research and development.

13.2 THE IMPORTANCE OF MANUFACTURING

Manufacturing industry varies in its importance from one country to another (Fig. 13.1).

- Manufacturing is least important in the world's poorest countries where it often employs less than 5 per cent of the working population.
- In MEDCs manufacturing usually employs at least 20 per cent of the working population. However, automation is reducing this figure.
- In countries undergoing rapid industrial development and in **newly industrialising countries** (NICs), manufacturing may employ up to 40 per cent of the working population.

Figure 13.1 *Global distribution of manufacturing industry employment.*

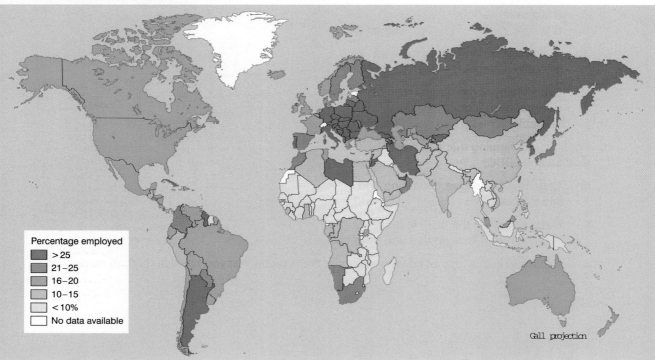

Percentage employed
- \> 25
- 21–25
- 16–20
- 10–15
- < 10%
- No data available

Gall projection

13.3 THE PURPOSE OF MANUFACTURING INDUSTRY

Manufacturing industries make products which have 'added value'. They do this in three ways: by refining raw materials; by processing materials into finished products; and by assembling components.

- Industries which refine raw materials are known as **processing industries**.

- Industries such as textiles, pottery and paper making fabricate materials to make finished products.

- **Assembly industries** purchase components and put them together to make new products, e.g. car industry and aircraft manufacture.

Check yourself

QUESTIONS

Q1 Study Figure 13.1. With the aid of an atlas:

i) Name the country in Africa which has more than 25% of its population employed in manufacturing.

ii) What percentage of the UK's population is employed in manufacturing?

iii) Describe the distribution of the countries which have more than 25% of their population employed in manufacturing.

Q2 What is meant by each of the following terms:

i) NIC?
ii) deindustrialisation?
iii) component?

REMEMBER! Cover the answers if you want to.

ANSWERS

A1
i) Libya.
ii) 16–20%.
iii) The major area is eastern Europe and the republics of the former Soviet Union. Libya is the only country in Africa and there are three countries in the Middle East. Only two countries in South America reach this percentage, Argentina being the largest.

TUTORIALS

T1
i) and ii) This type of questioning often forms the first part of a GCSE question. Remember to read the key carefully and write down exactly what is in it. For example, in part ii) the full range 16–20% must be given not a single figure. Figure 13.1 is an example of a choropleth map. You may be asked to shade a choropleth map. If you have to, there are two basic rules to remember. First, the maximum number of subdivisions should be five. Second, whether you use different densities of shading, or different colours, make sure that the higher values are represented by darker shades/colours.

iii) Use general locations like eastern Europe, but refer to individual countries as specific examples. Don't forget to mention exceptions.

A2
i) Newly Industrialising Countries.
ii) The shift from secondary to tertiary industries.
iii) A part which itself is the finished product of one industry which is 'assembled' with other parts to make a final product.

T2
i) *You can use the abbreviation NIC when referring to these countries in an examination. In a settlement question you can use CBD. However, as a general rule, do not use abbreviations.*
ii) *It is worth memorising an example of one country for the each of the stages: pre-industrial, industrial, post-industrial.*
iii) *This term is frequently examined in questions on industry. Make sure that you know the term 'assembly industry' too.*

13.4 THE LOCATION OF MANUFACTURING INDUSTRY

Many factors influence the location of manufacturing industry: raw materials, energy, labour, transport, markets, land, economies of scale and government policies.

THE UK IRON AND STEEL INDUSTRY

Iron and steel making is important to any modern industrial economy, because steel is an essential material for many other industries, e.g. car making, engineering.

There are three main operations in steel making:

- iron smelting in blast furnaces using iron ore, coke and limestone;
- refining iron to make steel;
- shaping steel into products, e.g. beams, rails.

In a modern integrated iron and steel works all three operations take place on the same site. This helps to reduce transport and fuel costs. Modern integrated works produce 3 to 4 million tonnes of steel a year and occupy an area of 6 to $7\,km^2$. These large plants keep the cost of making steel to a minimum by economies of scale.

Location of iron and steel making in the UK

Iron and steel making is a heavy industry. Its raw materials (coke, iron ore and limestone) are:

- heavy, bulky, and expensive to transport;
- low in value relative to their weight;
- undergo considerable weight loss in manufacturing.

These characteristics influence the industry's location. To keep transport costs down to a minimum, iron and steel making needs to be as close as possible to supplies of coke and ore.

- During the nineteenth century iron production favoured coalfield locations. Hence the development of the industry in South Wales, the West Midlands and central Scotland.

- In the late nineteenth and early twentieth centuries some works located close to sources of low-grade iron ore, e.g. Scunthorpe, Corby.

- Since 1945 steel making in the UK (and in most other MEDCs) has relied heavily on imported materials. New steelworks have located on the coast where bulk carriers bring in imported iron ore and coke (Fig. 13.2).

Redcar–Lackenby: a modern coastal steelworks

Redcar–Lackenby on Teesside is one of four integrated iron and steelworks in the UK. The availability of local materials gave the region its **initial advantage** (Fig. 13.3). Although local coke and iron ore are no longer used to make steel on Teesside, the deep water estuary of the River Tees has ensured the survival of steel making in the region. In 1976, a new iron works with its own deep water terminal, capable of handling 200,000-tonne bulk carriers was built at Redcar (Fig. 13.4).

The Tees estuary has other advantages for iron and steel making:

- large areas of flat, reclaimed land near the river mouth;

- the estuary is downwind from the main built-up area on Teesside, so that air pollution disperses over the North Sea;

- industrial processes can draw water from the estuary.

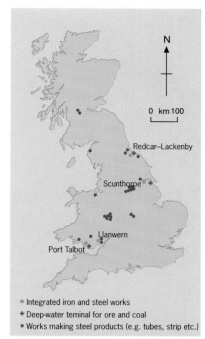

Figure 13.2 *Distribution of UK iron and steel industry.*

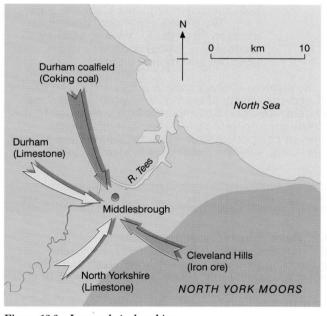

Figure 13.3 *Iron and steel making on Teesside.*

Figure 13.4 *Mouth of River Tees including Redcar–Lackenby.*

THE UK CAR INDUSTRY

Car manufacturing is an assembly industry. Components such as engines, radiators, and spark plugs are put together at an assembly plant. In 1997, huge **transnational corporations (TNCs)** dominated global car production, e.g. General Motors, Nissan. TNCs are so-called because they operate factories in many different countries.

215

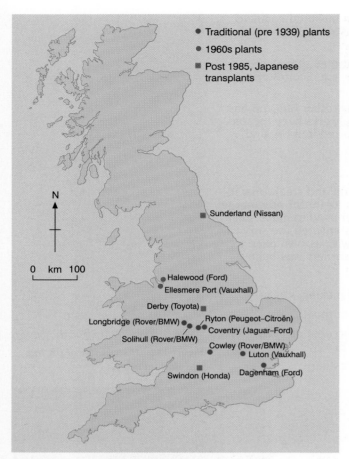

- Traditional (pre 1939) plants
- 1960s plants
- Post 1985, Japanese transplants

N

0   km   100

Sunderland (Nissan)

Halewood (Ford)
Ellesmere Port (Vauxhall)
Derby (Toyota)
Longbridge (Rover/BMW)
Ryton (Peugeot–Citroën)
Coventry (Jaguar–Ford)
Solihull (Rover/BMW)
Cowley (Rover/BMW)
Luton (Vauxhall)
Swindon (Honda)   Dagenham (Ford)

Figure 13.5   *Major UK car assembly plants, 1997*

The UK car industry employs over 200,000 people. In 1995, it produced exports worth £7 billion – second only to the electronics industry. Most of the world's leading car manufacturers have assembly plants in the UK (Fig. 13.5).

Distribution of the UK car industry

The following factors have influenced the location of the UK car industry: inertia; skilled labour; good communications; government assistance; and decisions by TNCs.

- The traditional centres for car making are the South-east and the West Midlands. The engineering skills needed to make bicycles and horse-drawn carriages years ago transferred to car making. These skills are less relevant now, but past investments in factories and machinery partly explains the survival of the car industry in these areas. This is an example of **industrial inertia**.

- In the early 1960s the government diverted new assembly plants to regions of high unemployment, such as North-west England and Central Scotland. In 1997, only two of these assembly plants survive (Fig. 13.5).

- Since 1984 three leading Japanese car makers – Nissan, Toyota and Honda – have built car assembly plants in the UK (Fig. 13.5). The UK is a convenient base from which to serve the EU market, and has relatively low labour costs, as well as generous government grants.

Three factors influenced the location of the Japanese plants within the UK: the quality of the local workforce; the quality of road communications; and the availability of large **greenfield** sites. Good transport links are essential to the Japanese companies because they operate just-in-time systems. These systems rely on the delivery of components just hours before they are needed. This reduces storage costs. Large sites are needed for modern factories.

UK HIGH-TECH INDUSTRIES

High-tech industries cover a wide range of activities, including micro-electronics, computers, telecommunications, biotechnology, and pharmaceuticals. One of the main differences between high-tech and other industries is the high level of investment in research and development (R & D).

Electronics is the leading branch of high-tech industry in the UK. The UK electronics industry is almost entirely controlled by foreign companies, e.g. IBM, Motorola, NEC, Compaq and Sony.

The location of high-tech industries in the UK

- Most high-tech products are high-value items relative to their weight and bulk. Thus transport costs are fairly low.

- Traditional locational factors such as supplies of materials and energy have little or no importance for the location of high-tech industries.

- With much greater freedom of location, high-tech industries are described as **footloose**.

Despite being footloose, most high-tech industries in the UK are concentrated in a handful of regions (Fig. 13.6). To understand why we need to know that there are two types high-tech enterprise:

- those which have important research and development functions and are concerned with developing new products;
- those which concentrate on routine production of standard products such as television tubes, desktop computers, silicon chips, etc.

The first type of high-tech industry is found mainly in southern England, especially along the M4 and M11 corridors between London and Bristol, and London and Cambridge (Fig. 13.6). The advantages of these locations are:

- access to a highly skilled workforce of scientists, technicians and managers;
- access to Heathrow international airport. High-tech is a global industry and most firms in the UK have their headquarters overseas;
- access to banks and other financial institutions in the City of London which invest in high-tech businesses;
- proximity to universities; aircraft, atomic energy and nuclear weapons research centres and other research institutions (Fig. 13.8).

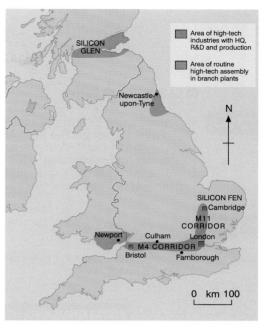

Figure 13.6 *Major concentrations of high-tech industry in the UK.*

Silicon Fen

Cambridge, or Silicon Fen, has developed as the UK's leading high-tech growth centre. It has over 600 high-tech firms which employ nearly 20,000 workers. In 1997, Microsoft decided to build its first research centre outside the USA in Cambridge. Cambridge owes its leading position in high-tech to:

- close links between university scientists and high-tech businesses (Fig. 13.7);
- the attractiveness of Cambridge as a place to live;
- good communications with London by road and rail.

Silicon Glen

High-tech enterprises concerned only with production (branch plants) do not require such highly skilled labour. In the UK high-tech branch plants have located mainly in assisted areas where government grants are available, the most popular regions being North-east England, Central Scotland and South Wales (Fig. 13.6).

Since the 1980s Central Scotland (Silicon Glen) has attracted huge investments from American, Japanese, Korean and Taiwanese TNCs. In 1997, Scotland's electronics exports were worth £8 billion a year. The industry employs 45,000 people; produces 35 per cent of all personal computers; and one-tenth of all silicon chips made in the EU.

In 1995, Chung Hwa invested £260 million in a plant near Motherwell to make television tubes. The plant is located on the site of the old Ravenscraig iron and steelworks which closed in 1992. The whole area is one of high unemployment. The site is part of a large Enterprise Zone (EZ). Here special tax concessions and simplified planning procedures operate to attract investment. This, together with other government incentives, and good road and rail links, persuaded Chung Hwa to locate in Central Scotland.

Figure 13.7 *The UK's first science park was established in Cambridge by one of the university colleges.*

217

Check yourself

QUESTIONS

Q1 i) Use Figure 13.4 to draw a labelled diagram to show the main features of the site of the Redcar–Lackenby integrated steelworks.

  ii) Use information in this chapter to add annotations to show the advantages of the site.

Q2 What is the meaning of each of the following terms:

TNC Industrial inertia Greenfield site Footloose industry?

Q3 Why is the car industry a good example of an assembly industry?

Q4 Why have many Japanese companies made the UK their European base?

REMEMBER! Cover the answers if you want to.

ANSWERS

A1 i) and ii)

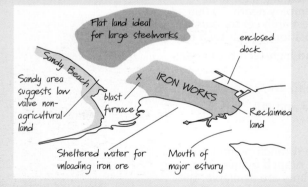

Flat land ideal for large steelworks
Sandy Beach
enclosed dock
Sandy area suggests low value non-agricultural land
X IRON WORKS
blast furnace
Reclaimed land
Sheltered water for unloading iron ore
Mouth of major estuary

A2 i) Transnational corporation.

A term used to describe the fact that some industries remain at their original sites even though the initial reasons or advantages of that site are no longer relevant.

A site that has not been used for industry before.

An industry which is not limited in its choice of location by traditional locational factors.

TUTORIALS

T1 *Drawing from a photograph is a skill that you may be tested on in a GCSE examination. Do not spend too long drawing minor detail. Sketch in the main features, trying to get the proportions roughly right. There will be relatively few marks for the quality of the drawing. The bulk of the marks will be for the labels and annotations. Remember the difference between a label and an annotation.*

T2 *The term multinational is still used for a TNC, but it is slowly being replaced.*

Some text books use the terms geographical inertia or historical momentum instead of industrial inertia.

The term 'brownfield site' is used to describe a new industrial enterprise built on the site of an old plant or factory that has been demolished.

ANSWERS

A3 A car is made by assembling large numbers of parts or components.

A4 The UK has relatively low labour costs and the Japanese factories qualified for generous government grants. The sites chosen have: plenty of land available; a skilled workforce; and good communications with the rest of the country and Europe. Having a factory within the EU means that the Japanese do not have to pay import tariffs to gain access to the EU market.

TUTORIALS

T3 *The early dominance of the car industry in the Midlands was because of its central position in the country. This made it easy to deliver components to the area. With improvements in transport, this is no longer relevant when considering the location of new car plants.*

T4 *Japanese, German, French, American and South Korean car manufacturers have all invested in the UK.*

13.5 GLOBALISATION

In the last 25 years new patterns of industrial location have appeared at global, national, regional and local scales.

Manufacturing industries are increasingly organised on a worldwide scale; so-called **globalisation**. One effect of globalisation has been the rapid growth of industry in LEDCs (Fig. 13.8). This **global shift** is set to continue. By 2010, China is expected to have the world's biggest economy.

Nowhere is the global shift of manufacturing more evident than in the Asian countries of the Pacific Rim. Industrialisation in this region began in Japan, in the 1950s. In the 1970s and 1980s, Japan was followed by four other NICs: South Korea, Taiwan, Singapore and Hong Kong.

EXPLAINING GLOBALISATION

Globalisation has occurred for the following reasons:

- giant TNCs can employ people, make products and buy services where they are cheapest;
- it gives TNCs access to the largest of all markets: the world;
- the world market allows economies of scale and makes TNCs more competitive;
- by locating overseas TNCs can avoid trade restrictions. Foreign investment in the UK avoids trade barriers which protect the EU market.

Globalisation has been made possible by huge advances in communications, e.g. satellites and computer networks.

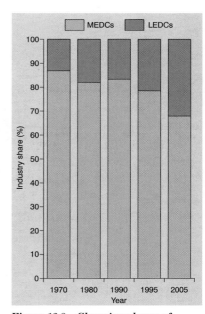

Figure 13.8 *Changing shares of global manufacturing, 1970–2005*

13.6 CHANGES AT THE NATIONAL SCALE: SOUTH KOREA

Since the early 1970s rapid industrialisation has made South Korea one of the fastest developing countries in Asia. The South Korean government planned the country's industrial development.

- It protected its own industries from foreign imports.
- Using subsidies and cheap loans it encouraged those industries making goods for export.
- It told firms what to make and where to build factories. Between 1973 and 1979 the government promoted heavy industries such as metals, machinery, and shipbuilding.

By the mid-1980s South Korea began to move away from heavy industries to cars, and high-tech products. A similar trend has occurred in other NICs. As skill levels improve and labour costs rise, labour-intensive industries have moved to neighbouring LEDCs with lower wage costs, such as Indonesia, Philippines, Thailand and Vietnam.

South Korean manufacturing industry is dominated by four huge companies or chaebols. Between them, Samsung, Hyundai, Daewoo and LG produce 60 per cent of the country's exports. The chaebols are involved in a wide range of industries. Samsung makes cars, semi-conductors, electronic watches, computers, video recorders, heavy machinery, ships, petrochemicals and medical equipment!

OVERSEAS INVESTMENT

In the 1990s South Korea's chaebols began to globalise. (Table 13.1). The four leading chaebols started to invest heavily in the USA and Europe, as well as in East Asia. The UK was the most popular location in Europe. In 1994 Samsung invested £450 million in electronics on Teesside.

Table 13.1 Globalisation of South Korean chaebols

CHAEBOL	INDUSTRY	COUNTRIES INVESTED IN
Daewoo	Vehicle assembly	China, India, Poland, Austria, Romania
Hyundai	Electronics, memory chips	USA
LG	Consumer electronics	Indonesia, UK, USA
Samsung	TV tubes	Germany, Mexico
	Silicon chips, computers	USA
	Consumer electronics, heavy machinery	UK
	Electronics	China

13.7 REGIONAL INDUSTRIAL CHANGE: NORTH-EAST ENGLAND

DECLINING HEAVY INDUSTRIES

In the nineteenth century North-east England was a prosperous industrial region, based on coal mining, steel making, shipbuilding, engineering and chemicals. For most of the twentieth century these industries have been in decline, resulting in high unemployment, and steady out-migration.

Yet as late as 1980 the North-east's traditional heavy industries remained prominent. County Durham still had 22 collieries, and 25,000 people worked in the iron and steel industry on Teesside and at Consett. Finally, in the 1980s, these industries collapsed.

This abrupt decline of the region's traditional industries is an example of **deindustrialisation**. Altogether 160,000 jobs in manufacturing disappeared in the North-east between 1970 and 1990.

REINDUSTRIALISATION

By the mid-1990s, the North-east had shed its old image of smokestacks, pit heaps and shipyards. In its place came the new North-east: a region of electronics, motor vehicles and modern business parks (Fig. 13.9).

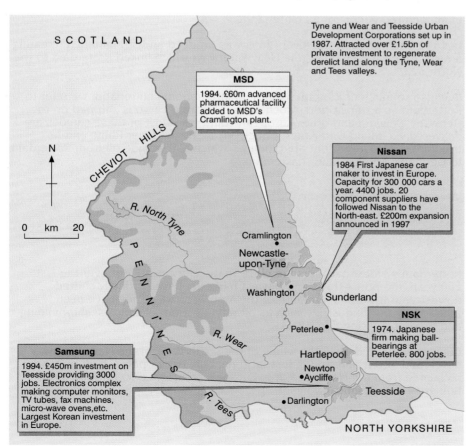

Tyne and Wear and Teesside Urban Development Corporations set up in 1987. Attracted over £1.5bn of private investment to regenerate derelict land along the Tyne, Wear and Tees valleys.

MSD
1994. £60m advanced pharmaceutical facility added to MSD's Cramlington plant.

Nissan
1984 First Japanese car maker to invest in Europe. Capacity for 300 000 cars a year. 4400 jobs. 20 component suppliers have followed Nissan to the North-east. £200m expansion announced in 1997

NSK
1974. Japanese firm making ball-bearings at Peterlee. 800 jobs.

Samsung
1994. £450m investment on Teesside providing 3000 jobs. Electronics complex making computer monitors, TV tubes, fax machines, micro-wave ovens, etc. Largest Korean investment in Europe.

SCOTLAND

CHEVIOT HILLS

R. North Tyne

PENNINES

Cramlington

Newcastle-upon-Tyne

Washington

Sunderland

Peterlee

R. Wear

Hartlepool

Newton Aycliffe

Darlington

R. Tees

Teesside

NORTH YORKSHIRE

Figure 13.9
The new North-east: major investments.

These changes came about through foreign **inward investment**. By 1995, 380 foreign companies were operating in the North-east. In 1997, the region was the biggest centre for investment in Europe by Pacific Rim companies. It all started in 1986 when Nissan, the Japanese car maker, opened its first European assembly plant at Sunderland. Nissan's success encouraged others. Companies were attracted by the region's skilled workforce; low labour costs; good communications; government grants and regional assistance (Fig. 13.10).

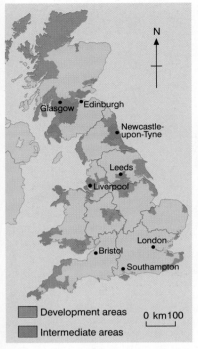

Figure 13.10 *Assisted areas in Britain.*

13.8 REGIONAL INDUSTRIAL CHANGE: ROTTERDAM

Rotterdam in the Netherlands is the world's number one port. In 1994, it handled nearly 300 million tonnes of cargo. More than three-quarters of this trade was bulk cargo such as crude oil, coal, iron ore and grain.

GROWTH OF THE PORT

Rotterdam owes its development as a port to its favourable geographical situation. Located near the mouths of two great rivers – the Rhine and Meuse (or Maas) – Rotterdam has unrivalled access to a large part of central Europe. We call this inland trade area the port's **hinterland**.

In the second half of the nineteenth century industrialisation began to take hold in Europe. Coalfield regions such as the Ruhr and Saarland in Germany, Lorraine in eastern France, and South Belgium grew rapidly. Rotterdam's trade expanded as it began to import the raw materials and export the manufactured goods for its hinterland.

In 1872, the mouth of the River Rhine was dredged and straightened, creating a new deep water channel (the New Waterway) which linked Rotterdam to the North Sea.

Because so much of its trade is with its international hinterland, we refer to Rotterdam as a transit port. Much of the imported cargo is shipped on to Germany, Belgium and other European countries. Most of these cargoes are delivered via inland waterways, principally along the River Rhine and its tributaries. Also important are pipelines which carry crude oil from Rotterdam to Germany, Antwerp and Amsterdam.

CHANGING LOCATION OF PORT ACTIVITIES

Rotterdam's oldest harbours are close to the city centre. But over the last 100 years the port's trade and busiest harbours have gradually shifted downstream towards the mouth of the New Waterway. They have been followed by port industries such as oil refining, petrochemicals, shipbuilding and food processing (Fig. 13.11).

Between 1955 and 1975 the whole of the south bank of the New Waterway developed into a port and industrial zone. This is Europoort: built on land reclaimed from the North Sea, it is Europe's greatest concentration of oil refineries and chemical works.

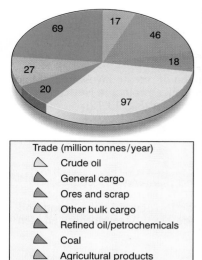

Trade (million tonnes/year)

△ Crude oil
△ General cargo
△ Ores and scrap
△ Other bulk cargo
◣ Refined oil/petrochemicals
◣ Coal
◣ Agricultural products

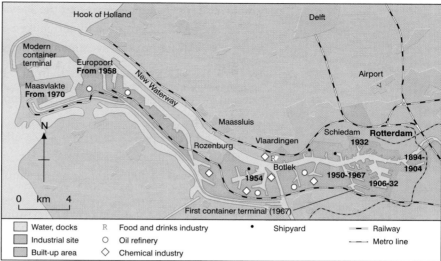

Water, docks	R	Food and drinks industry	•	Shipyard	——	Railway
Industrial site	O	Oil refinery			——	Metro line
Built-up area	◇	Chemical industry				

Figure 13.11 *Rotterdam, Europoort and trade*

The downstream movement of Rotterdam's port activities and industries has occurred for three reasons:

- a lack of space in the old, inner harbours;

- newer, larger ships need deeper water;

- new methods of cargo handling, e.g. containers, bulk cargoes, require more storage space.

THE CONTAINER REVOLUTION

General cargoes are mainly transported in standard-sized metal boxes or containers. The first container terminal was built at Eemshaven in 1967. A much larger terminal was built in Europoort in the 1980s. Ships carrying up to 4,000 containers can berth there. The advantages of containers are:

- cargoes can be loaded and unloaded faster;

- containers are a standard size and can be transferred easily between barges, trains and trucks;

- container handling is highly mechanised;

- cargoes are more secure and there are fewer spillages;

- goods stored inside metal containers require less packaging, reducing costs.

13.9 LOCAL INDUSTRIAL CHANGE

UDCS AND EZS IN NORTH-EAST ENGLAND

Deindustrialisation in the 1980s created a massive dereliction problem in the lower Tyne, Wear and Tees valleys. The government tackled this problem by setting up two urban development corporations (UDCs) and two enterprise zones (EZs).

The task of the Tyne-and-Wear and the Teesside UDCs was to:

- reclaim derelict land and make new sites for industry;
- attract private investment to regenerate these areas.

By 1995, the UDCs attracted more than £1.5 billion of private investment. Major schemes included the East Quayside leisure and office project in Newcastle; the Sunderland enterprise park; and the Hartlepool marina (Fig. 13.12).

The North-east's two EZs also cover derelict riverside sites in Newcastle and Sunderland. For a period of 10 years EZs offer:

- special tax allowances;
- fewer planning controls and simplified planning procedures.

Like UDCs, EZs aim to regenerate areas by attracting new manufacturing and service industries. The Chung Hwa television tube plant near Motherwell is in an EZ.

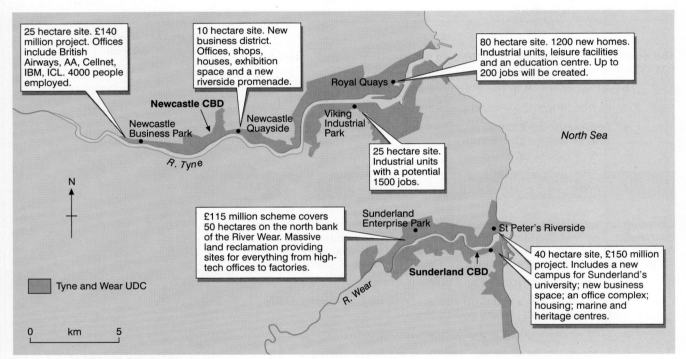

Figure 13.12 *Regeneration of the Tyne-and-Wear riverbanks.*

THE URBAN–RURAL SHIFT OF INDUSTRY

In the nineteenth century inner city locations had definite advantages for manufacturing industries:

- workers lived nearby;
- cities were highly accessible via roads, railways and docks.

Since 1960 manufacturing industry in inner city areas has declined sharply in most MEDCs. At the same time employment in manufacturing in many small towns and rural areas has increased. We call this trend the **urban–rural shift** of industry. We can explain this change through 'push' and 'pull' factors (Table 13.2).

Table 13.2 The urban–rural shift: push and pull factors

	Push factors (inner city)	Pull factors (small towns/rural areas)
Space	Sites in inner city areas are cramped.	Small towns and rural areas are more spacious.
Cost	Land, rent, taxes high.	Land, rent, taxes usually cheaper.
Access	Narrow roads and traffic congestion make access difficult for deliveries, employees.	Good access to motorways, A-roads, and by-passes.
Buildings	Factories are often multi-storey.	Single storey factories are more suitable for modern production lines. Industrial estates and business parks.
Environment	Often run down and derelict.	Attractive, purpose-built estates on greenfield sites. Levels of crime lower.

Check yourself

QUESTIONS

Q1 What is meant by each of the following terms:

globalisation   global shift   smokestack?

Q2 What advantages does South Korea have for industrialisation?

Q3 Why is South Korea likely to face increasing competition from other countries in future?

REMEMBER! Cover the answers if you want to.

ANSWERS

A1 Industry organised on a worldwide scale.

The movement of manufacturing industry from MEDCs to LEDCs.

The heavy basic industries such as coal mining, shipbuilding and chemicals.

A2 Originally the main advantage was cheap labour. However, the South Korean Government has planned the country's industrial development by protecting home industries from foreign imports, and using subsidies and grants.

A3 Costs in South Korea have risen, so the country has lost its competitiveness compared to other, less developed Asian countries.

TUTORIALS

T1 Sections testing the concept of globalisation and global shift are normally found at the end of questions. This is because they require an understanding of industry in a worldwide context.

T2 NICs are often referred to as the Asian Tigers. They all follow very similar industrialisation policies.

T3 The four original 'Tigers' were South Korea, Singapore, Hong Kong and Taiwan. The newly emerging industrial powers are Malaysia, Thailand, Indonesia and the Philippines.

EXAMINATION CHECKLIST

The facts and ideas you should know and understand after studying industry are:

- Economic activities can be subdivided into four groups: primary, secondary, tertiary and quaternary.
- The importance of manufacturing industries varies from one country to another.
- Manufacturing industries make products by refining raw materials, by fabricating processed materials and by assembling components.
- The importance of manufacturing changes as a country moves from the pre-industrial phase through an industrial phase and into the post-industrial phase.
- The location of industry is influenced by a variety of factors.
- The locational factors which influence the iron and steel industry.
- The car industry is an assembly industry.
- High tech industries are footloose and have fewer locational constraints than other industries.
- Globalisation involves a major global shift of manufacturing to the NICs in eastern Asia and to LEDCs.
- The globalisation of industry is associated with the emergence of TNCs.
- South Korea has been one of the main beneficiaries of this shift in industrial power.
- Some traditional industrial areas such as North-east England have undergone a dramatic change in the nature of their economies.
- Overseas investment has been instrumental in many recent industrial changes.
- Government policy and planning is now one of the most important factors influencing industrial location.
- The last quarter of the twentieth century has seen an urban–rural shift of industry.

Key words

These are the key words. Tick them if you think you know what they mean. Otherwise check on them.

primary	industrial inertia
secondary	greenfield site
tertiary	footloose
quaternary	globalisation
newly industrialising countries (NICs)	global shift
processing industries.	deindustrialisation
assembly industries	inward investment
initial advantage	hinterland
transnational corporations (TNCs)	urban-rural shift

EXAM PRACTICE

Sample Student's Answer and Examiner's Comments.

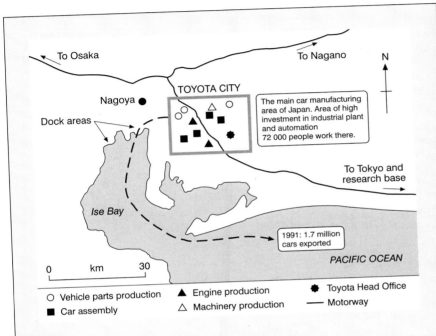

To Osaka
To Nagano
N

TOYOTA CITY

Nagoya ●

Dock areas

The main car manufacturing area of Japan. Area of high investment in industrial plant and automation 72 000 people work there.

Ise Bay

To Tokyo and research base

1991: 1.7 million cars exported

PACIFIC OCEAN

0   km   30

○ Vehicle parts production   ▲ Engine production   ✱ Toyota Head Office
■ Car assembly   △ Machinery production   — Motorway

1 Study the map of Toyota City. Using this information:

a) Explain how different types of <u>capital investment</u> (e.g. money spent on industrial buildings) have encouraged industry there.   (4 marks)

Infrastructure would have a great effect. Toyota City is a meeting point of motorways so access for trading is good for the firms. I also notice a research base is shown. Research and knowledge is used greatly in skilled industry, so this will also have been a positive point. Because Toyota City has been built in the centre it means that communications are good, e.g. between the head office, production of parts and the car assembly. This means that different parts of the car manufacturing industry can communicate easily. It also means that the transportation of the vehicle parts to where the car is assembled can be done cheaply and quickly.

b) Some areas have experienced economic growth (e.g. new factories, offices, jobs).
For an area you have studied, describe the economic growth which is taking place and explain why it is happening.   (6 marks)

Name of area: M4 corridor SE England.
Along the M4 various skilled industries have begun to set up and develop into business parks. There are various reasons for this. I think that the main reason is that the M4 motorway is a link to the many other motorways around the country. This makes communications good. It is also near to London where there is an

EXAMINER'S COMMENTS

a) *She gains full marks. This part is level marked but with only four marks the top mark is a Level 2 answer. The information has to be taken from the diagram, so she is not being tested on her knowledge of a case study. This candidate has recognised that the question asks for explanations and she supplies these by justifying the importance of the infrastructure and research base. She shows understanding of the assembly nature of the car industry and that site accessibility is important.*

She shows good examination technique by underlining 'capital investment' in the question. This is the key to the question and ensures that her answer sticks to the point. This technique is a useful habit to get into. The key words will include the command word, e.g. describe, explain, briefly, fully. The second key word will be the subject of the question, e.g. 'capital investment'.

She also makes good use of geographical terminology. The use of the word 'infrastructure' will help her SPaG mark.

b) *She reaches the top of Level 3 and gains full marks. Her example is very precise. Throughout her answer she shows that she understands the factors that are responsible for industrial growth in this area, i.e. good communications, proximity of towns, research centres and universities. This demonstrates she has clear understanding and enables her to reach the top of Level 2. She reaches the top of Level 3 by referring to actual examples relevant to the M4 corridor. The major towns Bristol, Swindon and London are named, as are examples of firms in the area.*

airport for trading abroad. Along the M4 a railway can be found which again could be used for trading or more likely the supply of labour. The M4 corridor is situated on flat land enabling firms to build there. It is surrounded by many major towns and cities, e.g. Bristol, Swindon and London. This is helpful for both the labour supply and for markets to trade in.

The final factor which I think is important is the research and knowledge which can be found in the area. There are many universities and research labs nearby which supply knowledge and skilled workers. Examples of industries set up there are Rolls Royce and British Aerospace.

c) **Industries sometimes decline (become less important). Using examples you have studied, explain why this happens.**

An example I have studied is South Wales. Here the coal and steel industries have closed down. One of the main reasons is fall in demand. Coal and steel are not as popular now so there is not as great a need for them. The second factor which I believe influences this, is the development of new sources, e.g. aluminium has been found to be light, easy to work with and free from rust. More industries are using aluminium, so not as much steel is needed. Technology is another factor. More machines (automation, etc.) do the work that labourers used to do more easily and more quickly, although this also means that more people are unemployed. A lack of natural resources used in the coal and steel industry, e.g. the coal itself, is also responsible. South Wales is rapidly running out of coal, so there is hardly any coal to mine. What is left is deep in the earth and very expensive to reach, making it not worth while for firms to mine. All this leads to decline in industry.

SEG, 1996

c) Again, she achieves full marks. She shows detailed understanding by relating general reasons for decline to specific examples within South Wales. These are the fall in demand for coal, iron and steel, associated with the development of new materials such as aluminium; increased automation; and exhaustion of local raw materials.

Notice that she has recognised the question asks for examples, and refers to more than one industry.

Questions to Answer

The answer to Question 2 can be found in Chapter 18.

2 There has been a shift of employment in North-east England from shipbuilding to car assembly.

i) What is the meaning of an 'assembly industry'? (1 mark)

ii) Why is it important for an assembly industry to have other industries near by? (1 mark)

iii) Suggest how the shift from the shipbuilding industry around Sunderland to the manufacturing car industry around Washington may have affected this part of the North-east England. (4 marks)

SEG, 1996

14.1 WHAT IS TOURISM?

Tourism is one way of spending leisure time. Tourism involves visiting places and staying away from home for at least one night. In the last 50 years the demand for tourism has soared. As a result tourism employs 120 million people worldwide and is one of the world's fastest growing industries (Fig. 14.1).

14.2 RESOURCES FOR TOURISM

Tourism depends on both natural and human resources.

- Natural resources include: warm, sunny climates; sandy beaches; mountain scenery; snow, etc.
- Human resources include local customs and culture; architecture; museums; night life, etc.

All of these resources provide opportunities for recreation and leisure.

14.3 TOURISM IN THE UK

Mass tourism in the UK began in the second half of the nineteenth century. Victorian seaside resorts such as Weston-super-Mare and Skegness grew rapidly to serve expanding industrial towns and cities. Two things made this possible.

- The development of the railways which provided cheap, rapid transport.
- The introduction of paid holidays.

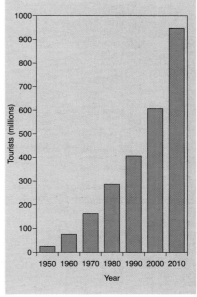

Figure 14.1 *Growth of international tourism, 1950–2010.*

CASE STUDY: BLACKPOOL

Blackpool is the biggest and most popular seaside resort in the UK. In 1995, 17 million visitors spent nearly £450 million in the resort, where 30,000 jobs depend on the tourism industry.

Until the mid-nineteenth century Blackpool was little more than a village, visited only by the well-off, who were attracted by the 'health-giving properties' of sea water and sea air. Between 1846 and 1900 Blackpool experienced massive changes.

- In 1846 the railway connected Blackpool to the fast-growing industrial towns of northern England. Almost overnight Blackpool became the first 'working class' resort, providing recreation for thousands of factory workers from Lancashire and Yorkshire.
- As Blackpool's popularity increased, so the town expanded (Fig. 14.2). Rows of terrace boarding houses were built. Soon the town sprawled in an untidy ribbon along the sea front, from Fleetwood in the north to Lytham St Annes in the south.
- By 1890 Blackpool's attractions drew over one million visitors a year. The town offered all manner of entertainments: amusement arcades, open-air dancing, music hall, firework displays and even steamer trips to the Isle of Man.

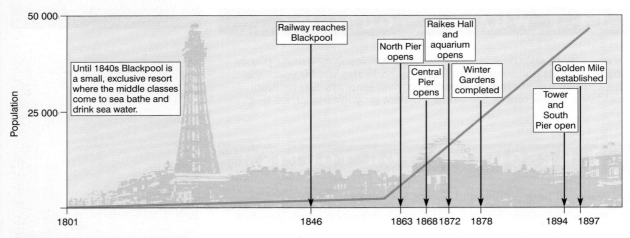

Figure 14.2 *Development of visitor attractions in Blackpool, 1801–1901.*

Declining popularity of British seaside resorts

Despite earlier successes, British seaside resorts have been in decline for many years. Cheap package holidays to the Mediterranean and Caribbean have eroded their popularity. Like other resorts, Blackpool now relies more on day trippers and short-break visits rather than long-stay visitors. Yet despite the general decline of British seaside resorts, Blackpool has retained its popularity. There are several reasons for this:

- Blackpool has continued to invest in new entertainments, e.g. the Pepsi Max roller coaster.
- Blackpool's illuminations help to extend the tourist season well into October.
- Blackpool has worked hard to capture the conference trade, which helps to fill guest houses and hotels out of season.
- Blackpool is easily accessible by motorway (Fig. 14.3).
- There is a population of nearly 10 million people within 90 minutes journey time.

Figure 14.3 *Relative location of Blackpool.*

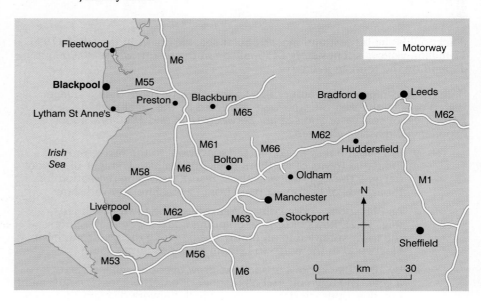

UK TOURISTS ABROAD

Foreign tourism has grown dramatically in the last 35 years or so. In 1995, Britons spent £14.5 billion on overseas holidays, with France, Spain and the USA being the most popular destinations. This has happened because:

- people have longer, paid holidays;
- they are generally better-off;
- there have been improvements in transport, particularly cheap air travel.

TOURISTS VISITING THE UK

Today, tourism in the UK is a huge industry (Fig. 14.4).

- In 1995, the UK received 23.5 million foreign visitors.
- The UK tourism industry is worth £37 billion a year.
- Tourism employs more than 1.5 million people (7 per cent of all employment) in hotels, restaurants, pubs, travel agencies, museums, sports centres, etc.
- Within a few years tourism will be the UK's biggest industry.

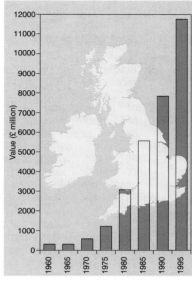

Figure 14.4 *Growth of foreign tourism in the UK, 1960–95.*

Check yourself

QUESTIONS

Q1 Name three types of tourist areas.

Q2 With the help of Figure 14.3 explain why Blackpool's situation favoured its growth as a major holiday resort.

Q3 Why is the development of tourism often so important for an area's economy?

REMEMBER! Cover the answers if you want to.

ANSWERS

A1 The three main types of areas are coastal areas, mountainous areas and cities.

TUTORIALS

T1 *Try to think of some examples of these types of areas. London attracts millions of tourists, and there are many other seaside resorts in the UK apart from Blackpool. Mountainous areas such as the Lake District and the Scottish Highlands attract tourists all year around.*

ANSWERS

A2 Blackpool lies on the coast. It has good motorway connections to a number of large centres of population. The conurbations of Liverpool and Merseyside, Greater Manchester and the West Yorkshire area around Leeds and Bradford are within 90 kilometres. The M55 provides direct access to the M6, the main north–south communication link. The M62 is the main east–west link . There are other motorways which make Blackpool accessible to people.

A3 The growth of tourism encourages the development of the infrastructure, particularly transport and communications. The development of tourist services/facilities provides employment. Local residents can use these services/facilities too. Money spent by tourists supports the local economy. Shops and services not directly related to tourism benefit from this money.

TUTORIALS

T2 *Notice that the question asks for an explanation of the suitability of Blackpool's situation. Also there is a difference between the site and the situation of a settlement (see chapter 10). Note the human and physical factors contained in the answer. The physical presence of the coast is Blackpool's main attraction.*

T3 *There are many disadvantages associated with the development of tourism. Employment may be very seasonal and consist of largely unskilled work. Increased traffic congestion, pollution, environmental damage and vandalism are other possible problems.*

14.4 NATIONAL PARKS

NATIONAL PARKS IN THE USA

The idea of National Parks started in the USA. Today, more than 140 countries have National Parks. In the USA National Parks are wilderness areas. Most of the USA's 54 National Parks occupy remote, mountainous areas in the Rockies and Alaska.

The US National Parks have two main purposes:

- to protect the natural environment (i.e. landscape and wildlife);
- to provide for the enjoyment of visitors in a way that does not damage the environment.

Yellowstone National Park

Yellowstone, established in 1872, was the world's first National Park. It occupies a remote area in the Rockies in Wyoming and Montana states (Fig. 14.5), and is comparable in size to North Yorkshire. Yellowstone forms part of a much larger conservation area which includes Grand Teton National Park and several adjacent national forest areas. Yellowstone is a high plateau lying between 2,000 and 2,500 metres, and has several outstanding features (Fig. 14.5):

- the world's largest concentration of geysers, hot springs, boiling mud pots and steam vents;
- spectacular canyons and waterfalls;
- abundant wildlife.

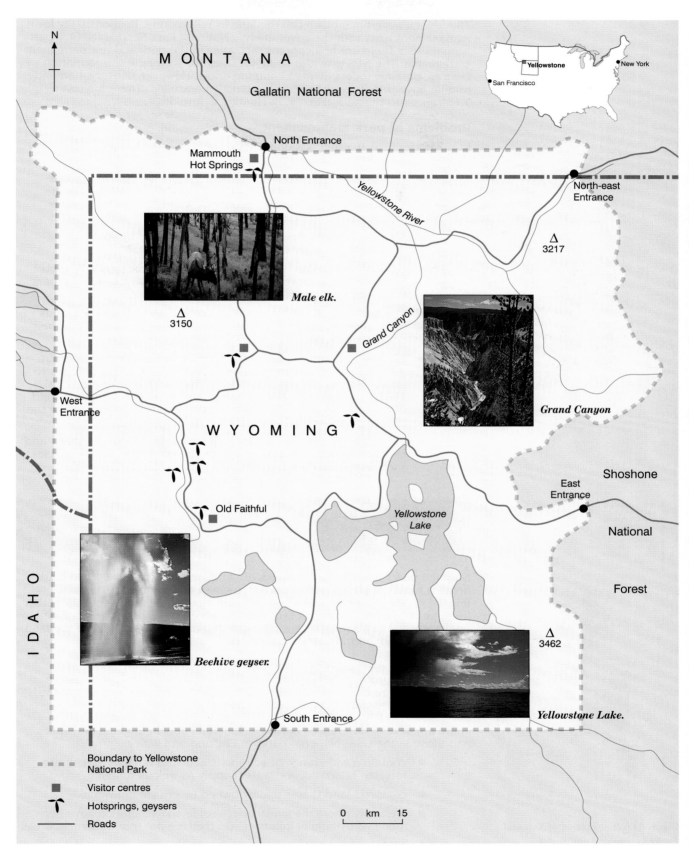

N

M O N T A N A

Gallatin National Forest

North Entrance

Mammouth
Hot Springs

Yellowstone River

North-east
Entrance

Δ
3217

Male elk.

Δ
3150

Grand Canyon

Grand Canyon

W Y O M I N G

Shoshone

West
Entrance

East
Entrance

National

Old Faithful

Yellowstone
Lake

I D A H O

Forest

Δ
3462

Beehive geyser.

Yellowstone Lake.

South Entrance

Yellowstone

San Francisco

New York

Boundary to Yellowstone
National Park

Visitor centres

Hotsprings, geysers

Roads

0   km   15

Figure 14.5 *Yellowstone National Park.*

233

The federal government owns all the land in Yellowstone. Responsibility for its management rests with the government's National Park Service (NPS). Apart from tourism there are no economic activities in the park and few permanent settlements. The NPS provides some facilities for visitors, e.g. information centres, parking, toilets, limited camping, trails. However, conservation and wildlife have priority. Visitor access is strictly controlled. There are just 5 entrances to the park (Fig. 14.5). Hunting is forbidden.

Problems of park management

In Yellowstone, as in other National Parks, conflicts arise between conservation, visitors and local people.

- Yellowstone receives over 4 million visitors a year. This causes overcrowding at popular attractions such as Old Faithful geyser; litter and sewage disposal problems; vandalism at hot springs and geysers; and accidental fires.

- A small number of visitors are injured or killed by some of Yellowstone's larger and more dangerous animals.

- Yellowstone's bison herds are infected with brucellosis. In winter, the herds often move to lower ground and stray outside the park. Here they may infect domestic cattle.

- The decision, in 1995, to reintroduce wolves to Yellowstone has been unpopular with local ranchers, who are worried about their cattle and sheep.

- Wildfire is a natural part of the Yellowstone ecosystem. Without it the native conifer trees cannot regenerate. Current policy is to allow wildfires to burn unless they threaten life or property. In 1988, huge wildfires swept through the park destroying one third of the forest. Local people who depend on tourism would like the NPS to guard against wildfires.

- Visitors have introduced alien fish species to the parks' rivers and to Yellowstone Lake. This threatens the survival of native species such as the cut-throat trout.

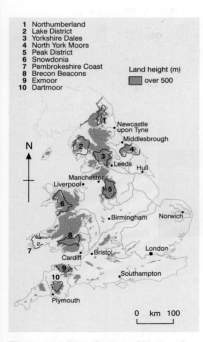

1 Northumberland
2 Lake District
3 Yorkshire Dales
4 North York Moors
5 Peak District
6 Snowdonia
7 Pembrokeshire Coast
8 Brecon Beacons
9 Exmoor
10 Dartmoor

Land height (m)
over 500

Figure 14.6 *Distribution of National Parks in England and Wales.*

NATIONAL PARKS IN ENGLAND AND WALES

National parks in England and Wales are large tracts of relatively wild land defined by act of parliament. Most are areas of mountain and moorland (Fig. 14.6). They are protected by legislation against development. Altogether there are 10 National Parks in England and Wales, plus the Broads in East Anglia which has a similar status. National parks cover 7 per cent of the land area of England, and 20 per cent of Wales.

Each park is looked after by a National Park Authority (NPA) whose main purpose is to protect the environment. NPAs also have a duty to promote 'quiet enjoyment and understanding of the parks', and take account of the economic and social needs of local people.

There are several differences between National Parks in England and Wales and those in the USA. National parks in England and Wales:

- contain a wide range of economic activities such as agriculture, forestry, quarrying and water supply as well as tourism;
- comprise land that is mainly owned by private individuals;
- are areas where the landscape, wildlife and vegetation have been modified by human influence, i.e. they are not true wilderness areas;
- contain many permanent settlements;
- are open freely to the public.

CONFLICTING LAND USES IN NATIONAL PARKS

Because conservation is not given the same priority in UK National Parks as in US parks, difficult management problems arise. Often there are conflicts between conservation and the different economic activities.

- Quarrying is important in several National Parks, e.g. Peak District, Yorkshire Dales. Yet quarrying destroys the very landscape National Parks are supposed to protect.

- Army firing ranges cover large areas of Northumberland National Park. These too have a destructive effect.

- The massive growth in visitor numbers places great pressure on the more popular parks such as the Lake District. Problems include traffic congestion at popular sites; footpath erosion on the fells; and noise pollution from speed boats on some lakes.

Check yourself

QUESTIONS

Q1 What is a National Park?

Q2 The following table shows the various people and animals found in Yellowstone National Park. The letter C shows that there is conflict between wild animals in the park and domestic animals.

	visitors	wild animals	domestic animals	local people
visitors	X			
wild animals		X	C	
domestic animals			X	
local people				X

i) Why is there conflict between the wild and domestic animals?
ii) Copy the table and mark any other conflicts.

Q3 Study Figure 14.6.
i) State to what extent you agree or disagree with the following statements on the location of the National Parks. They are to be found mostly:
 1. 'in the north and west of England and Wales'
 2. 'away from the centres of high population'
 3. 'close to the coastline'.
ii) Describe the location of the Brecon Beacons National Park.

Q4 What are the advantages and disadvantages of siting a quarry within a National Park?

ANSWERS

A1 National Parks are protected areas of great natural beauty. They were set up to provide for the enjoyment of visitors without damaging the environment.

A2

i) Brucellosis in wild bison can infect domestic cattle. Wolves may attack cattle and sheep.

ii)

	visitors	wild animals	domestic animals	local people
visitors	X	C		C
wild animals	C	X	C	C
domestic animals		C	X	
local people	C	C		X

A3

i)
1. This is true. With the exception of the Norfolk Broads the National Parks are found in the North and West of England and Wales.
2. This is not entirely true. The Peak District and the two National Parks in Yorkshire are near large centres of population. The Brecon Beacons are close to densely populated parts of South Wales. Other parks like those in South-west England, North Wales and Northumberland are more remote. The Norfolk Broads is in relatively sparsely populated East Anglia.
3. With the exception of the Yorkshire Dales and the Peak District all the National Parks are close to the coast.

ii) The Brecon Beacons National Park is in the highland area of South Wales.

A4 The quarry will be a source of employment in an area where there are likely to be few jobs outside of farming and tourism. The quarry will scar the landscape. Traffic associated with the quarry will cause congestion on small country roads, and there will be increased pollution from noise and dust.

TUTORIALS

T1 *Remember that there are considerable differences between National Parks in the USA and the UK.*

T2 *This is an example of a conflict matrix. It is a useful way of summarising information. Remember the examiner will accept a diagram as an alternative to a written description.*

T3 *These questions will help you to build up a good understanding of the distribution of National Parks in England and Wales.*

T4 *Quarrying is only one of the conflicting pressures on the National Parks in England and Wales. The demands for water from the National Parks and the use of the land by sheep farmers can cause problems for people using the parks for leisure and recreation purposes.*

14.5 TOURISM IN LEDCs

Although LEDCs account for only one fifth of world tourism, this proportion is increasing rapidly. In Africa, tourism has become the continent's fastest growing industry. For many poor countries tourism provides one of the few avenues for development. Tourism can bring many advantages (Fig. 14.7). However, without planning and sensitive development, tourism often does little to benefit local people.

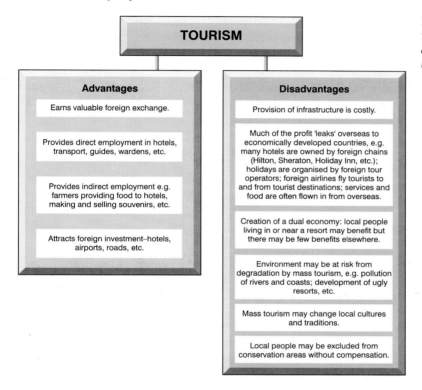

Figure 14.7
The advantages and disadvantages of tourism in LEDCs.

TOURISM

Advantages

Earns valuable foreign exchange.

Provides direct employment in hotels, transport, guides, wardens, etc.

Provides indirect employment e.g. farmers providing food to hotels, making and selling souvenirs, etc.

Attracts foreign investment–hotels, airports, roads, etc.

Disadvantages

Provision of infrastructure is costly.

Much of the profit 'leaks' overseas to economically developed countries, e.g. many hotels are owned by foreign chains (Hilton, Sheraton, Holiday Inn, etc.); holidays are organised by foreign tour operators; foreign airlines fly tourists to and from tourist destinations; services and food are often flown in from overseas.

Creation of a dual economy: local people living in or near a resort may benefit but there may be few benefits elsewhere.

Environment may be at risk from degradation by mass tourism, e.g. pollution of rivers and coasts; development of ugly resorts, etc.

Mass tourism may change local cultures and traditions.

Local people may be excluded from conservation areas without compensation.

CASE STUDY: ECO-TOURISM IN ZIMBABWE

Since 1990 the number of tourists visiting Zimbabwe in southern Africa (Fig. 14.8) has grown by 20 per cent a year. Tourism has brought considerable economic benefits to Zimbabwe.

- In 1996, 1.3 million tourists visited Zimbabwe, spending nearly £120 million.
- Tourism provides employment for 60,000 people in Zimbabwe.

Resources for tourism

Zimbabwe's greatest resource is its spectacular wildlife. National parks, game reserves and other wildlife conservation areas (Fig. 14.8) cover 10 per cent of the country - roughly the area of Denmark. In National Parks such as Hwange and Mana Pools (Fig. 14.9) tourists can see most of Africa's largest mammals, including elephants, rhinos, lions, giraffes, hippos, buffalo, zebra and antelope, as well as hundreds of species of birds. Other major attractions include the Victoria Falls on the Zambezi River and Lake Kariba (Fig. 14.9). Cultural and historical features also attract tourists. These include the ruined city Great Zimbabwe, and the capital, Harare, with its museums and art galleries.

237

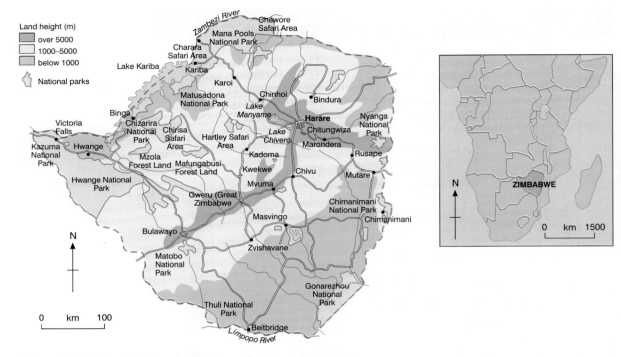

Figure 14.8 *National Parks and other conservation areas in Zimbabwe.*

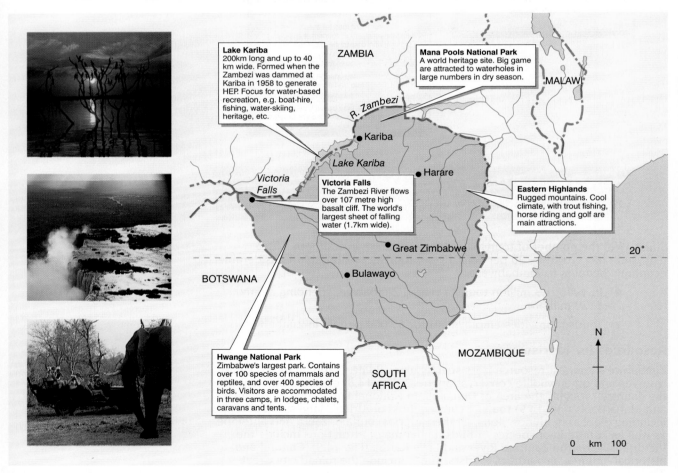

Lake Kariba
200km long and up to 40 km wide. Formed when the Zambezi was dammed at Kariba in 1958 to generate HEP. Focus for water-based recreation, e.g. boat-hire, fishing, water-skiing, heritage, etc.

Mana Pools National Park
A world heritage site. Big game are attracted to waterholes in large numbers in dry season.

Victoria Falls
The Zambezi River flows over 107 metre high basalt cliff. The world's largest sheet of falling water (1.7km wide).

Eastern Highlands
Rugged mountains. Cool climate, with trout fishing, horse riding and golf are main attractions.

Hwange National Park
Zimbabwe's largest park. Contains over 100 species of mammals and reptiles, and over 400 species of birds. Visitors are accommodated in three camps, in lodges, chalets, caravans and tents.

Figure 14.9 *Major tourism attractions in Zimbabwe.*

Eco-tourism

So far Zimbabwe has avoided mass tourism. Instead tourism is geared to small groups, on special interest holidays. These so-called **eco-tourists** include wildlife enthusiasts, bird watchers, botanists and photographers.

Investing in infrastructure

A successful tourism industry needs a good infrastructure as well as attractive resources. Tourists require accommodation, electricity, clean water, roads and airports. Zimbabwe has one of the best developed infrastructures in Africa.

- There are top-class hotels in Harare and Bulawayo mainly owned by international chains such as Holiday Inn and Best Western.
- In the National Parks accommodation ranges from luxury lodges to chalets and caravans.
- The road network is adequate compared with those in other LEDCs.
- There is an international airport in the capital, Harare.

Managing the resources for tourism

Without careful management the resources on which tourism depends are easily degraded. Zimbabwe aims to develop **sustainable tourism.** Protecting large areas of the country as National Parks and game reserves is part of this strategy.

Even so, the growth of eco-tourism has caused problems. Subsistence farmers living around the edges of the National Parks and game reserves often come into conflict with wildlife. These farmers are poor and with rapid population growth land is in short supply. In these circumstances:

- farmers are tempted to grow crops and to allow animals to graze inside conservation areas, destroying habitats there;
- wild animals destroy crops and threaten the livelihoods of local people.

The government's response has been to develop policies which give local people an interest in conserving wildlife. In 1984, the Zimbabwe government introduced its Communal Areas Management Programme for Indigenous Resources (CAMPFIRE) scheme.

- Money from game hunting fees – tourists pay up to £4,600 to shoot an elephant – and selling hides and meat, is given to local communities.
- Local communities receive cash payments for any crop losses caused by wild animals.

Thanks to CAMPFIRE the attitude of local people towards wildlife has changed. Now, because the wildlife provides them with an income, they have an interest in protecting it.

Recently there has been some concern about the nature of tourist developments in parts of Zimbabwe. Victoria Falls, the biggest single tourist attraction in southern Africa, has become increasingly commercialised. Bungee jumping, micro-light aircraft flights over the Falls, and the sale of cheap trinkets are giving the Falls a 'tacky' image.

The future

The problem at Victoria Falls highlights the dilemma facing countries wishing to expand their tourism industries. Do they promote more exclusive eco-tourism or mass-market tourism? Zimbabwe has chosen the former. It argues that it is not the volume of tourists that matters, but how much they spend.

Check yourself

Q1 What are the natural resources that attract tourists to Zimbabwe?

Q2 What is eco-tourism?

Q3 What is sustainable tourism?

Q4 How has Zimbabwe managed to avoid the worst excesses of modern tourism?

REMEMBER! Cover the answers if you want to.

ANSWERS

A1 Zimbabwe's greatest attraction is its wildlife. Lakes, waterfalls and mountains also draw tourists. The main attraction in its landscape is Victoria Falls.

A2 Eco-tourism encourages sensitive tourism that doesn't damage the environment. A country's flora and fauna are marketed in eco-tourism. Tourists tend to be wildlife enthusiasts, bird watchers, botanists, etc.

A3 Sustainable tourism is the careful management of a country's resources so that the impact of tourism does not harm the environment.

A4 Zimbabwe has set up National parks to protect the environment. The support of local people has been achieved through the CAMPFIRE programme. This programme ensures that local inhabitants recognise the economic value of the country's wildlife. The country decided to attract fewer tourists, who spend more money per head.

TUTORIALS

T1 *Make sure that you understand the difference between natural and human resources. Natural resources are those associated with relief, climate, vegetation, soils and the ecosystem.*

T2 *Eco-tourism is the opposite of tourism based on human resources such as historic sites, stately homes, castles, cathedrals, museums, etc.*

T3 *This is another example of the concept of sustainability. Look back at chapter 7 on ecosystems and compare the different approaches of Sarawak and Finland to their forest resources.*

T4 *Zimbabwe has not been totally successful in avoiding the worst excesses of modern tourism, e.g. the tourism at Victoria Falls.*

EXAMINATION CHECKLIST

The facts and ideas you should know and understand after studying tourism are:

- Tourism is one of the world's fastest growing industries.
- Tourism depends on both natural and human resources.
- Three main types of tourist areas have developed: coastal areas, mountainous areas and cities.
- The growth of seaside resorts in the UK began in the nineteenth century with the development of the railways and the introduction of paid holidays.
- Blackpool shows the main features of a British holiday resort.
- Tourism has become more international.
- National Parks have been established in different countries to try to protect the most scenic areas.
- There are eleven National Parks in England and Wales.
- The variety of interests in National Parks means that there is a need for careful management in order to reduce the possibility of conflict and damage to the environment.
- Tourism is growing rapidly in LEDCs.
- There are advantages and disadvantages in the growth of tourism in an LEDC.
- Eco-tourism and sustainable tourism may be the best way of developing the industry in LEDCs.

Key words

These are the key words. Tick them if you think you know what they mean. Otherwise check on them.

mass tourism
eco-tourism
sustainable tourism

EXAM PRACTICE

Sample Student's Answer and Examiner's Comments.

a) **i)**

This is correct. Other acceptable answers would be Corsica (even though it is French), Sardinia or Sicily.

ii)

This is correct.

iii)

This is incorrect. The correct answer is Sperlonga.

iv)

She has misunderstood the meaning of the word mainland. There are two marks for locating two named areas, i.e. Ospedaletti and Genoa. No mark was given for Venice because the mark scheme put a maximum on the list. However, the examiner really wanted evidence of a pattern. The word 'describe' should have suggested to the candidate that something more than a list was required. Possible points were: Blue Flag beaches not evenly distributed; more beaches in the north than in the south; biggest cluster in the North-west; other large clusters in the North-east and South-east. There is no credit for 'on the coast'. That is too obvious.

b) She gained three marks which is the bottom of Level 2. Her answer shows some clear understanding, but the information given is too general and not specific enough to Newquay for it to be considered a detailed Level 3 answer. The first sentence in the first section just reaches Level 2. There is an attempt to link the climate of the area to its location. This is very tenuous but it is just about sufficient. There are a number of misconceptions in this answer. For example, the reference to the human attractions in the first part despite it testing knowledge of natural attractions. The word 'natural' is in bold but the candidate has either ignored it or not noticed it. However, no marks are deducted for these irrelevant answers.

---

1 **a)** The 'Blue Flag' is an award given to European beaches which meet particular environmental and safety requirements. Study the map which shows some of the Blue Flag beaches in Italy.

i) Name one of the islands shown on the map. (1 mark)

Elba

ii) Name the most easterly Blue Flag beach in Italy. (1 mark)

Andrano.

iii) Which Blue Flag beach is nearest to Rome? (1 mark)

Naples.

iv) Describe the distribution of Blue Flag beaches on the mainland of Italy. (5 marks)

There are no flags on the mainland because there are no beaches, but there are many along the areas near Ospedaletti, Genoa, Venice, etc.

b) For any named coastal resort you have studied: (6 marks)

i) Describe its **natural** attractions, e.g. climate, landscape.

Chosen resort: *Newquay (Cornwall)*

It is in South-west England and has a variable climate during the summer, with both wet and warm weather. The landscape is sloping, flat and there are many attractions: beaches, surfing, swimming, discoteques, clubs, pubs, restaurants, etc.

ii) Show how the actions of the local council or developers have helped to attract tourists to the area.

The beaches are kept very clean with coast guards in constant attendance. The surrounding areas, shops and town are kept bright, inviting and interesting. The area is very accessible with many car parks and plenty of accommodation.

LEAG, 1993

Questions to Answer

The answer to Question 2 can be found in Chapter 18.

2 a) Nepal is a very poor, mountainous country on the edge of the Himalayas.
Study the diagrams which give some information about Nepal's tourist trade.

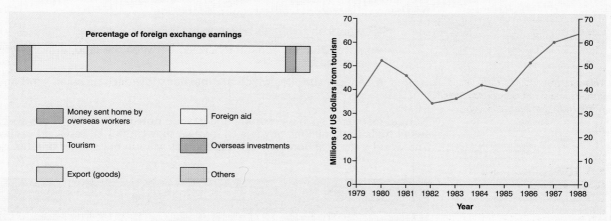

Percentage of foreign exchange earnings

Money sent home by overseas workers

Foreign aid

Tourism

Overseas investments

Export (goods)

Others

i)   What percentage of Nepal's foreign exchange comes from tourism?   (1 mark)

ii) Where does tourism rank in importance as a source of foreign income?   (1 mark)

iii) Describe how earnings from tourism changed between 1979 and 1988.   (2 marks)

iv) Suggest why countries cannot rely on tourism as a regular source of income, year after year. Use an example in your answer.   (4 marks)

b) Study the map which shows some of Nepal's main tourist attractions. Trekking, (walking in the mountains) is one of the main attractions.

i)   State one attraction other than trekking which might bring tourists to Nepal.   (1 mark)

ii) Which is the most popular area for trekking?   (1 mark)

iii) The area used for trekking is very small. What environmental problems might arise from so many people visiting such a small area?   (4 marks)

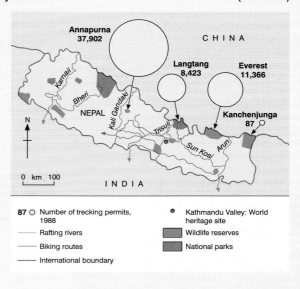

87 ○ Number of trecking permits, 1988

──── Rafting rivers

──── Biking routes

──── International boundary

● Kathmandu Valley: World heritage site

Wildlife reserves

National parks

c) Using examples you have studied in LEDCs describe three benefits and problems tourists may bring to people in the areas they visit. Do not refer to environmental problems again.   (4 marks)

d) Most visitors to Nepal are long-haul tourists from Europe

i)   What does long haul mean?   (1 mark)

ii) The number of long-haul holidays from Europe has risen sharply in the last 25 years. Using examples explain this increase.   (6 marks)

London, 1993

CHAPTER 15

MANAGING NATURAL RESOURCES

15.1 RENEWABLE AND NON-RENEWABLE RESOURCES

Natural resources are naturally occurring things which are useful to us. They include fuels such as oil and natural gas; and materials such as iron ore, and timber. There are two types of natural resource: renewables and non-renewables. **Renewable resources** include:

- plants and animals which follow biological cycles;
- water which is constantly cycled between the land, atmosphere, and seas;
- energy supplies which are inexhaustible such as solar, wind and geothermal power.

Natural resources such as coal, oil and gas are **non-renewable.** These so-called **fossil fuels** took millions of years to form so they cannot be replaced easily. The world's stock of non-renewable resources will run out sooner or later.

15.2 FOSSIL FUELS AND GLOBAL WARMING

In the twentieth century global temperatures have risen on average by 0.6°C. This is the most rapid increase since the end of the Ice Age. Most of this increase has occurred in the last 40 years (Fig. 15.1). Many scientists believe that the Earth's climate will get even warmer. By 2100 the average global temperature could be 3°C higher than today's.

Figure 15.1
Average global temperatures since 1853.

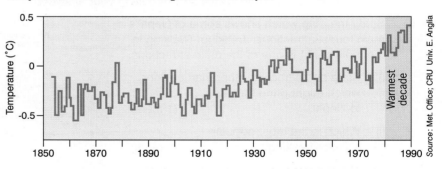

Source: Met. Office; CRU Univ. E. Anglia

Figure 15.2 *The greenhouse effect.*

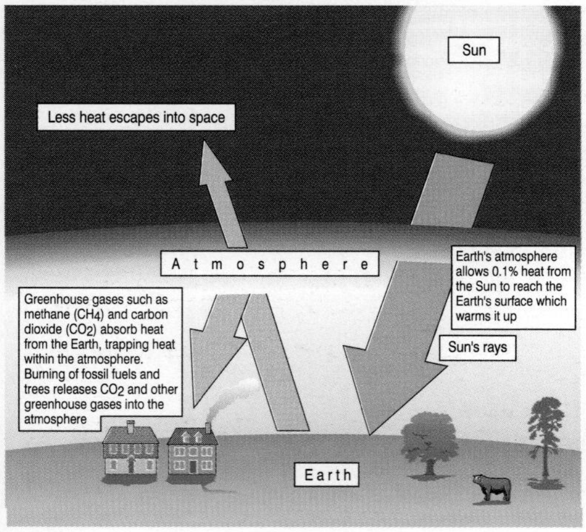

Sun

Less heat escapes into space

Atmosphere

Earth's atmosphere allows 0.1% heat from the Sun to reach the Earth's surface which warms it up

Sun's rays

Greenhouse gases such as methane (CH4) and carbon dioxide (CO2) absorb heat from the Earth, trapping heat within the atmosphere. Burning of fossil fuels and trees releases CO2 and other greenhouse gases into the atmosphere

Earth

CAUSES OF GLOBAL WARMING

Is global warming a natural event or is it the result of human influence? Until recently, scientists were divided over this question. However, by the mid-1990s the weight of evidence was sufficient for the Intergovernmental Panel for Climatic Change (IPCC) to announce that global warming was probably due to human activity.

Global warming is caused by the 'greenhouse effect' (Fig. 15.2). In the past 200 years, industrial development, population growth and rising prosperity have greatly increased the need for more energy. Most of this energy has come from burning fossil fuels. As a result levels of carbon dioxide, methane and other greenhouse gases in the atmosphere have increased dramatically, trapping more of the Earth's heat.

MEDCs such as the USA, Germany and the UK are mainly responsible for global warming. They consume large amounts of energy, relying heavily on **primary fuels** (i.e. coal, oil and natural gas) to produce **secondary energy** (i.e. electricity). Around 2 per cent of total carbon dioxide emissions produced each year by human activities come from the UK, mainly from coal-fired power stations.

THE CONSEQUENCES OF GLOBAL WARMING

Global warming has an effect at local, national (Fig. 15.3) and world scales (Table 15.1).

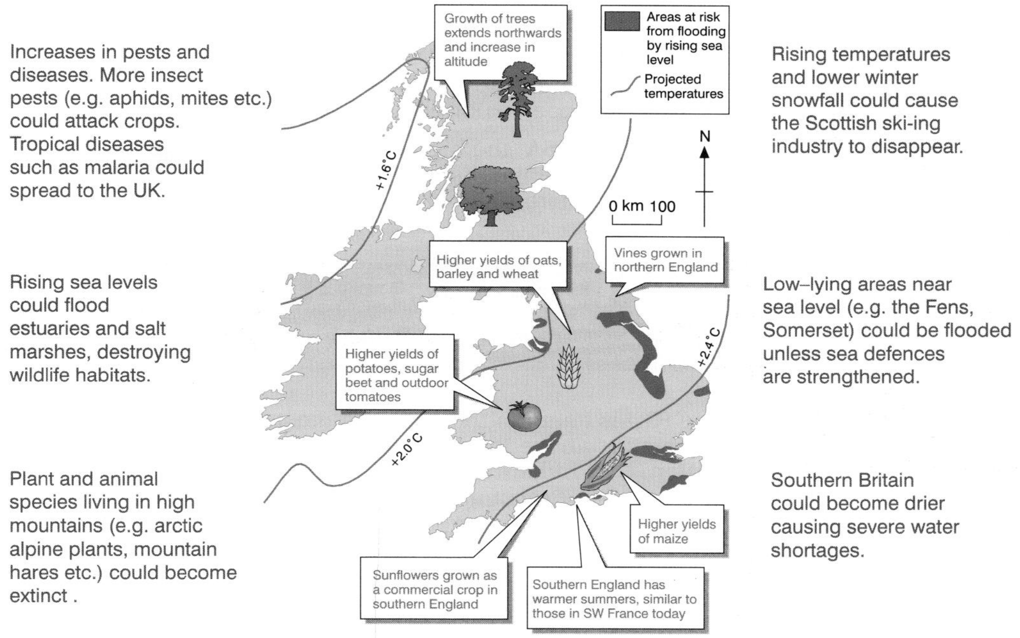

Figure 15.3 *The possible advantages and disadvantages of global warming in the UK.*

Increases in pests and diseases. More insect pests (e.g. aphids, mites etc.) could attack crops. Tropical diseases such as malaria could spread to the UK.

Rising sea levels could flood estuaries and salt marshes, destroying wildlife habitats.

Plant and animal species living in high mountains (e.g. arctic alpine plants, mountain hares etc.) could become extinct .

Growth of trees extends northwards and increase in altitude

Areas at risk from flooding by rising sea level
Projected temperatures

Higher yields of oats, barley and wheat

Vines grown in northern England

Higher yields of potatoes, sugar beet and outdoor tomatoes

Sunflowers grown as a commercial crop in southern England

Southern England has warmer summers, similar to those in SW France today

Higher yields of maize

Rising temperatures and lower winter snowfall could cause the Scottish ski-ing industry to disappear.

Low–lying areas near sea level (e.g. the Fens, Somerset) could be flooded unless sea defences are strengthened.

Southern Britain could become drier causing severe water shortages.

0 km 100

Table 15.1 The impact of global warming at the world scale

RISING SEA LEVELS	CLIMATE CHANGE
• Melting glaciers and ice sheets have caused a 25 cm rise in sea level since 1900.	• Drought, storms and floods could become more frequent.
• By 2100 sea level could be 50 cm higher than in 1998. Several small islands states, such as the Maldives and the Marshall Islands, could disappear.	• The Sahara Desert could leapfrog the Mediterranean Sea and extend into southern Spain and Sicily.
• Large parts of Egypt, Bangladesh and South China will flood, creating millions of refugees.	• Harvests could drop by one-fifth in Africa, and South and South-east Asia, causing further famine.
	• Siberia could become warmer allowing greater crop yields.
	• Ocean currents like the North Atlantic Drift could break down, giving much colder winters in North-west Europe.

MANAGING GLOBAL WARMING

Global warming affects all countries. And yet most seem either unable or unwilling to do anything about it. At the 1992 Earth Summit in Rio the world's richest countries agreed to stabilise carbon dioxide (CO_2) emissions at 1990 levels by 2000. By the mid-1990s it was clear that few countries would achieve this target.

Government attitudes to global warming depend on their interests.

- Low-lying islands such as the Maldives in the Indian Ocean could be swamped by a sea level rise of just one or two metres. They want greenhouse gas emissions cut immediately.

- Poor countries, such as China and India, whose rapid industrial growth is powered by fossil fuels, argue that most pollution comes from rich countries, and that these countries should cut emissions.

- Powerful TNCs involved in heavy industries oppose any reduction in burning fossil, fearing it would hit their profits.

- Major oil exporting countries, such as Saudi Arabia and Kuwait, and coal exporters, such as Australia oppose any reductions.

- The USA, the biggest energy consumer of them all, sees any reduction in its use of fossil fuels as a threat to its citizens' standard of living.

15.3 THE DISAPPEARING OZONE LAYER

Ozone (O_3) is found in the Earth's atmosphere. Concentrated between 20 and 30 kilometres above the surface, it absorbs a lot of the sun's ultaviolet (UVB) radiation. UVB radiation causes tanning in humans. However, large doses of UVB cause skin cancer and eye cataracts, and damages crops and plankton.

Chlorofluorocarbons (CFCs) threaten to destroy the ozone layer. CFCs have been used for the last 50 years as propellents in aerosols, refrigerants and plastic foam packaging. Each spring in the Antarctic and Arctic, a massive hole appears in the ozone layer. The hole is caused by complex chemical reactions between ozone, sunlight, and chlorine particles, from CFCs (Fig. 15.4). There is growing concern that the Antarctic ozone hole is widening over parts of Australia, New Zealand and southern Chile.

Like global warming, ozone depletion is a global problem which demands action by all countries. In the 1980s an international agreement limited production of CFCs. Even so, CFCs will remain in the atmosphere for many years to come.

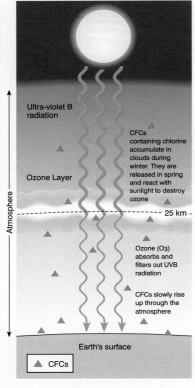

Figure 15.4 *Thinning of the ozone layer.*

Ultra-violet B radiation

CFCs containing chlorine accumulate in clouds during winter. They are released in spring and react with sunlight to destroy ozone

Ozone Layer

Atmosphere

25 km

Ozone (O_3) absorbs and filters out UVB radiation

CFCs slowly rise up through the atmosphere

Earth's surface

▲ CFCs

15.4 ACID RAIN

Much of the rain which falls in the industrialised countries of the northern hemisphere is highly acidic. The cause of this acid rain is air pollution. The main culprits are power stations and oil refineries which produce the waste gases sulphur dioxide (SO_2) and nitrogen oxides (NOx) (Fig. 15.5).

Acid rain has seriously harmed forests, soils, lakes, rivers and buildings. In Scandinavia large areas of coniferous forest are dying and thousands of lakes, acidified by pollution, are lifeless. The Scandinavian states blame the UK for this. They argue that prevailing south-westerly winds bring acid rain from the UK (Fig. 15.6).

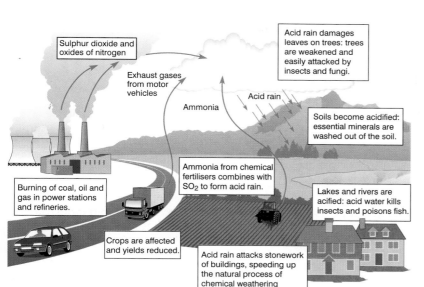

Figure 15.5
Acid rain: causes and effects.

Sulphur dioxide and oxides of nitrogen

Acid rain damages leaves on trees: trees are weakened and easily attacked by insects and fungi.

Exhaust gases from motor vehicles

Ammonia

Acid rain

Soils become acidified: essential minerals are washed out of the soil.

Ammonia from chemical fertilisers combines with SO_2 to form acid rain.

Burning of coal, oil and gas in power stations and refineries.

Lakes and rivers are acified: acid water kills insects and poisons fish.

Crops are affected and yields reduced.

Acid rain attacks stonework of buildings, speeding up the natural process of chemical weathering

Figure 15.6 *Power station producing smokestack pollution.*

Within the UK the areas worst affected by acid rain are uplands such as Snowdonia and the Lake District. These areas have:

- high rainfall and therefore large quantities of acid rain;
- hard, impermeable rocks which means that acid water runs straight into rivers and lakes. In areas where rocks are permeable and lime-rich (e.g. chalk and limestone), acid rainwater seeps into the ground, is neutralised and causes little damage.

In 1988, an EU directive called for a 40 per cent reduction in sulphur dioxide emissions within 10 years. The UK's emissions actually halved between 1970 and 1993, mainly because of the rising popularity of gas as a primary fuel.

Check yourself

QUESTIONS

Q1 What is the difference between a renewable and a non-renewable resource?

Q2 Explain what is meant by each of the following:
  i)   global warming?
  ii) ozone depletion?

Q3
  i)   What is the meaning of the term 'the greenhouse effect'?
  ii) Which two gases are most effective in trapping heat in the Earth's atmosphere?
  iii) Why is there increasing concern about the greenhouse effect?

Q4 Acid rain falling on Sweden is causing widespread environmental damage.
  i)   What is acid rain?
  ii) Name three factors which may cause acid rain.
  iii) Describe the damaging effects of acid rain.
  iv) How could the problems of acid rain be reduced?

ANSWERS

A1 Non-renewable resources cannot be replaced once they have been used.

Renewable resources are those which grow, are constantly recycled, or are inexhaustible.

A2 i) Global warming is the rise in average global temperatures.
ii) Ozone depletion is the destruction of the ozone layer. Ozone is concentrated between 20 and 30 km above the earth's surface.

A3 i) The greenhouse effect is the heating of the earth's surface because of the build up of carbon dioxide and methane gases in the atmosphere. The gases trap heat radiated from the earth.
ii) Carbon dioxide and methane.
iii) The greenhouse effect is responsible for global warming. There is a danger that the ice caps in the Arctic and Antarctic will melt, raising the sea level, and causing low-lying areas to flood. The world climate pattern could change too. This may cause desert areas to move northwards in the northern hemisphere. Ocean currents could change, giving much colder winters in North-west Europe

A4 i) Acid rain is acid rain water produced by the reaction of the water with pollutants such as sulphur dioxide.
ii) Three main causes are the burning of fossil fuels; industrial processes and vehicle exhaust emissions.
iii) Damage includes the contamination of water supplies; the destruction of vegetation, especially woodlands; and the killing of aquatic life in lakes.
iv) Greater international cooperation to control acid rain. The passing of clean air acts. Greater use of lead-free petrol in cars. Use of 'scrubbers' (filters) to remove acid rain producing pollutants from industrial emissions.

TUTORIALS

T1 *This is frequently asked at the start of a question on resources.*

T2 *The three topics global warming, ozone depletion and the greenhouse effect are frequently confused by candidates. Make sure that you understand the differences between these.*

T3 *The greenhouse effect has many implications. It is important to consider both the advantages and the disadvantages. Look back at Figure 15.3 to check these.*

T4 *i) You should memorise a precise definition of acid rain.*
ii) and iii) These two questions are the most likely ones you will be asked about for this topic.
iv) Sweden's acid rain problem is largely out of its control. International cooperation is essential to solve the problem.

15.5 COAL MINING AND THE ENVIRONMENT

At the local scale coal extraction also leads to environmental damage.

- Mountains of waste from coal mines form unsightly spoil heaps.
- Mine workings cause surface subsidence which can damage buildings and disrupt drainage.
- Water seeping from disused mines is often polluted.

Since the mid-1980s competition from gas and cheap coal imports have reduced the extent of the UK coal industry (Fig. 15.7).

- In 1997, coal accounted for less than one quarter of the UK's primary energy consumption.
- By 2001, there could be only a dozen collieries left.

Despite its decline, coal mining continues to affect the environment. This is because open-cast mining is still important. This involves quarrying coal from the earth's surface. It is cheaper than traditional deep mining but environmentally destructive. Open-cast operations often occupy huge sites and create holes up to 150 metres deep (Fig. 15.8). Great mounds of earth screen the sites in order to reduce the noise from blasting and shield against wind-blown dust.

Mining companies manage open-cast sites to minimise their effects on local residents and on the landscape. After completion of mining the sites are fully restored. However, it takes many years for agricultural land to return to its former state.

The arguments for open casting are:

- it is only temporary, e.g. 4 or 5 years;
- most open-casting is in areas already scarred by years of deep-mining;
- open-casting creates jobs, often where unemployment is high;
- open-casting provides cheap coal for industry.

15.6 ALTERNATIVE ENERGY RESOURCES

Our reliance on fossil fuels cannot continue indefinitely. These resources will eventually run out, and their use creates serious environmental problems.

NUCLEAR ENERGY

The fission of uranium in nuclear reactors produces nuclear energy (Fig. 15.9). Although uranium is a non-renewable resource, nuclear energy has two advantages over fossil fuels:

- supplies of uranium will last for many years to come;
- it does not produce greenhouse gases or acid rain.

Despite its advantages nuclear power is unpopular. Public concern centres around two issues: safety and the storage of radioactive waste.

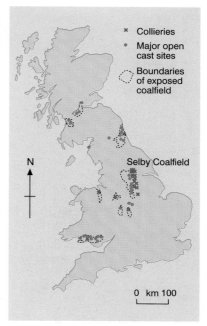

× Collieries
• Major open cast sites
Boundaries of exposed coalfield

N

Selby Coalfield

0 km 100

Figure 15.7 *Coalfields and coal mines in the UK, 1996.*

Figure 15.8 *Open-cast mining.*

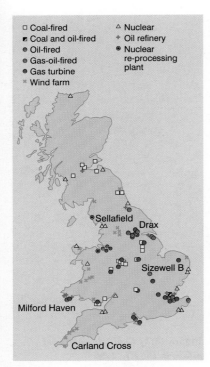

Figure 15.9 *Distribution of power stations in the UK, 1996.*

The main concern is safety. In 1986, the world's worst nuclear accident occurred at Chernobyl in the Ukraine. As a result hundreds of people in eastern Europe have died from radiation-related cancers. Even today parts of upland Britain remain contaminated with radioactive fall-out from Chernobyl.

The second major problem for the nuclear industry is the storage of radioactive waste. The most toxic, high-level waste will remain radioactive for thousands of years. Eventually, it will have to be put into specially designed storage areas, deep underground. However, people object strongly to the siting of storage areas near their homes.

In 1997, about 20 per cent of the UK's electricity came from nuclear power. With so little recent investment in new power stations this figure is bound to fall. Some of the oldest nuclear power stations have already closed down.

WIND POWER

In future coal, oil and gas fired power stations could be replaced by wind farms and other forms of renewable energy (Fig. 15.10). In 1997, there were 550 wind turbines and over 30 wind farms in the UK. In Europe, 4 million people get their electricity from wind power.

Two-fifths of Europe's usuable wind energy is in the British Isles. In theory, the UK could produce 20 per cent of its energy requirements from land-based wind farms (Fig. 15.11).

Wind power is efficient and non-polluting. Modern wind turbines occupy a small area, so that a wind farm can also be used for other activities, e.g. rearing livestock. Wind farms, unlike nuclear and thermal power stations, are also easy to build and to dismantle. However, wind power does have its disadvantages:

- wind turbines can spoil the appearance of a landscape;
- people who live close to wind farms complain about noise made by the turbines' blades;
- it is not always possible to generate electricity when it is needed.

Figure 15.10 *Other forms of renewable energy.*

Geothermal power
Feasible where hot rocks, because of volcanic activity, lie close to the surface. Iceland gets most of its electricity from geothermal power. Granite formations in South–west England have the potential for development.

Wave power
There is great potential on the UK's stormy western coastlines. Small wave machines are already working well in Norway.

Tidal power
The UK with its large tidal range, could produce huge amounts of electricity from barrages across estuaries. Disadvantages include the high capital costs; the disruption to navigation; and the destruction of important wildlife habitats (mud flats, salt marshes) in estuaries.

Solar power
Solar power can be used to heat water directly for domestic heating; to make steam to generate electricity; to generate electricity directly using photo–voltaic cells. Places in low latitudes with cloudless climates have the greatest potential although solar power is relevant even in cloudy, high latitude climates. But it is costly and solar power plants need large areas to collect sunlight. Also, power production stops at sunset.

Hydro–power
Hydroelectric power (HEP) already provides nearly 2 per cent of the UK's electricity. HEP is important in countries with high mountains and large rivers, e.g. Norway and Sweden. There are significant environmental costs, particularly where dams are built and valleys are flooded.

15.7 WATER RESOURCES

Water is constantly cycling between the atmosphere and the Earth's surface, so water is a renewable resource. There are two sources of fresh water:

- surface supplies from rivers, lakes and reservoirs;
- underground supplies from porous rocks or **aquifers.**

Currently the global demand for water doubles every 20 years. Its causes are:

- world population growth;
- the growth of intensive agriculture based on irrigation;
- rising standards of living which increase water consumption per person.

This demand is unsustainable. Large areas of the planet may run short of water in the next 30 years. The existing quality of water in many countries is poor. The United Nations (UN) estimates that dirty water causes 80 per cent of disease in LEDCs and kills 10 million people annually.

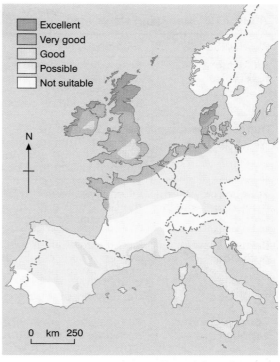

Excellent
Very good
Good
Possible
Not suitable

N

0   km   250

Figure 15.11 *Potential wind*

WATER RESOURCES IN THE UK

Every year around 250 billion billion m^3 of rain falls on the UK. Only about 5 per cent of this is used (Fig. 15.12). The remainder either evaporates or flows into the sea.

While the UK appears to have enough water, regional shortages are common. These water shortages occur for one of three reasons:

- drought years;
- the areas of highest rainfall (the North and West) (Fig. 6.9) do not correspond with the areas of greatest demand (the South and East);
- the uneven seasonal pattern of supply and demand. Water supplies peak in winter when rainfall is highest yet demand peaks in summer when most rainfall evaporates before it reaches rivers and aquifers.

MANAGING THE UK'S WATER RESOURCES

The UK's water companies manage our water resources. The demand for water has risen rapidly in recent years. Meeting this demand has proved both difficult and controversial. The water companies not only have to maintain supplies but also ensure that they are sustainable and do not damage the environment. There are three approaches to the problem (Table 15.2):

- increase the amount of water available by building more reservoirs, etc.;
- transfer water from areas of surplus to areas of shortage;
- conserve existing supplies by plugging leaks, metering. etc.

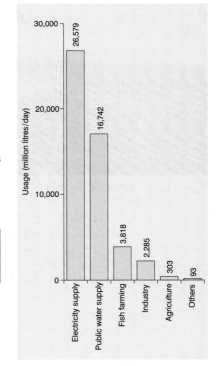

Figure 15.12 *Water use in the UK,*

Table 15.2 Managing water resources and the environmental impact

RESPONSE	EXPLANATION	ENVIRONMENTAL IMPACT
Build more reservoirs	Reservoirs store water and increase the amount of useable water available. They can be used for recreation, flood control and HEP. Building costs are high.	Building reservoirs floods farmland and other countryside. Rivers are controlled and cease to be natural.
Build a national water grid	Water could be transferred by aqueducts and rivers from regions of surplus to regions of shortage. More expensive than reservoirs. Grid may be used infrequently.	Transferring water between river basins can harm aquatic life, which is sensitive to temperature, acidity differences.
Take more water from rivers and bore holes	Often short-term response to drought in the UK. Quick and cheap, but not sustainable long-term.	Water tables fall and river flow falls or even dries up. Rivers look unsightly; less dilution of effluent; wildlife affected.
Reduce water pollution	Treat more effluent (sewage, chemical waste); reduce use of chemical fertilisers in agriculture; prevent contamination from landfill sites. These measures would increase the amount of useable water available.	None.
Conserve water supplies	Reduce water consumption by water metering; cut losses through leakage; introduce low-flush WCs, low-flow sprinklers, etc.	None.

Figure 15.13   Irrigation in Egypt.

EGYPT — RUNNING OUT OF WATER

Egypt is a water-poor country.

- Around 97 per cent of Egypt is desert.
- The River Nile is virtually Egypt's only source of water.
- The Nile is an international river, so Egypt shares its water with seven other African states.

Ethiopia and Sudan have agreements which guarantee Egypt 55.5 billion m^3 of water a year from the Nile. Today, so much water is taken from the Nile that only a tiny fraction of its flow reaches the Mediterranean.

Meanwhile, Egypt's demand for water continues to rise.

- Water consumption per person is high, because Egyptian agriculture depends entirely on irrigation.
- Egypt desperately needs more water to irrigate more land to feed its rapidly growing population (Fig. 15.13).

Water shortages are not new in Egypt. In the 1960s Egypt began building the Aswan Dam. Completed in 1971, the dam created the world's largest reservoir – Lake Nasser. The lake is so large that the whole of the Nile's annual floodwaters can be stored in it. Evening out the Nile's flow allowed farmers to irrigate more land, and grow more crops.

Now Egypt has a new plan – the New Valley project – to increase food output and relieve population pressure in the Nile Valley and delta. Only this time the plan may not succeed. The New Valley project aims to:

- irrigate 2,000 km^2 of desert and resettle millions of people there;
- pump 5 billion m^3 of water a year from Lake Nasser to Toshka and transfer it 200 km by pipeline to the New Valley.

However, the project's success depends on water supply. Already Egypt is using every drop of water it can from the Nile. And as demand for water continues to soar Egypt could have a 17 billion m^3 annual shortfall of water by 2025. Taking more water from the Nile might be the only option. Water could become so scarce that countries may fight over water in future.

Check yourself

QUESTIONS

Q1 Explain as fully as possible why:
i) Liverpool and Birmingham get their water from Wales;
ii) South-east England frequently suffers a hose pipe ban;
iii) holiday areas in South-west England suffer water shortages during the summer.

Q2 What is meant by the following statement?

Water is a renewable resource but its use must be sustainable.

REMEMBER! Cover the answers if you want to.

ANSWERS

A1
i) Liverpool and Birmingham both have large populations and are important industrial centres. Liverpool has quite a high mean annual precipitation, but Birmingham's is much lower. In both cities demand for water outstrips supply. Wales has a high precipitation and central and northern parts of Wales are sparsely populated. Surplus water can be transferred to Liverpool and Birmingham.
ii) South-east England is on the drier side of the country, situated in the rain shadow of the mountains to the west. There is a huge demand for water from the densely populated areas of London and the South-east. In particularly dry years water needs to be rationed.
iii) South-west England is one of the wetter parts of the country. In winter, the wettest time of the year, the resident population is relatively low. In summer, tourists swell the population when rainfall is lower.

A2 In the water cycle, water is constantly being recycled through evaporation and precipitation. The human use of water represents a temporary interruption to this cycle, in which water is used more quickly than it is being replaced.

TUTORIALS

T1 *The knowledge and understanding required to answer each part is the same in each case. All you have to do is relate water supply to the needs of each area.*

T2 *Sustainable development is covered in chapter 7. The information on the Finnish timber industry should give you an idea of what is required here.*

15.8 RECYCLING AND CONSERVING RESOURCES

In the natural world there is a constant cycling of energy and materials. Today, the challenge for humans is to design products which can be fully recycled in an economic system without waste (Fig. 15.14).

RECYCLING

Metals such as steel, copper and aluminium have been re-cycled for many years. Bottle banks and skips for waste paper and plastics have become familiar sights. Even so, large quantities of recyclable materials still end up on rubbish tips.

ENERGY CONSERVATION

We can conserve resources by using them more efficiently, e.g. by increasing the efficiency of furnaces and stoves. More than half the energy consumed in the UK is in buildings. Savings here can be significant. This may involve insulating the roof space or filling cavity walls with foam to reduce heat loss. Homes can be designed to be more energy efficient too. Heat rises so it makes sense to put the living areas on a higher floor.

Check yourself

QUESTIONS

Q1
i) What is the meaning of the term 'recycling'?
ii) Name one material that can be recycled.

Q2 Why is energy conservation becoming increasingly important in both LEDCs and MEDCs?

REMEMBER! Cover the answers if you want to.

ANSWERS

A1
i) The reuse of products or waste.
ii) Any one from aluminium, paper, glass, textiles, plastic.

A2 Both MEDCs and LEDCs are becoming more energy dependent with increasing demands in the home, at work and for transport.

TUTORIALS

T1 *The key word is reuse. The reuse of waste products is becoming increasingly important in manufacturing processes.*

T2 *In MEDCs more emphasis has been placed on energy conservation. However, it is also important that conservation is given high priority in LEDCs. Energy conservation can be made at both the supply and demand ends.*

EXAMINATION CHECKLIST

The facts and ideas that you should know and understand after studying the management of natural resources are:

- There are renewable and non-renewable resources.
- Fossil fuels are the most useful non-renewable resources for producing energy.
- Global warming is a feature of the twentieth century.
- It is accepted that human activity contributes to global warming, e.g. greenhouse gases.
- There are advantages and disadvantages of global warming.
- International cooperation is required to reverse the effects of global warming.
- The thinning of the ozone layer is a result of the widespread use of CFCs.
- Acid rain is a consequence of burning fossil fuels.
- Coal will remain an important source of energy in future.
- Coal mining has significant environmental effects.
- There are a number of problems associated with nuclear energy.
- There are a number of alternative sources of energy to fossil fuels.
- Alternative forms of energy are likely to remain uneconomic for some time.
- Water is an essential resource which needs to be conserved in both MEDCs and LEDCs.
- The UK and Egypt have adopted different ways of planning for their future water demand.
- Recycling and other forms of energy conservation will become increasingly important in future.

Key words

These are the key words. Tick them if you think you know what they mean. Otherwise check on them.

renewable resources	fossil fuels	secondary energy
non-renewable resources	primary fuels	aquifers

EXAM PRACTICE

Sample Student's Answer & Examiner's Comments

EXAMINER'S COMMENTS

a) ***i)***

He did not gain any marks as he did not recognise that wind power is used to generate electricity.
This is an example of a candidate failing to use a sufficiently precise definition of a technical term.
There was only one mark available so there was no credit for his simplified statement.

ii)

This is correct.
Notice that the question asks for the name of the site not the output or the number of turbines.

iii)

This answer reached the bottom of Level 3 and so gained 5 marks. He shows detailed understanding of the fact that fossil fuels are non-renewable and are used to produce energy, and that this causes an increase in the amount of carbon dioxide in the atmosphere. He does not use the term 'greenhouse effect' so he does not reach the top of Level 3. This shows how important it is to use technical terms.

1 (a) Study the diagram showing wind power sites in Great Britain.

Orkney
3 turbines
3.5 MW

Mynydd-y-Cemass
24 turbines
7.2 MW
(planned)

Kirkby Moor
15 turbines
4.5 MW
(planned)

Capel Cynon
25 turbines
8 MW

Addingham
4 turbines
1.2 MW
(planned)

Camarthen Bay
4 turbines
8 MW

Ovenden Moor
23 turbines
9.2 MW

Cold Northcott
23 turbines
7 MW

Huntington
1 turbine
0.2 MW

Delabole
10 turbines
3 MW

Richborough
1 turbine
1 MW

(i) What is wind power? (1 mark)

Power which is generated by the use of wind.

(ii) Which of the sites will have the greatest output? (1 mark)

Ovenden Moor.

(iii) Explain why there is an interest in the development of renewable energy resources. (6 marks)

The energy resources we use most at the moment are fossil fuels such as coal and oil. These fossil fuels are unrenewable, so once we use them up, there will be no more. By using resources such as wind and solar energy to create power, we are preserving the unrenewable resources. We create energy from fossil fuels by burning them. This causes an increased amount of carbon dioxide in the air which surrounds the Earth. This causes the sunlight and warmth to get trapped. If this continued at a fast rate, all the ice over the world would melt, causing an increase in water levels, and damage to settlements. By using renewable sources extra carbon dioxide is not produced, which is another reason why there is an interest in the development of renewable energy resources.

iv) Why are some people opposed to the development
of renewable energy resources?   (5 marks)

If the use of renewable energy resources developed, fuels such as coal and oil would no longer be needed in such great quantities. This would mean coal miners and people in the oil business would soon be out of work, as the demand for these fuels would decrease. These are some of the people who would be opposed to the development of renewable energy resources. Some governments would also be opposed because people in some areas may be coal miners, and so there would be high unemployment, which would not be good for the government. Shop owners in these areas would also be opposed to the development, because the unemployed would have less money to spend, so shop sales may decrease, causing shops to close. Power suppliers may also oppose the development, because renewable resources would give cheaper energy, and that would mean less profit.

SEG, 1993

Questions to Answer
The answer to Question 2 can be found in Chapter 18.

2 a) Study the information below on the numbers of coal miners in the UK.

Year	1947	1955	1965	1971	1976	1980	1984	1987	1996
Number of coal miners (thousands)	703	698	455	287	247	232	191	125	25

i) On some graph paper, plot the numbers of coal miners employed between 1947 and 1996.   (3 marks)

ii) Between which years was the fall in the numbers of coal miners most rapid?   (1 mark)

iii) Why has the number of coal miners fallen?   (3 marks)

b) i) Explain the term 'fossil fuel'.   (1 mark)

ii) Apart from coal, name one other important fossil fuel.   (1 mark)

iii) For the fossil fuel that you have named, explain the problems of extracting it from the ground.   (5 marks)

SEG, 1989

16.1 GLOBAL INEQUALITY

We live in a world divided between rich and poor nations (Fig. 16.1).

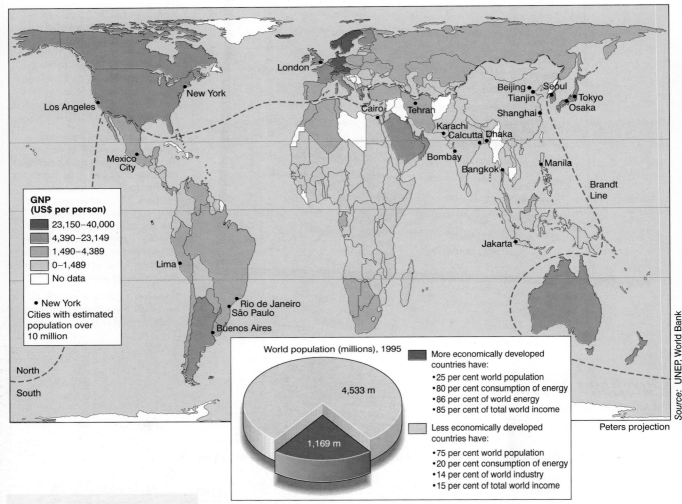

Figure 16.1 *Global inequality and the distribution of GNP per person, 1993.*

- The richest one-fifth of the world's population have 85 per cent of the world's income.
- The poorest one-fifth of the world's population have just 1.4 per cent of the world's income.

Throughout much of Africa, Asia and Latin America life is about survival. Here:

- 1.3 billion people live in absolute poverty;
- one child in three is malnourished;
- every year 12 million children die from causes that could be prevented for just a few pence (Fig. 16.2).

Moreover, between 1980 and 1996 these global inequalities widened. During this time the income of the poorest 1.6 billion people actually fell. Most of these people live in Africa, Latin America and the former Soviet bloc.

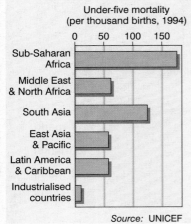

Figure 16.2 *Infant mortality by world region.*

16.2 WHAT IS DEVELOPMENT?

Development is about realising the natural and human resource potential of a country, a region or a locality. It is one way to reduce poverty and improve the quality of people's lives. There are two approaches to development:

- **economic development** aims to raise incomes by expanding and improving economic activities such as farming, manufacturing, tourism, etc;
- **social development** is about providing people with essential services such as education, training and healthcare.

16.3 MEASURING DEVELOPMENT

Many factors contribute to development. For instance, high levels of literacy, high incomes, good housing, clean water supply, adequate diet and healthcare are all associated with high levels of development. It is helpful to have one simple measure of development. **Gross national product** (GNP) per person per year is probably the simplest. GNP is the total value of goods and services produced by a country (including income from overseas) divided by its population (Fig. 16.1). However, this measure does have several weaknesses:

- it takes no account of the purchasing power of people's money;
- it is only an average measure;
- it does not take account of social welfare factors;
- it understates income in poor countries where many farmers grow crops for subsistence living.

Figure 16.3
Human development index (HDI), 1993.

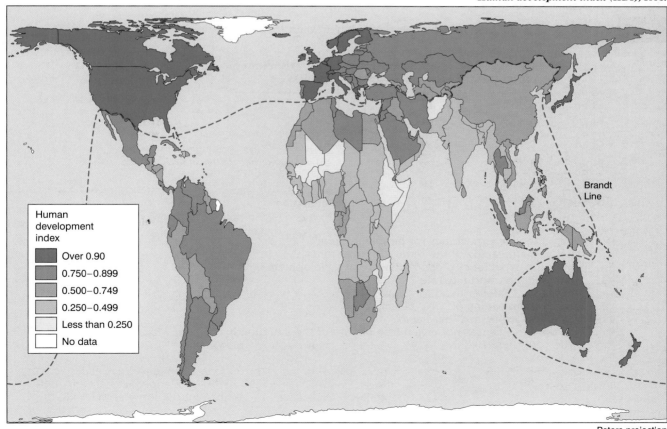

Brandt Line

Human development index

- Over 0.90
- 0.750–0.899
- 0.500–0.749
- 0.250–0.499
- Less than 0.250
- No data

Peters projection

To overcome these problems the United Nations has devised its own measure of human well being: **the human development index (HDI)**. The HDI combines data on average life expectancy, education and the purchasing power of incomes. Thus, the HDI measures social and economic progress. The index ranges from 0 to 1; higher numbers represent greater development (Fig. 16.3).

16.4 GLOBAL CONTRASTS IN DEVELOPMENT

The geographical distribution of wealth at a global scale is very uneven (Fig. 16.1).

- With the exception of Australia and New Zealand, the MEDCs are in the temperate zone of the northern hemisphere.
- The LEDCs are concentrated in the tropics and in the southern hemisphere.

The boundary which separates the rich 'North' and the poor 'South' is known as the Brandt Line (Fig. 16.1).

Check yourself

QUESTIONS

Q1 Study the following table which gives development data for six countries.

	GNP per head (US dollars)	Infant mortality (per 1000)	Life expectancy (years)
Cuba	2,509	14	75
Brazil	2,451	85	65
Chad	159	219	46
Japan	23,325	6	79
UK	14,477	10	76
Sweden	21,155	7	77

i) What is the life expectancy for people in Cuba?
ii) What is the meaning of the term 'life expectancy'?
iii) Why is life expectancy a good measure of development?
iv) What is 'infant mortality rate'?
v) What is the GNP per head for Brazil?
vi) What is the meaning of 'GNP per head'?
vii) Why is this expressed 'per head'?
viii) Why do these figures not give a true picture of the situation in these countries?

ANSWERS

A1
i) 75 years.
ii) The average number of years that a person can expect to live.
iii) The life expectancy can reflect the general level of health in a country. The health of the population gives some indication of the standard of healthcare and the availability of hospitals and doctors.
iv) The number of children in every thousand of the population who will die before they reach their first birthday.
v) $2,451.
vi) The gross national product per head is the total value of goods and services (including income from overseas) earned by a country divided by its population.
vii) So that the GNP for one country can be compared with another.
viii) The figures are only averages. They may hide great variations within the country.

TUTORIALS

T1
i) *Make sure that you always state the units if they are not included in the question.*
ii) *This term comes up frequently in GCSE geography examinations. 'Adult literacy' does too. Make sure that you understand these terms. Your examination syllabus will list the terms which you are likely to be tested on.*
iii) *You may be asked to state a good measure of a country's development. The best ones are those which imply things about a country. GNP per head is a very good measure. The higher the GNP per head, the more money there will be to spend on schools, hospitals and welfare facilities. Population is a poor measure of development, because it does not indicate how developed a country is.*
iv) *'Child mortality rate' is the number of children who die before their fifth birthday.*
v) *It is not necessary to add 'per head' because it is given in the question. The Latin equivalent of per head is 'per capita'. This term is used frequently as an alternative.*
vi) *You must know and understand this definition if you are answering questions concerned with contrasts in development.*
vii) *You would get a false picture of development if you compared the GNP of China with that of Norway without taking into consideration the vast difference in the populations of the two countries.*
viii) *In Brazil, the richest 20% of the population own 67% of the wealth, and the poorest 40% own just 8% of the wealth. There is a vast gap between rich and poor.*

16.5 OBSTACLES TO DEVELOPMENT

In the last 200 years economic and social development have allowed countries such as the USA, the UK, France and Germany to escape poverty. Since 1970 several newly industrialising countries (NICs) in East Asia have developed rapidly (chapter 13), and will be joined by others soon.

Despite this, the majority of countries are still poor, and without development will remain poor. These countries have to overcome a wide range of obstacles in order to develop.

GEOGRAPHICAL OBSTACLES

- Landlocked countries without a coastline are isolated from international trade. There are 15 landlocked states in Africa alone. Their physical isolation contributes to their lack of development.

- Soils are generally less favourable to farming in the tropics. Except for areas of volcanic soil, e.g. Java, soils are often acidic and infertile.
- Climate is often more extreme in the tropics. Devastating floods, droughts and storms slow development.
- Dense rainforest vegetation hinders communication and development in equatorial regions of Africa, Latin America and South-east Asia.

People living in LEDCs have poorer health than people in MEDCs.

- Tropical climates support more diseases and pests than temperate climates (Table 16.1).
- Poverty, malnutrition, overcrowded living conditions, and poor sanitation encourage diseases. Also, people cannot afford essential medicines and governments cannot provide adequate healthcare.

Disease and poor health can contribute to a lack of development. People who suffer from malaria lack energy and find it difficult to work. When malaria strikes young adults who have children to support, its economic effects can be severe. HIV infection and AIDS are also a growing problem in many LEDCs. Up to 60 per cent of the population of sub-Saharan Africa is thought to be infected with the HIV virus.

Table 16.1 Major diseases in LEDCs

DISEASE	CAUSES	TREATMENT AND CONTROL	NO. OF CASES AND DEATHS
Malaria	Malaria parasite spread by anopheles mosquitoes.	Spray breeding sites with insecticides. Drain stagnant water areas. Increasingly difficult to control drug-resistant strains.	300 million people infected; 107 million new cases and 2 million deaths per year.
Bilharzia	Larvae of bilharzia breed in water snails. Larvae penetrate skin of swimmers or people working in irrigated fields. Spread by poor sanitation.	Destroy snails. Very effective drugs exist but often do not reach people who need them.	200 million cases per year; approx. 200,000 deaths.
Sleeping sickness	Parasites spread to humans by tsetse flies which suck infected blood from cattle and wild animals. Causes nagana in domestic cattle.	Difficult to eliminate. Biological solutions which restrict breeding offer some hope. Two drugs are available but they are expensive.	50 million people at risk in Africa; 25,000 cases per year.
Filariasis	Parasitic disease caused by worms and their larvae. Spread by mosquitos, other blood-sucking insects. One strain causes blindness.	Insectides. Effective drugs exist to cure blindness.	Over one million cases per year.
Tubercolosis (TB)	Spread by air-borne bacteria when infected people cough or sneeze. Highly infectious in overcrowded conditions.	Risk and death toll increasing, as bacteria become drug resistant. Growing problem in MEDCs.	World's greatest killer of adults; 2–3 million deaths per year.

PESTS

Pests are animals or insects which consume and destroy crops. It is estimated that each year pests such as locusts, weevils and rats destroy up to one half of all the world's food crops. Most of these losses are in poor countries which cannot afford pesticides or secure food storage.

The wooded and grass savannas in sub-Saharan Africa are home to one of the world's greatest pests – the tsetse fly (Table 16.1). Huge areas of tropical Africa cannot support cattle. If the testse fly could be eradicated cattle farming could help to raise living standards in this region.

WATER SUPPLIES

There are two main issues concerning water supplies in LEDCs: water quality and water shortages.

- Around 2 billion people have no access to clean water.
- Rapid population growth, industrial development, expanding irrigation and the growth of tourism have increased demand for water. This, together with climatic changes, will cause serious water shortages in the next 30 years.

Water shortages act as a brake on development. However, water supplies can often be provided at low cost. Many aid agencies fund programmes to provide safe drinking water by sinking wells. Until 1980 few villages in Moyamba, an isolated rural area in Sierra Leone, had clean drinking water. Badly polluted streams and pools led to a high incidence of water-borne diseases such as diarrhoea and hookworm. A programme, supported by the UN, planned to sink 200 wells in the region, and improve sanitation. The result has been a dramatic improvement in people's health and in their quality of life.

FOOD SUPPLIES

A healthy adult needs to consume at least 2,500 kilocalories a day. Many people in LEDCs fall well below this level. This causes undernutrition and malnutrition.

- **Undernutrition** is a lack of sufficient food which eventually leads to death by starvation.
- **Malnutrition** results from an unbalanced diet. Millions of people in LEDCs survive on monotonous diets of cheap starchy foods such as rice, cassava and sweet potatoes. A healthy diet includes carbohydrates (e.g. cereals), protein (e.g. meat), fats and vitamins.
- Malnutrition is more widespread than undernutrition. Malnutrition can cause stunted growth, and impair mental development in children. In extreme cases it causes **kwashiokor** and **marasmus**.
- Millions of people in LEDCs do not have a reliable food supply – they have little **food security**.
- **Famine** occurs when food shortages are most acute. Even if food is available, poor people may starve because they cannot afford to buy it.

DEBT AND LACK OF CAPITAL

Lack of money for investment (**capital**) and borrowing are major economic barriers to development in many LEDCs (Fig. 16.4). Capital and **credit** are needed to exploit natural resources, improve agriculture, develop new industries and pay for roads, airports, schools and hospitals.

Capital for large investment projects comes from two sources:

- inward investment from large foreign companies or TNCs (chapter 13);
- loans from governments and banks in MEDCs.

In the 1980s, many poor countries borrowed huge sums of money to pay for development. Unable to pay the interest on these loans they soon got into debt. In 1997, 32 of the poorest 54 countries in the world had a severe debt problem. Thus, money which might otherwise be spent on hospitals, schools or housing had to be paid to MEDCs.

At the village level people also need to borrow money. Until recently local money lenders charging very high interest rates were the only source of credit. The micro-credit scheme aims to tackle this problem. A sum of money is collected from foreign aid, aid agencies and the savings of local people. The local people can then borrow small amounts of money at low rates of interest. The credit may be used to set up small businesses or finance improvements to farms and homes. In 1997, 16 million people belonged to micro-credit schemes. Nearly all loans are re-paid on time.

Figure 16.4
Economic obstacles to development.

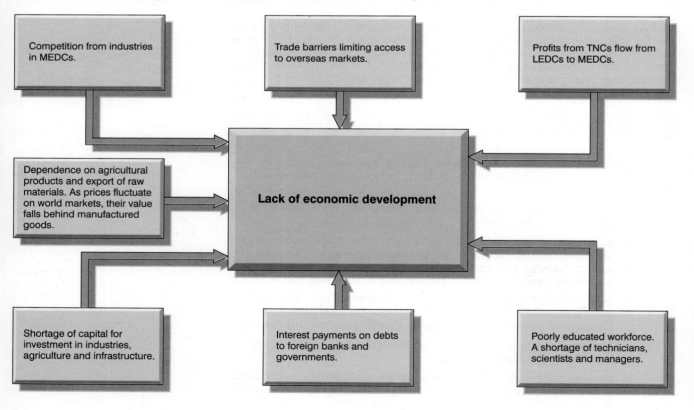

Competition from industries in MEDCs.

Trade barriers limiting access to overseas markets.

Profits from TNCs flow from LEDCs to MEDCs.

Dependence on agricultural products and export of raw materials. As prices fluctuate on world markets, their value falls behind manufactured goods.

Lack of economic development

Shortage of capital for investment in industries, agriculture and infrastructure.

Interest payments on debts to foreign banks and governments.

Poorly educated workforce. A shortage of technicians, scientists and managers.

TRADE

Most poor countries export **primary products** (food and raw materials) and import manufactured goods. This creates two problems.

- The prices of primary products fluctuate widely on world markets (Fig. 16.5).
- The prices of primary products have fallen consistently behind those of manufactured goods. Thus, poor countries get less and less for their exports and have to pay more for their imports.

Also, rich countries and economic groups such as the European Union use **tariff barriers** to protect their own industries against cheap imports from LEDCs.

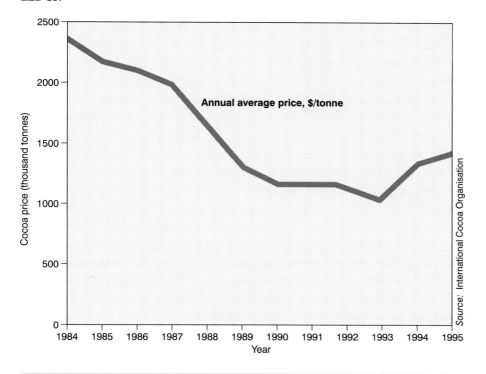

Figure 16.5
Changes in world cocoa prices, 1984–95.

POPULATION PROBLEMS

For many LEDCs population growth exceeds economic growth. Every year there are more mouths to feed, more jobs to provide, more demands for education and healthcare, yet less money per person to pay for these. However, the real problem is not population growth but poverty (Fig. 16.6). Poverty forces women to have large families which in turn can lead to a poverty cycle.

SOCIAL PROBLEMS

The rapid and successful development of several NICs in east Asia (e.g. Taiwan and South Korea) is partly because of investment in education there. Today, these NICs have workforces which are as highly skilled and educated as those in MEDCs. The contrast between Asia's NICs and other Asian countries such as Pakistan is striking. Pakistan has one of the lowest literacy rates in the world.

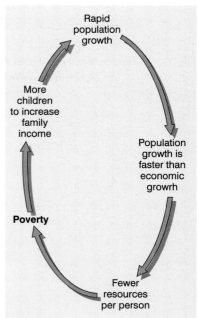

Figure 16.6 *Links between rapid population growth and poverty.*

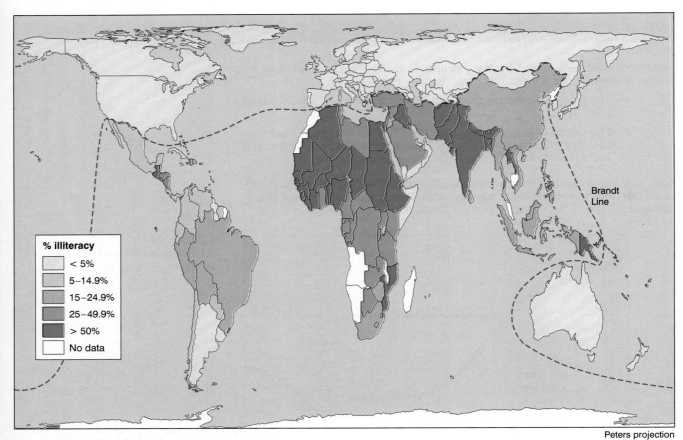

Figure 16.7 *Female literacy, 1995.*

In almost all LEDCs women are less literate than men (Fig. 16.7). This reflects the low status of women in many societies. Lack of education reduces women's chances of employment and of escaping poverty. In South Asia parents are reluctant to spend money educating daughters who leave home once they marry. And yet where women are literate infant mortality is lower, families are smaller and children have better health (Fig. 16.8).

Figure 16.8
Female literacy and infant mortality in India.

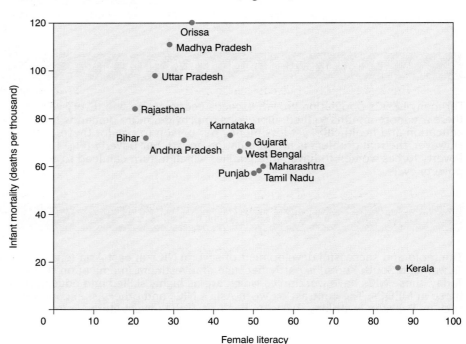

POLITICAL PROBLEMS

Many governments in LEDCs do not use their income to benefit the people.

- Smuggling and corruption within governments are common.
- Money is spent on weapons.

Political instability is another problem. Civil wars destroy essential infrastructure such as roads, pipelines and hospitals. Wars also disrupt food production and create millions of refugees.

The problems of corruption and war are worst in Africa. In the 1990s, there have been civil wars in Somalia, Sudan, Rwanda, Sierra Leone, Mozambique, Zaire and Liberia. This makes it hard for these countries to attract foreign investment.

Check yourself

QUESTIONS

Q1 Use Table 16.1 to explain the links between pests and diseases.

Q2 Why is a regular supply of good quality water vital if a country is to develop?

Q3 What is the difference between starvation and malnutrition?

Q4 Explain why each of the economic factors shown in Figure 16.4 are obstacles to a country's development.

Q5 Redraw Figure 16.6 to show what would happen if LEDCs managed to control their rapid population growth.

Q6 What do different literacy rates for males and females suggest about the status of women in society in different countries?

REMEMBER! Cover the answers if you want to.

ANSWERS

A1 The vast majority of diseases in tropical parts of the world are spread by pests (mainly insects). The most significant pests are the anopheles mosquito which spreads malaria, and the tsetse fly which is responsible for diseases in both humans and cattle.

A2 There needs to be a regular supply of water for drinking, washing and sanitation. The water needs to be of good quality to prevent the spread of disease. Water for irrigation helps to improve food supply.

TUTORIALS

T1 *Remember that the tsetse fly infects both humans and animals.*

T2 *The provision of a reliable supply of good quality water is one of the main forms of aid donated by MEDCs.*

ANSWERS

A3 Starvation is a lack of food. Malnutrition is the lack of a proper balanced diet.

A4 Competition from industries in MEDCs is intense, because these industries have economies of scale and are more efficient. They can produce goods more cheaply to undercut industries in LEDCs. The fluctuations in the price and demand for agricultural products and raw materials mean that LEDCs are never sure of the amount of income they will receive. The lack of capital means that LEDCs find it difficult to build new infrastructure, invest in new industries, provide training, or buy modern equipment. The trade barriers put up by MEDCs to protect their own industries mean that industries in LEDCs cannot easily gain access to markets in MEDCs. The interest payments on past debts mean that most of the money LEDCs make cannot be invested in future development. The profits that TNCs make from operating in LEDCs goes to the headquarters in MEDCs. The unskilled labour force means that people find it difficult to adapt to the technology of modern industry.

A5

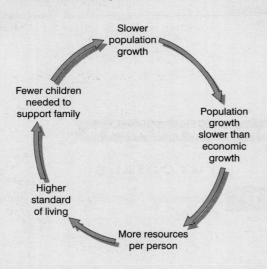

- Slower population growth
- Population growth slower than economic growth
- More resources per person
- Higher standard of living
- Fewer children needed to support family

A6 In many countries females are not seen as important as males. In these countries women's position in society is to stay at home and look after the family. For this reason women are not properly educated. Females are considered the 'property' of their husbands in many LEDCs.

TUTORIALS

T3 *It is important that you know the difference between these two terms. Remember a definition for each.*

T4 *These factors show how the balance between the rich and poor countries is so heavily stacked in favour of the MEDCs. The advantages of the MEDCs are such that the difference between them and the LEDCs is growing all the time. This is known as the Development Gap.*

T5 *Figure 16.6 is another example of the 'vicious cycle of poverty'.*

T6 *It is hoped that as women become more educated and more career-orientated this imbalance will decrease.*

16.7 REGIONAL CONTRASTS IN DEVELOPMENT

Just as there are contrasts in wealth *between* countries there are marked differences between rich and poor regions *within* countries. These regional contrasts are found in both MEDCs and LEDCs.

CASE STUDY: ITALY

No country in the EU has greater regional inequalities than Italy. There is a basic divide between the rich North and the poor South (Fig. 16.9). People in Tuscany are as prosperous as their neighbours across the Alps in Austria and Switzerland. The South by comparison is one of the poorest regions in the EU (Fig. 16.10).

Since 1950 the Italian government, and more recently the EU, has tried to reduce these regional inequalities. Huge sums of money have been poured into the South to improve agriculture, build roads and develop new industries. Despite these efforts, the differences in wealth between North and South remain.

Explaining Italy's regional inequalities

● The Italian South is on the edge or **periphery** of the EU. Its location is one reason why its development lags so far behind the North.

Other peripheral regions in the EU, such as the Scottish Highlands, western Ireland and the Greek islands, have similar problems. Generally, these peripheral regions are poorer than regions at the centre or core of the EU. A **core region** such as northern Italy grows at the expense of the peripheral South (Fig. 16.11).

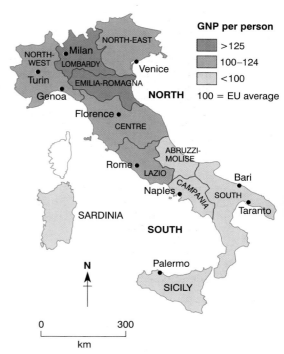

Figure 16.9 *Regional GNP per person in Italy.*

Figure 16.10 *Poverty in the south of Italy.*

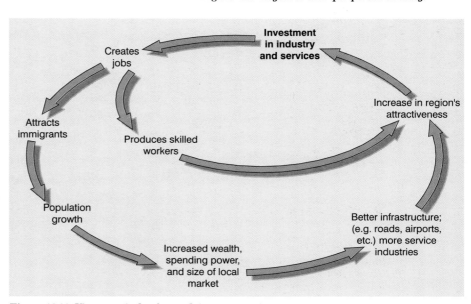

Figure 16.11 *Virtuous circle of growth in a core region.*

Apart from its location the South has other disadvantages which have hindered its development.

- Hot, dry summers make cultivation difficult without irrigation.
- Overcultivation and overgrazing in the past have produced eroded and exhausted soils.
- Much of the South is steep and mountainous.

During the twentieth century poverty has triggered massive migration from the South. People have flocked to the great northern cities, such as Milan and Turin, and even abroad to central and northern Europe, and the USA.

CASE STUDY: INDIA

India ranks 135 out of 174 countries in the UN's annual HDI. In India:

- 320 million people live in absolute poverty;
- 130 million lack basic health facilities;
- 226 million have no safe drinking water;
- around 480 million are illiterate.

Yet despite its poverty, India has made progress towards development in recent years.

- Food production has grown faster than population: there have been no famines in India since 1943.
- GNP per head has doubled in the last 30 years (albeit from a low base).
- Adult literacy increased from 34 per cent to 51 per cent between 1970 and 1996.

However, economic and social development have been uneven. Huge inequalities remain between urban and rural populations, and between men and women. There are also huge regional inequalities (Fig. 16.12).

Figure 16.12
Domestic product per person in India.

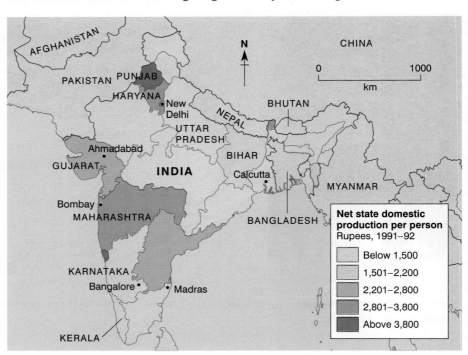

270

The better-off states (Fig. 12.12, p.206) which have achieved significant economic growth include:

- Punjab and Haryana. Both states have large areas of highly productive, irrigated farmland. They have benefited from massive increases in wheat production associated with the green revolution.

- Maharashtra and Gujarat. These have been the main industrial regions for many years. These regions have large cities and well developed infrastructure including good access to ports and the coast. More recently they have attracted foreign investment.

- Karnataka. Bangalore and its surrounding area has developed a successful software industry which serves world markets.

Table 16.2 Regional contrasts in development in India

	INDIA	KERALA	BIHAR
Life expectancy (females)	59.4	74.4	58.3
Infant mortality (per 1,000)	80	17	72
Births per woman	3.6	1.8	4.4
Literacy (% females)	39.3	86.2	22.9
Hospital beds (per million rural dwellers)	152	1,768	31

Although Kerala is one of India's poorer states (Fig. 16.12), in terms of social development it is the most advanced (Table 16.2). This reflects the priority given to education, family planning and healthcare by its socialist government. Life expectancy is similar to that in MEDCs; and the number of children born to each woman is the same as in the UK. In 1997, 60 per cent of all spending on education went to primary schools, thus raising adult literacy. This contrasts with the rest of India where higher education gets priority, which mainly benefits the better-off.

The poorest Indian states are in the North and East. States such as Uttar Pradesh and Bihar (Table 16.2) have attracted little outside investment. Social development has been slow too. Women, particularly in the northern Islamic states, have lower status than in the South. Female illiteracy, female fertility rates and infant mortality are all high (Fig. 16.8).

Check yourself

QUESTIONS

Q1
i) What is meant by 'core' and 'periphery'?
ii) Name the regions of Italy that appear to be the country's core.
iii) State one reason why the core has developed in this part of the country.
iv) Use Figure 16.9 to suggest why the Italian government encouraged the development of a few key areas such as Naples and Taranto.
v) Where do you consider the core of the UK to be?

Q2 Use information in this chapter to write a short account titled: 'India – a country of contrasts'.

ANSWERS

A1

i) The core is the economic centre of a country with the most successful agriculture and industry. The periphery is the area furthest away from the core, where the economy is stagnant or in decline.

ii) The regions of Lombardy and Emilia-Romagna is the core of Italy.

iii) This is the area nearest to the rest of Europe.

iv) The Italian government invested money in these urban areas, because they were the most likely to develop successfully in the periphery, compared to more rural areas. The government hoped that economic growth in these urban areas would perpetuate economic development there, and in the surrounding rural areas. The so-called virtuous circle of growth.

v) The core area in the UK is London and the South-east.

A2

India is a poor country: 320 million people live in absolute poverty. However, the country has made considerable progress towards development in recent years. This progress has not been evenly spread over the whole country. Most of the North and East remain very poor. The states of Bihar and Uttar Pradesh are landlocked and suffer from lack of investment. Here, the traditional way of life continues and there is poor female literacy, high birth rates and high infant mortality rates.

Industrial development around the large cities of Bombay, Ahmadabad and Bangalore has resulted in economic development in Maharashtra, Gujarat and Karnataka states. Economic development based on the green revolution has improved living standards in Punjab and Haryana. In contrast, the southern state of Kerala has given priority to social development. The emphasis on education, family planning and healthcare means that Kerala has a higher quality of life than other parts of India, despite it being one of the country's poorer states.

TUTORIALS

T1

i) Make sure that you know definitions for these two terms.

ii) These are the most prosperous regions, but the core also extends into the neighbouring regions of the North-west (around Turin) and the North-east (around Venice). A separate core has developed in northern Lazio around the capital Rome.

iii) This is not the only reason for this region's rapid development. Northern Italy has the largest area of lowland in the country. Irrigation from the River Po and its tributaries makes this area the most productive area of farmland in the country. Italy has few sources of energy, but the northern industrial cities of Milan and Turin are served by hydroelectricity produced in the Alps.

iv) These key urban areas are known as 'growth poles'. The Cassa per il Mezzogiorno (Southern Fund) allocated money to the South to encourage development there. Not all the growth poles were successful, e.g. Taranto.

v) With the opening of the Channel Tunnel it can be argued that the core has moved further south-east. The increasing importance of Europe will make northern and western parts of the UK even more peripheral. Peripheral areas can develop. The Irish republic is one of the most peripheral areas of Europe, yet it has undergone major development in recent years.

T2

You are more likely to be asked for this type of answer in a higher tier GCSE paper. You are unlikely to be asked to write a complete essay, but you may need to write a few paragraphs. You will have to base your answer either on facts and ideas you have learnt, or on information given in the question. Try to put the facts in your answer into a logical order. The point of this type of question is to see whether you appreciate the importance of particular information and whether you can draw any generalisations and conclusions based on the evidence.

EXAMINATION CHECKLIST

The facts and ideas you should know and understand after studying contrasts in development are:

- There are great contrasts in development between the richest and poorest parts of the world.
- Development is the realisation of the natural and human resource potential of a country, region or locality.
- There are two approaches to development: economic and social.
- There are many ways of measuring development.
- Measures of development include GNP per head, adult literacy rate, life expectancy rate and the human development index (HDI).
- All development measures are average figures, so they do not reveal any internal contrasts within countries.
- The world can be divided into the rich 'North' and the poor 'South' by the Brandt Line.
- Global contrasts reflect the advantages of MEDCs and the disadvantages of LEDCs.
- The disadvantages of LEDCs are both physical and environmental.
- Pests and diseases are more common in LEDCs.
- Improvements to the water supply are the key to raising living standards in many LEDCs.
- Many people in LEDCs still suffer malnutrition and starvation.
- LEDCs face considerable economic obstacles to development.
- Future economic development in LEDCs will depend on reducing population growth rates.
- Social problems such as female illiteracy need to be tackled in LEDCs.
- Development in LEDCs is often hindered by political instability and civil wars.
- There are contrasts *within* countries as well as *between* them.
- Internal contrasts exist within both MEDCs and LEDCs.
- Italy and India are good examples of countries with major regional contrasts in development.

KEY WORDS

These are the key words. Tick them if you think you know what they mean. Otherwise check on them.

economic development	food security
social development	famine
gross national product (GNP)	capital
the human development index (HDI)	credit
undernutrition	primary products
malnutrition	tariff barriers
kwashiokor	periphery region
marasmus.	core region

EXAM PRACTICE

Sample Student's Answer and Examiner's Comments

1 (a) Study the diagrams which show the age at death and the causes of death in the UK and Guatemala. (Guatemala is a LEDC in Central America.)

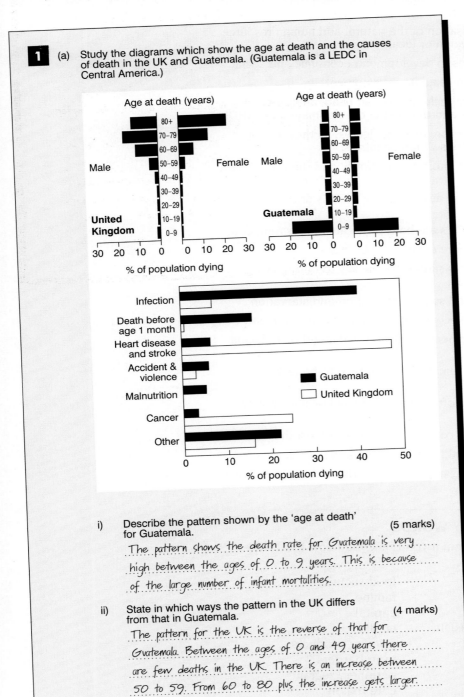

i) Describe the pattern shown by the 'age at death' for Guatemala. **(5 marks)**

> The pattern shows the death rate for Guatemala is very high between the ages of 0 to 9 years. This is because of the large number of infant mortalities.

ii) State in which ways the pattern in the UK differs from that in Guatemala. **(4 marks)**

> The pattern for the UK is the reverse of that for Guatemala. Between the ages of 0 and 49 years there are few deaths in the UK. There is an increase between 50 to 59. From 60 to 80 plus the increase gets larger.

EXAMINER'S COMMENTS

i)

He achieves 2 out of the possible 5 marks and so reaches Level 2. He has made some use of the diagram by recognising that there is a high level of infant mortality, and by referring to the death rate among 0-9 year olds in Guatemala. However, he has not used the diagram fully, and could have described the pattern in much greater depth. To reach Level 3, he needed to give a clear description of the pattern which showed understanding and made full use of the diagram. A Level 3 answer could be as follows:
'In Guatemala the overwhelming majority die when they are still young; 40% die before they reach 10 years of age. From 10 years old there is a more consistent and regular pattern.

ii)

This answer is of a very similar standard to part i). He gains 3 marks and so reaches the top of Level 2. He recognises that there is a difference and that the death rate among children in the UK is much lower, and that people live to an old age. He quotes specific age ranges from the diagram to support his answer. However, to reach Level 3 he needed to give a full, clear statement with at least two differences, making full use of the diagram. A Level 3 answer could be as follows:
'In the UK the majority live to reach old age. About 66% of people die at the age of 70 or over. There are clear signs that females live longer than males in the UK.

EXAMINER'S COMMENTS

iii)

He gains 4 marks to reach the top of Level 2. His answer shows some understanding but he tends to make statements without giving an explanation. He understands the reasons for the higher birth rates in Guatemala, but he does not relate this to death rates. He has misunderstood the diagrams, thinking of them as normal age–sex pyramids. His answer is more concerned with birth rates than death rates. A Level 3 answer would include at least two clear explanations, making use of the second diagram. A Level 3 answer might be: 'In Guatemala there is a high incidence of infectious diseases which affect the most vulnerable, such as the very young. There is a high incidence of deaths in infants. This may be the result of malnutrition as Guatemala is a poor LEDC. In the UK more people die of old age. The UK is a rich country which can control infectious diseases. Malnutrition is not a major problem. However, people living in richer countries are at greater risk of dying from heart disease, stroke or cancer.

iii) Explain why such differences exist between LEDCs and MEDCs.

(6 marks)

These differences exist between LEDCs and MEDCs, because MEDCs have a better standard of living, i.e. housing. Also, there is less need to have a lot of children in MEDCs than in LEDCs; in LEDCs parents need the children to work on the land. Some LEDCs see large numbers of children as a status symbol. The MEDCs have a good healthcare service and the LEDCs do not. The water supplies play a major part in the spread of infections and diseases in LEDCs. The MEDCs have a good, clean water supply which does not spread disease. In LEDCs such as parts of Africa there are no sewerage systems and raw sewage is in the water that people drink and wash their clothes in. The children play in the street where polluted water lies. The MEDCs, on the other hand, have a very convenient sewerage system which is separate from the drinking water.

275

Questions to Answer

The answer to Question 2 can be found in Chapter 18.

2 a) Study the map.

    i) Name one area with average weekly household spending below £210 per week.   (1 mark)

    ii) Area X has relatively high average weekly household spending and low unemployment. Suggest reasons for this.   (3 marks)

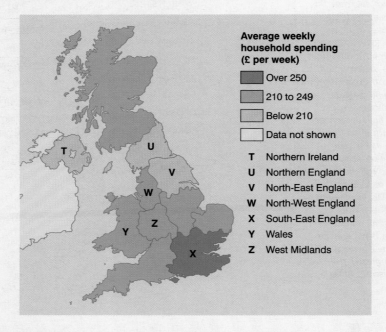

b) The amount of wealth in a country may be indicated by the average weekly household spending. Describe two other ways of indicating the wealth of a country. Explain how well each indicator works.   (8 marks)

17.1 INTERNATIONAL TRADE

International trade is the exchange of goods and services between countries.

- The goods and services that countries sell abroad are **exports**; those bought from other countries are **imports**.
- The difference between a country's exports and its imports is called its **balance of trade**.

Since 1970 there has been a huge expansion in world trade (Table 17.1). This expansion should benefit everyone and help narrow the gap between MEDCs and LEDCs (Fig. 17.1). However, not all countries have shared in the growth of world trade: the poorest have gained least. This inequality is evident in Figure 17.2.

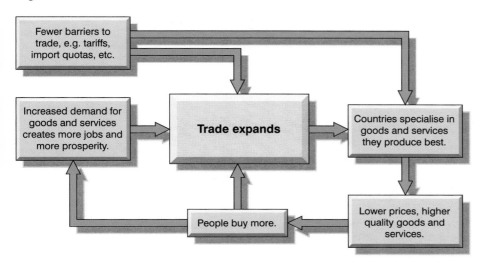

Year	Trade (billions US dollars)
1950	113
1960	232
1970	637
1980	4,095
1990	6,865
1993	7,480

Table 17.1 The growth of world trade, 1950–1993

Figure 17.1
Trade and prosperity.

17.2 INFLUENCES ON INTERNATIONAL TRADE

Many factors influence international trade (Fig. 17.3). Some, such as foreign investment and **free trade agreements** help to increase the volume of trade. Others, such as **tariffs** and **quotas** have the opposite effect.

TRADE BARRIERS

Most countries impose tariffs or tax duties on imported goods. There are two main reasons for this:

- tariffs make imports more expensive and thus protect a country's own industries from competition;
- by making foreign goods more expensive tariffs reduce the volume of imports, thereby strengthening a country's balance of trade.

Since 1947 the General Agreement on Trade and Tariffs (GATT) has reduced tariffs and promoted free trade between countries. Free trade is where tariffs, quotas and other barriers to trade are removed. This has given world trade an enormous boost. In 1995, the World Trade Organisation (WTO) replaced the GATT. The WTO has 122 member countries.

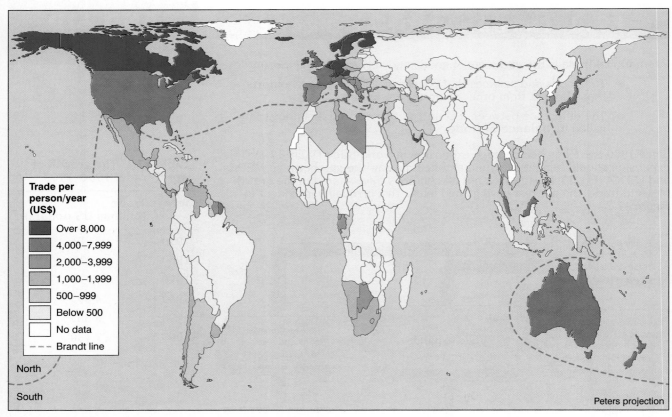

Figure 17.2 *Value of trade per person, 1993.*

Trade per person/year (US$)

- Over 8,000
- 4,000–7,999
- 2,000–3,999
- 1,000–1,999
- 500–999
- Below 500
- No data
- - - Brandt line

North
South

Peters projection

Yet even the total abolition of tariffs will not automatically lead to free trade. There are many other ways of blocking imports. They include:

- imposing fixed limits or quotas on specific goods, e.g. cars;
- insisting that imports meet certain technical standards;
- subsidising home industries to make their products cheaper than imports.

Figure 17.3
Influences on international trade.

Transport infrastructure

National government policies

Free trade agreements

Policies of transnational corporations, globalisation

International trade

Tariffs

Commodity price agreements

Economic and trade groups

TRADING GROUPS

Many countries have formed trading groups to promote trade between themselves (Fig. 17.4). The European Union (EU) with its 15 member states is the best known group. Within the EU there is:

- a single market with no tariffs blocking the movement of goods and services between member states;
- a common tariff on goods and services from outside the EU. This tariff protects EU industries from foreign competition. Without it many industries could go bankrupt and unemployment would rise.

GLOBALISATION

More and more transnational corporations (TNCs) are locating production worldwide. This globalisation of industry (chapter 13) has a number of advantages for TNCs:

- they can profit from lower labour costs or cheaper materials;
- they have direct access to markets which might otherwise be protected by tariffs and other trade barriers.

Globalisation has a direct effect on international trade. In 1997, around 40 per cent of all foreign trade took place within large companies. A growing proportion of this trade is between MEDCs and LEDCs as companies locate worldwide. Apart from its impact on world trade foreign investment spreads technology and skills, promotes economic development and provides jobs in LEDCs.

Figure 17.4
Main regional trading groups.

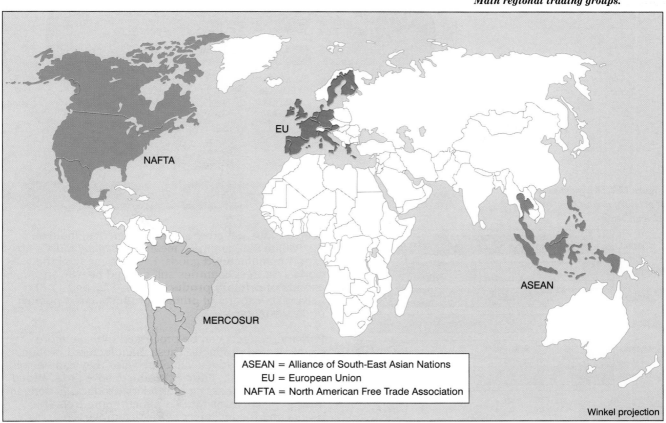

ASEAN = Alliance of South-East Asian Nations
EU = European Union
NAFTA = North American Free Trade Association

Winkel projection

Figure 17.5 *General Motors car factory in Brazil.*

South America has been particularly successful in attracting foreign investment (Fig. 17.5). In 1995, overseas companies invested 8 billion dollars in Mercosur (Fig. 17.4), mostly in the automobile industry. By 1996, Ford, VW, Renault and Fiat all had major car plants in Brazil.

Other regions in LEDCs have been less successful in attracting foreign investment. Sub-Saharan Africa received just 9 per cent of all foreign investment in LEDCs between 1990 and 1995 (see chapter 16 for reasons why). As a result this region, with 10 per cent of the world's population, accounts for just 1 per cent of the world's exports in money terms.

17.4 THE PATTERN OF WORLD TRADE

The MEDCs of the North dominate global trade (Fig. 17.6). Most of it takes place between MEDCs. However, trade between MEDCs and LEDCs is growing rapidly.

Figure 17.6
The pattern of world trade, 1994.

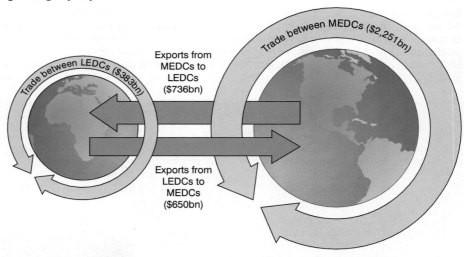

Trade between LEDCs ($383bn)

Exports from MEDCs to LEDCs ($736bn)

Trade between MEDCs ($2,251bn)

Exports from LEDCs to MEDCs ($650bn)

Figure 17.7 *Dependence on export of primary products in selected African states.*

TERMS OF TRADE

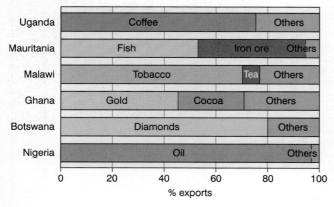

% exports

Recent industrial growth in Latin America, India and the Pacific Rim countries means that many LEDCs now export manufactured goods. Even so, many of the world's poorest countries still depend heavily on exports of **primary products** (Figs. 17.7 and 17.8). Relying on exports of primary products has a number of disadvantages.

Primary products can be processed to make more sophisticated products. These manufactured products have so-called 'added value' because they can be sold at a greater profit. Primary products have little 'added value'. Most processing of primary products is done in MEDCs. This means MEDCs benefit more from the profits and the millions of jobs this processing creates.

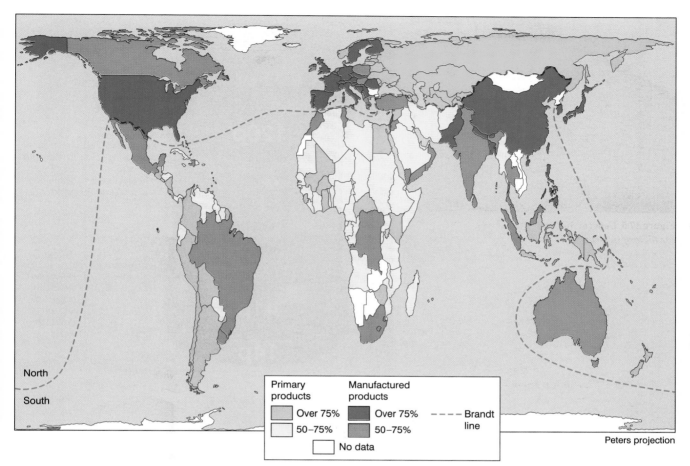

Figure 17.8 *World trade: the importance of primary and manufactured goods, 1994.*

Map legend:

Primary products	Manufactured products	
Over 75%	Over 75%	– – – Brandt line
50–75%	50–75%	
	No data	

Peters projection

North / South

Coffee is a classic example (Fig. 17.9). It is the second most valuable commodity worldwide. LEDCs such as Uganda, Ethiopia and Rwanda depend on coffee for more than half of their export earnings. And yet for every jar of instant coffee sold in the UK, the coffee producers receive less than 33 per cent of the supermarket price (Fig. 17.10). The coffee processing, packaging, advertising and retailing are all done in MEDCs.

- World prices for primary products often fluctuate wildly (see chapter 16). When commodity prices fall countries which export primary products receive less income. This makes it difficult for these countries to pay for imports and interest on foreign loans.

- Compared to manufactured goods, the value of primary products has fallen sharply in the last 30 years. This too harms the balance of trade for LEDCs.

The export profiles of the African countries in Figure 17.7 are not typical of all LEDCs. In fact, manufactured goods account for more than half of the value of exports from LEDCs. Although low-tech goods such as textiles, clothing and metals feature prominently, high-tech exports are becoming more important. Brazil, for example, exports chemicals, cars, electronic equipment and airplanes.

Figure 17.9 *Coffee growers in Columbia, South America.*

Figure 17.10
Value added on a jar of coffee.

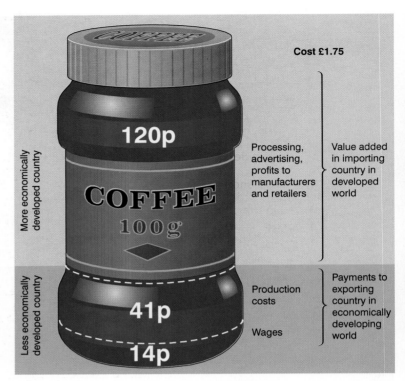

Check yourself

QUESTIONS

Q1 Explain what is meant by the term 'balance of trade'.

Q2 Study Figure 17.2. Describe the pattern of trade per person as shown on the map.

Q3 Study Figure 17.3
i) How do TNCs affect international trade?
ii) Why are commodity price agreements important in international trade?
iii) Why may national government policies work against international trade?
iv) What is the importance of the transport infrastructure?

Q4 Study Figure 17.6
i) Copy and complete the following table.

TRADE	VALUE in 1994 (billions US dollars)
LEDCs to MEDCs	?
	736
	2,251
LEDCs to LEDCS	?

ii) What conclusions can you draw from the completed table?

QUESTIONS

Q5
i) What are primary products?
ii) What is primary product dependency?
iii) Which of the African states shown on Figure 17.7 has the highest level of primary product dependency?
iv) What are the disadvantages of primary product dependency?

Q6 Figure 17.10 shows how each £1.75 spent on coffee is divided between groups involved in the coffee trade.

i) Which group receives least from the coffee trade?

ii) Which group takes most from the coffee trade?
iii) How much of the cost of a jar of coffee goes to LEDCs?
iv) Coffee growing countries earn £20 billion each year from their coffee exports. Explain why this sum is only a fraction of the total value of the world coffee trade.
v) Explain why a rise in the price of coffee in your local supermarket may not lead to a rise in the standard of living for the coffee grower.

REMEMBER! Cover the answers if you want to.

ANSWERS

A1 The difference between what a country exports and what it imports.

A2 With the exception of eastern European countries and the republics of the former Soviet Union, the Brandt Line separates the parts of the world where value of trade per person is high from those where it is low. In the 'South' exceptions are the Asian Tigers of Malaysia and Taiwan. In the 'North' Canada, Germany, Scandinavia, Australia and New Zealand have very high values of trade per person. South Asia, most of Africa, Brazil and the Andean countries of South America all have a very low value of trade per person. The only countries in Africa with a value above 500 US dollars are Libya, Tunisia and Algeria in the north; Gabon in central Africa; and Zambia, Botswana and South Africa in the south. There is a similar pattern in South America. The better-off are in the north (Venezuela, Guyana, Surinam and French Guyana) and the south (Argentina, Chile and Uruguay).

A3
i) TNCs are locating more of their operations in LEDCs which boosts the amount of trade between MEDCs and LEDCs. However, most of the profits go back to MEDCs. The TNCs' investments in LEDCs has been very selective, mostly in South America and South-east Asia. Areas such as Sub-Saharan Africa have attracted little investment and therefore little trade.

TUTORIALS

T1 *It should not be assumed that all LEDCs have a deficit on their balance of trade and all MEDCs have a surplus. It is a long time since the UK had a balance of trade surplus.*

T2 *This is a very common question at GCSE. A 'pattern' is a feature which is repeated over an area. Remember to state the general, the specific and any exceptions.*

T3
i) *The role of TNCs partly explains the imbalance in the volume of international trade between LEDCs and MEDCs.*

ANSWERS

A3

ii) When there is an internationally agreed price for a certain commodity, it stops one country undercutting another and gaining a larger share of the market.

iii) Governments like to protect their country's industries. Setting up tariffs makes foreign goods appear more expensive. This reduces demand for these goods. Governments may also impose quotas to limit foreign imports.

iv) Good transport is necessary to move goods profitably around the world. Similarly, a country must have a well developed transport infrastructure to get its goods to ports for export.

A4

i)

TRADE	VALUE in 1994 (billions US dollars)
LEDCs to MEDCs	650
MEDCs to LEDCs	736
MEDCs to MEDCs	2,251
LEDCs to LEDCS	383

ii) The bulk of the world's trade is between MEDCs. The MEDCs' exports to LEDCs is higher in value than exports from LEDCs to MEDCs. There is relatively little trade between LEDCs.

A5

i) Primary products are agricultural products such as food, and unprocessed raw materials.

ii) When a country's exports is dominated by just one or two primary products.

iii) Nigeria.

iv) Primary products have little 'added value'. Their price can fluctuate greatly and their value compared to manufactured goods has fallen sharply in the last 30 years.

TUTORIALS

T3

ii) *These agreements can help to stabilise prices and so cushion producers against fluctuations which would occur if there was a totally free market.*

iii) *Governments will always have to protect their own products to a certain degree. Totally free trade is therefore unlikely.*

iv) *The needs of the export trade often encourages the development of a country's transport infrastructure. Mauritania built an 800 kilometre railway into the desert to exploit the country's iron ore deposits.*

T4

i) *Changing information from one form to another is a common type of GCSE question. Be careful not to make careless slips.*

ii) *All you need to do here is to change the numbers into words. Do not just repeat the statistics. The only figures you should quote are any outstanding or exceptional examples.*

T5

i) and ii) *Make sure that you know both of these terms.*

iii) *Oil makes up 97 per cent of Nigeria's exports by value.*

iv) and v) *Both answers show how the balance of international trade is very much in favour of MEDCs.*

ANSWERS

A6

i) Coffee growers in LEDCs.
ii) Processing, manufacturing, advertising and retailing companies in MEDCs.
iii) 55 pence.
iv) Considerably more than £20 billion goes to other groups involved in the coffee trade, i.e. the retailers, shippers, and processors. The £20 billion that goes to coffee growing countries makes up only 27 per cent of the total coffee revenue.
v) Price increases benefit retailers, processors and distributors most. Only a tiny fraction goes to the growers.

TUTORIALS

T6

i) to iii) *The answers must be taken directly from the diagram. Take care because it is in these types of questions that simple slips are made.*
iv) *The command phrase 'comment on' allows you to express your opinion.*
v) *This is an important point to understand when studying international trade.*

17.5 FOREIGN AID

Foreign aid is the transfer of money, food, equipment and technical assistance from MEDCs to LEDCs. The United Nations (UN) recommends that MEDCs give 0.7 per cent of their GNP in foreign aid to LEDCs. However, few countries do (Table 17.2).

17.6 TYPES OF FOREIGN AID

Foreign aid takes several forms.

- **Short-term aid** is for immediate relief in emergencies such as famines, earthquakes, floods and droughts. Typically this aid includes money, food, blankets, tents and medical goods.

- **Long-term aid** is for economic and social development. Its purpose is to improve the quality of life for people living in LEDCs.

Table 17.2   Aid given by MEDCs to LEDCs, 1995

Country	Percentage of GNP given in aid to LEDCs
USA	0.16
Spain	0.23
UK	0.26
Italy	0.27
Japan	0.29
Austria	0.30
Australia	0.32
Switzerland	0.33
Finland	0.37
Germany	0.37
Belgium	0.38
Canada	0.48
France	0.62
Netherlands	0.81
Sweden	0.83
Denmark	0.87
Norway	0.92

Figure 17.11
Establishing a contour hedge to prevent soil erosion on Mount Oku, Cameroon. The A-frame is used to plot a level contour across the slope.

- **Multilateral aid** is assistance given by MEDCs to LEDCs through international bodies such as the UN, the World Bank, and the International Monetary Fund (IMF).

- **Bilateral aid** is aid given by a donor country directly to another. The aid provided by the British government through its Department for International Development (DFID) is mainly bilateral.

Charities such as Oxfam, Christian Aid and Save the Children are also important sources of aid. These **non-governmental organisations** (NGOs) rely on private donations and on government grants. They specialise in emergency relief aid and small-scale aid programmes. Often they support low-cost schemes, based on simple technology and local knowledge and skills (Fig. 17.11).

17.7 FOREIGN AID: WHO BENEFITS?

Foreign aid benefits both donor and recipient countries (Fig. 17.12). MEDCs give foreign aid for two reasons:

- For humanitarian reasons – to help people who live in misery in LEDCs.

- For the economic advantage of the donor country. For example, if the UK gives money to an LEDC it may insist that the money is spent on British goods. This is called **tied aid**. This type of aid can boost the donor country's exports and produce jobs. Sometimes, LEDCs are forced to buy goods which they could have purchased more cheaply elsewhere.

Tied aid increases the **dependency** of LEDCs on MEDCs. This is undesirable because LEDCs grow to rely on MEDCs, rather than establishing their own

Figure 17.12
Foreign aid: recipient countries.

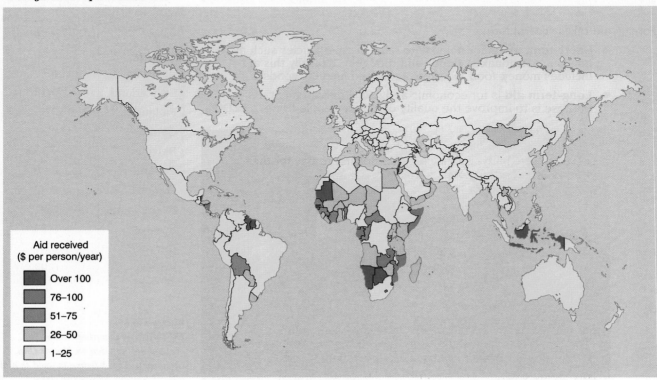

Aid received
($ per person/year)

- Over 100
- 76–100
- 51–75
- 26–50
- 1–25

industries and skilled labour force. Foreign aid does not always benefit LEDCs. Misuse of foreign aid in LEDCs is widespread. Often, aid ends up in the pockets of politicians, government officials and the better off.

17.8 INTERDEPENDENCE

Increasingly the developed countries of the North and the developing countries of the South depend on each another. North and South are linked by trade, investment, loans, interest payments, foreign aid and international migration (Fig. 17.13).

INTERDEPENDENCE AND MEDCS

Interdependence has many advantages for MEDCs.

- LEDCs supply commodities such as oil, mineral ores, timber and foodstuffs for manufacturing industries in MEDCs.
- Profits flow to MEDCs from investments by TNCs, banks and other organisations in LEDCs, and from interest payments on loans.
- Tied aid boosts exports and secures jobs in MEDCs.

However, interdependence does have disadvantages for MEDCs.

- As TNCs invest in LEDCs jobs may be lost in MEDCs.
- Competitive, new industries in LEDCs could destroy many industries and jobs in MEDCs.

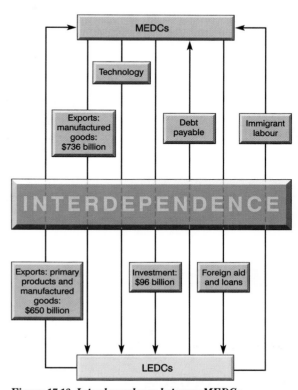

Figure 17.13 *Interdependence between MEDCs and LEDCs (figures are for 1994).*

INTERDEPENDENCE AND LEDCS

Interdependence also creates advantages and disadvantages for LEDCs. The main advantages are:

- LEDCs receive hard currency (e.g. US dollars) to pay for their imports by exporting goods to MEDCs.
- Investment by foreign TNCs provides jobs, promotes new skills, transfers modern technology, and allows LEDCs to use their cheap labour force to their advantage.
- Foreign aid.

The main disadvantages of interdependence for LEDCs are:

- The terms of trade often work against LEDCs.
- Foreign companies sometimes exploit raw materials at the expense of the environment. In Ogoniland, Nigeria, oil production by TNCs has caused massive oil spillages. The resulting pollution has damaged fish stocks, agricultural land, mangroves and water resources, and threatens the health of 6 million people.
- Foreign aid encourages dependency. Some LEDCs in Africa depend on foreign aid for one quarter of their income.

Check yourself

QUESTIONS

Q1 According to Table 17.2, which countries reached the UN's recommendation for the amount of aid MEDCs should give to LEDCs?

Q2 Study Figure 17.12.

i) Which countries received the highest amount of aid per person per year? Use an atlas to help you.

ii) Which of these countries appears to be the odd one out? Explain your answer.

iii) Many of these countries are (or were) colonies of European countries. Why do you think this is significant?

iv) In what respect can aid to these former colonies be considered as examples of tied aid?

Q3 Explain why the giving of aid to LEDCs may not be always successful.

Q4

i) What is 'interdependence'?

ii) State one advantage and one disadvantage of interdependence to MEDCs.

iii) State one advantage and one disadvantage of interdependence to LEDCs.

iv) Do MEDCs or LEDCs gain most from interdependence? Explain your answer.

v) What do you think is the meaning of the following cartoon?

"I have you under my control."

REMEMBER! Cover the answers if you want to.

ANSWERS

A1 Netherlands, Sweden, Denmark and Norway.

A2

i) Surinam, French Guyana, Mauritania, Namibia, Botswana, Israel and Indonesia.

ii) The odd one out is Israel. A lot of aid is given by Jews around the world.

iii) The colonies were established to provide the colonising countries with raw materials and other products. The colonising countries will have maintained close links with the colonies, including the giving of aid.

iv) In return for aid the colonising countries may expect preferential treatment in terms of prices of raw materials, and relaxation of tariffs or quotas.

TUTORIALS

T1 *The UN recommendation for aid giving is 0.7% of a country's GNP.*

T2

i) *In an examination you would not be expected to name as many as this.*

ii) *A lot of this aid is therefore given for religious reasons rather than economic or social ones.*

iii) *Surinam and Indonesia were formally Dutch colonies. French Guyana and Mauritania were colonised by France. Namibia was colonised by Germany until it was given to South Africa. Botswana was a British colony.*

iv) *The former British colonies are still loosely linked to Great Britain by the Commonwealth. The French colonies in the French Union are more closely tied to France. Some of the independent former colonies resent the continuing influence of the former colonial power.*

ANSWERS

A3 Not all the aid sent to LEDCs is suitable. Aid can be highly technical equipment which requires skilled personnel to use it. People in LEDCs may therefore be given equipment they cannot work. Some aid is given only with certain preconditions, which might not be desirable for people receiving the aid. Aid may end up with the wrong people or be spent on unsuitable projects, such as buying military equipment. If aid is given too freely it may discourage people from helping themselves, making them dependent on aid.

A4
i) Interdependence is recognition of the fact that MEDCs and LEDCs are so closely linked economically that they need to work together for their mutual benefit.

ii) The LEDCs provide a regular supply of cheap primary products for use in manufacturing industries in MEDCs. The growth of manufacturing industries in areas such as South-east Asia provides competition for industries in MEDCs.

iii) Investment by MEDCs allows LEDCs to develop their natural and human resources. The exploitation of raw materials in LEDCs can have a serious environmental impact.

iv) It is likely that MEDCs are gaining most from interdependence. The gap in development between the developed and developing countries is increasing. International trade is reinforcing the advantages that MEDCs have. Many LEDCs are finding it increasingly difficult to match MEDCs in development terms.

v) The cartoon is a visual representation of interdependence. If LEDCs do not provide MEDCs with the raw materials they need then industries in MEDCs will suffer. However, if LEDCs do not sell their raw materials to MEDCs they will not be able to develop. Neither group can totally dominate the other.

TUTORIALS

T3 *This type of question would be in a higher tier paper. On a foundation tier paper, the question would be reworded, for example:*
State two reasons why aid money does not always reach the people in a LEDC who need it most.

T4
i) *You should know a definition for this term.*
ii) and iii) *These are only examples. There are other advantages and disadvantages in this chapter.*
iv) *You will often be asked to give your opinion. Remember that there is no right or wrong answer. You will gain marks for the reasons you give to support your opinions.*
v) *The cartoon expresses what is meant by interdependence better than many written explanations.*

EXAMINATION CHECKLIST

The facts and ideas you should know and understand after studying trade and aid are:

- International trade is the exchange of goods and services between countries.
- A country's exports are the things it sells abroad. A country's imports are the things it buys from abroad.
- The difference between a country's exports and imports is its balance of trade.
- Foreign investment, free trade agreements and the creation of trading blocs increase the volume of trade.
- Quotas and tariffs may decrease the volume of trade.
- There has been rapid growth in world trade but this expansion has been greater in MEDCs than in LEDCs.
- NAFTA and the EU are examples of trading groups.
- TNCs have had a major impact on the development of world trade.
- MEDCs dominate world trade.
- Although manufacturing is increasing in LEDCs, many countries still suffer from primary product dependency.
- Processing primary products 'adds value' to them. MEDCs benefit most from this 'added value'.
- Aid is the transfer of money, food and equipment to countries that need these.
- There are four main types of aid: short-term aid, long-term aid, bilateral aid and multilateral aid.
- Both governments and non-governmental organisations (NGOs) give aid.
- Some aid is tied aid and gives advantages to countries that donate it.
- There is increasing interdependence between MEDCs and LEDCs.
- Interdependence brings both advantages and disadvantages to MEDCs and LEDCs.
- Not all aid benefits the countries receiving it. Aid may lead to increasing dependency.

KEY WORDS

These are the key words. Tick them if you think you know what they mean. Otherwise check on them.

exports	short-term aid
imports	long-term aid
balance of trade	multilateral aid
free trade agreements	bilateral aid
tariffs	non-governmental organisations (NGOs)
quotas	tied aid
primary products	dependency

EXAM PRACTICE

Sample Student's Answer and Examiner's Comments

1 (a) Study the diagram which shows information on the pattern of trade for countries around the shores of the Mediteranean Sea.

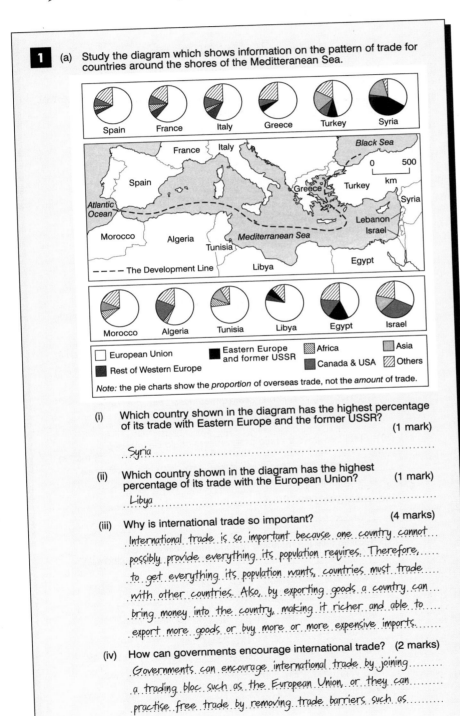

Note: the pie charts show the *proportion* of overseas trade, not the *amount* of trade.

(i) Which country shown in the diagram has the highest percentage of its trade with Eastern Europe and the former USSR?

(1 mark)

Syria

(ii) Which country shown in the diagram has the highest percentage of its trade with the European Union? (1 mark)

Libya

(iii) Why is international trade so important? (4 marks)

International trade is so important because one country cannot possibly provide everything its population requires. Therefore, to get everything its population wants, countries must trade with other countries. Also, by exporting goods a country can bring money into the country, making it richer and able to export more goods or buy more or more expensive imports.

(iv) How can governments encourage international trade? (2 marks)

Governments can encourage international trade by joining a trading bloc such as the European Union, or they can practise free trade by removing trade barriers such as tariffs and quotas.

a) ***i)***
This is correct.

ii)
This is correct.
In both cases she read the correct information from the diagram, showing that she can interpret pie charts and use a key correctly.

iii)
She gains three out of a possible four marks. The first mark is for recognising that a country cannot supply all its own needs. She reaches the next level for saying that trade brings in money to a country and that this money can be used to buy imported goods. She needed to give examples to support the points she made in order to reach Level 3 and gain full marks.

iv)
She has made three valid points and gains maximum marks. Marks are given for "joining a trading bloc"; "can practice free trade"; and "by removing trade barriers such as tariffs and quotas". She shows complete understanding.

b) *i)*

This is correct.
Notice how the examiner has made
reading the graph easier by making
the bar for the UK stand out.

ii)

Again, she has made three valid points
and gains maximum marks. Marks are
given for "the country receiving the aid
does something in return"; "buy the
donor country's goods"; and the final
sentence. It is a good idea to use the
marks allocated to a question part as a
guide when writing your answer. Don't
be afraid to write a little extra just in
case one of the statements you have
made is incorrect. However, don't write
excessive amounts and waste time. In
an examination paper, the examiner
will give you the number of lines that
it is needed to gain full marks,
whatever the size of your writing.

iii)

She gains both marks. The reduction
in the amount of tied aid given and a
greater emphasis on long-term aid are
both good suggestions. Notice how this
part is more open ended. This is
because it is towards the end of the
question.

iv)

Her answer reaches Level 2 and gains
two marks. The definition of long-term
development in the first sentence is
worth one mark. She has developed
this definition to show clear
understanding with the reference to
education improving standard of living
in the next generation.
The inclusion of another developed
point would have taken her to the
top of Level 2 with 3 marks. The
lack of a precise case study means
that she did not reach Level 3, and
so gain 5 marks.

She scored 20 out of the possible 25
marks which represents a Grade A
standard.

(b) Study the graph about aid programmes to LEDCs.

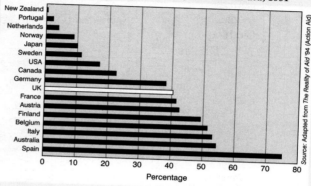

Tied aid as a percentage of total govermental aid, 1991

Source: Adapted from *The Reality of Aid '94* (Action Aid)

(i) The graph shows the percentage of each country's aid
programme that is given as tied aid. How much of the
UK's aid was given as tied aid in 1991? (1 mark)
40%

(ii) What is the meaning of the term 'tied aid'? (2 marks)
Tied aid is aid which is given to a country, so long as
the country receiving the aid does something in return,
such as buy the donor country's goods or pay the money
back with interest. It is aid with 'strings attached'.

(iii) State two ways that aid programmes could be improved.
(2 marks)
Aid programmes could give money with 'no strings attached'.
The receiving country would not have to pay back the
money. Also the countries could send people and experts
(such as teachers) instead of money.

(iv) Explain fully the meaning of 'long-term development'.
(You may use one or more examples that you have studied.)
(5 marks)
'Long-term development' means investing in a project which
over several years would help to improve a developing country.
Things such as education for example. By investing in
education the next generation will be much more educated
and able to help raise their country's standard of living. Also,
long-term development would stay in place for many, many
years to come. Using the example of education, once a good
system of education has been set up, it would stay in place
for many years, and improve a country's standard of living.

SEG, 1997.

Questions to Answer

The answer to Question 2 can be found in Chapter 18.

2 a) The table shows some of the types of aid sent from MEDCs to LEDCs.

SHORT-TERM AID	LONG-TERM AID
Food Aid	Education
Blankets and Tents	Training
Lorries	Capital Investment
Medicines	Infrastructure improvement
Clothing	
Water tankers	

i) Explain the meaning of the term 'short-term aid'. (1 mark)

ii) Why might long-term aid be of more use to a LEDC? (3 marks)

b) Study the diagram which shows how some LEDCs are dependent on primary products for their exports.

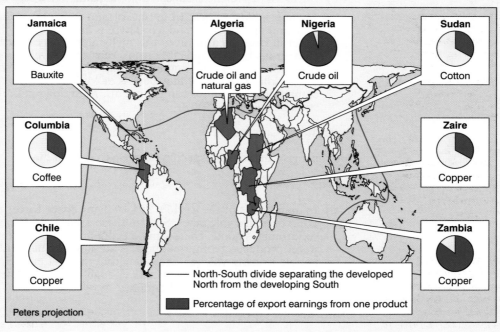

Jamaica — Bauxite

Algeria — Crude oil and natural gas

Nigeria — Crude oil

Sudan — Cotton

Columbia — Coffee

Zaire — Copper

Chile — Copper

Zambia — Copper

— North-South divide separating the developed North from the developing South

▮ Percentage of export earnings from one product

Peters projection

SEG (specimen paper)

i) What are 'primary products'? (1 mark)

ii) Use the diagram to analyse the pattern of primary product dependency in the world. (3 marks)

iii) What advantages does this pattern of primary product dependency bring to the MEDCs? (8 marks)

ANSWERS TO EXAM PRACTICE

CHAPTER 1 — EARTHQUAKES AND VOLCANOES

Answer

2 a) i) Possible examples are Surtsey or Tristan da Cunha on the North American/Eurasian plate boundary.
   ii) The location of volcanoes generally coincides with plate margins, but there are exceptions in East Africa, Russia, China and Hawaii.

   b) There is an extrusion of magma under the Pacific. Sea floor spreading is taking place as the Juan de Fuca plate moves towards North America. The Juan de Fuca plate is subducted under the North American plate at a destructive boundary. There is magma production in the subduction zone, some of which penetrates weaknesses in the crust. Magma under Mount St Helens has not solidified, so these processes are still continuing. The pressure builds up so that the volcano erupts periodically.

Examiner's Comments

Look for five separate points but bear in mind that more than one mark can be given for a developed point.

Answer

   c) If Mount St Helens is chosen a possible answer would be:

   There is a blast of heat from the volcano which leads to an avalanche of rock and melted snow and ice. There is an increase in the volume of water in rivers as a result of this meltwater. This can wash away bridges. Dangerous hot ash and cinders are released as well as clouds of poisonous gas. Homes and large areas of forest can be destroyed. People can be killed and there may be loss of wildlife habitats. The main communication routes can get cut off. Mud flows pollute rivers and streams killing the fish.

Examiner's Comments

You must give details of a specific example to get full marks.

Answer

   d) In many parts of the world a lack of living space forces people to live in areas of active volcanoes. Soils in these areas tend to be rich in minerals, so farming is good. There can be economic benefits from tourism. Hot water produces geothermal power. Sulphur can be extracted. Many people living in volcanic areas feel that they get enough warning before volcanoes erupt. This gives them enough time to escape. People argue that eruptions are very infrequent.

Examiner's Comments

There is single point marking for this question with a maximum of 1 mark for an example.

CHAPTER 2 — ROCKS AND LANDFORMS

Answer

2 a) i) Limestone pavement – B
          Swallow Hole – A
          Cavern – C.

ii) Fell Beck flows across mixed sedimentary rocks which are impermeable (1 mark), and then disappears down Gaping Gill (1 mark). This forms a waterfall (1 mark) until it reaches the impermeable slates (1 mark). After this, Fell Beck flows underground (1 mark) until it reappears (1 mark) at the surface at Clapham Beck (1 mark).

Examiner's Comments

Three different points are required. Notice that there are many different ways of achieving the three marks. The question asks only for description, so describe in as much detail as possible what you see in the diagram.

Answer

iii) Level 1 (1–2 marks) Basic understanding.
The answer is restricted to information in the diagram. The answer is largely concerned with the geology and merely states that a certain rock is permeable or impermeable.
Level 2 (3–4 marks) Clear understanding.
There is a greater depth of explanation, particularly of the words permeable and impermeable. Gaping Gill is explained as a swallow hole formed by limestone solution.
Level 3 (5–6 marks) Detailed understanding.
The answer shows an understanding of the weathering processes involved in the development of karst scenery. Rain water is described as a weak acid which chemically dissolves limestone or calcium carbonate. This changes the limestone to calcium bicarbonate which dissolves in the water. This attack takes place along the joints and bedding planes as limestone is a permeable rock.

b) People trampling on the ground will harm vegetation. This would result eventually in bare earth which could then be eroded by wind and rain. Visitors may cause pollution by dropping litter. The creation of a honeypot site with many visitors would cause traffic congestion and disruption to the life of the local inhabitants.

Examiner's Comments

Three developed points are required here.

CHAPTER 3 RIVERS

Answer

2 a) i) H – Slip-off slope or point bar
J – Ox-bow lake
M – Flood plain
N – River cliff or bluff.
ii) The river is flowing from the top left to the bottom right of the sketch (1 mark). There is turbulence on the downstream side of the weir. (1 mark)

Examiner's Comments
This is an example of a question where the examiner asks you to interpret what you can see on a sketch. A photograph is often used for the same purpose. Notice that there are two parts to this question. You must answer both parts to gain full marks. In an examination you would be asked to draw an arrow on the sketch to show the direction of flow.

Answer

iii) Level 1 (1 mark) Basic understanding.
The river cliff (or bluff) and the slip-off slope are identified but there is no attempt at explanation.
Level 2 (2–3 marks) Clear understanding.
There is clear understanding of the erosion on the outside and deposition on the inside of the meander. There is evidence of an understanding that the meanders move sideways. There is no explanation of how the processes of erosion, deposition and lateral meander shift lead to the formation of the river cliff (or bluff) and the slip-off slope.
Level 3 (4–5 marks) Detailed understanding.
There is detailed understanding of how the fast current migrates to the outside of the bend and undercuts the bank, causing the river cliff (or bluff) to migrate laterally; and that there is slower running water on the inside of the meander causing deposition of sediment on the point bar.

Examiner's Comments

Notice that the question specifically mentions river processes. To get the highest marks you must describe what the river is actually doing to form the features at H and N. Make sure you deal with both the river cliff and the slip-off slope. Don't assume that the examiner will guess what is happening on the side of the meander you do not describe.

Answer

iv) The weir helps to regulate the river flow. This makes the river less likely to break its banks. The flood control embankment attempts to stop the river covering the whole of the flood plain.

Examiner's Comments

Make sure that you look carefully for other pieces of evidence which may help you answer the question.

Answer

v) MEDCs have greater technical knowledge which means they have the ability to build successful flood control and prevention measures. More money is available in the MEDCs for flood control. In LEDCs more people are dependent on agriculture which means they are more likely to live and work on the flood plain where there are ample supplies of water and fertile soils.

Examiner's Comments

Note there are three developed points here. The question asks for three reasons which implies your answer will be point marked rather than in levels.

CHAPTER 4 GLACIATION

Answer

2 a) i) A – Ribbon Lake
B – Blea Water
C – Glacial trough
D – Arête – Riggindale Crag.

Examiner's Comments

This question tests your ability to look at two maps at the same time and cross reference information from one to the other. Sometimes the examiner will ask you to relate a diagram to a photograph or a map to a photograph.

Answer

ii) The western side of the valley has been cut into a series of tributary glaciers which have formed corries. At the back of these corries and between them there are steep rocky outcrops. The contour lines on the eastern side of the valley are close together showing the steep edge to the V-shaped valley. The eastern slopes consist of a straight, regular drop into the valley. There are truncated spurs left over from when the main glacier moved down the valley. Above 700 metres, on the eastern side, the slopes are more gentle. These are the remnants of the former river valley.

Examiner's Comments

When revising the main features of a glaciated highland (or upland) area, make sure that you can describe their appearance and recognise them from an Ordnance Survey map extract. It's a useful exercise to draw simplified contour maps showing the pattern of contours. Remember that the closer together the contours are, the steeper the slope.

Answer

b) There are a large number of acceptable answers. The spectacular scenery encourages tourism, so people can make a living in these areas. They could earn money from skiers in the winter and walkers in the summer. Highland areas are important for sheep farming. There are specific jobs related to highland areas such as forestry work and HEP production. The flat valley floors may be fertile, allowing some agricultural activity. Glaciologists may live there to study the ice. The pollution free air may attract people to these areas.

Examiner's Comments

There is little indication of how many reasons have to be given to gain full marks. However, the number of marks is the best indication. The fact that there are only three marks available suggests that the answer will be point marked. Generally there needs to be a minimum of four marks available for an answer to be level marked.

CHAPTER 5   COASTS

Answer

2   i)   A – Cliffs
        B – Beaches/pebbles/shingle
        C – Wave-cut platform
        D – Shingle/beach.

Examiner's Comments

Only one of the possible answers for each letter is required.

Answer

ii) Level 1 (1–2 marks) Basic understanding.

The answer does not define the erosion processes precisely. For example: 'the sea washes the foot of the cliffs and they fall down'.
Level 2 (3–4 marks) Clear understanding.
The answer contains detailed explanations of coastal erosion processes, or describes the sequence of events leading to cliff recession and the formation of the wave-cut platform.
Level 3 (5–6 marks) Detailed understanding.
The sequence of events leading to cliff recession is explained with precise reference to the erosion processes involved. A Level 3 response would be along these lines: 'The cliff face is attacked by the abrasive force of the sea. The sand and shingle carried by the sea erode the bottom of the cliff causing a cliff notch. This notch undercuts the cliff and eventually the overhang collapses...'

Examiner's Comments

It is important that you read the question carefully. There are two distinct parts to this question. These are 'processes' and 'cliff recession'. You need to refer to both and make the necessary links between them, if you are to reach Level 3. You can annotate the diagram to help you answer the question. The examiner is likely to mark the written part first and then see if any extra credit can be given for what has been added to the diagram. It may be possible to gain full marks from the written part. You do not have to use the diagram. Do not waste time adding things to the diagram which you have already written about.

Answer

iii) The cliffs may be eroded by people climbing them. There may be pollution from litter. Traffic may choke the narrow country lanes and the small village of East Quantoxhead. The presence of fields suggests that this is a farming area. The tourists may damage crops or frighten animals.

Examiner's Comments

The three marks allocated for this part of the question suggest that three reasons are required. Notice that use can be made of all the information in the field sketch. You do not have to confine yourself to the physical environment of the coast.

Answer

iv) Way-marking trails to keep visitors to footpaths. Providing tourist amenities away from the most sensitive areas.

Examiner's Comments

Notice that two suggestions are asked for. This tells you that the answer will be point marked rather than in levels.

CHAPTER 6 WEATHER AND CLIMATE

Answer

2 i) High pressure system or anticyclone.

Examiner's Comments

The answer can be taken directly from the map. It is better to use the correct technical term. The word 'High' may not be present on the map so you must be able to recognise an anticyclone from the pattern of its isobars. This is a typical anticyclone where the isobars make a roughly circular pattern. They are widely spaced indicating a gentle pressure gradient. The pressure is greater than 1012 mb.

Answer

ii) Warm front.

Examiner's Comments

The semi-circular marks along a front indicate a warm front. Triangles are found along a cold front.

Answer

iii) One okta of cloud. Temperature is 22 °C. There is a wind coming from the south south-east at a speed of 8–12 knots.

Examiner's Comments

An okta means an eighth, so only one eighth of the sky is covered with cloud. The direction of the wind is the most common mistake in this type of question. Remember that the 'shaft of the arrow' faces the direction that the wind comes *from*.

Answer

iv) The warm front is crossing this part of the British Isles (1 mark). This is where warm air is being forced above cold air. This causes water vapour in the air to cool, condense and produce rain (1 mark).

Examiner's Comments

The command word 'why' shows that the examiner is looking for an explanation. The two available marks show that recognition of the front alone is not sufficient.

Answer

v) Level 1 (1-2 marks) Basic understanding.
The answer only states that the weather would get wetter and colder. There is no attempt to relate changes in weather to the replacement of the anticyclone by a depression.
Level 2 (3–4 marks) Clear understanding.
Little or no attempt is made to make use of the information on the weather chart. There are no references to specific temperatures, wind direction, cloud cover or any other features of the weather shown on the chart. The answer concerns itself with the depression as a whole and does not recognise that the weather is influenced only by the cold front and cold sector parts of the depression.
Level 3 (5–6 marks) Detailed understanding.
The answer recognises that only part of the depression is affecting the British Isles, and that the eastern part of the country will be under the influence of the cold front. This will cause rain which will last for a few hours and is likely to be heavy. The rest of the country will be covered by the cold sector, so temperatures will drop and the air will become clearer. Any rain is likely to be isolated showers accompanied by bright periods.

Examiner's Comments

This question allows the best candidates to show their ability. It would be very easy to write a 'standard' description of the weather associated with the passage of a depression. You need to look carefully at information in the weather chart. The key to this question is the position of the cold front along the east coast.

CHAPTER 7 THE ECOSYSTEM CONCEPT

Answer

2 a) i)   The rainforests are distributed around the Equator.

Examiner's Comments

This type of straightforward question is often used as a lead. The answer may appear too obvious but don't be tempted to be too clever with your answer.

Answer

    ii) The temperature is fairly constant throughout the year. The average temperature is between 23–30°C.
    iii) The annual total is high, normally over 1500 mm. It rains throughout the year.

Examiner's Comments

Notice that parts ii) and iii) require simple facts about the climate of the rainforests. No credit will be given for explanation. Precise details are required. No credit would be given for generalisations such as 'very hot' or 'very dry'. Climatic statistics need to be quoted.

Answer

  b) i)   The relationship between living and non-living things.

Examiner's Comments

Notice that there are two marks for this question. This is very common in a question asking for a definition. The answer must be detailed and show full understanding. Avoid giving answers which are too simple. A simple answer would refer only to the animals and plants and not the relationship between them. The critical aspect of an ecosystem is the relationship or link between the animals, plants and non-living things.

Answer

    ii) In the rainforests there is a great variety of vegetation types. These vary greatly in scale, from large trees to small plants. Within the rainforest there are a large number of mini environments, each with their own characteristics and associated life forms. There is plenty of food because of the ideal growing conditions. This abundance of food supports a well developed food chain with plants, herbivores, omnivores and carnivores.

Examiner's Comments

This question allows you to show your understanding of the workings of an ecosystem, and the movements of energy and the recycling of nutrients through the system.

Answer

  c) Level 1 (1–2 marks) Basic understanding.
    The answer merely repeats information from the diagram, either by quoting a figure or indicating the cause of deforestation in a particular part of the world.
    Level 2 (3–4 marks) Clear understanding.
    Answer states there has been a decline in traditional rainforest activities, replaced by new activities. It mentions that activities such as cattle ranching and mining take money away from the native peoples. There

will be a loss of habitats and with this a number of rare species of animals and plants will die. The new activities may harm the native peoples of the area.

Level 3 (5–6 marks) Detailed understanding.

Answer recognises that tree felling will remove food sources and shelter. The loss of some species would have an impact on the food chain. The loss of exotic plants may mean the loss of genetic banks or medicines which may improve health. The introduction of non-traditional activities would mean the indigenous people losing their way of life and associated skills.

Examiner's Comments

The command words 'comment on' are normally used in one of the latter parts of an exam question. They make the question more open ended. This gives better candidates a chance to develop their answers more fully, to express opinions and make judgements. These types of question are usually level rather than point marked.

CHAPTER 8 THE GLOBAL DISTRIBUTION OF POPULATION

Answer

2 A – Migrants to Calcutta. There are a large number of 20–40 year olds.
B – MEDC city. The population is evenly balanced. There is a small proportion of young children which indicates a low birth rate. There is a large number of people aged over 60.
C – LEDC. There is a high birth rate and a high death rate. This is shown by the broad base and narrow peak to the pyramid.
D – Rural village. There are relatively few men, particularly between the ages of 20–30. The population consists of mainly females and older people.

Examiner's Comments

These are the most common population pyramids that you are likely to be tested on. In this question the examiner has used actual examples of places, because the syllabus was based on the locations named. Even if you have not studied these locations you should recognise the shapes of the pyramids from other places you have studied.

CHAPTER 9 MIGRATION

Answer

2 i) Four possible answers are: largest numbers of migrants are from South-east Europe; largest of all from Italy; there are migrants from nearly all western European countries; there are none from northern and eastern Europe.

Examiner's Comments

Four separate points are required. Reference could have been made to the large number of Turkish immigrants. When describing a pattern it is important to refer to the exceptional areas. In this case, the areas which do not appear to be a source of immigrants to West Germany. The question asks you to get your information from the map. Do not use any of your own knowledge which is not supported by the map details.

Answer

ii) Level 1 (1–2 marks) Basic understanding.
The answer merely lists a number of points. Answer is one-sided dealing only with advantages or disadvantages. Possible points are racial or cultural tension; housing shortage or overcrowding. Advantages include new take-away foods and source of labour.
Level 2 (3–4 marks) Clear understanding.
Simple points are developed further by giving explanations. For example, racial or cultural tensions can develop when people are housed in only basic or cheap accommodation, and are given only low paid and low status work.
Level 3 (5–7 marks) Detailed understanding.
In order to reach this level the answer needs to consider in detail both the advantages and disadvantages of the arrival of immigrants. The problem of poor housing and low status would be made worse by the increased distance from the supportive influence of families. The extended family, a feature of many areas, is likely to break down in the new country to which the emigrants have moved. There may be language difficulties and raised expectations which could lead to tension, dissatisfaction or crime. Higher ability candidates may also consider repatriation costs and political factors. On the positive side the new country would have a greater variety of items such as food, shops and clothing. There would be a greater appreciation of different cultural backgrounds which would broaden peoples' outlook. There are the economic advantages of a cheap, young labour force.

Examiner's Comments

In a higher tier paper, aimed at grades A* to D it is very important that you read the question carefully. It is likely that the question contains more than one command word or task. In a foundation tier paper there is only likely to be one command word per question. In this example you are asked to consider both advantages and disadvantages. In a foundation tier, this question would be subdivided into two subsections, one dealing with advantages ,the other with disadvantages. In a higher tier question you may be asked to describe and explain something.

CHAPTER 10 SETTLEMENT PATTERNS

Answer

2   i)   North-east, North North-east.

Examiner's Comments

The best way of answering this type of question is to line up a major feature on the photograph with the same feature on the map. This is easiest to do with a linear feature such as a road, a river or a railway. In this case use the River Tees.

Answer

ii) a) Works.
b) Museum.

Examiner's Comments

You need to use the map and the photograph in order to answer this question.

Answer

iii) The River Tees acts as a moat and so provides a defence on one side of the castle. The castle is built on a small hill which gives a better view of the surrounding area. The map shows that the straight (probably Roman) road crosses the river at this point. The castle would be able to control this bridging point.

Examiner's Comments

Notice the question asks you to use the map and the photograph. It is useful to show the examiner that you have done this by using expressions like "from the photograph I can see...", "the map tells me that...."

Answer

iv) The river appears to have restricted the growth of the town towards the south-west. Only Startforth is found on this side of the river. The layout of Startforth appears to be fairly modern, so this development may have happened comparatively recently.

Examiner's Comments

Look at the shape or layout of the town and take particular notice of the street patterns. This will give you clues to the stages in the development of the town.

Answer

v) The area around the castle.
vi) Reasons include: the town would have grown up around the castle near the bridging point of the river. Early housing would have been there in order to gain some protection from the castle. The grid-like pattern of the roads in this part of the town suggests that it is older. On the photograph and the map it is possible to see what appears to be a market or centre square which would be the main meeting point or focus of the town.
vii) The surrounding area is agricultural, so Barnard Castle probably acts as a market centre for the surrounding farms. The school appears to be a secondary school, serving not only the town itself, but also the surrounding rural area. As a bridging point of the river, the roads tend to focus on the town and this gives the settlement the function of a route centre. The castle ruins will attract visitors, so there could be tourist activities. The large museum in 0516 will bring people to the town. The Youth Custody centre in square 0416 is a source of employment. Some Works are shown on the map in square 0517, which suggests that Barnard Castle has some kind of industrial base.

CHAPTER 11   URBAN SETTLEMENT

Answer

2 a) i) Land in the city centre is expensive (1 mark). Land values rise as you get nearer the city centre (1 mark).

Examiner's Comments

To get both marks your answer must say how the land values change with distance from the city centre.

Answer

    ii) The city centre is easy to get to (1 mark). A site in the city centre can make more money than anywhere else; or many people are competing for a city centre site (1 mark)

Examiner's Comments

Again, a developed point is needed to get both marks. The high value of city centre sites is related to the competition between the different land uses which are prepared to pay highly for the ease of accessibility offered by a site in the CBD.

Answer

  b) Level 1 (1–2 marks) Basic understanding.
      The answer contains only general information that is not specific to any named example. It may largely consist of a description of the standard concentric model, possibly with a diagram. The mere mention of an example would not be sufficient to achieve Level 1.
      Level 2 (3–4 marks) Clear understanding.
      To reach this level you would need to make one point which is specific to your chosen example. For example, if you had chosen Southampton, you could mention that the position of the Rivers Test and Itchen means that the city does not have a simple concentric, circular pattern. You would need to make at least one point and give one reason specific to your chosen example to reach this level.
      Level 3 (5–6 marks) Detailed understanding.
      Your answer is very specific to your chosen example with more than one reason given in addition to descriptive material. A detailed description and explanation of, say, Figure 11.3 would be an ideal Level 3 answer.

Examiner's Comments

The question suggests you use a diagram. While it is not compulsory be assured that if the examiner gives you a hint like this, they think it is the best way of answering the question. Make sure you act on any advice given!

CHAPTER 12 AGRICULTURE

Answer

2 a) i)   Arable farming is the growing of crops or the cultivation of the land.

Examiner's Comments

The question asks for a definition, so just naming some crops would not be sufficient.

Answer

    ii) The largest area is in East Anglia, the area north of London and around Norwich. A second area is south-east of London, in central Kent. The area inland from Liverpool is also important arable land.

Examiner's Comments

Notice that the question refers to the whole of England and Wales. You must not restrict your answer to East Anglia. Make use of the location map by using the named towns as locating points. Remember to use proper compass directions: north, south-west, etc. not top, bottom, left or right.

Answer

iii) A – The summer warmth helps to ripen grain or make harvesting easier.
B – The winter frosts help to break up the soil or kill off pests.

Examiner's Comments

Notice the command word 'briefly'. The examiner is not looking for a long or detailed answer here.

Answer

iv) There are a wide range of possible answers including: capital investment, political factors, hard work, field enlargement, training, prices, agro-chemicals such as fertilisers of pesticides, and irrigation.

Examiner's Comments

Make sure you give only human factors. Don't list physical factors. Notice the command word is 'state'. There is no need to describe or explain the factors.

Answer

v) Reasons could include any of the following. The removal of hedgerows destroys wildlife habitats. The use of chemicals may have an effect on the wildlife. Fertiliser can run into water courses. The increasing use of machinery may cause job losses. Subsidised crops may spoil the natural look of the countryside. The increasing use of chemicals may have an effect on people's health.

Examiner's Comments

You need to give three reasons. Notice the question asks for explanations. You must therefore explain why the people may disagree with the changes in agricultural practices. It is not sufficient just to state that (say) hedgerows have been destroyed. It is the effect on wildlife that gains the mark here.

Answer

b) i) The type of farming and its location must be in a LEDC.

Examiner's Comments

The location must be specific, which means it must be a relatively small area or region. The name of a country or a general part of a country would not get a mark. For example, Punjab would gain a mark but North India or India would not.

Answer

ii) If the shifting agriculture of the Iban in Sarawak is your chosen example then the following would gain three marks: The Iban move from one place to another. They clear land by cutting and burning the forest. The cleared land is cultivated until the soil becomes infertile; then the Iban move on to a new area.

Examiner's Comments

Three descriptive points are required. The question asks for a description, so there are no marks for explanation. The question is asking 'what' rather than 'why'.

Answer

iii) Level 1 (1 mark) Basic understanding.
The answer gives simple statements about the climate and the traditional activity carried out. 'The Iban clear the forest when it is not raining.'
Level 2 (2–3 marks) Clear understanding.
The answer shows recognition of both the physical and human factors. 'The Iban clear the forest in June and July, and burn the leaves and branches in August, the driest time of year...'
Level 3 (4–5 marks) Detailed understanding.
The answer explains that the burning takes place in August, because it is the only relatively dry month. The details in Figure 12.5 would be very relevant here.

Examiner's Comments

Your answer must refer to your chosen example.

CHAPTER 13 INDUSTRY

Answer

2 i) The putting together of different parts (or components) that have been made elsewhere.
ii) If a factory is close to the suppliers of its components this saves time and transport costs. It is easier to maintain contacts and to ensure more regular supplies.
iii) Level 1 (1 mark) Basic understanding.
The answer consists of a simple statement about the balance of new jobs against job losses in Washington and Sunderland respectively.
Level 2 (2 marks) Clear understanding.
The answer shows that different skills are required. People moving to the car manufacturing factories in Washington will spend more time travelling to work. In Sunderland the increase in unemployment may lead to social problems such as crime.
Level 3 (3–4 marks) Detailed understanding.
The answer would show an appreciation of the knock-on effects of the changes mentioned in Level 2. There would be pressure on greenfield sites, as new factories would be required in Washington. There would be an increase in derelict sites in Sunderland that would become eyesores. The changes in employment prospects in the two towns would have an effect on the community, and on other economic activities such as retailing and other services.

CHAPTER 14 TOURISM

Answer

2 a) i) 19%
      ii) Third.

Examiner's Comments

These parts are testing your ability to extract information from the diagram. Be careful when reading values off a divided bar chart, particularly if the subdivision does not start at 0. In this case the start of the tourism subdivision is 5%, and the top is 24%. The difference between the two gives the answer, i.e. 24% – 5% = 19%.

Answer

iii) After rising from 1979 to 1980 the income dropped for the next two years. Between 1982 and 1988 the income increased. The increase has been particularly rapid from 1985 to 1988. The income in 1988 was 64 million US dollars.

Examiner's Comments

Notice the importance of describing the overall shape of the graph. Do not merely list numbers or values taken from the graph. Restrict comments to any outstanding years or values.

Answer

iv) Level 1 (1 mark) Basic understanding.
The account consists of general points which are relevant but not clearly linked to income or numbers of visitors, and there is no real appreciation of the need to have a more diversified economy. Statements are of the nature "There might be a war.' or "Sometimes there is less snow at the ski resorts." No example is given anywhere in the answer.
Level 2 (2 marks) Clear understanding.
The answer gives a clear reason linked to an example. For example, the drop in tourism in the former Yugoslavia because of the outbreak of civil war means a major source of income is lost from the economy. The seasonal nature of tourism could be mentioned here, as long as it is related to an area which deals almost exclusively with either summer or winter holidays.
Level 3 (3–4 marks) Detailed understanding.
The answer gives a fully developed account of one example. The decline in visitors to the UK at the beginning of hostilities in the Gulf War would be a good example, as long as the answer includes details of dates and which countries' tourists declined in number.

Examiner's Comments

Throughout this answer any mention of annual, seasonal or random fluctuations would be gain marks.

Answer

b) i) Any attraction taken off the map: rafting, biking, Kathmandu Valley/World heritage site, national parks, wildlife reserves. Names of mountains would not be acceptable.
ii) Annapurna.
iii) An example of a good answer is: Footpath erosion occurs when paths become worn away and ugly scars are left on the hillside. This happens because many people use the same paths. The vegetation gets trampled away making the paths wider and muddier.

Examiner's Comments

The problems need to be stated, then described and explained. The question asks for environmental problems, and at least two problems must be considered.

Answer

c) Level 1 (1 mark) Basic understanding.
The answer refers only to benefits or problems and the ideas are generalised and not specifically related to any examples in LEDCs.
Level 2 (2 marks) Clear understanding.
Both benefits and problems are considered with at least one of them linked to an example. For example: "People travel to look at the animals and so bring more income to the country. There has been conflict between subsistence farmers living near National Parks and the Parks' wildlife."

Level 3 (3–4 marks) Detailed understanding.
One benefit and one problem are carefully described and linked with examples. Details of (say) the crop damage by wildlife in National Parks are given. The increased income to the farmers as a result of, for example, CAMPFIRE programme is explained.

d) i) The definition should show an understanding that long-haul means holidays taken in another continent. A mention of people travelling thousands of miles would be acceptable.

Examiner's Comments

A simple statement such as 'a long way' is too vague to gain a mark.

Answer

ii) Level 1 (1–2 marks) Basic understanding.
The answers consist of a series of vague points about 'more money' or 'more time' with no clear explanations or examples.
Level 2 (2–4 marks) Clear understanding.
The ideas given in Level 1 are developed and an example is given. "More people are going to countries such as Zimbabwe, because they have at least three weeks annual holiday with pay."
Level 3 (5–6 marks) Detailed understanding.
There are at least three clear and explained reasons with examples. The reasons must be explicitly linked to the increase in holidays to long-haul destinations. "The increase in tourism in Zimbabwe can be partly explained by European visitors having more time and money". Other explanations include the increasing interest in environmental issues, and the decline in popularity of traditional holiday areas nearer home, because of over development. The improvement in the infrastructure and facilities in Zimbabwe may encourage some people to visit more remote areas. In places such as Nepal there is the other extreme, where young backpackers are prepared to 'rough it' off the beaten track in remote areas.

CHAPTER 15 MANAGING NATURAL RESOURCES

Answer

2 a) i) The points need to be plotted correctly and joined by a continuous line.

Examiner's Comments

The examiner will allow only a small tolerance for the points plotted. It is important that you have a sharp pencil to achieve the necessary level of accuracy to gain credit. This question illustrates the correct use of a line graph as it is shows continuous data over time. The four types of graph that you could be asked to draw in an examination are: a line graph, a pie graph, a bar graph or a scatter graph. Make sure you are familiar with each of these. As well as being able to draw these types of graph, you also need to understand which type of graph is appropriate for different forms of data.

Answer

ii) 1965–1971 or 1955–1971 or 1987–1996 or 1987–1996

Examiner's Comments

Use the gradient of the line to help you answer this.

Answer

    iii) There are a wide range of possible answers here. There has been an increase in the number of coal cutting machines in use (1 mark). This automation has occurred at the same time as the closure of a large number of pits (1 mark). There has been a decline in the consumption of coal because of competition from other forms of energy (1 mark). Other acceptable answers are the increasing concern for miners' health and safety, and the attractiveness of other forms of employment. The latter has occurred because many mining areas have been widening their industrial base as new industries have developed. Many coal seams in long established coal mining areas have become exhausted and there is increasing competition from imported coal. The USA and Australia are able to produce coal more cheaply.

Examiner's Comments

Notice how this is point marked which means three reasons are required. Each reason must be a well developed statement.

Answer

    b) i) An energy source which has been formed from dead animals and plant life.

Examiner's Comments

Make sure you define both 'fossil' and 'fuel'.

Answer

    ii) Any one from oil, natural gas, peat or lignite.
    iii) Your answer will depend on what type of fuel you have chosen.
        Level 1 (1–2 marks) Basic understanding.
        The answer consists of up to two simple statements which may not be specific to the fuel chosen. It is likely that a basic answer will concentrate on the dangers of the mining industry with reference to a collapse or a gas explosion in a mine (or an oil or gas blowout if another fossil fuel is chosen).
        Level 2 (3–4 marks) Clear understanding.
        The dangers of extraction are recognised and a reference to the increasing costs of extraction and of any technical difficulties involved. For example, the difficulties of bringing offshore oil to the mainland or the technical problems associated with deep shaft mining. Environmental issues would be relevant here, either with respect to the problem of waste disposal and storage, or the restoration of the landscape following open-cast working.
        Level 3 (5 marks) Detailed understanding.
        All of the above with depth of detail and related to a particular case study.

Examiner's Comments

Notice that the question is about the extraction of the fossil fuel and not the exploration. Many candidates explain exploration problems when they choose oil as their example.

CHAPTER 16 CONTRASTS IN DEVELOPMENT

Answer

2 a) i) There are three possibilities here: Northern Ireland, North-east England or northern England.

Examiner's Comments

You only need to give one example.

Answer

ii) Three separate points are needed. The average weekly household spending is largely dependent on the wages or income coming into a house (1 mark). The lower the unemployment rate the more people are in work earning a regular income (1 mark). This raises the level of average spending because people can afford more goods and services (1 mark).

b) There are a number of different indicators for the wealth of a country: gross national product, adult literacy rate, healthcare indices, percentage of car ownership.

Level 1 (1–3 marks) Basic understanding.
The answer consists of a series of brief points without any explanation. These points may be just a list of wealth indicators without any details on them. The question specifically asks for two measures, so the maximum number of marks for a list is two.
Level 2 (4–6 marks) Clear understanding.
Two indicators are described but the usefulness of neither one is fully explained. Alternatively the answer may describe only one indicator very well.
Level 3 (7–8 marks) Detailed understanding.
Two ways of measuring wealth are described fully, with a clear idea given of why the chosen indicators are a good guide to a country's wealth. For example, if the adult literacy rate is chosen, a possible Level 3 answer would be: "Literacy rate is the percentage of adults who can read or write. Only more developed countries have the resources to educate the mass of people. This is because of the high cost of providing schools, equipment and books. There is the additional cost of training and employing teachers. Literacy is a basic skill which is needed in both the manufacturing and service industries. Literacy is therefore important to developing a country's economy."

CHAPTER 17 TRADE AND AID

Answer

2 a) i) This is emergency aid or aid that is only provided for a short period.
   ii) Points could include: long-term aid helps a country to develop; capital investments may bring longer term developments and may help people to help themselves.

Examiner's Comments

This is point marked so there needs to be three developed statements.

Answer

b) i) Crops and raw materials that are not processed.

Examiner's Comments

A mark cannot be gained simply by giving an example.

Answer

ii) Three separate points need to be made. Primary product dependency is concentrated in the LEDCs. This is particularly true of countries in South America and Africa. Asia is an exception. Both large and small countries show primary product dependency. If the country's main export is agricultural then it is less primary product dependent than if the main export is crude oil or natural gas.

Examiner's Comments

Notice how the answer refers to the general pattern, as well as pointing out specific examples. It is important to mention exceptions to the general rule. The question is open ended enough to allow you to refer to the distribution of the countries with primary product dependency as well as commenting on the degree of dependency and the nature of the products involved.

Answer

iii) Level 1 (1–2 marks) Basic understanding.
Two simple statements such as MEDCs make more money from processing the primary products and that more jobs are created as a result.
Level 2 (3–5 marks) Clear understanding.
The answer recognises that the processing of primary products by MEDCs generates the greatest profits. This processing also encourages other MEDC industries such as steel and transport. The higher paid, management and marketing type jobs are likely to be in the MEDCs. LEDCs provide a ready supply of primary products.
Level 3 (6–8 marks) Detailed understanding
The processing company may be able to bargain for the lowest prices among competing raw material suppliers in LEDCs. There are few marketing groups for LEDC primary products. By ensuring that LEDCs continue to concentrate on primary product production, MEDCs do not encourage competition from other industries in LEDCs.

ACKNOWLEDGEMENTS

Published by HarperCollins*Publishers* Ltd
77–85 Fulham Palace Road
London W6 8JB

www.**Collins**Education.com
On-line support for schools and colleges

© HarperCollins*Publishers* Ltd 2001

First published 2001
Reprinted 2001

ISBN 0 00 711197 5

Michael Raw and Nicholas Rowles assert the moral right to be identified as the authors of this work.

British Library Cataloguing in Publication Data

A catalogue record for this book is available from the British Library.

Edited by Stuart Gill

Production by Kathryn Botterill

Picture research by Caroline Thompson

Cover design by Susi Martin-Taylor

Book design by Rupert Purcell and produced by Gecko Limited

Index compiled by Julie Rimington

Printed and bound by Scotprint

Acknowledgements

The Authors and Publishers are grateful to the following for permission to reproduce copyright material: *Yorkshire Post*: p. 47 (Fig. 3.13); *The Times*: pp. 85, 156 (Figs. 5.13 and 9.13 respectively); *Independent on Sunday*: p. 128 (Fig. 8.5); *The Economist*: pp. 178, 187 (Fig. 11.2 and table in exam question, respectively); Population Crisis Committee: p. 193 (table in exam question; *The Guardian*: p. 251 (Fig. 15.11); Unicef: p. 258 (Fig. 16.2), Action Aid: p. 274 (bar chart in exam question)

London Examinations, a division of Edexcel Foundation (pp. 90, 194, 242, 243) Edexcel Foundation, London Examinations accepts no responsibility whatsoever for the accuracy or method of working in the answers given.

Midland Examining Group (p. 15) The Midland Examining Group bears no responsibility for the example answers to questions taken from its past question papers which are contained in this publication.

Northern Examinations and Assessment Board (p. 143) The authors are responsible for the possible answers/solutions and the commentaries on the past questions from the Northern Examinations and Assessment Board. They may not constitute the only possible solutions.

Northern Ireland Council for the Curriculum, Examinations and ssessment (pp. 159–160, 210) Answers to questions are devised by ıe authors and have neither been provided nor approved by CCEA.

Southern Examining Group (pp. 14, 32–3, 34, 53–4, 55, 70–71, 89, 106–7, 122–3, 123, 141–2, 160, 176, 193, 211, 227–8, 257–8, 259, 293, 294) Answers to questions taken from past examination papers are entirely the responsibility of the authors and have neither been provided nor approved by the Southern Examining Group.

Welsh Joint Education Committee (p. 72)

Photographs

The Publishers would like to thank the following for permission to reproduce photographs (T = Top, B = Bottom, C = Centre, L= Left, R = Right): Aerofilms Ltd 89; Associated Press 6; J Allen Cash Ltd 21, 271; Dr E Pott/Bruce Coleman Ltd 116; Stuart Currie 182; P Hulme/Ecoscene 67; Tony Waltham Geophotos 9C, 50C, 81, 199, 249; Getty Images 111, 117, 125; N Cattlin/Holt Studios International 204; C Jones/Impact Photos 146; International Coffee Organization 284; London Aerial Photo Library 50B, 162, 167, 215, 217; NASA 42; J Hartley/Panos Pictures 155; Michael Raw 9B, 19, 39, 41, 50L, 56, 58, 62, 80, 171, 185, 207, 233; Science Photo Library 11, 100, 106; Southampton City Heritage Services 181; M Edwards/Still Pictures 189, 190, 197, 288; M Carwardine/Still Pictures 238B; Carew-UNEP/Still Pictures 238T; Klaus Andrews/Still Pictures 247; H Tin/Still Pictures 252; J Maier/Still Pictures 283; Tony Stone 238; C&S Thompson 151; Zefa Pictures Ltd 150.

Illustrations

Harvey Collins, Jerry Fowler, Gecko Ltd, Joe Little, Mike Parsons, Stephen Ramsay and Chris Rothero

Maps reproduced from Ordnance Survey 1:50,000 Landranger and 1:25,000 mapping with the permission of The Controller of Her Majesty's Stationery Office © Crown copyright (433772)

Every effort has been made to contact the holders of copyright material, but if any have been inadvertently overlooked, the Publishers will be pleased to make the necessary arrangements at the first opportunity.

You might also like to visit:
www.**fire**and**water**.com
The book lover's website

INDEX ▪